THE TECHNIQUE OF ACTING

The Technique of Acting

F. COWLES STRICKLAND

Department of Speech and Drama
Stanford University

McGRAW-HILL BOOK COMPANY, INC.

New York   Toronto   London   1956

THE TECHNIQUE OF ACTING

Library of Congress Catalog Card Number 55-11573

To EDIE AND TED
who badgered me
into writing this

PREFACE

For me to claim that the material of this book is my own would be a presumption; and yet it is impossible for me to give credit where credit is due in an orderly and factual accounting. I cannot honestly say that I learned timing from Donald Meek, or Ina Claire, or Walter Connolly, or Leo G. Carroll; but I learned much about timing, especially in comedy, from all of them. These four come to mind at the moment because I vividly remember rehearsals of *Broken Dishes* when Donald Meek patiently explained to younger members of the company that a line should be read one way and not another; and I remember attending all the rehearsals and all eight performances of a stock production of *Biography*, fascinated by Miss Claire's performance and eager to discover exactly what she was doing and how she was doing it; and there was the week when we did *Juno and the Paycock* and Walter Connolly and Leo Carroll worked out the business of the breakfast scene, deciding who should spear a sausage and when.

It is my impression that I absorbed the most about the total design of an acting performance from Aline MacMahon, years ago when she played in *The Royal Family* for me, and more recently when she did *The Madwoman of Chaillot* at Stanford University with an all-student cast. It was never my privilege to direct Madame Nazimova, or to work with her in an actual production, but there was one winter in New York when she graciously consented to meet regularly once a week with a group of us, all young actors and actresses, to discuss many of the problems of acting. I then realized that she could never begin work on any part of a play until she had decided what the total effect should be and that, with her tremendous power to create or recreate an emotion, she needed to know the form and the design of the final performance before she could begin to work on the content.

Of all the actresses I have known, the late Cissie Loftus seemed the most aware of the methods by which she achieved a characterization. Others, such as Patricia Collinge, Laurette Taylor, and Margaret Wycherly, may have been equally aware of their own technical methods, but Miss Loftus was kind enough to spend several evenings with the apprentices of the company, giving a program of her famous impersonations and explaining how she had worked to create them. Knowing how exact Miss Loftus' impressions were of such actresses as Ethel Barrymore and Minnie Maddern Fiske, whose work I had seen, I am particularly grateful to her because her great talent enabled me to gain some idea of the style and the manner and the personalities of Modjeska, Sarah Bernhardt, and Eleanora Duse, whose careers were over before I began going to the theater.

I am quite aware that in many instances, if I were to claim that I had learned this from one actor and that from another, the actors themselves might deny that I could possibly have learned a specific technique from them, since they, themselves, never knew it and never worked in the way it seemed to me they worked. Many actors cherish the illusion that everything they do is instinctive, the result of inspiration, when what has actually happened is that they have learned a technique so thoroughly that it has, in fact, become instinctive. In many cases I have worked with actors off and on, or observed their work, for a period of twenty years or more, and I have seen them when they had only the most rudimentary command of their technique and later when they had become master craftsmen. Whether or not they know they know the technique of acting, they have learned to use it.

Most experienced actors are eager and willing to assist less experienced actors who show a desire to learn. Margaret Wycherly and O. P. Heggie were especially kind to younger members of their companies; Walter Connolly gave much extra rehearsal time to helping Jane Wyatt; and Clarence Derwent spent hours helping Richard Eagan learn how to play comedy when they were appearing together in *The Rivals*. Aline Mac-Mahon goes out of her way to teach, to aid, and to assist young players to get established in the profession; Richard Eagan and Jack Palance owe her a special debt of gratitude for her help when she was an Artist-in-Residence at Stanford. The willingness of professional actors to teach newcomers is the rule, although the exceptions make the best stories and, therefore, are more widely known.

About four years after Alexander Kirkland and I had founded the Berkshire Playhouse, one of the first of the summer-stock companies and, under the able direction of William Miles, still one of the best, I found myself the director of the St. Louis Little Theatre. For a time I was directing talented amateurs in the winter and the best of the professionals in the summer. There is no question that the amateurs as individuals were as intelligent, as sensitive, and often as talented as the professionals. Frequently they were more experienced, for they played three or four roles every season, year after year, and few professionals ever have this opportunity. And yet the amateur performances looked like amateur performances, and the professional performances looked like professional performances—not that one was always better than the other, for the amateur performances sometimes achieve an excellence that the professional theater frequently misses.

Fundamentally there are four kinds of actors: professionals who act like professionals, professionals who act like amateurs, amateurs who act like professionals, and amateurs who act like amateurs. The first and last of these are unbearable. Stanislavski had devised his system of training to help the professional retain or regain the freshness and vitality of the amateur; but I could find little written material that would help the amateur gain the skill and the precision of the professional. To fill the gap, I organized a class, for which I made no charge. I invited some of the most experienced amateurs, and some of the least; some of the most sensitive members of the group, and some of the least; some of the most imaginative, and some of the least. Then I set about devising ways and means by which I could communicate to them the things I had heard professional actors teach beginning actors.

During the rehearsals of a play, the problems of acting do not necessarily present themselves in any orderly sequence. Part of my task, therefore, has been to arrange the lessons I have learned in a useful and meaningful sequence. Although the performance of any particular scene usually depends, not upon a single specific technique, but rather upon a complex use of several techniques, I have found it advantageous in teaching to isolate the various techniques, in so far as possible, and to study them separately, even though in performance they can never be used separately.

I have often observed experienced actors who have not themselves known exactly what they were doing or the reasons for doing it; in working with inexperienced actors, they have been able to demonstrate how a scene should be played, but unable to explain exactly what they have done. When a student has asked, "Why should it be played that way?" the answer has often been, "I don't know, but that's how you play it." I have been forced to suggest theories and deduce principles which, even though unproved, have been found useful.

Another difficulty in discussing acting techniques is the problem of terminology. Many actors have invented their own names for things. Leo G. Carroll talks about "balancing a line"; Aline MacMahon talks about "the spine of a performance"; Boleslavsky, Stanislavski, and Alexander Dean seem to mean entirely different things when they speak of "rhythm in acting"; and hundreds of people talk about "the style" of an actor, of a performance, or of a play without being able to say what "style" is, let alone how it is achieved. Because of this laxness in the use of terminology, I have frequently had to invent names for things which, to the best of my knowledge, never had names before. Some of the definitions which I have devised may not have wide acceptance, but they have been useful in clarifying discussions. If an actor uses the right techniques skillfully, the audience will forgive him if he uses the wrong names for those techniques.

Any definite acknowledgment of my indebtedness for the materials of this book would have to include a list of the hundreds of actors with whom I have been privileged to work and the thousands of actors whose performances I have observed. I am also grateful to the hundreds of students who have been my willing collaborators in working out the exercises in this book. Many who studied the technique of acting with me and who have since become directors and teachers themselves have urged me to attempt to put between the covers of a book the things we have learned in rehearsals and in classrooms. It is for them that this book has been written. With the disappearance of the opportunities for beginning actors to serve an apprenticeship with experienced actors, it falls to the teachers to pass on to the new generations of actors the skills and techniques which have been accumulated through the generations of actors who have preceded them.

I wish to thank the following publishers for permission to quote from copyrighted works:

Anderson House, for permission to quote from *High Tor, Winterset,* and *Saturday's Children,* by Maxwell Anderson.

Cambridge University Press, for permission to quote from Aeschylus, *Agamemnon,* translated by George Thomson.

Samuel French, Inc., for permission to quote from *The Show-off,* copyright, 1924, by George Kelly, copyright, 1951 (in renewal) by George Kelly, reprinted by permission of the author and Samuel French, Inc.

Henry Holt and Company, Inc., for permission to quote from *Cyrano de Bergerac,* translated by Brian Hooker.

William Heinemann, Ltd., for permission to quote from *A Doll's House,* by Henrik Ibsen, translated by William Archer.

Alfred A. Knopf, Inc., for permission to quote from *Of Thee I Sing* by George S. Kaufman and Morrie Ryskind.

MCA Management, Ltd., for permission to quote from *The Death of a Salesman,* copyright by Arthur Miller.

W. W. Norton & Company, Inc., for permission to quote from *Three Greek Plays,* translated by Edith Hamilton, copyright, 1937.

The Public Trustee and The Society of Authors, for permission to quote from *Candida* and *Arms and the Man,* by George Bernard Shaw.

Elmer Rice, for permission to quote from his play *Street Scene,* published by Samuel French, Inc., copyright by Elmer Rice.

Charles Scribner's Sons, for permission to quote from *The Collected
Works of Henrik Ibsen*, vol. 7, translated by William Archer; and from
The Sea Gull, by Anton Chekhov, translated by Stark Young, copy-
right, 1939, by Stark Young.

F. COWLES STRICKLAND

HOW TO USE THIS BOOK

THIS IS NOT a book to be read once and then put aside. Neither is it a book to be studied, for a mere intellectual understanding of the techniques of an art is of little use unless one acquires the ability to use those techniques. This book is an explanation of a series of suggested exercises and an explanation of what may be learned from practicing those exercises. The exercises are the core of the book, and they must be practiced regularly over a long period of time if the student is to derive any benefit from them.

It has been said that genius is one-tenth inspiration and nine-tenths perspiration. This book concerns itself with the corresponding nine-tenths of acting. The Stanislavski system of acting, as expounded in his two books *An Actor Prepares* and *Building a Character,* is devoted, as the author himself says, to devising a means "by which inspiration may be made to occur more frequently than is its wont." The system of training proposed in this book is designed to help the actor give an intelligent and competent performance, even when inspiration is lacking, and—equally important—to show him how to use an inspiration when he is fortunate enough to have one. The suggested exercises should aid the actor in acquiring those skills without which inspiration is useless—just as inspiration about the interpretation of a Beethoven sonata is useless unless it occurs to a person who also has the digital skill with which to perform it. It is my personal opinion that the inspirations of any artist in any field tend to be limited by his technical capabilities and that as he increases his ability to perform, he also increases the range in which inspirations are likely to occur.

To perform each exercise once is not enough. To perform each exercise until it is done correctly is not enough. Each exercise must be performed until the technique becomes easy and natural and instinctive; and then the student should select other scenes and plays and apply the specific techniques so that they become like familiar tools and he learns which technique is best suited to which purpose.

For the purposes of study, an effort has been made to isolate the separate techniques, and scenes have been selected for the exercises which depend

more upon a single technique than upon others, just as a musician may practice one piece to develop a legato and a long, sustained singing tone, and
another to develop a sharp, quick, staccato tone. Actually, there is a constant need for all the techniques, and the need for one is coexistent with
the need for others. The student would do well, having performed all
the exercises in their suggested order, to go back to the beginning and do
them all over again, applying to the beginning exercises the techniques
which are discussed and illustrated in the later chapters.

The student should be warned that if he has had considerable experience
in acting but has made no conscious effort to acquire technical knowledge
and technical skill, beginning a study of techniques may seem more of a
hindrance than a help, and for a while he will seem less capable than he was
before. This is natural and inevitable. When a person who has played
the piano "by ear" sets out to learn how to read music, for a time he will
play less well than he did before. But he will never become a real musician
until he has acquired the necessary technical skills, and the temporary
loss of performance skill is necessary if he is to go on to higher levels of
artistry. Until the techniques are both learned and forgotten and have
become instinctive and natural to him, the actor will never be the true
master of his art.

Unfortunately the art of acting cannot be practiced alone. The painter
can go to his garret and paint, and the musician can shut himself in his
room and practice; but acting is a cooperative art, and it must be studied
simultaneously by two or more people. The exercises in this book have
been selected with the hope that they will be practiced by a group of actors,
working together. Everyone in the group should perform every exercise
and every part in every exercise and should observe the performances of
others. Often one can convince himself of the correctness of a performance, or the faults in a performance, only by seeing others do it. Bobby
Burns's wish should be constantly in the mind of every actor:

> O wad some Power the giftie gie us,
> To see oursels as ithers see us!

Learning to observe and to evaluate the performances of other actors is
essential to the training of every actor. The ultimate aim of every performance is to create an impression upon the audience, and the more experience the actor has as a member of the audience, the better he will be
able to plan and execute his own performances. In many cases the effectiveness of a particular technique as a solution for a specific scene can be
assessed only by the audience, or by an actor who has a wide knowledge
of audience reactions. If this book is used by a class, the teacher should
assume the role of critic. Ideally the teacher should also be a sufficiently
skilled actor to demonstrate how the exercises should be done and how

they should not be done, but if the teacher is willing to learn along with the students, this is not necessary.

Most of the scenes which are discussed in the text to illustrate the technical problems of acting have been selected from a few of Shakespeare's plays: *Julius Caesar, Hamlet, The Merchant of Venice, Richard II,* and *Romeo and Juliet.* If the student is familiar with at least these five plays before reading the text, the illustrations and exercises will be more meaningful to him. To be familiar with a play, one must do something more than read it once. One must remember the details of the plot and the character relationships and must have formed some conception of the appearance and the emotional states of the characters in all the scenes in which they appear. The student of acting needs to cultivate the ability to form a mental image of the complete spectacle of a play as he reads it. This is not easy to do, but the knowledge acquired through performing the exercises suggested in this book will increase the student's ability to comprehend in a reading the total effect of the play in performance. Even if he never becomes an actor, this ability will increase his enjoyment in reading the great works of literature which have been written in dramatic form.

The five Shakespearean plays have been selected not because they offer better examples of technical problems than do other plays, for all plays present the same problems, but because they are plays with which any serious student of acting is likely to be familiar and because they are frequently used in literature courses in high schools and colleges. Frequently, however, a particular technical problem illustrated by a scene from one of these plays has also been illustrated by a scene from a play of another period to make it clear that the problems of acting in plays from one period are not different from those in plays of another period. When exercises have been suggested from plays other than the five by Shakespeare, an effort has been made to choose scenes that are self-explanatory or to provide enough explanation to make them intelligible. The student using this book, however, will also find it helpful to be familiar with *Arms and the Man* and *Candida* by George Bernard Shaw and with *The Sea Gull* by Chekhov.

Under no circumstance should an actor who has been cast in a play, with a performance date set and rehearsals about to begin, even read this book. At that point it is too late to worry about technical problems, and he must give that performance using only those techniques which he has already acquired and which come naturally to him. On the other hand, a director in a similar situation may find this book helpful, as he is frequently called upon to make up for the actor's lack of technical knowledge and technical skill. When a scene is not achieving the effect the director desires, he may be able to produce the desired effect by suggesting a different way of playing the scene. In the modern theater there are so many actors who have had no technical training and who have no knowledge of technique that the directors must be prepared to explain, and even to demonstrate, what is properly in the province of the actors.

This book is by no means a complete answer to the problems of the actor. It is not even a complete answer to the technical problems of the actor, for it assumes that the actor has already acquired complete technical mastery of his voice and his body. It also assumes a knowledge on the student's part of dramatic literature and the structure and form of drama, a knowledge of human nature, and an ability to understand and interpret character. Above all, it assumes that the student has emotional maturity and the ability to comprehend each and every author's interpretation of life as it is revealed in his work. If, however, an actor were to delay the study of technique until he had acquired all of these other skills and abilities, it would be too late. It is hoped that his pursuit of technical knowledge will aid and accelerate his acquisition of the other skills and the total knowledge which is essential if he is to become an artist.

F. C. S.

CONTENTS

Chapter 1. THE NATURE OF TECHNIQUE

THE ART of acting is probably the most popular of all the arts, and yet it is the one about which there is the least formal and organized knowledge. Its popularity is firmly established with those who enjoy it as spectators and those who enjoy actively participating in it, but there are no generally accepted criteria for judgment and evaluation on the part of the audiences, nor is there any generally accepted system of technique to aid the performer. It seems to be an art without rules, an art in which anyone is qualified to be an actor and everyone is an acceptable critic.

This lack of humility is not confined to those who want to be actors. Almost everyone in the audience feels himself to be a competent critic. In the lobbies of concert halls and in the art galleries, people are hesitant to express an opinion. They begin their criticism with apologetic phrases, such as, "Of course I don't know anything about art. I only know what I like . . . ," and then they pass judgment. But in the lobbies of the theaters, and in the living rooms where radio or television sets are turned on, the untrained critics express their opinions with a finality which is devastating. This kind of criticism is usually unsubtle. A show is good or it is bad.

The Myth of the Born Actor

This attitude of the general public toward the art of acting is not without some justification. Everyone has seen satisfactory and more than competent performances given by actors who are appearing upon the stage for the first time, and almost every year the motion-picture industry discovers a girl working as a waitress or a clerk and "builds" her into a star by having her pose in bathing suits on the beach at Santa Monica. If by any chance the young lady is given some acting lessons, the public is not informed of this, and so the myth of the "born actor" is given further credence.

There is quite generally a schizophrenic attitude toward acting, for while the theory of the born actor is widely accepted, so is the theory that acting is a difficult and complicated art which can only be learned

I

by years of devoted study.   Each season a few new actors are discovered, and their sudden emergence into the spotlight from previous obscurity seems to substantiate the theory that all anyone needs to be a successful actor is to be cast in a good role in a popular play.   The fact that these newly discovered actors have been studying their art for years in schools, in nonprofessional companies, and in smaller roles in less successful plays is not generally known.

It is unfortunately true that chance and coincidence play an important part in the rise to fame of almost every actor, but while the opportunity to play a given role is essential, it is also essential that the actor be ready to make the most of the opportunity.   For every actor who comes to prominence through the performance of a single role, there are dozens of others who were given the opportunity to play good roles but were not capable of playing them well enough to have their work praised.

The Lack of Training Opportunities

Any study of the techniques of acting would be futile if it could not be firmly established that these techniques are necessary.   If success in the art of acting is based upon the accident of being born with certain aptitudes and abilities, there is little need for formal study, and the beginning actor would do better to attend a school which pretends to develop charm, to pay strict attention to diet, if that seems to be necessary, to engage a good tailor or dress designer, and then to await discovery.   In many instances this seems to be the Hollywood method of developing new actors.

In the days when every medium-sized American city had a stock company, it was possible for the young person with a natural aptitude for the theater to get a job playing small parts first and gradually progress to larger parts.   With a new play to work on every week or every month, he gradually acquired certain skills from the more experienced members of the company and so became an actor.   In the present state of the theater, when the only jobs available are in New York productions, which have fabulous financial investments and must be immediately successful in order to pay off those investments, or in motion pictures, which have equally fantastic budgets, acting has become a little like parachute jumping; it is essential to get it right the first time.

Radio and television studios now offer the beginning actor an opportunity to learn the techniques of his profession by the apprentice system which used to be available in the stock companies.   The fortunate young person may get cast in a series of small roles and have the chance to work with more experienced actors, and so absorb the fundamentals of acting by a sort of psychological osmosis.   The professional theater has entirely lost its ability to offer this kind of training. If an uninitiated actor is lucky enough to get a small part in a Broadway production, the play will either close immediately, and the hopeful actor will be back where he was, trying to learn acting by sitting in a casting-agent's office; or it will run for four years, and endless repetition of the same role does not offer any great variety of learning experience.

School, college, university, and community theaters, which have been drawn into the vacuum created by the disappearance of the professional stock company, have been trying to give the young actor the necessary training and experience. In addition to offering some formal courses in acting, they have been able to create opportunities for the actors to play a varied succession of parts, but most of these institutions have been forced to omit the most valuable ingredient of the old stock-company training—close association with more experienced actors.

The Lack of Knowledge concerning Technique

No one seems to have any precise knowledge about the things which a young actor is supposed to learn from the more experienced actor. This is especially true of the actors themselves. Morton Eustis, in his interesting book *Players at Work*, reports interviews which he had with established and successful actors in an effort to discover exactly how they practiced their art. There is no reason to suspect that the reporting is not accurate, but the result is a series of essays which are full of mystical generalities and poetical self-analyses that offer very little tangible aid to the person who would like to learn the art of acting.

Toby Cole and Helen Chinoy in *Actors on Acting* have industriously made an invaluable collection of essays, discussions, and arguments which actors, from the Greeks to the moderns, have written about their art, but the result is not simplification or clarification of the art of acting, but rather increased confusion. Dozens of aesthetic principles are argued and discussed with fervor and enthusiasm, and anyone who is interested in acting will find much that is stimulating but little that is concrete. The old adage, "You learn to act by acting," seems to be true, but apparently no one is willing to say what it is you learn.

The Modern Revolution in the Art of Acting

Part of the confusion concerning the nature of the technique of acting arises from the fact that at the beginning of the nineteenth century all the arts of the theater—playwriting, scene design, stage directing, as well as acting—underwent changes which, at the time, seemed more revolutionary than evolutionary. Goethe's *Rules for Actors*, one of the few serious attempts to pass on from one generation of actors to another the accumulated experience which should be the basis for the technique of the art, were devised for plays that were frankly theatrical. The concept of the fourth wall and the theory that actors should behave as though they did not know the audience was present had not yet been invented. Goethe's insistence that "the actor must constantly remember that he is on the stage for the sake of the audience" and must never play in profile or turn his back to the audience was obviously inappropriate to the new type of play. Some of his rules, such as his instruction that an actor who is suffering from a cold should carry a handkerchief, seem not only naïve, but downright foolish.

Throughout Europe, from Ireland to Russia, the new schools of playwriting, now generally identified as "realistic" or "naturalistic," demanded a new kind of acting. It seems more than coincidence that in many countries the new actors to act the new plays were frankly and proudly amateurs—that is, untrained and unskilled and belligerently nonprofessional. Frank Fay of the Abbey Theatre in Ireland was scornful of the professional theater, and William Butler Yeats said, "I think the theatre must be reformed in its plays, its speaking, its acting, and its scenery." Antoine in Paris boasted that his company was composed of housewives, clerks, and laborers, and warned that any knowledge of the professional theater was both useless and dangerous. The famous Moscow Art Theatre had begun as a society of amateur actors. The break with the past was complete and definite. It was frequently stated, and often believed, that there was absolutely nothing that had been learned in two thousand years of acting which was worth preserving and handing on to the next generation.

The Purpose of the Stanislavski System

The new amateur companies immediately set about devising systems to train their actors. The most widely accepted of these systems is the one evolved by Constantine Stanislavski. Contrary to the uses to which the Stanislavski method has been put by many of his enthusiastic converts, the system was never intended to cause a revolution; it seems to have been honestly conceived as an attempt to foster an evolution in the art of acting. Stanislavski did not rail against the acting of his day, but against the spirit with which it was done. For the most part, or at least for the part which has aroused the most enthusiastic response from the students and teachers of the system, he devised a discipline, the object of which was to increase the sensitivity and emotional capacity of the actor and to give him a control of his emotions.

In *My Life in Art* Stanislavski relates that he asked himself the question, "Are there no technical means for the creation of the creative mood, so that inspiration may appear oftener than is its wont?" His method of training was devised as an answer to that question. His first volume, *An Actor Prepares*, is appropriately titled, for it is not a book on how to act but rather a book on how to be an actor. To use the book as a manual on acting is rather like using a manual on how to make a violin as a method of instruction for learning to play the violin.

It should be remembered that Stanislavski was himself a well-trained and skillful actor before he felt the lack in himself which led him to the studies from which he finally evolved the exercises and the discipline which have come to be known as the Stanislavski method. His autobiography is very clear on this point. Through experience, learning by trial and error, by observing great actors and frequently imitating them, he had learned the technique of acting and then had found that technique was not enough. But he never claimed that technique was not essential.

Unfortunately, many young actors who have never had the opportunity to learn the technique of acting have devoted themselves to the Stanislavski method in the mistaken belief that it is the complete and final answer to the study of acting. They have convinced themselves that if they succeed in training themselves so that "inspiration may appear oftener than is its wont" they therefore have learned how to act, and that this inspiration may be substituted for skill.

In the United States it was the Group Theatre that became the most famous and for a time the most successful disciple of the Stanislavski system of actor training. Stella Adler, one of the most brilliant actresses of the Group Theatre and one of the teachers in its training school, gives eloquent testimony that the Stanislavski system is best adapted to the purposes for which it was devised, that is, to provide advanced training for actors who have already acquired considerable skill rather than to provide training for actors with little or no experience. She freely admitted that "the system chiefly benefited the more experienced actors." What had this experience taught them? Speaking of the more experienced actors of the Group Theatre, Miss Adler says, "They knew they could act—had already done it—had fulfilled the requirements needed in the professional theatre. They were able to bring an independence, therefore, which they had achieved through experience." But she does not say what specific knowledge had been acquired through experience.

The fact that there actually exists a definite technique of acting which has been learned, consciously or unconsciously, by many of the most successful actors is established by the frequency with which actors refer to their technique. Minnie Maddern Fiske said, "Genius is the great unknown quantity. Technique supplies a constant for the problem."

Alla Nazimova spoke of the "conscious technical effort" which the actor must make. John Barrymore said, "A man isn't an actor until he commands a technique which enables him to get an impression across into the heart of an audience." E. H. Sothern advised, "We should surely study the results achieved by the great actors, the means by which they secured their effects, just as one studies the old masters of painting or the giants of literature." Ellen Terry said, "I feel more strongly than ever how important it is to master these principles [scientific principles of acting]. There is all the difference in the world between departure from recognized rules by one who has learned to obey them, and neglect of them through want of training or want of skill or want of understanding." Obviously the actors themselves are aware of the existence of a technique of acting, even though they make no effort to say exactly what that technique is.

Technique Obscured by the Actor's Appearance

There are several reasons why the techniques of acting are not so obvious and so easily recognized by either actors or audiences as the techniques of other arts. Perhaps the most important of these is that in the art of acting the artist himself becomes his own instrument, his own medium. The violinist is never confused with either his violin or the musical composition he is playing. Stradivarius created a violin capable of beautiful tone, but his art is not confused with the art of a Kreisler or a Menuhin who plays the violin and brings forth the tone; for it is easily demonstrated that a less capable violinist cannot produce as beautiful a tone from a Stradivarius violin as can a virtuoso and that a master violinist can produce a good tone from a less satisfactory instrument.

Although the violinist who uses a Stradivarius is not necessarily considered a good violinist, the actor with a beautiful voice is usually judged a better actor because of this special ability. A good voice is certainly an asset to an actor in certain roles, but an unpleasant voice can also be an asset to an actor in certain other roles, as Jean Arthur's rather unpleasant, rasping voice was to her in playing Peter Pan. It should be obvious, even though critics and audiences are often confused, that the test of the abilities of an actor should not rest with the possession of a voice of any particular quality, but rather with the use he makes of it and the suitability to the role which he is playing.

Just as one distinguishes between the quality of an instrument and the skill of the musician, it is easy to differentiate between a painting and its original. The smile of the *Mona Lisa* is known to have belonged to the model, but the skill, the technique, the artistic ability to render it into an everliving thing of paint and canvas belong to Leonardo da Vinci. Helen Hayes has a charming, whimsical smile, which becomes the smile of Viola in *Twelfth Night* or of the young Queen Victoria in *Victoria Regina*. The ability to smile in this particular way is a great asset to Miss Hayes, for it allows her to play many roles in an inimitable manner and helps her win friends and influence audiences and critics; but it is not a test of her abilities as an actress. Judith Anderson has never been particularly admired for her smile, but she is not therefore either a greater or a lesser artist than Miss Hayes, although audiences may prefer one to the other for no other reason.

Since the versatility of every actor is ultimately limited by such characteristics as his height and weight, his voice and smile, and all the evasive and intangible things which make up his physical personality, any young actor will do well to do everything in his power to cultivate those qualities which will be most useful to him in the portrayal of a variety of roles. It is difficult, however, to say what those qualities are. Donald Meek found it a great asset to be bald. Josephine Hull is usually cast in a role because she is stout. Mary Wicks got her first part on Broadway because she was tall and thin, and a dozen actresses in Hollywood get jobs because they look well in bathing suits. None of these physical attributes has anything to do with the skill or ability with which he uses those attributes.

Technique Obscured by Conflicting Emotions

The unique complexity of emotional states which must be coexistent during any dramatic performance has also tended to obscure both the need and the nature of the technique of acting. First, there is the fundamental and basic emotion of the playwright, the mood he wished to express. Second, in most modern productions, there is the director's interpretation of the author's concept. Ideally, the director is a person of sensitivity whose artistic intention is identical with that of the playwright, but this ideal is not always achieved. Third, there are the varied emotions of the different characters in the play. The emotions of the characters are almost always different from the emotional attitude of the author. It is clear, for example, that Shakespeare regarded Polonius as a garrulous, boring old man uttering endless platitudes, but this could not be the opinion which Polonius has of himself. When he gives his fatherly advice to Hamlet, he himself must think that it is important, significant, and profound. Fourth, there is the emotion of the actor playing the part, who must on the one hand assume the emotions of the character, or at least seem to do so convincingly, and on the other hand see that he creates the impression intended by the author, or suggested by the director, even though the character he is playing is unaware of the effect to be created and in many cases is actually trying to create a completely different effect—as the artistic intentions of Shakespeare and Polonius are opposed to each other.

No other art presents such a tangled complex of emotional states which must somehow be unified and reconciled with one another to present to the audience the emotional attitude of the playwright. In the Stanislavski system this final effect upon the audience envisaged by the playwright is called the "super-objective." The task of reconciling these various and conflicting emotional states is so prodigious that it has obscured the fact that there must also be a technique by which the emotion of the actor and of the character must be projected to the spectators, so that they, in turn, will have the emotional response which was the aim of the author when he wrote the play.

Just as the audience inevitably identifies the physical personality of the actor as belonging to the character that he is playing, so the emotional personality of the actor becomes associated with the character that he plays. When the physical and emotional characteristics of an actor are carefully matched to the physical and emotional characteristics of the role, the result is often a reasonably satisfactory substitute for the art of acting. Casting actors in roles which are suited to their own emotional and physical personalities is normal practice in all branches of theater, professional and nonprofessional, stage and motion pictures, radio and television. The fact that an actor is "typed" to the part he is going to play has nothing to do with his capabilities as an actor. It simply means that it is possible for him to seem to be a capable actor without his having any special knowledge of the techniques of acting. If he is fortunate enough also to have skill in the art and technique of acting, his performance will be better, but his audiences may not be aware of the reason.

Importance of the Actor's Personality

It does not follow that the test of acting is the ability of an actor to disguise his own personality and completely assume that of another, although many people seem to think so. In living-room conversations about the relative merits of different actors, the proof that any given actor is not an actor at all is the statement that he is always the same in every part. The ability to play many different kinds of roles is undoubtedly a sign of versatility in an actor, but it is by no means a sign of greatness. Ina Claire is not a lesser actress because her personality is ideally suited to a certain type of comedy, nor is Judith Anderson an inferior actress because she plays tragedy instead of comedy. The same amateur critics who damn one actor for lack of versatility will become devotees of another actor whose personality they happen to like. In either case they are judging an actor, not on his abilities, but rather on his personality. The test of the art of an actor should be the way in which he uses his personality, not the personality itself.

In all other arts the personality of the artist, together with his techniques is called his style, and each artist is praised for developing a style which is individual and recognizable. One likes the style of a certain author and prefers that all his books, while they may be about different subjects, should be marked with his own style and personality. No one expects Wagner's music to sound like Beethoven's, or vice versa. An El Greco or a Rembrandt or a Titian painting is prized because it has the unmistakable qualities of the painter. As long as a painter paints in the manner of some previous master, which he is likely to do in his early student days, he is not considered a great painter; but as soon as his work begins to reflect his own personality, as soon as his personal attitude toward life becomes apparent through carefully evolved techniques which are adapted to the adequate presentation of his own thoughts and emotions, he is taken seriously as an artist. His work is judged on the truth and profundity of his observations of life and on his technical skill in using his medium to communicate those observations effectively.

If the analogy of acting to the other arts is valid, it would seem that the actor should not strive to submerge or disguise his personality, provided personality is understood to include the thoughts and emotions of the actor as well as his physical appearance. The confusion concerning the nature of the art of acting is caused by the fact that the artist-actor is, in a sense, his own medium. It is so dangerously easy to substitute the personality of the actor for the personality of the character and to leave the rest to the playwright and the director that even conscientious actors have often tried to obliterate their own thoughts and feelings. To do so would be to fulfill Gordon Craig's dream of the Über-Marionette; it would mean that the actor had abdicated the role of the artist and become content to be merely an instrument in the hands of other artists.

The aim and the object of the art of acting is to explain human behavior. Its subject material is the human heart and the human mind. Its purpose is to reveal man in his relations to other men, to society, and to his gods in such a way that audiences will understand and believe. It is the duty of the artist, therefore, to see the truth and to be able to communicate that truth to others, and the stature of an artist is measured by his understanding of life and his ability to communicate that understanding. If an actor obliterates his own thoughts and feelings, then he obliterates himself as an artist, and he has become, not the violinist playing Brahms, but the violin itself; not the painter observing life and communicating to others what he has seen with his artist's eye, but paint and canvas being used by another.

Analysis of the Actor's Problem in the Role of Julius Caesar

A specific example may help to clarify the problem of the actor. In Shakespeare's *Julius Caesar*, Caesar—having refused to reconsider the banishment of Cimber—is stabbed, first by Casca and then by others. Finally Brutus stabs him, and Caesar says, "Et tu, Brute? Then fall Caesar," and dies. Shakespeare gives the actor no further instructions. Undoubtedly the director will plan where the various actors are on the stage and where Caesar should be at every given moment, but the actor still has the problem of deciding what Caesar thinks and feels during the appreciable seconds from the moment when Casca stabs him until the moment when Brutus stabs him. Is he brave? Is he, suddenly confronted with physical opposition, frightened? Is he bewildered? He says nothing, but he has not yet lost the power of speech, for in a moment he does speak. Does he try to escape? Does he fight back? The adjectives "brave" and "frightened" do not describe exact opposites of human behavior, for the "brave" man who is not frightened to some extent is merely fearless, and fearlessness is quite different from bravery. Innumerable subtle variations of bravery in relation to fear are possible, and the actor must decide the exact emotion that is appropriate to Caesar in this scene.

The personal emotional experience of the actor will be of little use to him at this moment, for Caesar has probably never been played by a man who has been stabbed even once, let alone many times. Nor is it likely that the actor will ever have witnessed a stabbing. Probably no living actor can authoritatively interpret this moment from either his own experience or his own observation.

Even if the actor who plays Caesar is fortunate or unfortunate enough to have had experiences which have seemingly brought him face to face with death, so that he knows that he has been either fearful or fearless in such a situation, he will not know which emotion is appropriate to Caesar. Caesar, of necessity, has borrowed the physical appearance of the actor playing the role, but he does not necessarily have the same emotional reactions as the actor.

The Stanislavski system of training has helped many actors to comprehend, and even to experience, the emotions of the characters that they are playing, but there is always the danger that the student-actor will reverse the process, substituting the emotions which would be natural to the actor. The interpretation of this moment must depend upon the emotions of Caesar, not those of the actor.

Caesar has a total of forty speeches, the majority of them quite short— not more than 1 or 2 lines. He speaks a total of 148 lines, if one counts a broken line as a full line. These 148 lines must supply most of the evidence upon which the actor will base his conclusions about the emotions of Caesar, not only in his final scene, but also in all the other scenes in which he appears.

In the second scene of the play, when Caesar makes his first appearance, the Soothsayer warns him, "Beware the ides of March," and Caesar says, "What man is that?" Is this question motivated by fear, bravery, or idle curiosity? The Soothsayer repeats the warning. Caesar says, "He is a dreamer; let us leave him;—pass." Is the motivation fear or bravery, or is he genuinely and arrogantly disinterested? Certainly Shakespeare has been unspecific. The artist-actor is faced with a decision of interpretation.

Whatever emotional motivation the actor may decide is the right one for these two lines to the Soothsayer will have a bearing upon the emotions of Caesar in the stabbing scene, for the audience will recognize the Soothsayer's warning as the threat of death, even if Caesar does not do so. If the character of Caesar is to be presented in a manner which is believable to the audience, there must be a relationship between his reaction to the threat of death and to death itself.

The actor cast as Caesar cannot avoid a decision concerning Caesar's valor or cowardice, for Shakespeare himself has raised the problem in the often quoted passage:

> Cowards die many times before their deaths;
> The Valiant never taste of death but once.
> Of all the wonders that I yet have heard,
> It seems to me most strange that men should fear:
> Seeing that death, a necessary end,
> Will come, when it will come.

This speech suggests that Caesar does not think himself a coward who fears death, but in the next breath (or possibly in the same breath), he asks the servant what the augurers have predicted. Were his fine words on the subject of valor and cowardice merely words to hide an inner fear? All the omens and portents have predicted Caesar's death, and he has been advised not to go to the Senate, but he remains adamant in his determination: "Caesar shall go forth." But in another moment he has yielded to his wife's pleading: "I will stay at home."   The omens and portents are reinterpreted for him, and he has changed his mind again: "Give me my robe, for I will go."

Caesar is an enigma, an enigma which must be solved by the actor for in the next scene Caesar will actually face the daggers.   It is the test. The enigma must be solved by the actor's own understanding of life, by his own emotional comprehension of the problem of man in relation to his fate, by his knowledge of human behavior.   Shakespeare has left plenty of room for the creative actor-artist.   The stabbing scene is a test both for Caesar and for the actor.

Unfortunately, Shakespeare did not write stage directions to indicate the manner in which he expected the lines to be spoken or the actions to be performed as the lines are spoken.   A thoughtful study of other plays by Shakespeare, such as *Coriolanus, Macbeth,* and some of the history plays, may shed some light on what Shakespeare thought about kings and rulers, the proper functions of government, and the ideal character of those who rule; but any deductions based upon this material will be inconclusive.

In a modern production it is likely to be the director who will decide that Caesar should be presented as an admirable or a despicable man. He can be and has been played both ways.   The decision concerning the kind of man Caesar is will have a tremendous effect upon the performance and upon the interpretation of Brutus and the other conspirators; for if Caesar is presented as admirable, then the assassination becomes an evil deed, but if Caesar is presented as despicable, the assassination may be considered necessary and justifiable.

The problem has been oversimplified in this discussion, for men are not all good or all evil.   It should be clear, however, that the decision concerning the character of Caesar cannot be based solely on the personal experiences and observations of the person cast in the role or on the internal evidence deduced from the 148 lines assigned to Caesar, but rather upon a valid concept of the dramatic values of the entire play, the function of the character of Caesar, the structure of the play, and the ultimate effect of the characterization of Caesar upon the interpretation of the other roles.

The question of Caesar's bravery or cowardice is fundamental to the characterization because Caesar himself is preoccupied with the subject, as many of his speeches indicate.   The ultimate test of his cowardice or bravery is in the assassination scene, where he meets physical danger and death; but the resolution of this problem, while fundamental to the characterization of Caesar, may not be fundamental to the play.   Since Shakespeare himself has devoted no lines and no time to a delineation of the thoughts and feelings of Caesar at this crucial moment, the director, with or without consultation with the actor concerned, may decide to stage the scene in such a way that the assassins crowd around Caesar, hiding him from the audience, in which case the enigma of the character will be passed on to the audience.

The actor's ultimate decision regarding the appropriate and the necessary characterization of Caesar will reflect the emotional and intellectual personality of the actor, as distinguished from his physical personality. The quality of the actor as an artist will be judged, in part, on his ability to reconcile his own thoughts and feelings with those of the character as presented by the author and interpreted by the director.

The process of study and analysis by which the actor hopes to arrive at an emotional and intellectual understanding of the character he is to play is at once so essential, so complex, and so absorbing that it has tended to obscure the fact that it is only half of the function of the artist. There remains the whole problem of the ways and means by which the actor's interpretation of the role is to be projected to the audience so that they will grasp the meaning and the intention of the actor, and will see and know the character as the actor intended them to do. It will profit the actor little to know in his own mind, to feel in his own heart, what Caesar thought and felt if he does not have a technique for communicating those thoughts and feelings to the audience.

The Relation of Content to Form

All works of art must have both content and form. In the finished work of art the content and the form are so interrelated and so interdependent that they are inseparable, but in the process of creating the work of art they clearly represent two separate problems. This analysis of the character of Caesar has dealt exclusively with the content of the finished performance. Nothing has been said of the means by which the results of the actor's analysis can be made clear and comprehensible to the audience.

It is obvious that the actor who has command of the techniques of the medium in which he is working, who knows the various ways and means by which concepts of character may be projected to an audience, who understands the relative effectiveness of different methods of playing a role, will be a more eloquent actor; he will be capable of expressing his thoughts and feelings about a character with greater force and with more subtlety; he will be able to play his role in closer relationship to the other characters in the play and to adapt it to the dramatic structure of the whole play.

Nothing could be more futile than to argue the relative importance of content and form in any work of art, for both are absolutely essential.

The artist must have something to say and be capable of saying it. There are many works of art—novels, paintings, symphonies, and poems —in which the force and vigor of the original concept have overcome lack of skill on the part of the artist; there are others in which the greatest interest and pleasure for the beholder, the listener, or the reader lie in the skill with which the artist has rendered his concept, rather than in the concept itself; but the greatest satisfaction comes from those works of art in which the form is so ideally suited to the concept that the two seem inseparable.

It is curious that while in most arts the student is taught techniques but left to himself to discover and solve the problems of concept, the process is usually reversed in acting courses. The beginning actor spends most of his time learning how to arrive at a concept of character and is left to himself to discover the techniques by which that concept may best be expressed.

The Materials of the Actor's Art

It is the actor's obligation to present to his audience a character that will be believable and understandable and to perform his role, as a part of the whole play, so that it contributes its share to creating a predetermined emotional response on the part of the audience. The materials with which he must work are: (1) his physical personality; (2) his emotional and intellectual personality; (3) the words he has been given to say by the author; (4) the physical actions which have been assigned to him by the author or the director, or invented by himself; and (5) the space within which the performance is being given. The technique of an actor consists of the ways in which he combines these materials and the skill with which he accomplishes his aim of presenting a believable character in a way that will have a calculated effect upon the audience.

Naturally each actor will wish to work with the best materials possible; he will constantly strive to train his body and his voice so that they become more maleable and adaptable; he will do all that he can to develop his own emotional and intellectual comprehension of the roles he is to play and of the plays in which they appear. Any study of the technique of acting should in no way hinder the actor's efforts to improve the materials with which he works.

The Physical Personality of the Actor

It should be understood at the beginning that there is no particular physical personality which is more suitable to the art of acting than any other. There is an easily understandable misconception that only young people of great personal beauty can hope to become successful actors. But plays are written about all types and ages. Richard III is ugly and misshapen; Falstaff is fat; Cassius has a "lean and hungry look." It is quite true, of course, that most plays have parts for a young man and a young woman who fall in love with each other, and it is best that the actors playing these parts should not be conspicuously unattractive; for the action of the play must be believable to the audience, and audiences— particularly modern American audiences, who seem to be conditioned by reading the advertisements of thousands of different beauty prepara- tions—are unwilling to credit the emotion of love to any except those who are physically attractive. This attitude may be contrary to their own observation of life, since there is scarcely a person so unattractive that there is not someone to fall in love with him, but they are right in so far as it is improbable that Romeo and Juliet would experience love at first sight if either or both were noticeably unattractive.

Beginning actors must learn to assess their own physical personalities and be willing to play the parts which are suitable to them. If they are overweight, they must either reduce or play roles where overplumpness can be an asset. An actor is limited by his physical personality only to the extent that it affects an audience's willingness to accept him as the type he is trying to portray. An actress who was noticeably past thirty once asked Mrs. Patrick Campbell about the role of Liza Doolittle in *Pyg- malion*, which Mrs. Campbell had played in the original production. The inquiring actress said, "The director won't let me play Liza. He says that I am too old, that Shaw says Liza should be sixteen; but you weren't sixteen when you played it, were you, Mrs. Campbell?" Mrs. Camp- bell replied, "No, dear, but they'd believe me. They'd never believe you."

The Intellectual and Emotional
Personality of the Actor

The intellectual and emotional personality of an actor is less tangible and more difficult to measure than his physical personality. The intel- lectual stature of an artist cannot be computed. Some actors are by nature more suited to comedy and others to tragedy. No matter what his subject material, Thackeray's ironic and satiric view of life colors almost everything he wrote. In one sense this personal style is a limita- tion, but in another it opens roads no other artist can travel without seem- ing to follow. Every role which Beatrice Lillie plays is tinged with the color of her own personality. She may be a limited artist, but she is not thought to be a lesser artist because she can do one thing better than anyone else can do it. Much lip service has been paid to the theory that every actor should be able to play every type of part. This is a degree of versatility which is not demanded of an artist in any other field. The glory of the Moscow Art Company or the Old Vic Company or any other company is not that all of the actors can play all of the parts, but that all of the actors can play their own parts excellently.

A young actor should do everything he can to increase his understanding, his sensitivity, and his comprehension; he will never be able to give a performance which he cannot think of in the first place. Much of the Stanislavski system of actor training, as expounded in his book *An Actor Prepares*, is devoted to suggested exercises by which an actor may hope to develop his emotional and intellectual comprehension of the roles which he is to play.

Training for an Actor's Voice

The actual lines written by the playwright and spoken by the actor are, in a sense, the one unalterable ingredient of any acting performance. Actors with different physical characteristics and different interpretations of the role may be cast as Hamlet, but the words will still be those written by Shakespeare. And yet the words themselves are capable of conveying many subtle variations in meaning according to the manner in which they are spoken by the actor. Ever since the beginnings of drama in early Greece, a good voice has been considered a requisite for an actor.

The vocal training of the actor should be such that it enables him to gain complete control of his voice in regard to volume, tone, pitch, rate, and clarity of diction, for his ability to interpret various characters will be limited by the qualities of his own voice and the facility with which he can use it. The training of a good speaking voice is a whole subject in itself, but for the purposes of this study of acting techniques it must be assumed that the actor has a trained and flexible speaking voice and is capable of using it in any way which he deems necessary for his interpretation of a given role.

The Physical Actions

An actor needs training in the control of the movements of his body as much as he needs voice training; for his actions, the things which he does on the stage, provide him with the greatest opportunity for creative work. Again, the actor will find that his ability to play certain roles is limited by his ability to perform the actions required by the part and that this ability is in turn limited by his physical personality. An actor who cannot fence or learn enough fencing to give the impression that he is an expert fencer cannot play the role of Cyrano or Hamlet. An actor who cannot handle test tubes and laboratory equipment in what seems to be a professional manner cannot play several of the roles in *Yellow Jack*. Alfred Lunt had to learn a tap-dance routine for his part in *Idiot's Delight*. The list of special physical skills and aptitudes which an actor may be called upon to have is limitless.

It is difficult to prescribe the kind of physical training most suitable for an actor, for it will differ with each individual, depending upon his own physical, emotional, and intellectual personality. Some actors have found Dalcroze eurythmics helpful. Ballet and other forms of dance also offer a kind of training which is beneficial to the actor. Fencing, for both men and women, develops a precision of muscular control which is valuable. If an actor is naturally suited by the limitations of his physical, intellectual, and emotional personality to play stolid business-men, there is no reason why he should be able to perform intricate ballet steps or to walk with the agility of an athlete; but he will need precise muscular control to use his body in a way appropriate to his own physical personality and to the type of character he portrays.

The Use of Space

The space in which a performance is to be given is to the actor as a piece of paper or a canvas or a wall is to a painter, or as a piece of wood or a block of stone is to a sculptor. It is both a limitation and an opportunity. The subject material of an etching, a water color, an oil painting, and a mural may be identical, but the techniques used in creating each piece of work will be vastly different. Hamlet can be effectively produced as a radio play or in a huge outdoor amphitheater, but the techniques used by the actor in the two performances will be almost diametrically opposed to each other: on the radio the actor must rely exclusively upon vocal techniques while in the amphitheater he will be forced to use large pantomimic action.

In the motion-picture performance of *Hamlet*, when Hamlet has thought of the plan to use the players to trap the King into betraying his guilt, Laurence Olivier elected to show Hamlet's elation by running down the long corridor of the palace and leaping into the air as he said, "The play's the thing." This is a valid and effective bit of action in that particular setting, but it could not be used in a television performance, and Hamlet's elation would need to be revealed through other means. In a motion-picture close-up or in a small, intimate theater a slight change in facial expression can become a dynamic and powerful means of expressing an emotion, but in a large auditorium the same emotion would need to be expressed by other means. The actor's techniques must be suitable not only to his own personality and to the character that he is playing but also to the space in which the performance is being given.

The technique of acting is the skill with which the actor combines the materials of his art to create an emotional or intellectual response on the part of the audience. No one can arbitrarily say that an actor should play a particular role in any particular manner or with any particular techniques; but it is possible for the young actor to learn that there are certain well-established ways of reading a line or performing an action and that each method of reading the line or performing the action will have a different effect upon the audience and will create a different impression of the character. It remains for the actor-artist to decide which effect he wishes to create and then to know the best methods by which that effect can be created.

Chapter 2. A BEGINNING EXERCISE

THE FIRST EXERCISE in acting technique will illustrate to the beginning actor the complicated interrelationship between the various elements from which an acting performance must be constructed.

Presuppose that the stage on which the performance is to be given is approximately 28 feet wide. The action is that two characters appear at one side of the stage, as though the scene were set in a street or in the corridor of some office building, and walk across the stage. Only one of the characters speaks, and so it is best that the exercise be performed for the first few times only by the speaking actor, the second character being imagined. The lines to be spoken are:

> I am going on a vacation.
> I am going to New York.
> I have a friend there.
> He is an interior decorator.

The personal pronoun in the last sentence should be that of the opposite sex from the person who is doing the exercise.

The lines have been intentionally selected to be as banal as possible, and they are completely unrevealing as to the kind of person who is saying them. Nothing in the lines particularly suggests the size, age, appearance, or emotional or intellectual qualities of the speaker. If, in the performance, any sense of the character of the speaker is communicated to the audience, it must be that the characterization was supplied by the actor and not by the author.

If the actor who speaks the lines is of normal height and walks with a normal step, not having either extra-long or extra-short legs, he will immediately discover that the lines do not fit the space. If he speaks the lines without any pauses between the sentences and walks with a natural, unbroken rhythm, he will have finished speaking the lines approximately four steps before he disappears on the opposite side of the stage. The exact amount of time between the ending of the spoken line and the end of the pantomimic action will vary slightly according to the size of the step of the actor, but he will immediately feel embarrassed if he finds himself on stage, even for a few seconds, with nothing

19

to say and nothing to do. A vacuum will have been created, and he will feel compelled to invent something to fill this gap which will hold the attention of the audience.

Drama is a concentrated form of art. The playwright and the actors have the attention of their audience for two or three hours only, and during that time every second must be made to count in the creation of the emotional experience for which the spectators have paid their money and given their time.

Changing the Position of the Pause

Several technical devices for solving the problem posed by this exercise will readily suggest themselves. The actors may decide to take one or two steps without speaking when they first enter. The moment during which the audience is receiving no new sensation will be less noticeable and less objectionable at the beginning of the scene than at the end of the scene because the spectator, seeing two characters enter, will sense that they are about to say something or do something and his own curiosity will seem to fill the pause.

It is also possible to spread the gap throughout the little scene by having the actors take one step after each sentence. This device splits the pause into three tiny segments, which may easily pass unnoticed by the audience. The fact that the actors have been upon the stage for measurable moments without communicating anything to the audience has not been changed. It has merely been disguised.

Changing the Rate of Speaking and Walking

Another possible solution to the problem is for the actor to talk more slowly or walk more quickly. Either of these alternatives will not only eliminate the pause but introduce the elementary beginnings of characterization and interpretation. If the actor talks more slowly than is natural to him, the audience will assume that the character is either a different type of person from the actor playing the part or in a different emotional state. A slower rate of speech may be justified by assuming that the character is either a more deliberate or thoughtful person or that for some reason he is giving the matter of a vacation and where he will go considerable thought. In the same way, the audience will interpret a change in the actor's speed of walking as an indication that the character is naturally an energetic person or that for some reason he is in a hurry.

Actors must accustom themselves to the fact that audiences will always make their own interpretations of what is said and done upon the stage. They will assume that every character is doing and saying what is natural to him in the specific situation and they will base their interpretations upon their own experience and observation. In this particular exercise the audience will be certain that the character hurries because he is eager either to get away from one place or to arrive at another place.

When Olivier, in his motion picture *Hamlet*, runs the length of the palace corridor and leaps into the air as he shouts, "The play's the thing," those in the audience understand that he is excited and exuberant and eager, for in their experience they have never seen anyone act that way, and have not acted that way themselves, unless these feelings were present. No amount of sepulchral intoning that *Hamlet* is the tragedy of a man who cannot make up his mind will convince them that at this particular moment Hamlet is suffering from any doubts or uncertainties.

Since the audience will inevitably assign a reason to any change in the character's rate of speaking or walking, it follows that the actor must not change the rate without a reason which is consistent with his interpretation of the character. Since this particular exercise is not taken from a play, the actor is free to invent as many reasons as he is capable of imagining to explain the change of rate. Were it an excerpt from a play, his choice of reasons would be limited to those which were consistent with his interpretation of the role in all the other scenes of the play.

If the actor elects both to increase the rate of walking and to decrease the rate of speaking, he may find himself faced with a slight problem of coordination. If the scene were to be played on a large stage with a proscenium opening of 40 feet, this problem would be almost certain to arise. There is a natural tendency for one to increase his rate of speaking as he increases his rate of walking. Not to do so is a little like trying to do the parlor trick of patting the head while rubbing the stomach. It can be done, but it will not seem natural on the first try.

Filling the Pause

Instead of eliminating the pause by a change of rate, the actor may elect to fill the pause with something which will have interest for the audience and which will help him delineate the character. As the character enters and begins to speak he may, for example, start searching his pockets for something. If he continues the search while talking and walking, he will find that the search itself will hold enough interest for the audience to allow him to take the necessary two or three steps without speaking and without losing their attention.

Having introduced the subject of searching to the audience, it will be best if he completes the search and finds whatever he is looking for. Merely searching is extraneous business and, while it may trick an audi-

ence into paying attention, it will add nothing of value to the performance. But if the actor finds a card just as he says, "I have a friend there,"
reads it during the pause, and then says, "She's an interior decorator," he
will seem to have amplified the role considerably. The audience will
understand that he was searching for the card because he needed to re-
fresh his memory, and the line spoken after he reads the card will seem
to have been motivated by the card. Now the friend in New York has
become a very casual acquaintance, someone who gave the character a
business card and probably said, "If you ever come to New York, look
me up." The friendship between the character and the unidentified
friend has been clarified for the audience.

Any other piece of business which the actor feels is appropriate to
the character may be introduced into this little scene. If, for example,
the character is smoking as he enters, merely taking a puff at some point
during the scene will occupy the time for the extra steps. "I'm going on
a vacation." He takes a short, nervous puff. The audience will see
that he is nervous and think he needs the vacation. "I'm going to New
York." He takes a long, easy puff. The audience will see that he is
contemplating the vacation with pleasure and has already begun to re-
lax. "I have a friend there." He flicks the ashes from his cigarette.
The audience will suspect that he doesn't care much for the friend.
"She's an interior decorator." He tosses the cigarette away. The audience will understand that he has no intention of looking up the friend.
The width of the stage and the time allowed for crossing will not permit
the actor to use all four of these little bits of business. He will be forced
to choose that one which he considers most appropriate to the character
and most useful for the play as a whole.

The Process of Selection

The necessity, and the opportunity, of selecting one piece of pantomimic action to be inserted into the scene permits the actor to make his
own emotional and intellectual comprehension of the character and of
the character's relationship to the play clear to the audience. The pantomimes suggested, searching for a card and smoking a cigarette, are trite
and banal. The actor-artist, drawing upon his own observation of life
and upon his own emotional experience, should be able to think of an
action which will more deftly define the character and which will clearly
show his own understanding and estimation of the character.

The creative process by which the actor invents pantomomic actions
suitable for each character and each scene is similar in many ways to
the methods of the poet. Wordsworth, contemplating a sunset, had cer-

tain thoughts and experienced certain emotions which he wished to communicate to others through the medium of a poem.   The fourteen iambic-
pentameter lines of a sonnet set the dimensions of the poem, just as the
size of a stage and the length of a scene set the dimensions for the actor.
The poet's selection of specific words to express his thoughts and feelings
is similar to the actor's selection of specific actions through which he, too,
may reveal his thoughts and feelings.   Wordsworth wrote:

> It is a beauteous evening, calm and free.
> The holy time is quiet as a nun,
> Breathless with adoration.

The peculiar appropriateness of such words as "calm" and "free" become the measure of the poet.   The sentence, "It is a beautiful evening,
still and clear," means approximately the same thing as Wordsworth's
opening line, but the freshness and the originality have gone.

In the same way, an actor imagines a character which he wishes to express, an emotional relationship between characters which he wishes to
make clear.   In addition to the words which the author has given him
to speak, he may invent the necessary action to go with the words.   The
actions need not be unusual, but they must be effective and true to the
character, the situation, and the actor's interpretation of the character
and the situation.

Changes in Technique Dictated
by the Character

It has thus far been assumed that the physical personalities of the actor
performing this exercise and the character he portrays are not dissimilar
and that the rate of speaking and walking natural to the actor is also
natural to the character.   If their personalities are dissimilar, the exercise
will raise the same technical problems, but to a different degree.   If,
for example, the character in the scene is assumed to be an octogenarian
or a partial invalid, the rate of walking will be slowed, and the time the
actor will be on stage may be doubled.   Although he will have more
time for pantomimic action, his choice of action suitable to the character
will be more restricted.

Any other change in the personality of the character, either physical
or psychological, will automatically make a change in the timing of the
scene.   If a change in the action will change the meaning of a scene,
then a change in the meaning of the scene will of necessity change the
action.   All that remains constant is the lines that the author has written
and the width of the stage which must be crossed.

Creating New Action

It is possible that the actor, in planning or rehearsing the scene, will think of some action which has so much dramatic value that he will wish to include it in the performance even though the time involved in crossing the stage is not sufficient to allow for it. In this case, he will search for a sound psychological reason for interrupting the walk to gain time for the new bit of action. The actor must use as much care in deciding whether to include or exclude an action of this sort as the playwright would use in deciding whether or not to write another line for the character. Such an action, to be worthy of being included in a performance, should be interesting to an audience because it is true to the character and indicative of his thoughts or feelings. In the finished performance it must be so carefully incorporated into the scene that it will seem an integral and wholly necessary part of it.

Change of Rate during a Scene

There is one other possible technical solution of this particular scene. Thus far, a slow rate, a fast rate, and an interruption in the rate to include an extra bit of action have been considered. The last alternative is to play the scene with a change of rate during the scene. The actor may enter slowly and exit hurriedly or vice versa. This device has interesting psychological implications for the audience because it is understood that no one changes his rate of walking unless there has been some change in his thinking or in his emotions.

If the actor enters slowly, as he says, "I'm going on a vacation. I'm going to New York," and then increases his speed as he says, "I have a friend there. She's an interior decorator," the audience will understand that the character had not thought about the friend until just that moment and that the thought has increased the character's interest in the coming vacation. If the change in rate occurs after the first sentence, then the audience will understand that the character has just thought of something which has made him decide that New York is the place for a vacation, and the last two sentences will become the explanation of the reason for his decision. If the change of rate is from fast to slow, however, it will seem that suddenly remembering the friend in New York has somehow taken the enjoyment out of anticipating the vacation.

All consideration of this exercise has been concentrated on its technical aspects, and all possible technical variations of the scene have been considered. It must be played with the walk at a steady rate or at a changing rate or with the walk interrupted to include some special action. A steady rate must be fast or slow, and the slower it is the more necessity there will be for the invention of hand and facial action which will contribute to the total meaning of the scene. If the walk is interrupted for the inclusion of special action, then that action must also be a part of the scene and a valuable addition to the scene. A change in rate during the scene should be made only if the actor is willing to have the audience understand that there has been a change in the emotional attitude of the character.

The Nontechnical Approach

If the actor now reverses his attitude toward the scene and considers it, not from a technical aspect, but from the emotional and creative aspect, he will find that his interpretation of the scene whatever it may be, will fall into one or more of the technical patterns that have been suggested. It has been stressed that the audience will interpret any change in action as indicative of a change in meaning, but the reverse is also true. Any special or individual interpretations of the character or the character's emotional reactions or thoughts, any change in meaning dictated by the actor's concept of the part, will usually be expressed in a change in the physical action of the scene.

The actor may, if he chooses, approach the scene exclusively from his intellectual and emotional understanding of the character. He may use whatever devices he has to stimulate himself to the desired emotional state, but having done so, he must cast the result into a technical pattern. Then he must rehearse the physical action, just as he rehearses the lines. In the actual performance he must strive to motivate the actions which he has decided to perform exactly as he will strive to motivate the lines the author has written.

Technique as a Stimulus for Imagination

Many actors will find that an awareness of the technical problems of a scene stimulates their imaginations. The knowledge that the stage is too wide and the lines too few for the scene to time easily forces the actor to try to think of an appropriate and useful pantomimic action to fill the space. Similarly, the size of a canvas is a stimulus to the painter. The space is there, and it must be filled with something which contributes to the whole picture. The fourteen lines and the predetermined rhyme scheme of a sonnet are not bothersome limitations for the poet, but an aid in the control of his inspiration. If the poet knows the sound of the word and the size of the word for which he is searching, he may more easily find the exact word to convey his specific meaning and fulfill the needs of his poetic form.

In the same way, if the actor knows that any pantomimic action he invents must be performed in a certain limited time and space, the very limitations help him to think of the action which will satisfy these technical needs and, at the same time, be both appropriate and useful for the delineation of the character that he is playing. Even if he chooses to concentrate on the character and work from the emotional impulses of the character, it will help him to know that, of the hundreds of pantomimic manifestations of the character which occur to him, only those which can be fitted into the time and space of the scene will be useful. The known dimensions of a needed inspiration may spur inspiration.

This relationship of character portrayal to time and space is not artificial. It exists in drama because it also exists in life. If two friends have a subject which they wish to discuss, and decide to take a walk while they discuss it, they will instinctively tailor the length of the walk to the length of the subject. If the walk is finished before the conversation is finished, they will probably walk around the block once more. Two friends meeting in a railroad station will be conversationally limited by the clock, and only those subjects which can be discussed in the time allowed are likely to be introduced into the conversation. Businessmen with five-minute appointments force their thoughts and actions into a five-minute form, aware that whatever impression they wish to create must be made in that time.

So the actor creates his characterization in terms of its size, in terms of the duration of the time allowed to the scene. If this exercise scene is the only scene for the character, then there can be no full, complete characterization. There can be only a vignette, only an impression. The effect must be achieved by a few simple but carefully selected touches.

Technique Affected by Other Actors

No consideration has been given to the silent figure in the exercise, who walks along with the speaker. His is a more difficult and, at the same time, an easier part to play. Since he has not been aided by words from the author to indicate who he is, what he is thinking, and what his reactions are, he is free to invent his own character as he chooses, but his invention must make a valuable contribution to the scene and to the entire play.

The nonspeaking actor cannot begin on his problem until the speaking character has indicated how the scene is to be played. Both actors have almost identical limitations of time and space, but the time it takes to play the scene will be dictated by the rate of speech and the rate of walking selected by the speaking actor. Although the necessary pauses in the speeches to give the required time for the extra steps are also a problem for the silent actor, he has lost the power to decide where those pauses shall occur—at the beginning of the scene, at the end of the scene, in the middle of the scene, or in smaller fragments of time scattered throughout the scene.

In timing the scene, the nonspeaking actor must decide whether to enter a step ahead of the speaking character, a step behind, or simultaneously. Suppose, for a first trial, that he enters a step behind and exits a step ahead. In this case his rate of walking cannot be identical with that of the other actor, but must be faster, no matter what the rate of the speaking actor. Now the scene also includes the necessity of passing the other actor, and it will be necessary to decide at which moment it is most advantageous to pass. It will probably seem more comfortable if the pass is placed directly after any one of the first three lines. It immediately becomes obvious that this will perceptibly change the meaning of the lines, for words spoken backward over the shoulder do not convey the same emotional connotations as words addressed to the back or the shoulder of a person in front.

The decision about where to place the passing should be based on a sure knowledge of the meaning and intention of the scene, the characters to be portrayed, and the relationship between the characters; but this decision cannot be made intelligently unless the actors also have a sure knowledge of the technical devices which are available to them and the probable interpretation which the audience will place upon each varying action which might be introduced into the scene.

There are endless other variations of the scene. If the silent actor enters slightly ahead of the speaking actor and then turns to listen, the turning will make whichever line directly precedes it seem much more important, because the audience will understand that the line had sufficient significance to make the listening character stop. "I'm going on a vacation"; the listener stops. This announcement must have been sufficiently startling to cause him to stop. If he continues walking, then the information is less important. "I'm going to New York." Stop. Now it is the speaker's destination which is startling, and the lines which follow become an explanation of the surprising news.

All the technical devices suggested for the speaking actor are also possible devices for the silent actor. He, too, may use a kind of walk and a rate of walk with which to suggest both the type of character and his emotional state, or introduce self-invented pantomimic action to explain and clarify the character further, or use a change of pace to indicate a change in the emotional state of the character. But the two performances must now be coordinated, for the action of each becomes a motivation for the further action of the other. These are not problems which each actor, from a study of the play and from the study of his character, can solve for himself without consultation with the other. There must be mutual agreement about the meaning and the intention of the scene and about the best plan of action to convey that meaning to the audience.

In a sense, the pantomimic action of each actor comes into competition with the actions of the other actor. If the action of the nonspeaking actor is so interesting that it absorbs the attention of the audience, then they will not pay attention to the lines. In most instances this would not be desirable, but there are exceptional cases when this would be the best method of playing the scene.

EXERCISES

1. One actor crosses the stage, speaking to an imaginary companion, saying the lines:

> I'm going on a vacation.
> I'm going to New York.
> I have a friend there.
> He [or she] is an interior decorator.

Imagine the stage to be at least 28 feet wide. If this much space is not available, then either the first or last line should be omitted.

   a. Play the scene once with no pauses between the spoken lines, so that the extra steps which must be taken appear at the end of the scene.
   b. Take the extra steps at the beginning of the scene before speaking, so that the last word is spoken just before the exit.
   c. Repeat with pauses between the sentences, so that the extra steps are placed between the sentences.
   d. Repeat, speaking the lines at a rate which is natural to the actor, but increasing the rate of walking.
   e. Repeat, walking at a rate which is natural to the actor, but slowing the rate of speaking.
   f. Repeat with a rate of speaking and walking which is natural to the actor but with the pauses appearing in different places in the scene.
   g. Invent appropriate actions which add meaning to the lines, explain the personality of the character, or reveal his emotional state and which will fill the pause in the lines, wherever the pause is placed.
   h. Repeat using a change in the rate of walking, from slow to fast and then from fast to slow.
   i. Repeat using the characterization of a person who would move at a rate faster than is normal for the actor.
   j. Repeat using a characterization of a person who would move at a rate slower than is normal for the actor.

 k. Repeat all of the above exercises with the nonspeaking character played by a second actor, instead of merely imagined by the speaking actor.

 l. Permit the second actor to invent actions which will reveal his character or emotional state. Fit these actions into the scene and note how this limits the time for actions to be performed by the speaking actor.

 m. Repeat the exercise with each member of the class trying to present the same characterization which has been used by another member of the class.

2. Sequence from *Street Scene* [1] by Elmer Rice.

Work out all the possible technical solutions of the following scene. The scene shows:

The exterior of a "walk-up" apartment house, in a mean quarter of New York. It is of ugly brownstone and was built in the "90's." Between the pavement of large, gray flagstones and the front of the house, is a deep and narrow "areaway," guarded by a rusted, ornamental iron railing. Spanning the areaway is a "stoop" of four shallow, stone steps, flanked on either side by a curved stone balustrade. Beyond the broad fourth step, another step leads to the double wooden outer doors of the house; and as these are open, the vestibule, and the wide, heavy glass-panelled entrance door beyond are visible.

 Rose is seated on one side of the stoop as Miss Cushing enters from one side of the stage.

ROSE: How's your mother today, Miss Cushing?

MISS CUSHING: She's not feeling so good today.

ROSE: It's too bad she's not feeling well.

MISS CUSHING: I'm afraid it's her heart. At her age, you know—!

(*Miss Cushing exits into the house.*)

NOTE: For purposes of the exercise, this scene may be performed by two men, Miss Cushing becoming Mr. Cushing, etc. If steps are not available, they may be marked out on the floor, or it may be assumed that the door to the house is on the same level as the street.

3. In the same play, two college girls of nineteen appear at the right, cross the stage, and exit at the left, speaking as they go.

FIRST GIRL: (*as they appear*) I don't understand it.

SECOND GIRL: Convex is this way; and concave is this way.

FIRST GIRL: That I know.

SECOND GIRL: When you're near-sighted, they give you convex glasses, and when you're far-sighted, they give you concave.

[1] Copyright by Elmer Rice.

FIRST GIRL: That I didn't know.

SECOND GIRL: Of course, you know it. Didn't we have it in Psychology?
(*Exit.*)

4. Scene from *Winterset* [2] by Maxwell Anderson.

The scene is the bank of a river under a bridgehead. To the left is an
apartment house with room for an exit between the house and the proscenium
arch. There is also an entrance from the right around an outcropping of
rock. In the center of the stage but toward the back, against the masonry
support of the bridge, is a shack in which Lucia keeps his street-piano. Trock
and Shadow have been talking and are on stage as Lucia, the street-piano
man, comes in right from behind the rock and goes to the shed where he
keeps his piano. Piny, the apple-woman, follows and stands in the entrance.
Lucia speaks to Trock, who still stands facing Shadow.

LUCIA: Morning.

(*Trock and Shadow go out round the apartment house without speaking.*)

PINY: Now what would you call them?

LUCIA: Maybe something da river washed up.

PINY: Nothing ever washed him—that black one.

LUCIA: Maybe not, maybe so. More like his pa and ma raise-a heem in da
cellar. (*He wheels out the piano.*)

PINY: He certainly gave me a turn.

LUCIA: You don' live-a right, ol' gal. Take heem easy. Look on da bright-a
side. Never say-a die. Me, every day in every way I getta be da regular
heller.

(*They exit.*)

5. Sequence from *Romeo and Juliet*, Act I, Scene 3.

Juliet, Lady Capulet, and the Nurse are on stage as a Servant enters.

SERVANT: Madam, the guests are come, supper served up, you called, my
young lady asked for, the nurse cursed in the pantry, and everything in ex-
tremity. I must hence to wait; I beseech you, follow straight.

LADY CAPULET: We follow thee. (*Exit Servant.*) Juliet, the county stays.

NURSE: Go, girl, seek happy nights to happy days. (*Exeunt.*)

Take care that Juliet, Lady Capulet, and the Nurse are placed on the stage in
an arrangement that makes it logical for the Servant to speak to them in
the order in which he does. If the scene is not carefully worked out, the
three actresses will find themselves standing in the middle of the stage,
after the lines have been spoken, with nothing to do except to walk off.

[2] Copyright by Anderson House.

6. Sequence from *Romeo and Juliet*, Act I, Scene 5.

A hall in Capulet's house. Enter Servingmen, with napkins.

FIRST SERV.: Where's Potpan, that he helps not to take away? He shift a trencher? He scrape a trencher!

SEC. SERV.: When good manners shall lie all in one or two men's hands, and they unwashed too, 'tis a foul thing.

FIRST SERV.: Away with the joint stools, remove the court-cupboard, look to the plate. Good thou, save me a piece of marchpane; and, as thou lovest me, let the porter let in Susan Grindstone and Nell. Antony and Potpan!

SEC. SERV.: Ay, boy, ready.

FIRST SERV.: You are looked for and called for, asked for and sought for, in the great chamber.

SEC. SERV.: We cannot be here and there too. Cheerly, boys; be brisk awhile, and the longer liver take all.

The Servingmen are apparently making ready for the party. A great variety of actions may be invented to suit the scene. For instance, let the two servants enter carrying a table between them, upon which are placed two stools. Let them set the table down in a predetermined place and then set the stools beside it and finish the scene standing behind the table, ready to serve people.

a. Repeat the scene several times inventing various characterizations for the Servingmen. For instance, let them both be young, energetic, and brisk, or let the First Servingman be an old retainer who is slow and sullen.

b. Repeat the scene several times changing the essential physical action. For instance, let the table they are carrying be all set with serving dishes and goblets which must be carried slowly and carefully.

c. Repeat the exercise using three men instead of two, assigning the last two speeches of the Second Servingman to the Third Servingman. Have the Third Servingman enter as he says, "Ay, boy, ready," and bring with him additional articles of serving.

Chapter 3. THE ENTRANCE

YOU ENTER. These are the pleasantest words in the actor's dictionary. But what do you do when you enter? The actor should carefully analyze the problem and decide the exact impression which he wishes to make, both on the characters who are already upon the scene and on the audience, for the adage about first impressions being lasting is as true in the theater as it is in life.

Entrances differ from one another in that each involves a different actor, a different character, and different physical conditions, but all entrances raise essentially the same problems. Sometimes the author has left the manner of entering entirely to the discretion of the actor; but sometimes, as in the case of Romeo's entrance, the author has been explicit and definite concerning the first impression to be created.

The Entrance of Romeo

Just prior to Romeo's entrance, Benvolio gives a description of Romeo's actions, a description which must be fulfilled by the actor if the audience's expectations are to be satisfied:

> Many a morning hath he there been seen,
> With tears augmenting the fresh morning's dew,
> Adding to clouds more clouds with his deep sighs.

The precise moment that Romeo appears will vary according to the discretion of the actor and the director, for Romeo may enter just before Benvolio says, "See where he comes," or at any convenient time during the next four lines, at which point Benvolio greets him, "Good morrow, cousin." The space allotted to the entrance is also variable. In a production on an Elizabethan stage, Romeo might enter from the side and cross on the front of the stage, thus having as much as 30 feet in which to perform a pantomimic action, while the other characters observe him from upstage and speak the four lines. In a modern production he might enter upstage from an arch, and his action might be confined to 12 feet or less.

Within the time and space selected, the actor may invent whatever action he thinks appropriate to a lovesick youth. He may cry or sigh, for example, as Benvolio has said he does. Benvolio has also told how Romeo starts and runs away whenever anyone approaches him. This pantomime might also be included in the action, if the director and the other actors place the characters on the stage in such a way that it is plausible for Romeo to enter without being aware of the other characters during their speeches. And yet he must see them at some point, for he later asks if that was his father who "went hence so fast."

The amount of time and space and the specific details of pantomimic action will depend upon the first impression the actor wishes to create. If he takes the full time, he must behave in a manner similar to that described by Benvolio. But the actor may think that the description is sufficient and may choose to delay the entrance until the actual moment when he is addressed.

The Parts of an Entrance

The maximum that any actor can hope to accomplish in his entrance is to (1) establish the character, (2) indicate what the mood or emotional state of the character was before he came on stage, (3) establish contact with the play and the other characters, and (4) indicate the new mood or emotional state which is evolved from that contact. Each of these objectives becomes a separate entity to be examined and studied by itself, very much as each measure of music is a separate entity with its own technical problems, although it is part of a larger whole and must make its own contribution to the larger musical phrase or melody.

The establishment of character will, of necessity, be achieved first by physical means, that is, by the physical appearance of the actor playing the role, aided and abetted by his costume and make-up. Added to this is the use which the actor makes of his physical appearance and his costume and make-up. He will strive to achieve a stance, a posture, a way of moving which he considers typical of the character and which he hopes the audience will recognize as typical of a certain kind of person.

Most actors seem to be afraid to classify either themselves or the characters they play as types, as if to do so would in some way belittle the art of acting. Establishing the character type, however, is an unavoidable procedure, for audiences are trained, either consciously or unconsciously, to think of people as falling within certain classifications. That is the way they judge character.

Establishing the Type

Everyone is a type. To begin with, everyone is classified by sex and age. If a man of forty seems, in appearance and actions, to be either thirty or fifty, he is judged to be of the age group with which his appearance and actions are associated. A character who acts and dresses either younger or older than is suitable for his actual age becomes a type which audiences easily recognize, for they have seen such persons in life.

People are also typed according to occupation. College professors are easily differentiated from farm laborers by their clothes, their habits of speech, and their physical posture. Probably there are college professors who act like farmers and farmers who act like college professors, but the very fact that such persons are considered exceptions establishes the fact that there are recognizable types. O'Neill's *Beyond the Horizon* deals with a situation in which the brother who should have been a farmer goes to sea and the brother who should have been a sailor stays and works the farm. The whole power and force and poignancy of the drama will depend upon the actors' ability to seem to be types who are unsuited to the kind of work they are doing.

Establishing the Individuality

All broad, general classifications are broken into smaller classifications, which, in turn, are subdivided again and again until one arrives at the specific and the individual. Romeo is a man. He is a young man. He is a sad young man. He is a sad young man who sighs. This much the actor can show in the entrance scene. Hamlet, too, is a man, and a young man, and a sad young man; but he probably does not sigh because his sadness is of a different kind, and of a different intensity, and for a different cause. Thus the actor moves through the more general classifications to which the character belongs and so arrives at the individual.

In most modern productions, Hamlet is discovered on the scene as the curtains open. Although he does not have an entrance, he does sit or stand for a considerable time while the King proceeds with the matters of court, and in his physical appearance and in his manner of sitting or standing, he must convey to the audience the type of man he is, even before he speaks. Shakespeare has not made it easy for the actor who plays Hamlet, for in a moment Hamlet himself says that no actions can reveal his grief:

> Tis not alone my inky cloak, good mother,
> Nor customary suits of solemn black,
> Nor windy suspiration of forc'd breath,
> No, nor the fruitful river in the eye,
> Nor the dejected haviour of the visage,
> Together with all forms, modes, shews of grief,

That can denote me truly; these, indeed, seem,
For they are actions that a man might play;
But I have that within, which passeth shew;
These but the trappings and the suits of woe.

According to Benvolio's description and Hamlet's own testimony, the actions of both Romeo and Hamlet have recently included sighing and weeping. So far the two characters are similar. They are the same type. This fact does not deny that they are also both individuals, dissimilar in hundreds of important and unimportant ways; but their individuality begins after, and is in addition to, their resemblance to a type which is easily recognizable to an audience. Their importance and significance as characters, their universality, their humanness depends upon audience recognition of their kinship to other sad young men.

A Pause in the Action

Technically the first impression of the character will be given to the audience by means of his walk from wherever the entrance may be to the prearranged place on the stage where he first comes into contact with the situation of the play. The entrance will be more effective—that is, the impression made upon the audience will be more definite and clear— if the actor interrupts the walk and allows the character to become motionless for at least a split second, for as long as the character is moving —is doing something—the audience will pay more attention to what he is doing than to who he is. An audience can more easily observe and comprehend the qualities of a new character if there is a moment when he is not in motion. The moment need not be long. It can, if the actor so desires, be so infinitesimal that the audience is never consciously aware of it. But, however long or short it may be, it must be properly motivated, so that it seems the natural and inevitable thing for the character to do.

The pause is like a stress in music. A German band thumping out a waltz tune will pound the *one*, two, three, *oom*-pah-pah-*oom*-pah-pah, but a symphony orchestra, observing the same beat and making the same stress, will have the technical facility to communicate the rhythm without making the listeners aware of the means by which the effect has been created.

To say that one method of playing a scene is more effective than another does not mean that it is better. In any play there will be many entrances which will be best performed if the character does not make any special effect upon the audience and which, therefore, should not include a pause in his action. In such cases the actor should hurry the character directly into the play and wait for a later moment for the audience to become consciously aware of the character.

It is questionable that Benvolio, hearing the noise of fighting in the streets and rushing to see what is the matter, needs the split second to establish his character, and yet it would be simple to include it. He could easily rush on, see the fighting, stop, draw his sword, and say "Part, fools!" If this entrance is performed without the stop, it will be less effective, but not therefore less good.

One line later Tybalt enters. Whether or not the actor playing the part wants to include the momentary stop, he will probably be forced to, for he must have time to see, not only that there is fighting in the streets of Verona, but also that Benvolio is seemingly fighting with serv-ingmen. He may rush on, stop, say, "What, art thou drawn among these heartless hinds?" draw his sword, and say, "Turn thee, Benvolio." Should Tybalt elect to omit the stop, then he must either continue to rush or begin to draw his sword as he speaks the first line. In either case the moment in which the audience has a chance to see who he is and what kind of man he is would be slurred over. A few lines later Lord and Lady Capulet enter; one more line, and the Montagues have entered. Certainly if all these characters enter, make a momentary pause, and then continue, there will be an effect similar to the German band's *oom*-pah-pah, *oom*-pah-pah.

The important thing for the actor to remember is that a character is more effectively established in the awareness of the audience if the actor in some way motivates a pause in the action, a moment in which the character is static in a physical position that clearly states the kind of person he is. The actor who can contrive to have this moment ex-press the character's unmistakable individuality, as well as his general type and mood, will have achieved brilliance. Every student-actor, however, should also practice the ineffective entrance, for there will probably be many more times in his acting career when his taste and discretion, and the nature of the character and the play, will require him to make this kind of entrance.

First Entrance Does Not Reveal Total Character

In this first entrance scene, where the actor has his first opportunity to establish the character, he will, of course, strive to establish the character as the type of person he should seem to be at that particular point in the play, not necessarily as the type of person he actually is. When Nora first enters in Ibsen's *A Doll's House,* she is already an independent and responsible person. She has already signed the papers and borrowed the money and spent it on a health cure for her husband. But to the audience, and to her husband, she must seem to be the kind of person who would be incapable of such action. She must seem to be the "little squirrel" of a wife which her husband believes her to be. The play is called *A Doll's House*, and she must seem to be the doll wife. Later her true character will appear.

Ibsen has taken care of the first impression, for he says that Nora enters humming gaily, laden with Christmas packages, and accompanied by a porter, whom she tips generously, giving him a crown and telling him to keep the change. Perhaps these actions should be enough to establish the character, but Ibsen also says that she nibbles a macaroon and continues to hum. Then she tiptoes to the door of her husband's study and listens, saying, "Yes, he is at home." Then she begins humming again. Having established Nora as a gay and irresponsible person, the actress may choose to use the pause, the moment when she listens, to show a sudden seriousness and thus indicate the character of Nora as the audience will eventually discover her to be. Whether or not the pause should be used in this way is a matter of artistic interpretation at the discretion of the actress, but it is clear that the first impression must be one of untroubled happiness.

Off-stage Mood

The off-stage mood of a character can be considered to extend from the moment of entrance until such time as the character establishes contact with the play. In many instances the off-stage mood is either irrelevant or nonexistent; in others, it is of the greatest importance. Each actor will be forced to decide for himself what that mood is, how important it is in establishing his interpretation of the character, and how much time he will need to project the mood so that the audience will understand it.

When the off-stage mood has great importance, the author has usually provided for it in the script. Shakespeare allows Romeo to enter and gives lines to Benvolio and the Montagues during which Romeo may continue to act as though he were alone. Not until he sees them talking does he establish contact with the play. But the actor must decide the precise moment at which he will become aware of the others. He could, if he wished, notice them immediately upon his entrance, in which case his remaining near them would place an entirely new interpretation on his actions. Now Romeo, instead of avoiding his friends, would be inviting them to discover him. This is an entirely plausible interpretation, for many lovesick young men derive a morbid pleasure from discussing their unhappiness with their friends. The important thing for the actor to realize is that a glance in the direction of Benvolio will break the off-stage mood and that technically the actor may place that glance at any moment he chooses.

In Nora's entrance the humming, the Christmas packages, and the tipping of the porter are all clearly part of the off-stage mood. These actions give a brief picture of what Nora has been doing. The nibbling of the macaroon may also be a part of this mood, but it may also be a part of the on-stage mood if the actress wishes to interpret it this way. A glance toward the door of her husband's study will establish her contact with the play. If this occurs before she eats the macaroon, then she does so in defiance of her husband's objections. If the order is reversed, then her eating the macaroon becomes another example of her thoughtless, irresponsible action.

The entrances of Benvolio, Tybalt, Montague, and Capulet, which have been briefly considered, do not involve an off-stage mood. The noise of the fighting has already drawn them into contact with the play. Where they were and what they were doing before they heard the noise are not indicated and are entirely irrelevant. There would be no technical means by which the actor playing any one of these parts could convey the off-stage mood even if he wished to do so.

The Off-stage Mood of Juliet

The first entrance of Juliet poses still another problem. Lady Capulet asks the Nurse where Juliet is. The Nurse replies:

> Now, by my maidenhead, at twelve year old,—
> I bade her come. What, lamb! what, lady-bird!
> God forbid! where's this girl? what, Juliet.

Obviously Juliet is busy doing something, but Shakespeare never says what. Why doesn't she come when first called? What is her off-stage mood? And is it relevant to the play? Is she engaged in some innocent amusement, such as reading a book or placidly embroidering? Is she a gay and cheerful young lady before the tragedy begins? Or is she, already, a sullen, willful girl, as her father later claims? The answers to these questions are matters of artistic interpretation and can be left to the taste and the understanding of the actress.

Technically the actress must convey the answer by the manner of her entrance, as she says, "How now! who calls?" Is she happy? Is she angry and petulant at having been disturbed? The Nurse answers, "Your mother." Now Juliet is in contact with the action of the play. From this moment on, her emotions and moods will in some way indicate her relationship to her mother. Her gaiety or her sullenness may continue past this point, but if it does, it has a new dramatic value, because it is a gaiety or sullenness which remains unaffected by the presence of her mother.

Later in the play it is possible for the actress playing Juliet to make considerable differentiation between her feelings for her mother and her feelings for the Nurse. Since this is so, it may be advantageous to begin to show that differentiation here. In this case it will be essential to distinguish the off-stage mood clearly from the new mood which is engendered by the news that it is her mother who has called her.

In order to study the technical problems involved in this entrance, presuppose that Juliet will appear through a door or arch in the center of the back wall of the stage picture and that Lady Capulet will be approximately 6 feet away to one side and the Nurse 6 feet away on the other side of the door. Juliet may enter, half-running and half-skipping, and go directly to the Nurse, as she says, "How now! who calls?" When the Nurse replies, Juliet may turn to her mother and cross slowly to her, dropping a curtsy as she says, "Madam, I am here. What is your will?" Or she may enter, appearing in the center of the arch, and look from one to the other when she asks who is calling. When the Nurse says it is her mother who wants her, Juliet may do any one of a number of things that might occur to the actress. She may stand where she is and say, with a toss of her head, "Madam I am here. What is your will?" Or she may rush to her mother's side and put her arms around her as she speaks. Or she may skip toward her mother and curtsy in order to suggest both her joy in seeing her mother and her willingness to be obedient.

To include or exclude the curtsy, or some other sign of filial respect, is an important decision for the actress, for Juliet's filial duty is a crucial consideration in any interpretation of the role. Either of these entrances includes both an off-stage and an on-stage mood, clearly differentiated from each other. But if the off-stage mood is considered unimportant or irrelevant, Juliet may ask who calls before she even appears and, knowing it is her mother who wants her, enter in whatever mood the actress may think appropriate to that situation. Then the off-stage mood will have been omitted.

Candida's Entrance

That George Bernard Shaw was wise in the ways of acting and directing, as well as playwriting, is well illustrated by his stage directions for the first entrance of his title character in *Candida*. She appears at the end of a sequence in which Morell has been arguing with his father-in-law, Burgess:

BURGESS: Our quarrel's made up now, isn't it?

A WOMAN'S VOICE: Say yes, James.

(*Startled, they turn quickly and find that Candida has just come in, and is looking at them with an amused maternal indulgence which is her characteristic expression.*)

Nothing is said of Candida's off-stage mood. The actress playing the role must have entered at least a step into the room, but certainly she can't have come far, or her arrival would have interrupted the scene seconds sooner. But she has stopped. She has come to a momentary pause in a pose which Shaw says is characteristic of her, "an amused maternal indulgence." Shaw goes on to note, as any audience would also do, what she looks like as she stands there—her physical personality:

> *She is a woman of 33, well built, well nourished, likely, one guesses,* [the audience guesses] *to become matronly later on, but now quite at her best, with the double charm of youth and motherhood. Her ways* [may one understand that Shaw means her actions?] *are those of a woman who has found that she can always manage people by engaging their affection, and who does so frankly and instinctively without the smallest scruple. So far* [Shaw is indicating that this is a first impression and not a complete characterization], *she is like any other pretty woman* [type] *who is just clever enough to make the most of her sexual attractions for trivially self-ish ends; but Candida's serene brow, courageous eyes, and well set mouth and chin signify largeness of mind and dignity of character to ennoble her cunning in the affections.* [Obviously the actress playing the part will find it easier to portray Candida according to Shaw's directions if she has some of these physical features in her own personality.] *A wise-hearted observer* [Shaw means an intelligent audience] *looking at her, would at once guess that whoever had placed the Virgin of the Assump-tion over her hearth did so because he fancied some spiritual resemblance between them, and yet would not suspect either her husband or herself of any such idea, or indeed of any concern with the art of Titian.*

In this description of Candida's entrance Shaw shows a keen awareness of the effect which the actress should have on the audience and of the fact that the total effect will be compounded of her appearance, her pos-ture and manner of moving, and the expression on her face, as well as what she says. His interest seems to be concentrated almost exclusively upon establishing the character, not at all upon indicating an off-stage mood and only slightly upon conveying an on-stage mood. The off-stage mood is irrelevant, and the on-stage mood will be developed later.

In *Arms and the Man* Shaw handles the entrance of Raina very dif-ferently. The scene shows the bedroom of Raina with doors opening onto

a balcony. Catherine, her mother, comes rushing into the room calling
to her and expecting to find her in bed:

> CATHERINE: Why where—(*Raina looks into the room.*) Heavens! child,
> are you out in the night air instead of in your bed? You'll catch your
> death. Louka told me you were asleep.
> RAINA: (*Coming in*) I sent her away. I wanted to be alone. The stars
> are so beautiful! What is the matter?
> CATHERINE: Such news. There has been a battle!
> RAINA: (*Her eyes dilating*) Ah! (*She throws the cloak on the ottoman,
> and comes eagerly to Catherine in her nightgown, a pretty garment, but
> evidently the only one she has on.*)

In this entrance the off-stage mood is of great importance, for Shaw
has given the mother the descriptive line about Raina being out in
the night air and Raina the line about wanting to be alone to look at the
stars. Both lines are spoken before Raina esablishes contact with the
play by asking what is the matter. Whatever means the actress may
select to present a picture of a young girl in a romantic reverie will obviously continue until she asks this question. Is the question itself still
part of the languorous mood which the actress is trying to establish? It
would seem so, for Shaw, who is generally meticulous about these things,
specifically indicates that her eyes dilate upon hearing the news of the
battle. This is the moment when the off-stage mood is broken and the
first step in establishing the new mood is taken. Here again Shaw shows
his reliance upon the physical action as well as upon the spoken word.

Shaw's stage directions have carefully directed the attention to the
off-stage mood and the contrasting new mood, but he has taken no trouble to say anything of Raina's character beyond giving us a description
of what she is wearing. Perhaps the reason for this is that the character
of Raina is not fully revealed, or at least exposed, until the third act
when Bluntschli says to her, "When you get into that noble attitude
and speak in that thrilling voice, I admire you; but I find it impossible to
believe a single word you say." After gasping in protest, she sits beside him and, with a complete change of manner "from the heroic to the
familiar," says, "How did you find me out?" In a play that devotes
a climactic scene in the third act to exposing the character, it would
be wise for both the author and the actress not to be definite and specific
about the character on her first entrance but rather to allow the audience
to make its own estimate of her character according to the things she
says and the things she does. The actress playing Raina, or Candida, or
Juliet, knows the total and final effect which the character should have
upon the audience, but her sole concern at the moment of entrance is the
necessary first impression.

The Analysis of an Entrance

In all the entrance scenes discussed, the existence or nonexistence of the off-stage mood is of prime importance. For Romeo, Hamlet, Nora, and Raina the off-stage mood is clearly demanded by the author, for it is defined and described either in the spoken lines of other characters or in the stage directions. For Benvolio, Tybalt, and especially for Juliet, it is optional and at the discretion of the actor. For Candida, Montague, and Capulet, it is nonexistent.

Once the actor has determined that an off-stage mood is essential or desirable, his next step is to invent the means by which the mood is to be conveyed to the audience. The duration of the mood will be an important controlling factor in the selection of the best means of stating it. Hamlet is on stage for sixty-three lines before the King directs the attention of the court, and the audience, to him. Attention is already focused on Romeo when he enters, but thereafter only four lines are spoken before he is directly addressed and must make an answer.

The time allowed to Raina is optional. It can be lengthened or shortened at the discretion of the actress and the director, for she is on stage at the opening of the play, and her mother's entrance can be delayed as long as the actress playing Raina has anything of importance or interest to communicate through her pantomimic action. In addition, she must sustain the mood through Catherine's opening speech and her own first line.

Nora's entrance is made easier for the actress because Ibsen has already indicated the action by giving Nora Christmas packages to bring in, a Christmas tree to be placed, a porter to be tipped and, if she chooses to sustain the off-stage mood somewhat longer, a macaroon to be nibbled. If the actress playing Juliet is to establish an off-stage mood, she must, in a sense, steal the time from the coming scene. Three steps, five steps, or seven steps used to convey the off-stage mood are so many steps which cannot be used to establish her new mood, which is engendered by the presence of her mother.

The precise moment of establishing contact with the scene is frequently left to the interpretation of the actor. Romeo may notice Benvolio whenever it best suits the actor's artistic conception of the part to do so; Nora may use the macaroon action as part of her entrance mood or as part of her reaction to her husband; Hamlet can participate in the King's scene with the ambassadors and with Laertes by breaking his attitude of moody silence and physically indicating a reaction to the proceedings. Raina could, by a glance, show that she is cognizant of her mother's entrance the moment the door opens.

The actor will discover that the only way to indicate to the audience that he has established contact with the scene, at whatever moment he chooses to do so, is by some change in the physical action. The specific change, how large or how slight, how sudden or how gradual, must be left to the imagination and inventiveness of the individual actor. Obviously the change will be a physical action which the actor considers natural and appropriate to the character in the situation in which he finds himself and the emotional state indicated by the author. In addition, this action must necessarily be one which the actor is capable of performing—he must be able to make the turn of the head, the hunch of the shoulders, or the change in facial expression in a way which will seem natural to the character. Shaw has suggested that Raina's eyes should dilate when she hears the news of the battle, and the actress playing the role must either be able to do this or substitute some other physical action which will create the same effect.

The moment when the character establishes contact with the scene frequently coincides with the moment when the actor also establishes the first clear impression of the character. This is likely to be true if the technique used to establish the contact includes a momentary pause in the physical action. When the actor elects to use this method of playing the scene, he should take particular care that the physical attitude—his facial expression and the posture of his body—is the one best calculated to create the impression on the audience which he most desires.

Immediately after this moment of establishing contact, the actor will take on the on-stage mood or emotion. Indeed, this moment is often not a separate and distinct action, but merely the shift from the off-stage to the on-stage mood. Perceiving that such a shift has occurred, the audience will tend to think that the motivation for the emotional shift is the character's awareness of the new situation in which he finds himself. Again the actor will need to select a physical means by which the new emotional state can be projected, and again the selection will be made according to the actor's own interpretation of the character and according to his own taste, sensitivity, and intellectual and emotional understanding.

Frequently the off-stage and the on-stage emotional states are similar or identical. If the difference between them is almost imperceptible, and if the change has any significance at all for the audience's proper understanding of the character, the actor must devise some means of making the audience notice the change, slight though it may be. Actresses will find little difficulty in indicating the strongly contrasting emotional states of Nora, who drops her Christmas gaiety when she first thinks of her husband, and of Raina, who drops her reverie and romantic contemplation of the stars when she hears the news of the battle; but actors will find that Romeo and Hamlet, whose grief continues in a similar way through a more extended length of time, must be played with deft and precise technical skill. Each move must be as carefully chosen for its exact effect upon an audience as a poet selects the individual words of a sonnet.

When the actor portrays the on-stage emotional quality of the character as identical with his off-stage emotional state, even though a moment of contact with the play has occurred, the audience will understand that there actually has been an emotional change. A grief like Romeo's, which persists unchanged even in the presence of his father and mother and friend, must be, so the audience will think, a greater grief. Experience and observation will have taught the audience that almost any emotional state will be changed or modified by a new stimulus, however irrelevant it may be, and that any mood which continues unchanged in defiance of a new situation is exceptionally strong and dominating. The dramatic device of showing a strong and powerful emotion by having it persist against new stimuli is a favorite among playwrights. Romeo's grief at the loss of Rosalind continues even though Benvolio tries to cajole him out of it, and Hamlet's grief continues in spite of the blandishments of both the King and the Queen.

Emotional Motivation

No analysis of the technical problems of a scene, and no understanding of the technique to be used in playing a scene, will obviate the necessity for the actor to have at his command the ability to experience, or at least seem to experience, the emotions which he has decided are appropriate to the character. As a matter of fact, the techniques devised for the playing of an entrance scene, or any other scene, are invented for the express purpose of conveying to the audience the emotions which the actor has decided are appropriate and essential to a full understanding of the character. The actor's technical analysis of a scene should even help him to experience or to seem to experience the appropriate emotion, for he can more easily do so if he knows precisely what that emotion is, its intensity and duration, and the exact moment when it may be made apparent to the audience.

Establishing the Correct Characterization

Because every actor has certain limitations and potentialities which are dictated by his own physical appearance and his emotional and intellectual personality, great care must be taken to ensure that he uses the various facets of his own personality for the portrayal of the character he is playing, instead of using the character as a means of setting forth his own personality. Shaw has indicated that the actress playing Raina should dilate her eyes at a specific moment. If she is not able to do this, then she must find some other action, which she is capable of performing, to convey to the audience the fact that Raina is surprised, pleased, and excited by the news that there has been a battle. The alternative action might be a slight, sudden intake of breath with the mouth left open; it might be some sudden gesture of the hands. An actress who is able to dilate her eyes can use this ability to advantage when she plays Raina, but she should not therefore use the same facial expression for the entrance of Juliet. If she did, she might perform the entrance of Juliet with great technical skill, but she would be making the wrong entrance and would be establishing the wrong characterization.

One of the reasons why people like Antoine and Copeau were so distrustful of technical skill was that too frequently the actor used his technical knowledge to give an impressive but a wrong performance. In a production of *The Merry Wives of Windsor*, Mrs. Fiske and Henrietta Crossman, who were playing the wives, made entrances which were technically brilliant but magnificently wrong. Shakespeare has been very unkind to the actresses who play Mistress Ford and Mistress Page, for he has provided them with the most ineffective entrances imaginable. Part way through the first scene of the first act, with no preparation in the dialogue, there is the stage direction, "Enter Anne Page, with wine; Mistress Ford and Mistress Page, following." They remain on stage during five speeches, neither of the ladies saying a word, although Falstaff kisses Mistress Ford. If ever there was a scene in which taste and discretion require an unostentatious performance, this is the scene.

Mrs. Fiske and Miss Crossman, however, were famous actresses, and the audiences had paid their money to see them. Possibly because the actresses were aware of this and knew that there would be some demonstration on the part of the audience when they appeared, or possibly because they wished to encourage such a demonstration, they elected to make entrances, not in the characters which they were playing, but rather in their own characters. First Miss Crossman came swiftly onto the stage and went directly to the footlights, paused a moment as though surprised that the audience was already assembled and, as the applause broke out, curtsied deeply and then rose smiling and retired to one side of the stage while Mrs. Fiske made her entrance in the same manner and received her own ovation. When this was over, the play proceeded.

While one could admire the warmth and brilliance of the personality of each of these actresses and appreciate the technical skill with which the entrances had been performed—each step, each gesture, each facial expression carefully chosen to produce the desired effect—one suspected that the final effect was not what Shakespeare had in mind when he wrote the scene and that the impression created was not that either Mistress Ford or Mistress Page had entered, but rather that two great actresses had come to receive the approbation of their devoted followers.

EXERCISES

1. Make an entrance in which no off-stage mood is expressed and in which there is no moment of contact with the scene. *Example:* You enter a room which is familiar to you for the purpose of picking up some object which you have left there, and you speak to some person who is known to you and whom you are not surprised to see there.

   NOTE: To achieve the desired effect, the actor will tend to maintain a steady rate of movement, for any change of rate or any pause in the movement will create the impression that the entering character is disturbed or surprised to some degree by either the place or the other character on stage.

2. Repeat the same exercise changing the distance from the place of entrance to the place where the object is to be picked up.

3. Repeat the same exercise trying to establish differing emotional states for different characters. *Example:* A young person who is sad, gay, or indifferent; then an older person who is sad, gay, or indifferent.

4. Make an entrance in which there is an off-stage mood clearly differentiated from the on-stage mood and in which there is a definite moment of contact with the scene. *Example:* Enter backwards, fearfully, as though trying to escape from someone or to avoid someone; then become aware that the person you are trying to avoid is already in the room you have just entered; assume an attitude of forced bravery and say, "What are you doing here?"

5. Repeat exercise 4 limiting the expression of the off-stage mood to a movement which does not include more than two steps, but use at least six steps in establishing the on-stage mood.

6. Repeat exercise 4 using at least six steps for the off-stage mood, but limit the on-stage mood to no more than two steps.

   NOTE: If the actor has invented interesting and appropriate actions that reveal both the off-stage mood in exercise 5 and the on-stage mood in exercise 6, it is not possible to include the full statement of both moods in a single entrance, unless the time or space allowed for the entrance is extended. The actor is forced to select those actions which he considers most interesting in themselves and most useful to the performance as a whole.

7. Sequence from *Romeo and Juliet*, Act I, Scene 1.

Montague, Lady Montague, and Benvolio are talking together. Montague is speaking.

MON.: Could we but learn from whence his sorrows grow,
   We would as willingly give cure as know.
(*Enter Romeo.*)
BEN.: See, where he comes: so please you, step aside;
   I'll know his grievance, or be much denied.
MON.: I would thou wert so happy by thy stay,
   To hear true shrift.   Come, madam, let's away.
(*Exeunt Montague and Lady Montague.*)
BEN.: Good morrow, cousin.
ROMEO: Is the day so young?

a. Let Montague, Lady Montague, and Benvolio be stage right. Have Romeo enter through an arch, center up, and move to a bench which is down left, sitting on the bench in an attitude which conveys sadness. Let the action be continuous and unbroken from the time he appears to the time he arrives at his seated position, the action continuing during the speeches of the others.   He does not look toward the others, even when Benvolio speaks directly to him.
   NOTE: Performed in this way, the off-stage mood continues on into the scene and maintains itself despite the stimuli of coming into the presence of the others and being spoken to by Benvolio.

b. Keep the same arrangement of the stage, but let Romeo stop as he appears in the arch and sigh after Benvolio says, "Step aside," and before he says, "I'll know his grievance."   Let Romeo complete the action as above, going to the bench and sitting, while Montague says the next speech and exits.   Do not have Romeo look toward the others, even when Benvolio speaks to him.

c. Let Montague, Lady Montague, and Benvolio be upstage and toward the left in a position from which they can look through the arch and see Romeo's approach.   Delay Romeo's entrance until after Benvolio has said, "Step aside," and the three other actors have moved from their position, up left, to their former position down right.   Let Romeo carry out his action as in exercise 7a—an unbroken cross and no look toward the others.

d. Repeat as in 7c, but allow time after the three actors have crossed to down right for Romeo to enter, stop, and sigh. Let him resume his cross down to the bench as Benvolio says, "I'll know his grievance."

e. Repeat the action as in 7a, but have Romeo sigh after Montague has said, "To hear true shrift," and before he says, "Come, madam, let's away."

f. Repeat the action as in 7*d,* but include a second sigh as in 7*e.*

g. Repeat 7*b,* but let Romeo, instead of sighing, look toward the other characters.

h. Repeat 7*d,* but again substitute a look toward the others for the sigh.

i. Repeat all the above exercises, using one sigh and one look in each.

j. Repeat all the above exercises, but have Romeo suddenly rise and start to leave just after Montague says, "Let's away."

NOTE: The object of these exercises is to discover all the possible ways in which the scene may be played and to have the actors decide which is the most interesting and effective. The exercises should never be performed perfunctorily and without feeling, but the actor should decide which method of playing the scene can best convey to the audience the character of Romeo and the emotions which he is experiencing. Experiments should be made to discover other gestures which might more effectively portray the characters and their emotions than the actions suggested here.

8. Examine the entrances of Romeo in all the other scenes of the play. Decide the off-stage mood in each scene and how it may be revealed by Romeo's actions. Decide the most effective moment for establishing contact with the new scene, which is the moment when the off-stage mood is broken. Decide what the new, on-stage mood should be and by what means, in addition to speaking the words supplied by the author, the actor may reveal it.

Example: In Act I, Scene 4, Romeo's off-stage mood does not differ from his on-stage mood. Whatever his thoughts and emotions may be, they have been established long before the scene begins in which Romeo sets out with the revelers. The actor will probably wish to use an "ineffective entrance," playing the scene with a continuous flow of action, unbroken by any stops or sudden shifts in rate, thus hoping to establish an over-all, sustained mood.

On the other hand, it seems quite clear that Romeo's first line in Act II, Scene 2, "He jests at scars that never felt a wound," is in relation to the off-stage mood; the lighted window becomes the stimulus for the new on-stage mood, and the moment of contact with the scene may be placed just before Romeo says, "But, soft! what light through yonder window breaks?" or just after that line and before the next, "It is the east, and Juliet is the sun."

9. Sequence from *Romeo and Juliet,* Act I, Scene 1.

Work out the appropriate entrances for Benvolio, Tybalt, Capulet, Lady Capulet, Montague, Lady Montague, and the Prince. Entrances for the Citizens may also be worked out.

(*Enter Benvolio.*)

GREGORY: (*Aside to Sampson*) Say "better": here comes one of my master's kinsmen.

SAMPSON: Yes, better, sir.

ABRAHAM: You lie.

SAMPSON: Draw, if you be men, Gregory, remember thy swashing blow. (*They fight.*)

BENVOLIO: Part fools! (*Beating down their weapons.*)
        Put up your swords; you know not what you do.

(*Enter Tybalt.*)

TYBALT: What, art thou drawn among these heartless hinds?
        Turn thee, Benvolio, look upon thy death.

BENVOLIO: I do but keep the peace: put up thy sword,
        Or manage it to part these men with me.

TYBALT: What, drawn, and talk of peace! I hate the word,
        As I hate hell, all Montagues, and thee:
        Have at thee, coward! (*They fight.*)

(*Enter several of both houses, who join the fray: then enter other Citizens and Peace-officers, with clubs.*)

CITIZENS: Clubs, bills, and partisans! strike! beat them down! Down with the Capulets! down with the Montagues!

(*Enter old Capulet in his gown, and Lady Capulet.*)

CAPULET: What noise is this? Give me my long sword, ho!

LADY CAPULET: A crutch, a crutch! Why call you for a sword?

CAPULET: My sword, I say! Old Montague is come,
        And flourishes his blade in spite of me.

(*Enter old Montague and Lady Montague.*)

MONTAGUE: Thou villain Capulet! Hold me not, let me go.

LADY MONTAGUE: Thou shalt not stir one foot to seek a foe.

(*Enter Prince Escalus, with his train.*)

PRINCE ESCALUS: Rebellious subjects, enemies to peace,
            Profaners of this neighbor-stained steel,—
            Will they not hear? What, ho! you men, you beasts,
            That quench the fire of your pernicious rage
            With purple fountains issuing from your veins,
            On pain of torture, from those bloody hands
            Throw your mistemper'd weapons to the ground,
            And hear the sentence of your moved prince.

NOTE: There is some doubt about the exact moment when the Montagues enter since the dialogue indicates that they are on the scene prior to the printed instruction for them to enter. The actresses will find that there

is no time or place for them to do very much about establishing the characters of Lady Capulet and Lady Montague. The actors who play the
Citizens may establish any characterizations they choose to imagine. If
the actor playing the Prince considers the off-stage mood to be worry, concern, fear for the consequences of the fight, or excitement, and the on-
stage mood to be the showing of his power and of the dignity and authority
of his office, the actor will find that he can play the off-stage mood in
pantomime and establish the on-stage mood before the first line is spoken,
or he may use the first eight lines or any portion of them for the off-stage
mood and leave the establishing of the on-stage mood until as late as the
ninth line.

10. Sequence from *A Doll's House*.[1]

Work out the problems of making entrances and establishing characters
for the four roles in the following scene from *A Doll's House*. The scene
may be arranged in any way that suits the space available, but Ibsen suggests
the following:

*A room, comfortably and tastefully, but not expensively, furnished. In
the back, on the right, a door leads to the hall; on the left another door
leads to Helmer's study. Between the two doors a pianoforte. In the
middle of the left wall a door, and nearer the front a window. Near the
window a round table with arm-chairs and a small sofa. In the right wall,
somewhat to the back, a door, and against the same wall, further forward,
a porcelain stove; in front of it a couple of arm-chairs and a rocking-chair.
Between the stove and the side-door a small table.*

*A bell rings in the hall outside. Presently the outer door of the flat is
heard to open. Then Nora enters, humming gaily. She is in outdoor
dress, and carries several parcels, which she lays on the right-hand table.
She leaves the door into the hall open, and a porter is seen outside, carrying
a Christmas-tree and a basket, which he gives to the maid-servant who
has opened the door.*

NORA: Hide the Christmas-tree carefully, Ellen; the children must on no
account see it before this evening, when it's lighted up. (*To the porter, taking out her purse.*)   How much?

PORTER: Fifty ore.

NORA: There is a crown. No, keep the change.

*The porter thanks her and goes. Nora shuts the door. She continues
smiling in quiet glee as she takes off her outdoor things. Taking from
her pocket a bag of macaroons, she eats one or two. Then she goes on
tip-toe to her husband's door and listens.*

NORA: Yes; he is at home. (*She begins humming again, crossing to the
table on the right.*)

[1] Copyright by Charles Scribner's Sons.

HELMER: (*In his room.*)   Is that my lark twittering there?
NORA: (*Busy opening her parcels.*)   Yes, it is.
HELMER: Is it the squirrel frisking around?
NORA: Yes.
HELMER: When did the squirrel get home?
NORA: Just this minute. (*Hides the bag of macaroons in her pocket and wipes her mouth.*)   Come here, Torvald, and see what I've been buying.
HELMER: Don't interrupt me. (*A little later he opens the door and looks in, pen in hand.*)   Buying, did you say?   What!   All that?   Has my little spendthrift been making the money fly again?

NOTE: The actors playing the roles of the Porter and Ellen may work to establish any characterizations which they choose to imagine. Are they friendly or sullen?   Are they annoyed at being called upon to perform these duties, or do they enter into Nora's mood and the Christmas spirit?

Does Nora's mood of gaiety and Christmas excitement continue throughout the scene, or is it broken by her concern for her husband?   Ibsen indicates that the humming stops and is resumed.   Does this change the mood momentarily?   Is the humming resumed in the same manner, or is it resumed with the intention of attracting Helmer's attention?   How will the audience know the motivations for the resumption of the humming? How will the audience know whether the tiptoe cross to the husband's door is done in the same spirit of gaiety or in a more serious mood of concern lest the husband disapprove?

Ibsen says that Nora comes into the room and sets down the parcels before she pays the Porter.   If she sets them down with a sigh of relief and brings her actions to a momentary pause, the actress will have established contact with the scene.   If the actress is famous and the audience has come particularly to see her, the applause of greeting will come at this moment.   If the actress who is playing the role, whether or not she is famous, wishes to avoid this applause, she can set the parcels down without any pause in the action and turn immediately to the Porter.   In spite of Ibsen's directions, the actress may speak as she enters, setting the parcels down as she speaks.   The first pause in the action could be played just before or after she says, "How much?"

Ibsen's instruction that there is a considerable pause in the lines after Helmer says, "Don't interrupt me," and before he enters, presents a very serious problem which can be solved only by the imagination and invention of the actress playing Nora.   What happens on the stage during this pause?   Should Nora delay removing her outdoor things until this time?   Can the actress think of some interesting pantomime which will hold the attention of the audience?

The actor playing Helmer, being off-stage, will be forced to establish the first impression of his character through vocal techniques only. If his mood is one of pleased and amused tolerance of his wife's frivolity, is there a new mood of concern when he enters and says, "Buying, did you say?" or does the first mood continue? If there are two moods, is the "Don't interrupt me" part of the first or the second mood?

11. Sequence from *Romeo and Juliet,* Act I, Scene 3.
Work out the entrances for Lady Capulet, the Nurse, and Juliet. It should be decided whether or not Juliet has an off-stage mood which differs from her on-stage mood. The actresses should experiment with establishing different characterizations. *Example:* Lady Capulet could be played as an austere and dominating person or as a warm and affectionate person; Juliet may be sweet and docile and obedient, or she may be willful, resentful, and antagonistic toward her mother.

The scene is a room in Capulet's house.
(*Enter Lady Capulet and Nurse.*)
LADY CAPULET: Nurse, where's my daughter? call her forth to me.
NURSE: Now, by my maidenhead, at twelve year old,
       I bade her come. What, lamb! what, ladybird!
       God forbid! Where's this girl? What, Juliet!
JULIET: How now! who calls?
NURSE: Your mother.
JULIET: Madam, I am here. What is your will?

12. Scene from *Candida* [1] by George Bernard Shaw.
Let Candida enter as described in Shaw's directions, which are quoted in this chapter. Do the scene once so that her action has stopped and she is motionless when she speaks her first line, "Say yes, James," and once when she does not stop moving after she has spoken the line.

MORELL: (*Decisively—offering his hand.*) Shake hands, Burgess. Now you're talking honestly. I don't think they'll make me a bishop; but if they do, I'll introduce you to the biggest jobbers I can get to come to my dinner parties.

BURGESS: (*Who has risen with a sheepish grin, and accepted the hand of friendship.*) You will have your joke, James. Our quarrel's made up now, isn't it?

A WOMAN'S VOICE: Say yes, James.

13. Sequence from *Arms and the Man.* [2]
Work out the entrances for the two characters in the following scene:

Night. A lady's bedchamber in Bulgaria, in a small town near the Dragoman Pass. It is late in November in the year 1885, and through an open

---

[1] Copyright by The Public Trustee and The Society of Authors.
[2] Copyright by The Public Trustee and The Society of Authors.

window with a little balcony on the left can be seen a peak of the Balkans, wonderfully white and beautiful in the starlit snow. The door is on the right.

The window is hinged doorwise and stands wide open, folding back on the left. Outside a pair of wooden shutters, opening outwards, also stand open. On the balcony, a young lady, intensely conscious of the romantic beauty of the night, and of the fact that her own youth and beauty is a part of it, is gazing at the snowy Balkans.

Her reverie is interrupted by her mother, Catherine Petkoff, a woman over forty, imperiously energetic, with magnificent black hair and eyes, who might be a very splendid specimen of the wife of a mountain farmer, but is determined to be a Viennese lady, and to that end wears a fashionable tea gown on all occasions.

CATHERINE: (*entering hastily, full of good news*) Raina—(*she pronounces it Rah-eena, with the stress on the ee*) Raina—(*She goes to the bed, expecting to find Raina there*) Why, where—(*Raina looks into the room.*) Heavens! child, are you out in the night air instead of in your bed? You'll catch your death. Louka told me you were asleep.

RAINA: (*coming in*) I sent her away. I wanted to be alone. The stars are so beautiful! What is the matter?

CATHERINE: Such news. There has been a battle!

RAINA: (*her eyes dilating*) Ah! (*She throws the cloak on the ottoman, and comes eagerly to Catherine in her nightgown, a pretty garment, but evidently the only one she has on.*)

CATHERINE: A great battle at Slivnitza! A victory! And it was won by Sergius.

RAINA: (*with a cry of delight*) Ah! (*Rapturously.*) Oh, mother! (*Then, with sudden anxiety*) Is father safe?

Experiment with various poses, bodily attitudes, and pantomimic actions which will establish the character of Raina. Play "What is the matter?" as part of the romantic first mood and also play it as an excited response to her mother's entrance. Play Catherine with the momentary pause for character establishment after the first "Raina." Omit the pause at this moment and place it instead after the "Why, where. . . ." Play Catherine with no pause for character establishment.

Chapter 4. PHRASING ACTIONS
IN RELATION TO THOUGHTS

THE CLOSE examination of the dialogue of a scene from any play will reveal the fact that normally a character is given three or four sentences, depending upon their length, in which to express a single thought or feeling. If, for instance, in a greeting there is some reason why the audience should know the degree of warmth in the greeting it is apt to be expressed in several sentences; as "Hello. How are you? I'm glad to see you again. Where have you been?" If the greeting is expressed in a simple "Hello," then the actor would assume that the author did not think it necessary to define the relationship between the characters.

The Structure of Dialogue

There is an old rule of playwriting that if you want an audience to know anything you should repeat it three times. There is something about the psychology of an audience which requires that the attention be directed onto a given subject for a certain length of time for a large group of people to be impressed with the subject. If two characters merely greeted each other by saying "Hello" there would not be sufficient time for the greeting to become effective in the consciousness of the audience, but the more extended form of the greeting which includes several more sentences allows the audience time to be aware of the fact that the two characters have seen each other and have experienced a certain degree of pleasure or displeasure in so doing.

A simple exercise will illustrate the problem. Let one character greet another character, saying, "Hello. How are you? I'm glad to see you again. Where have you been?" Invent whatever actions seem appropriate to these lines. Then repeat the exercise using only one word of greeting, "Hello," but assume that the character's thoughts and feelings remain the same—that he is equally glad to see his friend, that the thought passes through his mind that he hasn't seen his friend for a long time, and that he wonders where the friend has been. The actor will immediately discover that it is impossible to convey these thoughts to the audi-

54

ence without either speaking the extra words or inventing pantomimic action, which would require approximately as much time as it would take to speak the words.

The amount of time which the audience needs to comprehend a thought or an emotion is also affected by the size of the auditorium in which the play is being performed. The larger the auditorium, the longer the time that will be required for the effective presentation of a thought—possibly because it takes sight and sound longer to travel the length of a large auditorium, possibly because people sitting at a greater distance from the stage tend to concentrate less strongly on the play. Whatever the reason, the actor will soon learn from experience that he must vary his acting rhythm according to the size of the theater in which he is appearing if his performance is to be equally effective.

A comparison of the script of a motion picture with the script of the play from which it was adapted will reveal the fact that screen writers tend to cut down the amount of dialogue used for the expression of each thought or emotion. Since the characters in a motion picture are enlarged on the screen, the audience, even those who are sitting at a considerable distance from the screen, receive the same impression they might receive if they were watching the performance in a theater from a seat close to the stage.

The use of the close-up makes it possible for every member of the audience to be as near to the actors as the camera is, the camera becoming, as it were, the eyes of the audience. With the camera a few feet from the face of the actor, it is possible for him to express the full meaning of his greeting, even though the script permits him to say only, "Hello." In such a situation, a twinkle in the eye or a faint smile may be enlarged so that everyone in the audience, no matter how far he is sitting from the screen, can be made aware of it, while the same facial expression used by an actor playing in a large theater would go unnoticed except by those in the first few rows. Later the appropriate size of a performance will be discussed, but for the moment we are concerned only with the amount of time necessary to express a thought or an emotion adequately.

The Duration of Action in Relation to the Duration of Thought

It is natural for a person to change his facial expression and his bodily attitude as he experiences new thoughts or new emotions. In the present exercises the new thought and the new emotion are engendered by seeing another person whom the character knows but has not seen for a considerable time. The actor, upon receiving this stimulus, will respond to it by changing his facial expression to one which he considers appropriate to the emotion he is now attempting to express, and he will begin to perform a bodily action which he considers appropriate to the character he is playing and expressive of the character's emotional relationship to the person he has just seen. If the actor considers the character a reserved, quiet, and placid type, the change in facial expression and physical attitude may be very slight. If he wishes to portray the character as effusive and enthusiastic, then the change will be larger and more noticeable.

Whatever the change, the new expression and the new bodily attitude will be sustained as long as the character is dominated by the thought and the emotion that stimulated the change, which will be until he receives some new stimulus. In the present exercise the actor will need a bodily action which can be continued for the length of time which it takes him to say, "Hello. How are you? I'm glad to see you again. Where have you been?"

The invention and selection of the appropriate action will also be conditioned by the space relationship of the two characters upon the stage. If, for instance, the characters are 5 feet apart, or 10, or 15, at the moment when they see each other, and if the author or the director requires that they meet and shake hands, then the appropriate action will be slightly different according to the number of steps which must be taken.

If the actors are 20 feet apart when they see each other and if the speaking character must move across the stage to shake hands with the other character, then the problem is similar to the one posed by the walking exercise discussed in Chapter 3. Great care must be taken to time the action scene so that the speech lasts as long as it takes to complete the action, the handshake being completed with the last line of the speech. To illustrate the technical problem involved, the actor might try the action including a 20-foot cross and a handshake but omitting the last two sentences, saying only, "Hello. How are you?" In this instance the actor is likely to be embarrassed when he finds that he has completed the speech before he has completed the action.

The problem of inventing an appropriate action is completely changed if the director decides that the speaking character should remain stationary and the other character should cross the stage to meet him. Now the speaking actor will be forced to use only hand and arm gestures and to rely more upon a change of facial expression to express his thought and his emotional reaction, while the other actor will be forced to time his walking to the speech of the first actor.

A little experimentation with the various ways of playing this scene will reveal that it is very difficult to play the scene in different ways and still have it convey precisely the same meaning. A shorter walk, say 5 feet instead of 20, will make it seem that the character is less pleased to meet the other character again. If the character is allowed to take only two steps toward the other person, the actor will find that he is forced to extend the handshaking into a hand pumping, or to add some back-slapping.

Action Used to Phrase the Thought

If it is normal and natural for a person to continue the same bodily action or attitude as long as he is motivated by the same thought or emotion, it follows that a change of thought or emotion can be indicated to the audience by a change of bodily action. If, in the present exercise, the two characters are approximately 10 feet apart when they first see each other and if the speaking actor waves a greeting while he says, "Hello. How are you?" and then begins to walk toward the other actor as he says, "I'm glad to see you again. Where have you been?" the audience will understand that the character has suddenly remembered that he had not seen the other person for a considerable time. Phrasing the scene this way gives it a slightly different meaning. The actor can rephrase the scene by smiling as he says, "Hello," and beginning the walk at that point.

A very different meaning will be conveyed if it is the nonspeaking character who begins to move after the "Hello" or after the next sentence. Now it will be understood that the speaking character had not intended to go on with the rest of the speech but was motivated to do so by the approach of the other character.

Using Action to Phrase a Scene from The Merchant of Venice

Making a change in the physical action or the bodily attitude of a character, since this tends to indicate a change in his thought or emotion, is one of the actor's most useful devices for projecting his interpretation of a role. In *The Merchant of Venice*, Act I, Scene 3, Bassanio and Shylock enter, and the following dialogue takes place:

SHY: Three thousand ducats; well?
BASS: Ay, sir, for three months.
SHY: For three months; well?
BASS: For which, as I told you, Antonio shall be bound.

SHY: Antonio shall be bound; well?

BASS: May you stead me? Will you pleasure me? Shall I know your answer?

SHY: Three thousand ducats, for three months, and Antonio bound.

BASS: Your answer to that.

SHY: Antonio is a good man.

The scene continues with Shylock's explanation of what he means by saying, "Antonio is a good man."

Suppose the director works out the action so that Shylock enters first, followed by Bassanio, and that the two move approximately 20 feet, or eight normal-sized steps, from a point up left or right to a place further downstage and on the opposite side of the stage. There are, as always, an infinite variety of ways that this action may be combined with the lines, and each change in the phrasing of the words in relation to the actions will project a different meaning to the audience.

First of all, the structure of the dialogue should be noted. Shylock's first three speeches are a statement of the problem. Then Bassanio asks for his answer in three sentences. Shylock recapitulates the problem in a three-clause statement, mentioning the money, the time, and the security. Bassanio again asks for his answer, and Shylock replies by introducing a new subject.

The scene can be played with Shylock walking slowly and meditatively through his first three speeches, pausing, and then continuing to walk, not only on his own speeches, but also on those of Bassanio. The stop in the walk will indicate to Bassanio that the proposition has been clearly stated and understood and will motivate him to press for an answer. As an alternative, Shylock may move only on his own speeches. In this plan each stop becomes a separate stimulus to motivate each of Bassanio's speeches, and the scene is divided into three separate little scenes. A further variation is for Shylock to stop his walk just before he says each of the "well's" and, if the actor chooses to do so, to turn his head slightly toward Bassanio as he says each of the "well's." This will create the impression that Bassanio needs urging to continue his proposition, and he will therefore seem hesitant or embarrassed, although the actor playing Bassanio has not himself done anything to create this effect.

The actor playing Bassanio will have the option of following Shylock as he crosses or of holding back on the opposite side of the stage. If he stays back during the first speeches, then he will be able to move toward Shylock as he says, "May you stead me? Will you pleasure me? Shall I know your answer?" If he elects to play it this way, he has the additional option of walking toward Shylock on all three of the questions, or only on one or two of them, in which case Shylock's failure to reply to either the first or the second question will seem to have irritated Bassanio.

Dividing the action creates the effect of dividing the thoughts or emotions, making two or more separate but related thoughts; playing the scene without breaking or dividing the actions makes the characters seem to be motivated by only one thought, which is sustained for a longer time.

If it has been planned that Shylock will turn and look at Bassanio before he says, "Antonio is a good man," the actor playing Shylock will have the option of making the turn as he says, "Antonio will be bound, well?" or on his next speech, or on the one after that. Each change in the action will make a slight change in the audience's interpretation of Shylock's thoughts and emotions.

Using Action to Phrase a Scene from Romeo and Juliet

Act I, Scene 5, of *Romeo and Juliet* provides another example of the way in which physical action may be used to indicate to the audience the precise moment when a new thought or new emotion begins. The guests are leaving after the ball, and Juliet and the Nurse are watching them go:

> JUL.: Come hither, Nurse. What is yond gentleman?
> NURSE: The son and heir of old Tiberio.
> JUL.: What's he that now is going out of door?
> NURSE: Marry, that, I think, be young Petruchio.
> JUL.: What's he, that follows there, that would not dance?
> NURSE: I know not.
> JUL.: Go, ask his name.

This scene, like the Shylock-Bassanio scene, is also constructed on a series of three questions and answers. It may be played as one continuous thought if Juliet, standing in a place where she can observe the departing guests, asks all three questions with no particular change in her physical attitude; or it may be broken into three smaller units by having her turn to look back at the Nurse for each answer; or it may be played so that the first two questions and answers are a unit and the last question, which is, of course, the most important one, is distinguished from the others by some new physical attitude.

Juliet, in this scene, is dissembling for the Nurse; the assumed curiosity of her first two questions is intended to disguise the real curiosity in her third question. It is a matter of artistic interpretation for the actress to decide whether or not Juliet is clever enough to conceal her emotions from the Nurse, or from the audience, as she asks the last question. If the actress elects to show Juliet's feelings at this point, thus making it clear to both the Nurse and the audience that the third question has a different and more important emotional motivation, then the actress playing the Nurse must decide whether or not she should observe the change in Juliet's manner, as the audience will observe it, or whether she should so contrive her actions that she is not looking at Juliet when Juliet asks the question and reveals her feelings.

If this were all there was to the scene, it would probably be considered absolutely necessary for Juliet to reveal her feelings to the audience when she asks the third question; but in the moment when the Nurse goes to discover the identity of the guest, Juliet says, "If he be married, my grave is like to be my wedding bed." This sentence adequately satisfies the necessity of keeping the audience informed of the character's feelings and thoughts, and therefore the decision to reveal or hide the emotions which Juliet presumably experiences as she watches Romeo leave may be left to the discretion of the actress playing the part.

Using Action to Phrase a Speech from Julius Caesar

This method of analyzing the structure and form of a dialogue to discover the characters' thought and emotion sequences may also be applied to a longer speech of a single character. Brutus' speech in the Forum in Act III, Scene 2, of *Julius Caesar* is an excellent example of a theatrical speech constructed with approximately three sentences devoted to the expression of a single thought or emotion. Having quieted the citizens, Brutus begins:

> Hear me for my cause; and be silent, that you may hear: believe me for mine honour, and have respect to mine honour, that you may believe: censure me in your wisdom, and awake your senses, that you may the better judge.

This is the end of his first thought. He continues:

> If there be any in this assembly, any dear friend of Caesar's, to him I say, that Brutus' love to Caesar was no less than his. If then that friend demand why Brutus rose against Caesar, this is my answer: Not that I loved Caesar less, but that I loved Rome more.

The next sentence is an extension or a fuller explanation of the preceding thought:

> Had you rather Caesar were living, and die all slaves, than, that Caesar were dead, to live all free men?

Now follows a perfect threefold sentence structure, with an effective fourth phrase in sudden contrast to the beginning of the sentence:

> As Caesar loved me, I weep for him; as he was fortunate, I rejoice at it; as he was valiant, I honour him; but as he was ambitious, I slew him.

The same structure is repeated in the next sentence:

> There is tears for his love; joy for his fortune; honour for his valour; and death for his ambition.

Brutus concludes the speech with the third repetition of the threefold structure:

> Who is here so base that would be a bondman? If any, speak; for him have I offended. Who is here so rude that would not be a Roman? If any, speak; for him have I offended. Who is here so vile that will not love his country? If any, speak; for him have I offended. I pause for a reply.

In this speech, Brutus reveals himself to be a master of the art of persuasion; and it must be presumed that he is as careful in the selection of his physical attitudes as he is in his choice of words. It is his aim to have his arguments appear logical, so that the assassination of Caesar will seem to have been inevitable and justified. Brutus is trying to make the right impression upon the citizens of Rome; but the actor playing the part will want to make the right impression, not only on the citizens of Rome, but also on the audience, and the two impressions are not necessarily identical.

The actor playing the role of Brutus will be limited in his selection of physical attitudes—first, by his own physical appearance and by those gestures which he is capable of performing; second, by his interpretation of the character of Brutus, who in this scene seems to be making an effort to appear as a simple, direct, and logical man who is making an appeal to the reason rather than to the emotions of the crowd; third, by the physical arrangements of the scene, which will probably provide a platform on which Brutus stands, a podium for him to stand behind, and sufficient space around the podium so that he may also stand on either side of it and possibly in front of it; and finally, by the situation, for Brutus is supposed to be addressing a large group of Romans and so his gestures, though restrained, must be large enough to be easily seen by the entire crowd. The size of the theater in which the play is to be performed will also have a bearing upon the size of the gestures to be used, for the spectators in the last rows of the gallery, as well as the Romans in the play, must see and understand the gestures and the words.

The various techniques suggested for the Bassanio-Shylock scene and

the Juliet-Nurse scene are also possible alternatives for the actor playing
Brutus: he may combine the three parts of each thought together, speaking all three sentences while performing one gesture or action, or while
remaining in one physical attitude; or he may have a separate gesture or
attitude for each of the three parts of the thought; or he may combine
two of the thoughts together, separating them from the final one in order
to make it a separate point.

It should be obvious—if not, a little experimentation on the part of the
student will quickly make it obvious—that to play all four of the sequences with the same technical method will make the scene seem ridiculous and the actor unresourceful and unimaginative. Certainly the second
method, that of using a separate gesture or attitude for each of the parts
of the thought, quickly reduces the speech to an absurdity. The actor
will soon discover that it is to his advantage to make use of all the technical methods available to him, a different one for each of the sequences.

The similarity in the structure of the two sentences beginning, "As
Caesar loved me," has been noted—each sentence having three similar
phrases followed by a fourth phrase, the meaning of which contrasts
with the thought of the beginning phrases. The actor might conclude
that it would be best to assign a new gesture or physical attitude to the
last phrase of each sentence in order to emphasize the contrast in the
meaning; but this would be contrary to the aims of Brutus, who must
wish the Romans to consider the last phrase a logical conclusion to the
preceding phrases. It is probably best, therefore, to play each of these
sentences with a single appropriate gesture which is large enough to include all four of the phrases, or with a single physical attitude which can
be maintained while the four phrases are being spoken.

Once the actor has decided that these two sentences, or any other sequence or sequences, should be played in a particular manner, he can
proceed to assign specific technical methods to the remaining passages.
Possibly the first sequence, beginning, "Hear me for my cause," and the
last sequence, beginning, "Who is here so base," might be treated in such
a way that they are divided into their separate component parts.

If the actor would like to try this method of playing the scene to
see whether the technical devices are adequate for the entire scene, he
might play it in the following manner. Brutus, standing behind the
podium, might look toward the audience (his Roman audience), who are
on his left, his right, and in front of him, as he delivers the first sequence,
turning his head or his whole body to the left, the right, and the front
as he speaks each of its three parts.

During the second sequence he might move forward and to the side
of the podium, as though he wished to speak more simply and more di-

rectly to any individuals in the audience (still the Roman audience), who might have felt as he did toward Caesar. The extra phrase, "Had you rather Caesar were living . . . ?" could be delivered from the same position, but with a body turn toward those who are on the opposite side.

The two crucial sequences which explain the reason for Brutus' part in the assassination might be delivered from the same place, each played with an appropriate hand gesture to be invented by the actor. Then the final sequence might be delivered with Brutus turning, or even moving, toward a different part of his Roman audience on each phrase, as was suggested for the first sequence. These moves could easily be worked out in such a way that Brutus finishes the speech either behind or in front of the podium, depending on which position seems the more advantageous for playing the scene which follows.

Whether the actor invents a floor pattern and technical plan for playing a scene before he begins rehearsals or after he has rehearsed the scene a sufficient number of times to become familiar with the exact thoughts and emotions he is trying to project will depend upon the preference of the individual artist.

EXERCISES

1. Two characters greet each other, one character saying, "Hello. How are you? I'm glad to see you again. Where have you been?"

   a. Perform the scene with the two characters approximately 20 feet apart when they see each other and with the speaking actor crossing to the silent actor and shaking his hand.

   b. Repeat the exercise, but omit the cross, the speaking actor remaining in place. There is no handshake.

   c. Repeat the exercise, maintaining the same thoughts and emotions and the same action as in a, but saying only the "Hello."

   d. Repeat, keeping the action as in b, but saying only the "Hello."

   e. Repeat as in a, but change the distance between the actors to 15 feet; to 10 feet; to 5 feet.

   f. Repeat all the above exercises with the speaking actor remaining in place and the nonspeaking actor performing the cross and initiating the handshake.

   g. Repeat all the above exercises, including f, with as many changes in characterization as possible. *Example:* Two society ladies at a tea, two businessmen at a smoker, a society lady and a businessman at a dance, two octogenarians, two high school students, a high school student and a former teacher, etc.

h. Repeat as in *a* and in *f,* but begin the cross toward the other actor while saying, "Hello."

i. Repeat as in *h,* but begin the cross after saying, "Hello.   How are you?"

j. Repeat as in *h,* but begin the cross after saying, "Hello.   How are you? I'm glad to see you again."

NOTE: Beginning the action at a later moment seems to indicate that the action has been stimulated, not by seeing the person, but by a thought concerning the person which occurs momentarily later.   The first greeting becomes more perfunctory, and the emotion reveals itself when the action starts.

2. Sequence from *The Merchant of Venice,* Act I, Scene 3.

Bassanio and Shylock enter.

SHY.: Three thousands ducats; well?

BASS.: Ay, sir, for three months.

SHY.: For three months; well?

BASS.: For which, as I told you, Antonio shall be bound.

SHY.: Antonio shall be bound; well?

BASS.: May you stead me?   Will you pleasure me?   Shall I know your answer?

SHY.: Three thousand ducats, for three months, and Antonio bound.

BASS.: Your answer to that.

SHY.: Antonio is a good man.

a. Shylock and Bassanio enter and cross from up left to down right.   Shylock moves slowly, meditatively, and continuously while he speaks, as well as while Bassanio speaks, until he finishes the line, "Antonio shall be bound; well?"   Bassanio follows, slightly behind Shylock, also moving continuously and at the same rate as Shylock.

b. Shylock has the same business as in *a,* but Bassanio stops walking as he delivers his first speech.   Then Bassanio crosses to Shylock on the speech beginning, "May you stead me?" moving continuously through the whole line.

c. Shylock moves a few steps on his first line, followed by Bassanio on his first line.   Shylock stops and looks at Bassanio on Shylock's second line, and Bassanio is also stopped on his second line.   Shylock begins to move away again on "Antonio shall be bound; well?"   Bassanio also moves on his next line, thus having a shorter cross for this speech than in *b,* but longer than in *a,* where he could have no more than a step.

d. The curtain rises with both characters on stage, standing near each other. Neither one takes any steps throughout the scene.

e. They enter as in *a;* Shylock moves a few steps on his first line, turning to look back at Bassanio as he says, "Well?"   Bassanio moves toward

Shylock as he says, "Ay, sir, for three months." Shylock turns thoughtfully away from Bassanio but does not move away as he says, "For three months; well?" Bassanio moves behind Shylock and to the other side of Shylock as he says, "For which, as I told you, Antonio shall be bound." Shylock moves a few steps in front and to the other side of Bassanio as he says, "Antonio shall be bound; well?" Bassanio moves to beside Shylock as he says, "May you stead me? Will you pleasure me?" and again crosses behind Shylock as he says, "Shall I know your answer?" Shylock moves away from him in the opposite direction as he says, "Three thousand ducats, for three months, and Antonio bound." Bassanio moves after him on the next line, "Your answer to that."

NOTE: Exercise *d* will seem too static, while *e* will seem too busy and will almost have a comic effect.

f. Work out other plausible patterns of movement and select the one which seems to accord best with your interpretation of the scene and to make the best sequence of thoughts and emotions, not breaking the thoughts into too many separate bits, and not leaving a thought too extended to sustain audience interest.

3. Sequence from *Romeo and Juliet*, Act I, Scene 5.

Juliet and the Nurse are watching the guests leave.
JUL.: Come hither, Nurse, What is yond gentleman?
NURSE: The son and heir of old Tiberio.
JUL.: What's he that now is going out of door?
NURSE: Marry, that, I think, be young Petruchio.
JUL.: What's he, that follows there, that would not dance?
NURSE: I know not.
JUL.: Go ask his name.

a. Play the scene so that Juliet's lack of interest in the first two men is clearly differentiated from her interest in the last. Have this difference noticed by the Nurse.

b. Play the scene for the same values as in *a*, but in such a way that the audience, but not the Nurse, would be likely to notice the difference in Juliet's emotions.

c. Play the scene so that Juliet does not reveal the change in her emotions to either the audience or the Nurse.

d. Play the scene as in *a*, *b*, and *c*, but eliminate as far as possible any use of movement, gesture, or change in physical attitude on the part of either actress. Rely as much as possible on vocal techniques only.

NOTE: The actresses will find this exercise difficult, if not impossible to do. In trying to do it, they will probably find that they are using small actions, gestures, and facial expressions.

e. Play the scene so that Juliet does not reveal the change in her emotions to either the audience or the Nurse, but presuppose that the Nurse already suspects Juliet's interest in Romeo and knows what the questions mean and to what they are leading.

4. Sequence from *Arms and the Man,*[1] Act II.

Raina, a very romantic young lady, is talking with her mother, Catherine. They have just heard that a Swiss soldier whom Raina had saved by hiding him in her room while the soldiers searched for him has told the episode as a funny story to the man Raina is engaged to marry and to her father. Raina had given him a coat in which to escape and had also fed him some chocolate creams.

CATHERINE: Imagine their meeting that Swiss and hearing the whole story! The very first thing your father asked for was the old coat you sent him off in. A nice mess you've got us into!

RAINA: (*gazing thoughtfully at the gravel as she walks*) The little beast!

CATHERINE: Little beast! What little beast?

RAINA: To go and tell. Oh, if I had him here, I'd stuff him with chocolate creams till he couldn't ever speak again!

CATHERINE: Don't talk nonsense. Tell me the truth, Raina. How long was he in your room before you came to me?

RAINA: (*whisking round and recommencing her march in the opposite direction*) Oh, I forget.

CATHERINE: You cannot forget! Did he really climb up after the soldiers were gone, or was he there when that officer searched the room?

RAINA: No. Yes, I think he must have been there then.

CATHERINE: You think! Oh, Raina, Raina! Will anything ever make you straightforward?

a. Work out the scene according to Shaw's stage directions.
b. Do the "whisking round" business in the previous speech, after saying, "To go and tell!" and before saying, "Oh, if I had him here . . . !"
c. Now do the same action in a later speech, after saying, "No," and before saying, "Yes."
NOTE: Changing the placement of the action seems to change the place in which Raina's emotions begin and end.

5. Sequence from *Winterset,*[2] Act I, Scene 3.

The scene is a poor tenement section of New York, down under the abutments of a large bridge. Mio and Carr, road boys of seventeen or so, come round the apartment house.

CARR: Thought you said you were never coming east again.

[1] Copyright by The Public Trustee and The Society of Authors.
[2] Copyright by Anderson House.

MIO: Yeah, but—I heard something changed my mind.

CARR: Same old business?

MIO: Yes. Just as soon not talk about it.

CARR: Where did you go from Portland?

MIO: Fishing—I went fishing. God's truth.

CARR: Right after I left?

MIO: Fell in with a fisherman's family on the coast, and
went after the beautiful mackerel fish that live in the
beautiful sea. Family of Greeks—Aristedes Marinos
was his lovely name. He sang while he fished. Made the
pea-green Pacific ring with his bastard Greek chanties.
Then I went to Hollywood High School for a while.

CARR: I'll bet that's a seat of learning.

MIO: It's the hind end of all wisdom. They kicked me out
after a time.

CARR: For cause?

MIO: Because I had no permanent address, you see. That
means nobody's paying taxes for you, so out you go.

a. Play the scene once with as little action as possible.

b. Play it indicating the changes in thought by changes in action. Invent
some action for Mio as he says, "Just as soon not talk about it," and just
before he says, "Then I went to Hollywood High School for a while."

c. Play it again, putting Mio's first move as he says, "Fishing," and the
second move just before he says, "They kicked me out after a time."

d. Repeat the scene with Mio not moving appreciably, but have Carr move
on "Where did you go from Portland?" and on "I'll bet that's a seat
of learning."

e. Combine Mio's moves in *b* with Carr's moves in *d*.

f. Combine Mio's moves in *c* with Carr's moves in *d*.

g. Experiment with different physical attitudes for Mio to show changes
in his emotional state. Find a way to suggest his remembered pleasure
of the fishing adventure and his remembered displeasure of the high school
episode.

6. Sequence from *Julius Caesar*, Act III, Scene 2.

*Brutus is addressing the assembled citizens who have come to the funeral
of the assassinated Caesar.*

BRUTUS: (*speaking from the rostrum*) Romans, countrymen, and lovers!
hear me for my cause, and be silent that you may hear: believe me for mine
honour, and have respect to mine honour, that you may believe: censure me
in your wisdom, and awake your senses that you may the better judge. If
there be any in this assembly, any dear friend of Caesar's, to him I say, that

Brutus' love to Caesar was no less than his.   If, then, that friend demand why
Brutus rose against Caesar, this is my answer: Not that I loved Caesar less,
but that I loved Rome more.   Had you rather Caesar were living, and die all
slaves, than that Caesar were dead, to live all freemen?   As Caesar loved me,
I weep for him; as he was fortunate, I rejoice at it; as he was valiant, I honour
him; but as he was ambitious, I slew him.   There is tears for his love; joy for
his fortune; honour for his valour; and death for his ambition.   Who is here so
base, that would be a bondman?   If any, speak; for him have I offended.   Who
is here so rude, that would not be a Roman?   If any, speak; for him have I
offended.   Who is here so vile, that will not love his country?   If any, speak;
for him have I offended.   I pause for a reply.

    a. Divide the speech into its component parts and select a movement, a
       gesture, or a physical attitude appropriate to each and capable of being
       sustained for the duration of the thought with which it is associated.
       Example: One action, attitude, or gesture for the first sentence, beginning,
       "Hear me for my cause," and ending, "That you may the better judge."
    b. Subdivide each of the major component parts of the speech which were
       used in *a,* and select an appropriate movement, action, or gesture for each
       of these subdivisions.   *Example:* One movement, action, attitude or ges-
       ture for "Hear me for my cause, and be silent that you may hear," and
       another for "Believe me for mine honour, and have respect to mine
       honour, that you may believe."
    c. Whenever possible, make a further subdivision and again select ap-
       propriate actions.   *Example:* One attitude or gesture for "Hear me for
       my cause," and another for "And be silent that you may hear."
    d. Play the scene as statically as possible, using only one physical attitude
       for the entire speech.
    e. Play the scene using the attitudes selected for the major component parts
       of the speech.
    f. Play the scene observing all the first subdivisions of the major thoughts.
    g. Play the scene observing all the smallest subdivisions of the thoughts.
    h. Play the scene in many different ways, using various combinations of the
       above exercises.   *Example:* Play one part of the scene as in *e,* another
       as in *f,* and another as in *g;* then play the first thought as in *g,* the
       second as in *f,* and the third as in *e.*
    i. Devise what you consider to be the best way to play the scene, and
       then rehearse it until you can perform it perfectly.

7. Sequence from *The Merchant of Venice,* Act IV, Scene 1.

    Portia is speaking to Shylock before the assembled court.   One may presume
    that she also has a rostrum from which to speak.   Portia says:
            The quality of mercy is not strain'd,

It droppeth as the gentle rain from heaven
Upon the place beneath: it is twice bless'd;
It blesseth him that gives and him that takes:
'Tis mightiest in the mightiest: It becomes
The throned monarch better than his crown;
His sceptre shows the force of temporal power,
The attribute to awe and majesty,
Wherein doth sit the dread and fear of kings;
But mercy is above this sceptred sway;
It is enthroned in the hearts of kings,
It is an attribute to God himself;
And earthly power doth then shew likest God's
When mercy seasons justice. Therefore, Jew,
Though justice be thy plea, consider this,—
That in the course of justice, none of us
Should see salvation: we do pray for mercy;
And that same prayer doth teach us all to render
The deeds of mercy.

a. Study this speech in the same manner as suggested for Brutus' speech
and deliver it in the various ways described in exercise 4.

Chapter 5. PROGRESSIONS

THE SKILLFUL playwright arranges any sequence of lines devoted to the expression of a single emotion or thought in such a way that the least important or consequential part of the thought is stated first and each following sentence is an extension or an amplification of the thought, with the most important sentence placed at the end of the sequence.   In the Bassanio-Shylock scene, for example, the amount of money and the duration of the loan are of less importance to the plot and the character relationships than is the fact that Antonio is to be bound, which is presented as the third of the three conditions.   In the Juliet-Nurse scene quoted in Chapter 4, only the stranger who would not dance, the subject of Juliet's final question, has any significance in the story.

The Need for Technical Progressions

Just as the author has taken infinite pains to arrange the dialogue in such a way that it constantly seems to be moving toward a climax, so the actor must constantly speak the lines in such a way that they always seem to be moving forward, to be advancing the plot or amplifying the characterizations.   That which follows must always be made to seem more important and more interesting than that which has preceded. Theater audiences are intolerant of any lessening of interest or any sense of retrogression.   Even an attempt to maintain the same level of interest will not satisfy an audience.   A play that does not seem to be moving forward will tend to bore an audience almost as much as it would if it were moving backwards.

Actually, the dialogue of a play does not and cannot move constantly forward and upward in an unbroken line.   What happens is that a thought is introduced and developed to its own climax and then a new thought is introduced, which must begin immediately to move toward its climax.   Possibly there will be a drop in interest after the climax of the first thought, but this will not worry an audience, or even be apparent, provided the next thought is immediately introduced and the development toward a new climax immediately begun.

70

The Limited Number of Technical Devices

Although the actor has only a limited number of technical devices by which to develop a progression corresponding to, and exactly suited to, the progression in the dialogue, the number of possible combinations of these devices is almost infinite, so that there seems to be practically no limitation on the different ways of playing a scene. Every art is subject to similar limitations, a thorough knowledge of which opens up limitless possibilities. A painter is limited by his palette; everything he paints must be red, orange, yellow, green, blue, violet, brown, black, or some combination of these, plus white, and of these colors only three—red, yellow, and blue—are actually primaries, the others being already combinations; and yet the skillful painter can achieve a limitless number of shades, hues, and tones. [A composer is limited by the eight notes of a scale, but from these he may compose an unlimited number of melodies and harmonies.] Not true !! A composer can use note that are not in the scale. He can even create his own scale,

The Division between Vocal Techniques and Physical Techniques

In acting the technical devices are divided into two main groups, since acting is itself a combination of speaking and doing: the vocal techniques and the physical techniques. Almost constantly the actor will find it necessary to be using some vocal technique in combination with some physical technique. Only in pantomime scenes will he be able to use physical techniques without vocal ones, and only in a medium like radio will he be able to use only vocal techniques; for if he stands absolutely motionless and expressionless while he is speaking a line, that fact will have connotations and meaning for an audience, and will be considered to be a manifestation of the character in relation to the dramatic situation. In a sense, such a moment in acting is like a rest in music, or the use of white or black in a painting; the separation of the vocal from the physical becomes in itself an important and an effective technical device.

The Vocal Techniques

I. INCREASE IN VOLUME

The most frequently used and the most obvious vocal technical device is a gradual increase in the volume. There are many scenes, particularly quarrel scenes, in which it is natural and almost inevitable that each actor speak each line slightly louder than he did the preceding one. The sequence between Abraham and Sampson in the first scene of *Romeo and Juliet*, for example, plays easily in this manner:

ABR.: Do you bite your thumb at us, sir?
SAM: I do bite my thumb, sir.
ABR.: Do you bite your thumb at us, sir?
SAM: (*aside to Gregory*) Is the law of our side if I say ay?
GRE: (*aside to Sampson*) No.
SAM: No, sir, I do not bite my thumb at you, sir; but I bite my thumb, sir.

The easiest way, and possibly the most natural way, to play this scene is for each actor to speak each sentence louder than the last, with the exception of the two speeches which are spoken aside. Even the asides may be brought into the gradual progression by volume if Gregory stands several paces to one side and Sampson crosses to him to ask the question and then crosses back to Abraham to renew the quarrel.

In doing the "Hello. How are you?" exercise described in Chapter 4, the actor will discover that if he is required by the action to remain standing in one place he can still create the effect of having a hearty interest in the other character by increasing his volume as he speaks. In this case the increase in volume becomes a substitute for the action. It is quite probable that the first time the actor performs this exercise he will naturally and unconsciously use an increase in volume together with the action. It will increase his control of his technical abilities, however, to try making the cross but being careful to maintain the same volume.

2. IN RAISING THE PITCH

Since it seems natural for the voice to rise in pitch as it increases in volume, the actor will experience little difficulty in playing many scenes in this manner. He may, however, find it difficult to play a scene in which he must increase the volume without raising the pitch. The Abraham-Sampson scene is one which may be played this way.

If the actor playing Abraham speaks the second "Do you bite your thumb at us, sir?" with a considerable increase in volume but no change in pitch, he will seem more angry than he would if his voice rose in pitch, but he will also seem to be controlling his anger. The increase in volume suggests an increase in his emotion, but since it is normal in such a case for the pitch to rise with the volume, the fact that Abraham has not allowed his voice to follow the normal pattern will create the impression that his anger is greater, but partially concealed. The actor will find few instances, however, in which it seems appropriate to play a scene with a gradual rise in the pitch of the voice without a corresponding increase in the volume. The ability to control volume and pitch separately is one of the most necessary skills for the actor.

3. INCREASE IN THE RATE OF SPEAKING

In addition to increasing the volume of a speech and raising the pitch, an actor may also gain variety by changing his rate of speaking. One place where this technique might be used for a comic effect is in *As You Like It*, Act V, Scene 4, when Touchstone is asked to nominate in order the degrees of the lie:

> The first, the Retort Courteous; the second, the Quip Modest; the third, the Reply Churlish; the fourth, the Reproof Valiant; the fifth, the Counter-check Quarrelsome; the sixth, the Lie with Circumstance; the seventh, the Lie Direct.

Any considerable acceleration in the rate of speaking is likely to decrease the audience's comprehension of the lines. The actor who uses an increase in rate on this passage substitutes the humor of Touchstone's glibness for the humor of the lines themselves.

In the motion-picture version of *Hamlet*, Laurence Olivier used an extreme acceleration of speech in his scene with the Queen, Act III, Scene 4. Even though every word was spoken with great clarity, the sense of the words was lost on an audience; Olivier had chosen to communicate Hamlet's excitement and anger rather than the actual sense of his words. This is a completely justifiable treatment of certain lines, for there are circumstances in which it is natural to speak in this manner; but it is dangerous for an actor to use the device often, since the audience is likely to feel frustrated if words are being spoken which cannot be understood.

4, 5, AND 6. DECREASE IN VOLUME, PITCH, AND RATE

The three vocal techniques discussed—an increase in volume, a rise in pitch, and an increase in rate—may all be effectively used in reverse—that is, a decrease in volume, a lowering of pitch, and a decrease in rate. In the speech of the Prince in Act I, Scene 1, of *Romeo and Juliet*, it would seem appropriate for the first few lines to be spoken with a gradual increase in volume and for the next few lines to be spoken with a decrease in volume after the citizens and the Montagues and Capulets have begun to listen.

> Rebellious subjects, enemies to peace,
> Profaners of this neighbor-stained steel,—
> Will they not hear? What ho! you men, you beasts,
> That quench the fire of your pernicious rage
> With purple fountains issuing from your veins,
> On pain of torture, from those bloody hands

> Throw your mis-tempered weapons to the ground,
> And hear the sentence of your moved prince.

If the actor attempts to play this entire speech with an ever-increasing volume, he will find that he has reached his maximum volume long before he has finished the speech. If, on the other hand, he increases the volume through "What ho! you men," or even through "You beasts," he can build to a climax until he has been heard above the noise of the fighting; the remainder of the speech will gain in effectiveness and create a sense of power and authority in the Prince if it is spoken with a gradually de-creasing volume, the actor reaching normal volume at the end of the speech.

In practicing such a passage, the student may discover that his voice is not yet capable of achieving the volume required for the climax, in which case he must go back to beginning exercises to increase the power of his voice. The Prince's speech is an excellent one to practice with an increase and decrease in volume and with no appreciable change in pitch. If the actor cannot increase the volume without raising the pitch, he will find that the scene very quickly gets out of control, giving the impression that the Prince has lost control of himself and has been reduced to an im-potent rage.

A lowering of pitch without any considerable change in volume is an infrequently used technical device that is most effective in creating the impression that the volume has been decreased without actually decreas-ing it. The theater often demands that the characters in a play seem to be speaking in hushed voices, even though they are completely audible in the last rows of the balcony.

In Act I, Scene 1, of *Hamlet*, when Bernardo, Marcellus, and Horatio are keeping watch at midnight, Marcellus interrupts Bernardo's story by saying, "Peace! break thee off: look, where it comes again!" The actor playing Marcellus may find it very useful to be able to speak each phrase with a slight lowering of pitch and with no change in volume. The next six lines might well be spoken by all the actors involved in the scene with an unnaturally low pitch but with no loss of volume and audibility:

> BAR.: In the same figure, like the king that's dead.
> MAR.: Thou art a scholar; speak to it, Horatio.
> BAR.: Looks it not like the king?   Mark it, Horatio.
> HOR.: Most like: it harrows me with fear and wonder.
> BAR.: It would be spoke to.
> MAR.:   Question it, Horatio.

When Horatio speaks to the ghost in the next speech, he will naturally both raise the pitch and increase the volume.

Once when Richard Hale was playing Mercutio in *Romeo and Juliet*, he delivered the Queen Mab speech with a gradually decreasing volume and pitch, so that the entire passage of forty lines became quieter and lower; he was careful, however, not to slow the rate. Mr. Hale was able to do this because he possesses a carefully trained voice. This technique is ideally suited to the Queen Mab speech because it enhances the lightness and the delicacy of the poetry, but not many actors have such subtle control of their voices that they would be able to play the entire passage in this manner.

Just as an increase in the rate of speech tends to decrease the emphasis upon the sense of the speech, so a slowing of the rate tends to place greater emphasis upon the meaning of the words spoken. Almost everyone has learned to speak more slowly when he wishes the listener to pay careful attention to the words. The actor will have frequent need for this device since he must use it not only when the character he is playing wishes to be emphatic but also when it is particularly important for the audience to comprehend the full meaning of his speech, even though the character may not attach a similar significance to the words.

The actor playing the Prince in *Romeo and Juliet* will want to use a slow, measured rate, with little change in either volume or pitch, as he delivers the following lines, which come soon after the passage already quoted:

> If ever you disturb our streets again
> Your lives shall pay the forfeit of the peace.

The next five lines may be delivered more easily, more freely, more casually, and with a slight increase in both rate and pitch:

> For this time, all the rest depart away:
> You, Capulet, shall go along with me;
> And, Montague, come you this afternoon
> To know our further pleasure in this case,
> To old Free-town, our common judgement-place.

Each phrase of the concluding sentence, however, may well be spoken with an increase in volume and pitch but with a decrease in rate.

> Once more, on pain of death, all men depart.

7. CHANGE IN TIMBRE OR QUALITY OF THE VOICE

In addition to varying his speech pattern in volume, pitch, and rate, the actor can change the quality or the timbre of his voice by changing the placement of the voice and the areas where the resonance is created. An actor can learn by practice, with the help of a competent

voice teacher, to use or not to use a nasal resonance or a chest resonance and to speak with his words forming well forward near
his lips or farther back in the middle of his mouth. Nearly every
actor discovers very definite limitations in the quality of his voice caused
by the physical structure of his mouth and throat. Constant study and
practice, however, can definitely increase his ability to change the quality
of his voice.

Actually very few characters require any considerable change in the
quality of the voice, except in those plays that involve a considerable
lapse of time and present the characters at several different ages. Most
people acquire a definite habit of speech, and so their voices have a more
or less constant quality, which changes only as time makes actual changes
in their physical being.

The various vocal qualities discussed—resonance, volume, pitch, and
rate—cannot be separated from one another, since, of necessity, all these
qualities are present in every sentence that is spoken. What concerns
the actor is the change which may occur in any or all of these qualities.
He will frequently find sentences, or whole scenes, in which changing
one or all of these qualities will be an effective means of portraying the
emotions of the character.

Since it is natural to vary three of the qualities—volume, pitch, and
rate—whenever any one of them varies, the actor will find that a large
part of any role will need to be spoken in this manner. But drama frequently concerns itself with either exceptional people or normal people
in exceptional situations for whom the natural speech pattern may not be
appropriate. *Romeo and Juliet* does not show us the everyday home life
of the Prince, but rather his manner of dealing with the third street brawl
occasioned by the Montagues and Capulets. We do not see Marcellus
and Bernardo on an ordinary night watch, but on a night watch in which
they see the Ghost. Under these circumstances the characters experience extraordinary emotions and consequently speak in an extraordinary
manner; the actor, therefore, must practice all the vocal techniques, so
that he may convey these emotions to an audience in a manner which is
natural to the character experiencing them, but which would not be natural to the character under ordinary circumstances.

Physical Techniques

Coexistent with every sentence spoken, there must be, except in radio
drama, a visible physical attitude on the part of the speaker. In one sense,
there must always be change in the physical attitude, since speaking the
words necessitates a movement of the lips and the muscles of the jaw,
but for purposes of study and analysis it is convenient to disregard the

minor changes in facial expression caused by speaking the lines and to concentrate on voluntary movements.

The Need for Relaxation and Concentration

Inevitably, the audience will understand and interpret all movement or lack of movement on the part of the actor as a manifestation of either the character's habits or his thoughts and emotions, but during every performance each actor is, of course, subject to impulses for movement stimulated by his own thoughts, emotions, and habits. Perhaps the most important and certainly the most frequent of these stimuli are the nervousness and excitement caused by the fact that he is standing upon a stage in front of an audience and that he is being judged by what he is doing. The inexperienced and untrained actor is almost always subject to a more or less constant twitching of the fingers or wiggling of the feet. The actor is nervous, and so he acts nervously.

One large part of the Stanislavski system is devoted to a series of suggested exercises by which the actor may hope to gain relaxation and thus relief from the impulse to move in response to his personal emotions, rather than to those of the character he is playing. Other exercises are suggested to help the actor develop a power of concentration, so that he can force himself to think the thoughts of the character rather than his own thoughts, the theory being that he will then move naturally in response to the thoughts and feelings of the character. Obviously an actor who is not sufficiently in control of his body to avoid moving in response to his personal thoughts and feelings is not prepared to act and should pursue a course of study and training to help him achieve that control.

On many occasions the actor will find that the most effective way to play a scene is to speak his line or lines with no physical movement. A scene in which one character does not wish the other characters on the stage to know or see what he is feeling is the most obvious example of a situation in which this technical device is appropriate. Hamlet's first line, Act I, Scene 2, can be effectively played in this manner.

The court is assembled, and Hamlet sits or stands apart, paying very little attention to the proceedings. At last the King turns to Hamlet and addresses him:

KING: And now, my cousin Hamlet, and my son—
HAMLET: (*aside*) A little more than kin, and less than kind.

The speech is not intended to be heard by the King or the other members of the court. It is spoken almost involuntarily and is the expression of Hamlet's thoughts: he is unmoved, unchanged, by the words of the King. Persisting unmoved and unchanged in his thoughts and feelings, the actor may well deliver the line with as little motion as possible, continuing in whatever physical attitude he has chosen for the beginning of the scene.   The King continues:

> KING: How is it that the clouds still hang on you?
> HAMLET: Not so, my Lord; I am too much i' th' sun.

Hamlet still makes no noticeable movement.   Now the Queen speaks to him:

> QUEEN: Good Hamlet, cast thy nighted color off,
>   And let thine eye look like a friend on Denmark.
>   Do not forever with thy vailed lids
>   Seek for thy noble father in the dust:
>   Thou know'st 'tis common; all that lives must die,
>   Passing through nature to eternity.
> HAMLET: Ay, madam, it is common.

The speech of the Queen clearly requires that Hamlet be looking at the ground, not raising his eyes to look at anyone or anything; and Hamlet's third speech is spoken with no change in this physical attitude.   It is in Hamlet's next speech that he first makes an effort to communicate his thoughts and feelings to the other characters on the stage, and so it is in his next speech that he first begins to move.

The Various Kinds of Movement

For the purposes of discussion and illustration, movement has been arbitrarily divided into five classifications:

1. Change of level, including anything from a slight raising of the head to movement from a reclining position on the floor to standing on the highest level provided by the scenery

2. Turning, including the turning of the head, the torso, or the whole body

3. Walking, including all movement from one area of the stage to another

4. Gestures, including any movement of the hands, arms, feet or legs which does not involve moving from one area of the stage to another

5. Facial expressions

1. CHANGE OF LEVEL

Each movement, carefully selected to give effective expression to the emotion which the actor is attempting to convey to the audience, is capable of being performed in such a way that it will enhance the sense of the forward motion of the scene and the progression of the dialogue. It has been suggested that Hamlet's first scene be played with the actor avoiding any movement. If, however, he chooses to use some movement to help project the emotions of the character, he may well use a change of level as a technical device.

If he is sitting in a dejected manner with his arms resting on his knees and his head bowed throughout the opening scene, in which he does not participate, he may, when the King first speaks to him, start to lift his head, raising it a little higher as he speaks each of the three sentences. Somewhat the same effect could also be created if the change in level were accomplished, not by a simple raising of the head, but by raising the whole torso from the hips up. Or the two movements might be combined, so that the actor would raise his torso for the first and second lines and raise his head for the last line, when he answers his mother.

Just as each of the vocal technical devices may be performed in both directions—that is, from soft to loud or from loud to soft—so the physical movement can be used from down to up or from up to down. Another method of performing this particular sequence of lines from *Hamlet* would be for the actor to be sitting staring at the court, but not reacting to it. As the King speaks, Hamlet might begin the downward motion of his head, or of his head and torso, in which case he would be staring at the ground by the time the Queen speaks the lines referring to that attitude. The actor rehearsing this sequence will discover that each variation in the technical method of playing the scene conveys a slightly different emotion, or a variation in the degree of the same emotion.

Any large movement involving a change of level is more likely to be the invention of the director than of the actor, but it remains for the actor to incorporate the movement into the scene in the most advantageous manner. Suppose that a 6- or 8-foot-high platform, with a flight of stairs leading up to it, has been provided for Act I, Scene 4, of *Hamlet,* which takes place on the parapet of the castle, and that the director has decided that the Ghost shall be seen walking along this platform, while Hamlet and the others appear below. Since Hamlet exits following the Ghost, at some time during the scene the actor playing Hamlet must go up the steps. There are several different ways in which this action may be incorporated into the scene.

It will be noted that Hamlet does not follow the Ghost until the fourth time that he says he will. After the Ghost first beckons to Hamlet, there are three speeches by Horatio and Marcellus, and then Hamlet says, "It will not speak; then, will I follow it." At the end of his next speech Hamlet again says, "It waves me forth again; I'll follow it." After Horatio's next speech Hamlet says, "It waves me still. Go on, I'll follow thee," and at the end of the next sequence of lines, Hamlet throws off the restraining hands of his friends, saying, "I say, away! Go on, I'll follow thee."

Certainly the first three times that Hamlet says he will follow, it is essential that he make some motion in the direction of the Ghost, but the motion can be very small, leaving the big action of actually going up the steps for the very last speech. In this case the actor will find that the final movement is too large to be completed during the actual speaking of the lines and that the words must be spaced so that he can move between some of the phrases—for instance, "I say, away," then a few steps; "Go on," and a few steps; "I'll follow thee," and the number of steps necessary to bring the actor to the top of the platform and the exit.

Instead of playing the scene this way, however, the actor may choose to reach the top of the platform before he says, "I'll follow thee"; or he may elect to complete the speech at the bottom of the steps and leave the business of mounting the steps as an action to be performed separately for its own emotional values. Another variation of the scene would be for the actor to go up a few steps each time he says, "I'll follow," so that he is already on the top of the platform and near the exit when he comes to the last speech. The scene could also be played with the Ghost entering on the stage level, and Hamlet and his friends entering above. The change of levels would then be used in reverse, Hamlet coming down the steps instead of going up them.

An interesting problem in the use of levels occurs in *King Richard II*, Act III, Scene 3, when Richard appears on the wall of Flint Castle. The scene seems to have been written so that on an Elizabethan stage Richard would enter in the "inner above" and then exit and reappear on the stage level. In a modern staging of the play, however, the designer would probably provide stairs which the actor could use on stage. The descent would have to be accomplished in relation to Richard's speech:

> Down, down, I come; like glistering Phaethon,
> Wanting the manage of unruly jades.
> In the base court? Base court, where kings grow base,
> To come at traitor's calls and do them grace.
> In the base court? Come down? Down, court! Down, king!
> For night-owls shriek where mounting larks should sing.

Considering that the play deals with the downfall of a king, it would seem advantageous for the actor to make a visible descent. He uses the word "down" five times in a single speech, and if he is to suit the action to the word, it would seem appropriate for the action of coming down to be incorporated into the scene. The actual technical method of doing this would depend upon the actor's interpretation of the character, the

number of steps provided by the scene designer, and the actor's decision
about the most effective relation of the action to the words.

2. TURNING

Turning the head, the torso, or the whole body during a sequence of
lines is one of the most useful technical devices because it allows the
actor to indicate a growing or changing emotional state both effectively
and unobtrusively. When, for example, Benvolio first speaks to Romeo
in Act I, Scene 1, the actor playing Romeo may be looking away on the
first line, gradually turn to face Benvolio on the third line, and then turn
away again during the next three lines.

> BEN.: Good morrow, cousin.
> ROM.:   Is the day so young?
> BEN.: But new struck nine.
> ROM.:   Ay me! Sad hours seem long.
>   Was that my father that went hence so fast?

The turn toward Benvolio is completed on Romeo's third line.

> BEN.: It was. What sadness lengthens Romeo's hours?
> ROM.: Not having that, which having, makes them short.
> BEN.: In love?
> ROM.: Out—
> BEN.: Of love?
> ROM.: Out of her favor, where I am in love.

And the turn away from Benvolio is completed on the last line. To see
the advantage of this technical device, the actors might rehearse the
scene with Romeo looking away throughout the sequence and making no
turns, and again with Romeo turning back toward Benvolio on each line
and then immediately away again. In the one case the scene will lack
variety and tend to be monotonous, and in the other it will seem jerky.

The most frequent use of the turning movement is to break long
speeches into smaller units by completing the turn between two sequences
and thus indicating to the audience that the character has moved on to a
new thought or new emotion. It will be remembered that in suggesting action which might be appropriate to the Brutus speech in *Julius Caesar*, turns
toward one portion of the citizens and then toward another were proposed.
The actor playing Richard II will also find this technical device useful
in delivering the famous speech, in Act III, Scene 2, beginning, "Of
comfort no man speak."

Ten lines into this speech the King is required to sit, since he says,
"For God's sake, let us sit upon the ground." From there to the end of
the speech, the actor will find it helpful to divide the speech into its

various thought sequences and deliver each sequence of lines in a slightly
different direction, the turns being motivated by a desire to address different members of the listening group, who are gathered around him.

> For God's sake, let us sit upon the ground
> And tell sad stories of the death of kings;
> How some have been depos'd, some slain in war,
> Some haunted by the ghosts they have depos'd,
> Some poison'd by their wives, some sleeping killed;
> All murder'ed. . . .

On each of these phrases the actor might wish to turn slightly in another direction, or he might choose to play the entire sequence facing
the same way, using instead some vocal technique to develop the passage.
It will be advantageous to the actor, however, to motivate as many turns
as possible in this passage, for the next sequence of lines is a relatively long
passage devoted to a single thought:

> for within the hollow crown
> That rounds the mortal temples of a King
> Keeps Death his court, and there the antick sits,
> Scoffing his state and grinning at his pomp,
> Allowing him a breath, a little scene,
> To monarchize, be fear'd, and kill with looks,
> Infusing him with self and vain conceit
> As if this flesh which walls about our life
> Were brass impregnable: and humour'd thus
> Comes at the last, and with a little pin
> Bores through his castle wall, and farewell king!

This speech is obviously all one thought—one concept; for the audience to understand it as such, it must be delivered in one line and one
direction, and the progression of the thought must be sustained with
vocal techniques, facial techniques, and hand and arm gestures.

3. MOVEMENT FROM AREA TO AREA

Like the changes in level, all the large movements from one area of
the stage to another will be planned by the director. Smaller moves—
a step or two—may be left to the discretion of the individual actor.
Frequently, however, when a large movement has been dictated by the
director, it will remain for the actor to decide the most advantageous
time to make the movement. Whenever such a movement is called for,
it becomes a technical device to be used by the actor to assist in projecting the emotions of the character, for the audience will always understand that such a movement has been motivated by the thought and
emotions of the character.

Fundamentally, the actor must choose one of two alternative ways of relating such a movement to the lines: he may make the movement between sequences of lines, or he may make the movement while a line or a series of lines are being spoken. Since those in the audience will understand that the movement is made because of a reaction to some stimulus, they will also understand that the lines spoken during the time that the movement is being made are in relation to the same stimulus.

Suppose that in Act III, Scene 2, of *The Merchant of Venice*, Bassanio, who is about to choose the casket, is standing near the caskets and at some distance from Portia. According to Portia's own words, it is her desire to delay the choosing; it may therefore be assumed that she will wish to cross to a position near Bassanio. Such a movement might be made on the first words of the speech, "I pray you, tarry," or it might be made directly after those words, or it might be made to extend through her first three lines:

> I pray you, tarry: pause a day or two
> Before you hazard; for, in choosing wrong,
> I lose your company: therefore, forbear a while.

Actually the same emotion and desire motivates Portia throughout the entire speech of twenty-three lines, for in the ninth line she says, "I would detain you here some month or two," and in the last line she tells Bassanio that she speaks "to stay you from election." Since the same emotion motivates the entire speech, it would be appropriate for Portia to make a move to detain Bassanio from the caskets at any time during the first three lines, in relation to the ninth and tenth lines, or at the end of the speech. If the scene is rehearsed in all the various arrangements that have been suggested, a sensible decision may be reached as to the most effective manner of playing it.

4. GESTURES

The choice of hand and arm gestures is left almost exclusively to the discretion of the actor, although once in a while the author will indicate some action of this sort which is essential to the plot, such as stabbing or kissing. When an author has a character say, as Romeo does in Act III, Scene 3,

> Then mightst thou tear thy hair,
> And fall upon the ground, as I do now,
> Taking the measure of an unmade grave,

it becomes absolutely necessary that the actor act as he describes himself; but for the most part the actions of the character are the invention and creation of the actor. He will select those gestures and bodily attitudes which best convey his interpretation of the character, based upon his own knowledge of human behavior.

As a technical device, movement of the hands and arms is used, like other kinds of movement, to indicate the beginning, the development, and the end of a thought or an emotion.   One of the most frequent faults of the inexperienced actor is that he allows his gestures to become redundant.   He makes a gesture which he considers appropriate to the thoughts or feelings which he is expressing, and then, having made it, finds that the lines indicate a continuation of the same thought or emotion, so that he feels it necessary to repeat the gesture or to make another similar gesture.   As a result, the action becomes choppy and jerky, and the dialogue begins to sound repetitious because the gestures have become repetitious.

In the speech of the Prince in the first scene of *Romeo and Juliet*, the actor might consider it appropriate to raise his right hand as high as possible above his head in order to attract the attention of the citizens. In doing so, he might immediately raise his arm as high as he is ever going to raise it and hold it there through the first three phrases:

> Rebellious subjects, enemies to peace,
> Profaners of this neighbor-stained steel.

On the other hand, the actor might raise his arm, but not to its highest point, on the first phrase and smoothly and gradually extend it to full height while he speaks the three phrases; or he might raise it a little higher as he begins each of the phrases, thus giving the gesture a certain sense of pulse, rather than a smooth, continuous motion.

The wrong way to perform the gesture would be to raise the arm and then, at the end of each phrase, lower it slightly before carrying the gesture to its next highest point.   An audience would immediately sense that this gesture, or series of gestures, as it has now become, is false and unnatural.   Since the emotion of the Prince is a continuing and developing one, with no drop in the emotional level, it would be unnatural to allow a drop in the gesture.

The problem of the extent and duration of a gesture as related to the thought of the character can perhaps best be illustrated by an example from music drama, in which the thought, supported and developed by the music, is likely to be sustained even longer than in ordinary drama.   In the chorus of the title song from *Of Thee I Sing*,

> Of thee I sing, baby,
> Summer, autumn, winter, spring, baby,

the actor may feel it necessary to make some gesture with his hands. To use a simple, unimaginative, and banal example, he may wish to extend first his right and then his left hand slightly forward with open palm. The first impulse might be to move the right hand on "of" and then the left hand on "thee," since both of these words are slightly accented in the music. If he does this, he will have nothing left to do but repeat the same gestures on "sing" and "baby," and to repeat them again in the next line.

The next possible extension of the gesture would be to start the right-hand gesture on the "of" but to continue it through the "thee," and only begin the left-hand gesture on "sing," continuing it to the end of the line. The same gestures would be repeated for the second line, but now there is only one repetition of each gesture, not three. The next extension of the gesture would be to use only the right hand on the whole first line, saving the left-hand gesture for the second line.

At the end of the Prince's speech in *Romeo and Juliet*, the actor playing the role might wish to point toward Montague as he addresses him:

> And, Montague, come you this afternoon
> To know our further pleasure in this case,
> To old Free-town, our common judgement place.

It is possible that the actor might drop the gesture, returning his arm to his side, immediately after he has spoken Montague's name. In this case, the command to Montague would be separated from the gesture of attracting his attention. To drop the gesture after the word "afternoon" would seem completely unnatural. It might possibly be dropped after the word "case," but this would suggest that the Prince had finished his sentence and his thought, and the next line would seem unrelated, unmotivated, and unnecessary. It seems logical to sustain the gesture as long as the thought is sustained and to drop the gesture on the word "place," which is the actual end of the thought. When played in this way, the last line seems an integral part of the speech and of the thought which it expresses.

Since the exact relationship between the duration of a gesture and the duration of the thought or the emotion is one of the most important considerations in the technical use of gesture, the actor will need to be alert to discover and invent appropriate gestures which can either be performed in as brief a time as necessary or sustained and extended for as long a time as required.

Not all gestures will seem, at first glance, to be capable of being extended and sustained for any length of time. A little experimentation, however, will soon reveal that many gestures which are, in themselves, small and of brief duration may nevertheless appear to be sustained. A hand placed on the shoulder of another character as a sign of friendship or as a gesture of restraint may be left there during the whole sequence of lines related to that particular emotion. There are several places where such a gesture might be appropriate to Benvolio and Romeo, or to Horatio, Marcellus, and Bernardo. A hand placed threateningly upon the hilt of a sword may be left there, giving the sense that the gesture has been continued and sustained through several speeches; several of the characters in both *Hamlet* and *Romeo and Juliet* have opportunities for this gesture—the four servants, for example, in the opening scene of the latter play.

In more realistic plays, almost any gesture may seem to be continued. A glass or a cup may be held in the hand and toyed with; smoking a cigarette or a pipe creates certain hand and arm movements which may, in a sense, be interrupted by the lines, and the hand or arm left poised for the time required to express the thought; reading a letter, a book, or a magazine creates gestures which may be used as technical devices to clarify the structure of the dialogue and to assist the actor in indicating to the audience when new thoughts or new emotions begin to dominate the character. The student-actor will soon discover that almost any activity permitted to the character will lend itself to being used in this manner; even if his activity is only sitting and listening, the actor can discover several different bodily attitudes which might be appropriate to the character in the situation, and shifting from one attitude to another can be made to reflect his changing reaction to the scene.

5. FACIAL EXPRESSIONS

Certain scenes and certain characters do not lend themselves to the use of any considerable amount of either movement or gesturing. Such scenes become a special challenge to the actor and require a most economical use of the few small devices available. The actor who is playing a character who is not, either by nature or habit, given to any display of emotion will find that it is difficult to convey and project the emotions of the character to the audience, since the character himself is controlling those emotions so as not to allow them to be seen. Under such circumstances, the actor will find that he is forced to rely primarily upon vocal devices and facial expressions.

The part of Brutus in *Julius Caesar* is a good example of a role that must be played with a minimum of large gestures, particularly in the tent scene, Act IV, Scene 3, for one of the main points of both the scene and the characterization is that Brutus, for the most part, keeps his temper and makes no display of his emotions. In the last scene of the play, Antony says of Brutus, "His life was gentle," and the actor who plays Brutus must have so interpreted the role that Antony's statement will seem justified.

When threatened by Cassius, Brutus refuses to allow himself either to become angry or to show fear:

> Must I give way and room to your rash choler?
> Shall I be frighted when a madman stares?

And in the next speech, he says:

> Must I budge?
> Must I observe you? must I stand and crouch
> Under your testy humour?

The extent to which Brutus controls his emotions may be deduced from the fact that, having refused to lose his temper with Cassius, he suddenly lets his anger flare at the poet. When Cassius, remarking that Brutus has suddenly lost his temper for an inconsequential reason, says:

> Of your philosophy you make no use
> If you give place to accidental evils,

Brutus replies, saying:

> No man bears sorrow better: Portia is dead.

There has been no previous mention of his sorrow at his wife's death, and he does not now allow himself to give way to grief. But the audience must not be left to think that since he will neither let himself become angry with Cassius nor show grief for his wife's death, he is unfeeling and insensitive. Denied the use of any large movements by Brutus' "gentle" nature and with no speeches to express either his anger or his grief, the actor must rely almost exclusively upon facial expressions and vocal techniques. The eloquent actor will diligently search out portions and sequences of the scene which will allow him to express the very emotions that the character is trying to conceal and will attempt to find appropriate technical devices by which to do so.

Another scene which will tax the technical skill, the ingenuity, and the inventiveness of the actor is the scene in Act II of *The Sea Gull* in which Trigorin, the disappointed writer, explains what his life is like. There are no sizable movements which are germane to the scene. The intensity of the character's emotion is implied but never expressed in words. His feelings, if they are to be expressed at all, must be revealed to the audience through the subtle use of facial expressions, vocal techniques, and the most economical use of small hand gestures and slight changes in position. If the scene is difficult for the actor playing Trigorin, how much more difficult it is for the girl who only sits and listens but who must find ways and means to show, at least to the audience, her love and admiration and hero worship.

Each of the technical devices based upon physical action is capable of being varied, just as the vocal qualities can be varied. It has already been noted that a change in level may be from up to down or from down to up, but it may also be performed from slow to fast or from fast to slow. If Hamlet, mounting the platform to follow the Ghost, begins quickly and impulsively and then slows to a walk, one effect will have been created and Hamlet's emotions will be understood to be of one kind; if, on the other hand, his first moves are slow and tentative and his last steps are taken quickly, so that he leaps up the steps, his emotions will be judged to be of a different kind. In the same way, Romeo may either turn slowly toward Benvolio and then suddenly face him or begin the movement quickly and finish it slowly. Any hand or arm gesture may also be performed at a steady rate or with a change in tempo during the gesture. Even certain facial expressions may be accelerated or retarded, as a smile may begin tentatively and then suddenly spread into a grin.

Each change in tempo will seem to the audience to reflect a change in the emotional status of the character. The student should practice each movement in each exercise until he is able to perform it at a steady, unchanging rate and with different degrees of acceleration or deceleration and until he becomes aware of the different meanings and interpretations of the character which may be created by variations in tempo.

EXERCISES

1. Greet another character saying, "Hello. How are you? I'm glad to see you again. Where have you been?"
   a. Say the lines without any physical movement but increase the volume and raise the pitch.
   b. Repeat, increasing the volume but not raising the pitch.
   c. Repeat, raising the pitch, but not increasing the volume.
      NOTE: Exercise c is likely to seem unnatural and therefore difficult.

2. Sequence from *Romeo and Juliet*, Act I, Scene 1.

   ABRAHAM: Do you bite your thumb at us, sir?
   SAMPSON: I do bite my thumb, sir.
   ABRAHAM: Do you bite your thumb at us, sir?
   SAMPSON: (*aside to Gregory*) Is the law of our side if I say ay?
   GREGORY: (*aside to Sampson*) No.
   SAMPSON: No, sir, I do not bite my thumb at you, sir; but I bite my thumb, sir.

   a. With Gregory standing at some distance from Sampson, practice speaking each speech with a slight increase in both the volume and pitch.
   b. Repeat, using an increase in volume, but maintaining the same pitch.
   c. Repeat, with the actor playing Abraham maintaining a constant volume and pitch, but the actor playing Sampson using an increase in volume and pitch.

d. Repeat, with the actor playing Abraham increasing the volume, while the actor playing Sampson maintains a constant level.

e. Move Gregory closer to Sampson and use an increasing volume on all the speeches except the lines spoken aside, lowering both volume and pitch for these two lines. Be careful to make the last line louder than the first three lines of the scene.

3. Sequence from *Romeo and Juliet*, Act II, Scene 5.

JULIET: Now, good sweet nurse,— O Lord, why look'st thou sad?
　　　　Though the news be sad, yet tell them merrily;
　　　　If good, thou sham'st the music of sweet news
　　　　By playing it to me with so sour a face.
NURSE: I am a-weary, give me leave a while:
　　　　Fie, how my bones ache! what a jaunce have I had!
JULIET: I would thou hadst my bones, and I thy news.
　　　　Nay, come, I pray thee, speak; good, good nurse, speak.
NURSE: Jesu, what haste? can you not stay awhile?
　　　　Do you not see that I am out of breath?
JULIET: How art thou out of breath, when thou hast breath
　　　　To say to me that thou art out of breath?
　　　　The excuse that thou dost make in this delay
　　　　Is longer than the tale thou dost excuse.
　　　　Is thy news good, or bad? answer to that:
　　　　Say either, and I'll stay the circumstance:
　　　　Let me be satisfied, is't good or bad?

Perform the scene, using as little physical action as possible, attempting to build the progression of the scene by vocal techniques only.

a. Attempt to play the entire sequence with a gradually increasing volume to show the increasing irritation and anger.

b. Repeat as in a, but have Juliet increase the volume of the beginning of each speech, allowing the second part of each speech to revert to a lower volume level.

c. Play the entire scene on a constant volume level, except Juliet's last three lines, which should be delivered with a gradual increase in volume.

d. Repeat as in c, using a decrease in volume for the last lines, as though Juliet were wheedling the nurse.

e. In any of the foregoing exercises, when an increase in volume has been naturally accompanied by a rise in pitch, attempt to play the scene with the same increase in volume without allowing the pitch either to rise or to fall.

f. Substitute changes in rate to create the same effect as changes in volume and pitch, using a decrease in rate wherever there was an increase in volume.

g. Repeat, using an increase in rate where there had been an increase in volume.

4. Sequence from *As You Like It*, Act V, Scene 4.

JACQUES: Can you nominate in order now the degrees of the lie?
TOUCHSTONE: O sir, we quarrel in print, by the book; as you have books for good manners: I will name you the degrees. The first, the Retort Courteous; the second, the Quip Modest; the third, the Reply Churlish; the fourth, the Reproof Valiant; the fifth, the Countercheck Quarrelsome; the sixth, the Lie with Circumstance; the seventh, the Lie Direct.

Practice Touchstone's speech for speed and for acceleration in rate.

5. The Prince's Speech from *Romeo and Juliet*, Act I, Scene 1.

> Rebellious subjects, enemies to peace,
> Profaners of this neighbor-stained steel,—
> Will they not hear? What, ho! you men, you beasts,
> That quench the fire of your pernicious rage
> With purple fountains issuing from your veins,
> On pain of torture, from those bloody hands
> Throw your mistemper'd weapons to the ground,
> And hear the sentence of your moved prince.
> Three civil brawls, bred of an airy word,
> By thee, old Capulet, and Montague,
> Have thrice disturb'd the quiet of our streets,
> And made Verona's ancient citizens
> Cast by their grave beseeming ornaments,
> To wield old partisans, in hands as old,
> Canker'd with peace, to part your canker'd hate:
> If ever you disturb our streets again.
> Your lives shalt pay the forfeit of the peace.
> For this time, all the rest depart away:
> You, Capulet, shall go along with me:
> And, Montague, come you this afternoon,
> To know our further pleasure in this case,
> To old Free-town, our common judgement-place.
> Once more, on pain of death, all men depart.

a. Use increasing volume on the first three lines and a decrease in volume on the next four.

b. Attempt to use increasing volume on the first seven lines.

c. Use a slow rate of speaking for the ten lines beginning with the line, "Three civil brawls. . . ."

d. Starting on the same line, use a slow but increasing rate for seven lines: then use a slower and decreasing rate for the next three lines.

6. Sequence from *Hamlet*, Act I, Scene 1.

(*Enter Ghost*)

MARCELLUS: Peace, break thee off; look where it comes again!
BERNARDO: In the same figure, like the king that's dead.
MARCELLUS: Thou art a scholar; speak to it, Horatio.
BERNARDO: Looks it not like the King?   Mark it Horatio.
HORATIO: Most like: it harrows me with fear and wonder.
BERNARDO: It would be spoke to.
MARCELLUS: Question it, Horatio.
HORATIO: What art thou that usurp'st this time of night,
        Together with that fair and warlike form
        In which the majesty of buried Denmark
        Did sometimes march? by heaven I charge thee, speak!
MARCELLUS: It is offended.
BERNARDO: See, it stalks away!
HORATIO: Stay! speak, speak!   I charge thee, speak!   (*Exit Ghost*)

a. Play the scene, using a decrease in volume on the first six lines.
b. Repeat, using a decrease in pitch, but no decrease in volume.
c. Use an increase of volume and rate on the last three lines.
d. Use an increase in volume, but none in rate on the last three lines.
e. Use a lowering of pitch and a decrease in rate, but no change in volume, on the last three lines.

7. Sequence from *Romeo and Juliet*, Act I, Scene 4.
Learn and rehearse Mercutio's Queen Mab speech.
NOTE: This is one of the most difficult passages to sustain.   From a technical point of view, it is usually broken into a series of smaller passages, each one dealing with a separate image or with closely related images.   Then each passage is treated separately but with a constant awareness that the parts must be joined to make a whole.   To deliver this speech in an actual performance, the actor will need more techniques than have yet been discussed in this book; but, since he will have little opportunity for large movements, the most important techniques will be gestures and vocal devices.
a. Divide the speech into logical sequences.   Assign to each section a vocal technique, such as an increase or a decrease in volume or rate or pitch.   Try to discover which techniques are best suited to each section. This exercise may be performed by both men and women.

8. Sequence from *Hamlet*, Act I, Scene 2.

KING: But now, my cousin Hamlet, and my son,—

HAMLET: (*Aside*) A little more than kin, and less than kind.

KING: How is it that the clouds still hang on you?

HAMLET: Not so, my lord; I am too much i' the sun.

QUEEN: Good Hamlet, cast thy nighted color off,
And let thine eye look like a friend on Denmark.
Do not forever with thy vailed lids
Seek for thy noble father in the dust:
Thou know'st 'tis common; all that lives must die,
Passing through nature to eternity.

HAMLET: Ay, madam, it is common.

a. Play the scene with as little physical movement as possible on the part of Hamlet.

NOTE: This scene is discussed further in a later chapter, where it is used to illustrate a problem in emphasis through movement.

b. Play the scene with Hamlet using a change of level, from down to up, or from up to down.

c. Play the scene with Hamlet using a body turn, from toward the King to away from the King.

d. Play the scene with Hamlet using only a turn of the head.

9. Sequence from *Hamlet*, Act I, Scene 4.

(*Ghost beckons Hamlet*)

HORATIO: It beckons you to go away with it,
As if it some impartment did desire
To you alone.

MARCELLUS: Look, with what courteous action
It waves you to a more removed ground:
But do not go with it.

HORATIO: No, by no means.

HAMLET: It will not speak; then I will follow it.

HORATIO: Do not, my lord.

HAMLET: Why, what should be the fear?
I do not set my life at a pin's fee;
And for my soul, what can it do to that,
Being a thing immortal as itself?
It waves me forth again:—I'll follow it.

HORATIO: What if it tempt you toward the flood, my lord,
Or to the dreadful summit of the cliff,
That beetles o'er his base into the sea,
And there assume some other horrible form,
Which might deprive your sovereignty of reason
And draw you into madness? think of it:

> The very place puts toys of desperation
> Without more motive, into every brain
> That looks so many fathoms to the sea
> And hears it roar beneath.

HAMLET: It waves me still.
> Go on, I'll follow thee.

MARCELLUS: You shall not go, my lord.

HAMLET: Hold off your hands.

HORATIO: Be ruled; you shall not go.

HAMLET: My fate cries out,
> And makes each petty artery in this body
> As hardy as the Nemean lion's nerve.
> Still am I call'd.—Unhand me, gentlemen.—
> By heaven, I'll make a ghost of him that lets me!
> I say, away!—Go on; I'll follow thee.

(*Exeunt Ghost and Hamlet*)

a. Play the scene with the Ghost on platform up left and Hamlet down right.

b. Let Hamlet make a move of at least several steps each time he says, "I'll follow."

c. Play the scene with no actual steps toward the Ghost until after the last "I'll follow thee."

NOTE: In both *a* and *b*, use as little increase in volume or as little change in rate as possible in speaking the lines.

d. Repeat *a* with Hamlet above on the platform and the Ghost down right.

e. Repeat *b* and *c* with the physical positions as in *d*.

NOTE: Exercise *d* is likely to seem more effective than exercise *a* because Hamlet, moving downstage and forward, comes into closer contact with the audience and his facial expressions become more effective. Exercise *e* is likely to seem more effective than *b* and *c* because Hamlet stays in the better acting area longer.

f. In Horatio's long speech, use an increase of rate for the first six lines to the word "madness," and a slower rate for the remainder of the speech.

g. Have Horatio reverse the techniques of *e*, using first a slow, measured speech and then an increase in rate.

h. Work out several different vocal techniques for Hamlet's last speech, using changes in volume, pitch, and rate in different combinations.

NOTE: The four times that Hamlet says he will follow the ghost divide the dialogue and the action into four parts, plus Horatio's warning. Each part should be studied to determine which technical devices are best suited to it, remembering that the total scene includes a long cross and either going up- or downstairs and that this action can itself be divided into smaller parts or performed all at one time, depending upon the actor's decision as to the most effective way to play the scene.

10. Richard's speech in *Richard II*, Act III, Scene 3.

> Down, down, I come; like glistering Phaethon,
> Wanting the manage of unruly jades.
> In the base court? Base court where kings grow base,
> To come at traitor's calls and do them grace.
> In the base court? Come down? Down, court! Down, king!
> For the night-owls shriek where mounting larks should sing.

a. Have Richard appear at the top of a visible flight of steps. Work out the passage in several different ways, each way incorporating the descent of the stairs in conjunction with different lines.

11. Sequence from *Romeo and Juliet*, Act I, Scene 1.

BENVOLIO: Good morrow, cousin.
ROMEO: Is the day so young?
BENVOLIO: But new struck nine.
ROMEO: Ay me! sad hours seem long.
           Was that my father that went hence so fast?
BENVOLIO: It was. What sadness lengthens Romeo's hours?
ROMEO: Not having that, which having, makes them short.
BENVOLIO: In love?
ROMEO: Out—
BENVOLIO: Of love?
ROMEO: Out of her favor, where I am in love.

a. Play the scene with Romeo turned away from Benvolio during the entire sequence.

b. Have Romeo slowly turn toward Benvolio, the whole turn taking the time of the entire scene.

c. Play the scene with Romeo making a turn toward Benvolio during the first four speeches, and away again during the remainder of the scene.

d. Play the scene with Romeo faced toward Benvolio at the beginning, turning away during the first four speeches, and turning back during the remainder of the scene.

12. Sequence from *Richard II*, Act III, Scene 2.

Learn Richard's speech, beginning, "No matter where; of comfort no man speak. . . ."

a. Have Richard's followers placed in various positions on the stage on both sides of Richard. Have Richard make as many moves as possible, taking steps toward a different follower as he introduces each new idea in the first eleven lines.   He could make a move before the second line, the third, the fifth, the sixth, the eighth, and the ninth.

NOTE: The scene will seem very jerky when played this way, but it will also suggest that Richard is frantic.

b. Play the scene as in *a*, but use only body turns with no steps.

c. Play the scene using some steps and some body turns.

d. Play the scene using only half as many turns or movements.

e. Play the scene with the first eleven lines addressed to one person and with no turns or movements.

f. Work out the next five and a half lines in the same manner, but with Richard sitting on the ground, so that only body turns are possible.

g. Invent some gesture, such as Richard pointing to his own temples, which can be sustained for the eleven lines beginning, "For within the hollow crown. . . ."

h. Use turns with each separate thought in the last six lines, making turns from one follower to another on such small phrases as "feel want," "taste grief," and "need friends."

NOTE: All the possible turns of the head or body are too many.   The actor will also want to decide at which place in the lines it is most advantageous to get up again.

13. Sequence from *The Merchant of Venice*, Act III, Scene 2.

Learn Portia's speech beginning, "I pray you, tarry; pause a day or two. . . ."

a. Play the scene, having Portia cross from one side of the stage to a position near the caskets, where Bassanio is standing.   Try the cross at the beginning of the scene and at the end of the scene, and also with the cross divided into smaller parts to be used at several places in the scene.   Decide which use of the cross is the most effective.

14. Sequence from *Romeo and Juliet*, Act I, Scene 1.

Practice various hand and arm gestures for the Prince's speech, quoted in exercise 5.

a. Raise an arm to attract attention at the beginning of the speech and keep it raised throughout the first eight lines.

b. Use the same gesture, but sustain it through only two lines.

c. Use the same gesture, but begin it in the middle of the third line and sustain it for the next five lines.

d. Use the same gesture beginning on the line, "If ever you disturb our streets . . . ," and sustain it—first for two lines, and then for three.

15. Sequence from *Saturday's Children*,[1] Act I.

Florrie is explaining to her sister, Bobby, how to get Rims to propose.   Rims

[1] Copyright by Anderson House.

is in love with Bobby, but has been offered a job in South America and is planning to leave soon. Florrie is afraid that he will forget Bobby if he doesn't propose before he goes. Bobby is reluctant to trick him into a proposal.

FLORRIE: Darling, if you knew just half a dozen sentences to say that would make him propose to you, would you say them?

BOBBY: No, I wouldn't.

FLORRIE: It's so easy— When he asks if you weren't really going out with somebody, tell him you were going out with Fred—has he ever seen Fred?

BOBBY: No, but you're just wasting your time, Florrie.

(Florrie gets a pad and pencil)

FLORRIE: Look, dear, I'm writing it down—can you read my shorthand?

BOBBY: I could if I wanted to—

FLORRIE: You're going with Fred to a dance or a supper-club—you see? and then Rims will come in and ask you to stay with him this evening—and you'll say yes, you'll call it off when Fred telephones—and then I'll telephone—isn't it easy?

BOBBY: It doesn't interest me.

FLORRIE: Then he'll ask you to go somewhere with him and you'll suddenly take out your hanky and begin to cry a little and say you don't want to go anywhere.

BOBBY: Me—cry—me?

FLORRIE: Yes, darling, you. You'll weep a little and he'll ask you what's the matter and try to comfort you, and—

BOBBY: I can't cry on order.

FLORRIE: Oh, yes, you can, dear.

BOBBY: Anyway, I never cry.

FLORRIE: Well, he'll ask you what's the matter, and then you'll say, "Oh, I'm so tired of—of everything, Rims—and I'm afraid I'm not very good company," —and he'll say, "Oh, yes, you are" and he'll put his arm around you—or would he?

BOBBY: How could he help it?

FLORRIE: Well, after that it gets easier all the time—you just say, "Rims dear, sometimes you're the only person in the world I can talk to—sometimes I can't bear to be with anybody else."

BOBBY: I simply couldn't—

FLORRIE: But that's exactly what you've got to say—and then you go right on and say, "Rims, don't you ever get tired of poor me,—ever?"

BOBBY: And then he'll say "Never" of course.

FLORRIE: Of course—and you say, "You're such a darling—and it's going to be awfully hard"—

BOBBY: What is?

FLORRIE: That's exactly what he'll say— "What is" and you'll say, "Marrying somebody else!" Then he'll draw back and say, "You getting married?" and you'll say, "Oh, Rims, a girl has to get married sometime, you know, while she's got chances," and he'll say, "How many chances do you get in a week?" or something like that, and you'll say, "I've had two every other week for two weeks," or something, and he'll say "Now kid, you don't mean you're set to marry somebody?" and then you'll say—

BOBBY: Oh, no, I won't—

FLORRIE: Yes, you will, dear, you'll say, "Fred wants me to marry him, and he's awfully in love with me, and I don't want to go on working forever," and he'll say, "Well, if you're getting married this season, why not marry me?" —and there you are—

BOBBY: No, because he wouldn't say it—

FLORRIE: Why not?

BOBBY: Because he isn't such a sap for one thing, and for another I don't think it's fair and I wouldn't do it.

FLORRIE: My darling, how do you think people get married?

BOBBY: I don't know.

FLORRIE: I'll say you don't—

BOBBY: Honestly, do you think a person of any sense would fall for a deliberate trap like that?

FLORRIE: Why, honeybunch, hundreds of thousands of them fall for it every year. (*The doorbell rings.*) There's one coming now. I'm running along, dear. And, look, I'm leaving those notes—see?—

BOBBY: You'd better take them—

FLORRIE: Shut the note-book if you feel scrupulous—you'll probably remember the system anyway—it comes natural—

a. Using the business of Florrie writing in the shorthand book and sitting and thinking with the pencil poised in various attitudes, work out the best possible phrasing of this scene. *Example:* If Florrie writes during the speech beginning, "You're going to a dance. . . ." and stops writing when she says, "And then I'll telephone," and then she doesn't write again until she says, "Oh, yes, you can, dear," the speeches between will be treated as a unit. On the other hand, if Florrie writes during all the speeches, the scene will lack variety, and the separate emotional or thought units will not be made clear to the audience. Whenever the actress playing Florrie wishes to indicate that several speeches are a continuation of the same thought, she needs only to continue the same action through them; and whenever she wishes to indicate that a new thought has begun, she needs only to begin a new action.

16. Sequence from *The Sea Gull*,[2] Act II.

NINA: It's a marvellous world! If you only knew how I envy you! Look how different different people's lots are! Some have all they can do to drag through their dull, obscure lives; they are all just alike, all miserable; others— well, you, for instance—have a bright, interesting life that means something. You are happy.

TRIGORIN: I? (*Shrugging his shoulders*) H'm—I hear you speak of fame and happiness, of a bright, interesting life, but for me that's all words, pretty words that—if you'll forgive me saying so—mean about the same to me as candied fruits, which I never eat. You are very young and very kind.

NINA: Your life is beautiful.

TRIGORIN: I don't see anything so very beautiful about it. (*Looks at his watch*) I must get to my writing. Excuse me, I'm busy—(*Laughs*) You've stepped on my pet corn, as they say, and here I am, beginning to get excited and a little cross. At any rate let's talk. Let's talk about my beautiful, bright life. Well, where shall we begin? (*After reflecting a moment*) You know, sometimes violent obsessions take hold of a man, some fixed idea pursues him, the moon for example, day and night he thinks of nothing but the moon. Well, I have just such a moon. Day and night one thought obsesses me: I must be writing, I must be writing, I must be— I've scarcely finished one novel when somehow I'm driven on to write another, then a third, and after the third a fourth. I write incessantly, and always at a breakneck speed, and that's the only way I can write. What's beautiful and bright about that, I ask you? Oh, what a wild life! Why now even, I'm here talking to you, I'm excited, but every minute I remember that the story I haven't finished is there waiting for me. I see that cloud up there, it's shaped like a grand piano—instantly a mental note— I must remember to put that in my story—a cloud sailing by—grand piano. A whiff of heliotrope. Quickly I make note of it: cloying smell, window's color—put that in next time I describe a summer evening. Every sentence, every word I say and you say, I lie in wait for it, snap it up for my literary storeroom—it might come in handy— As soon as I put my work down, I race off to the theatre or go fishing, hoping to find a rest, but not at all—a new idea for a story comes rolling around in my head like a cannon ball, and I'm back at my desk and writing and writing and writing. And it's always like that, everlastingly. I have no rest from myself, and I feel that I am consuming my own life, that for the honey I'm giving to someone in the void, I rob my best flowers of their pollen, I tear up those flowers and trample on their roots. Do I seem mad? Do my friends seem to talk with me as they would to a sane man? "What are you writing at now? What shall we have next?" Over and over it's like that, till I think all this attention and praise is said only out of kindness to a sick man—deceive him, soothe him, and then any minute come

[2] Copyright by Charles Scribner's Sons.

stealing up behind and pack him off to the madhouse. And in those years, my young best years, when I was beginning, why then writing made my life a torment. A minor writer, especially when he's not successful, feels clumsy, he's all thumbs, the world has no need for him; his nerves are about to go, he can't resist hanging around people in the arts, where nobody knows him, or takes any notice of him, and he's afraid to look them straight in the eyes, like a man with a passion for gambling who hasn't any money to play with. I'd never seen my readers but for some reason or other I pictured them as hating me and mistrusting me, I had a deathly fear of the public, and when my first play was produced it seemed to me all the dark eyes in the audience were looking at it with hostility and all the light eyes with frigid indifference. Oh how awful that was! What torment it was!

a. Work out small hand gestures, facial expressions, etc., for both Nina and Trigorin which can be used to indicate where the different thoughts and emotions begin and end, and practice sustaining one gesture or physical attitude through that portion of the speech which deals with a single subject. *Example:* Select one gesture or attitude which can be sustained from the time Trigorin says, "Let's talk about my beautiful bright life," until he says, "What's beautiful and bright about that, I ask you?" Then break this passage in two parts by having one attitude for the man obsessed by the moon and another for the man obsessed by writing.

Chapter 6. THE USE OF TECHNIQUES
TO BUILD A CLIMAX

Every scene may be divided into a series of progressions, each sequence of lines making a definite contribution to the total scene. The actor must decide the exact purpose of each sequence and the impression it is to convey to the audience, noting carefully the precise moment at which a new thought begins, a new emotion is revealed, or another facet of the character is portrayed. The duration of each sequence is of particular importance to the actor because he must select technical devices for the playing of each sequence which will be suited to both its purpose and its length.

The actor's first task is to decide which techniques will be appropriate to the scene as a whole. How much movement from one area to another is permissible and desirable? How many gestures may be used and how many are required? To what extent may he rely upon facial expressions? Which vocal techniques are appropriate? Just as the author has arranged the thoughts and emotions of the scene so that it seems to move constantly toward a climax, the actor will wish to arrange his techniques in a climactic order, selecting a method of playing each sequence that will create a different effect from that of the sequence which precedes and the one which follows.

Techniques Which May Be Combined Easily

Certain fundamental techniques of acting combine easily and are frequently used together. Based upon what is recognized as the normal behavior of the normal person, these combinations are much like the notes in music which combine to produce harmony as contrasted to the notes which cannot be used together without producing dissonance. It is easy for the student-actor to discover which techniques combine naturally, since such combinations are as natural to the actor as a person as they are to the character that the actor is attempting to portray. It has already been noted how difficult it is to use an increase in volume without using a rise in pitch, and vice versa. In the same way, large gestures or an in-

crease in the size or the rate of movement is likely to be combined with
an increase in the volume of the spoken line and an increase in the rate of
speech.

The normal person, when angry, raises both the volume and pitch of
his voice and increases his rate of speech. At the same time, his facial
expression shows his anger, and the size of his movements and gestures,
as well as the vigor with which they are performed, is also likely to increase. In playing a scene in which anger is the chief emotion, however,
the actor will need to be economical in his use of the appropriate technical devices, lest he attain the maximum display of the emotion long before the scene is finished. This problem occurs in *Romeo and Juliet* in
the scene in which Capulet is angry because Juliet refuses to marry Paris,
a scene which cannot be kept in control and steadily progressing toward
a climax without taxing the technical facilities of the actor playing
Capulet.

Technical Analysis of Capulet's Scene

Capulet's anger begins in Act III, Scene 5, when Lady Capulet informs
him that Juliet has said she will not marry Paris:

> Ay, sir; but she will none, she gives you thanks.
> I would the fool were married to her grave.

There follows a speech of five lines in which Capulet's anger begins to
rise, but the lines express his unbelieving indignation and consternation
rather than his anger:

> Soft! take me with you, take me with you, wife.
> How! will she none? doth she not give us thanks?
> Is she not proud? doth she not count her blest,
> Unworthy as she is, that we have wrought
> So worthy a gentleman to be her bridegroom?

Surely the actor will need to use some increase in pitch and some accompanying increase in volume during this speech, but the actor will
need to keep careful control of his voice, lest he use a volume which is so
great that he will not be able to develop the following speeches with the
necessary sense of progression and increase of emotion. He will be wise
if he restrains himself from any considerable use of gesture or movement,
for these devices, too, will be more needed later. If the scene is directed
so that it is feasible to do so, the actor might address most of this speech to
Lady Capulet and then turn to face Juliet, possibly on the words, "Unworthy as she is."

Juliet now confirms what her mother has said:

Not proud, you have; but thankful, that you have:
Proud can I never be of what I hate;
But thankful even for hate, that is meant love.

At Juliet's words, Capulet gives way to his anger, and that anger is expressed in three speeches—the first of nine lines, the second of nine lines,
and the third of twenty-one lines.   At the end of the first speech Capulet's anger has become so great that Lady Capulet feels it necessary to attempt to intervene, and Juliet kneels before him to beg for patience.   At the
end of the second speech the Nurse dares to intervene, and the scene includes a short sequence in which Capulet vents his anger on the Nurse before turning back to Juliet.   The third and longest speech finishes with
Capulet's exit.

Before attempting to play this scene, the actor will do well to consider
all the technical devices appropriate to both the scene and the character,
and to decide how he can use them most effectively.   Some potentially
violent physical action will be needed at the end of the first speech to
provide proper motivation for Lady Capulet's speech and Juliet's action.

CAP.: How now! how now, chop-logic!   What is this?
         "Proud," and "I thank you," and "I thank you not;"
         And yet "not proud;" mistress minion, you,
         Thank me no thankings, nor proud me no prouds,
         But fettle your fine joints 'gainst Thursday next,
         To go with Paris to Saint Peter's church,
         Or I will drag thee on a hurdle thither.
         Out, you green-sickness carrion! out, you baggage!
         You tallow face.
LADY CAP.: Fie, fie! what, are you mad?
JULIET: Good father, I beseech you on my knees,
         Hear me with patience but to speak a word.

Does Capulet strike her?   Does he threaten to strike her?   Does he
lay violent hands upon her and so force her to her knees?   These are
questions of interpretation which affect the characterization and also affect the audience's reaction to the character.   What is certain is that at
this point there must be some physical action which may be composed
mostly of gestures or which may include a larger action of crossing the
stage toward Juliet, in which case the effect of threatened violence can
be created without using arm gestures to any great extent.

In the middle of Capulet's next long speech there is another hint of
threatened violence, "My fingers itch."

Hang thee, young baggage!   Disobedient wretch!
I tell thee what, get thee to church o' Thursday,

> Or never after look me in the face.
> Speak not, reply not, do not answer me;
> My fingers itch.   Wife, we scarce thought us blest
> That God had lent us but this only child;
> But now I see this one is one too much,
> And that we have a curse in having her.
> Out on her, hilding.

Looking ahead into Capulet's next and final speech, we find that there are no other lines which suggest that Capulet is making threatening gestures toward Juliet; therefore, these two places—"Out, you green-sickness carrion . . . ," and "My fingers itch"—are the only lines on which it is necessary to use a gesture such as raising the arm as though to strike.

The short dialogue between Capulet and the Nurse is an interlude which need not be considered at this time, since it is more in the nature of an interruption of the main scene than an integral part of it.

Capulet's final speech is redundant, repetitive of the ideas which he has previously expressed.   It begins with a restatement of the idea that Paris is a "worthy" gentleman; it mimics Juliet, as was done in the "chop-logic" speech; it repeats the instructions that Juliet is to be ready to marry Paris on Thursday, making a total of three times that these instructions have been given; and it finishes with the final threat, which is not one of physical violence but rather a threat of disownment and disinheritance:

> God's bread! it makes me mad.
> Day, night, hour, tide, time, work, play,
> Alone, in company, still my care hath been
> To have her match'd;
>
>   And having now provided
> A gentleman of noble parentage,
> Of fair demesnes, youthful, and nobly train'd,
> Stuff'd, as they say, with honourable parts,
> Proportion'd as one's thought would wish a man;
>
> And then to have a wretched puling fool,
> A whining mammet, in her fortune's tender,
> To answer "I'll not wed; I cannot love,
> I am too young; I pray you, pardon me."
>
> But, as you will not wed, I'll pardon you:
> Graze where you will, you shall not house with me:
> Look to't, think on't, I do not use to jest.
> Thursday is near; lay hand on heart, advise.

An you be mine, I'll give you to my friend;
An you be not, hang, beg, starve, die in the streets,
For, by my soul, I'll ne'er acknowledge thee,
Nor what is mine shall never do thee good.
Trust to't, bethink you; I'll not be forsworn.

This speech can be devided into at least five sections. The first four and a half lines are devoted to Capulet's version of the amount of time and effort he has expended on arranging the match; the next four and a half lines extol Paris' qualifications; the next four are given over to scorn of Juliet's attitude; the next four are a threat to disown Juliet unless she marries Paris on Thursday; and the last four are a threat to disinherit her. The actor can use the last line as a means of getting himself near the exit, so that he will not be left with a long cross to make after he has finished the speech.

Since each of Capulet's three big speeches includes a statement of the idea that Juliet must marry Paris on Thursday—"Fettle your fine joints 'gainst Thursday next," "I tell thee what, get thee to church o' Thursday," and "Thursday is near"—the actor would do well to select the technical device or devices best suited to these lines before he works out the techniques to be used for the rest of the scene.

This detailed analysis of the Capulet scene has been included to illustrate how an actor uses his knowledge and understanding of fundamental techniques to plan a method of playing a scene. Certainly the actor will want to shout, but not through the entire scene, lest his lines become ranting; he will want to use some large movements from one area of the stage to another, but not all the time, lest the movements lose their effectiveness. By relying first upon one technical device and then upon another, the actor can give the scene variety, clarify the different ideas and distinguish between the different gradations of his emotion, and at the same time sustain the fundamental emotion of the scene for the length of time required by the dialogue.

Much of the effectiveness of any particular technique depends upon the manner in which it is combined with other techniques. If, for example, the actor elects to use a loud tone and some large gesture as he says, "God's bread! It makes me mad," and then suddenly uses a smaller and a staccato tone, along with an increase in rate, on the next line, "Day, night, hour . . . ," he can create the impression that Capulet is making an effort to control his anger and to be reasonable. It is certainly more interesting and effective to play the scene this way than to use the more normal and more natural way of speaking the lines, which would be to deliver the four-line sequence with a gradual increase in both volume and rate.

A marked change in the techniques used for consecutive passages creates a startling effect, but the actor must use this device with taste and discretion. There are many roles and many plays in which it would not be appropriate. There would be little opportunity for this kind of acting in the major plays of Chekhov or in *Pelléas and Melisande*, although these plays require a more subtle use of the same techniques. It is unlikely that an actor playing Hamlet would use sudden contrasts in the "To be, or not to be" soliloquy, but he would very possibly want to use them in the "Oh, what a rogue and peasant slave" speech. To be the master of his art, the actor must be the master of all of its techniques and must understand the relative values of each method of playing a particular sequence.

Technical Analysis of Juliet's Potion Scene

Another scene which demands careful technical analysis and which requires great technical skill, as well as profound emotional comprehension, is Juliet's potion scene in Act IV, Scene 3, of *Romeo and Juliet*. The whole scene readily divides itself into several clearly defined sections as Juliet, left alone on the night before she is supposed to marry Paris, imagines the possible consequences of drinking the potion which the Friar has given her. Since each possibility, as she thinks of it, motivates a different emotion or a different degree of emotion, the actress will need to discover those techniques of bodily action and the use of the voice which will reveal to the audience the emotions which Juliet is experiencing. In searching for the variety of technical means necessary to play the scene effectively, the actress must take care that all the devices she selects are consistent with the character of Juliet and that they are arranged in such a way that the entire scene will have flow and continuity.

It is immediately apparent from a first reading that the scene begins in relative inaction and finishes in relative animation, for at the beginning of the scene Juliet says,

> I have a faint cold fear thrills through my veins,
> That almost freezes up the heat of life,

and at the end of the scene her imaginings have induced an emotional state close to frenzy as she fancies she sees Tybalt's ghost and crys, "Stay, Tybalt, stay!" Technically then, the scene must somehow be played with an increase in action—more movement about the stage, an increase in the size and vigor of gestures, or an increase in the number and the frequency of gestures.

Although the need for an increase in volume is less obvious than the need for an increase in action, it is certainly plausible that the scene might be played from soft to loud, the sequence beginning with a tone which is

barely—but, of course, clearly—audible and gradually rising in volume
as Juliet's fears and terrors mount, reaching a climax with the actress
using the maximum volume that she can command. But the ability to
increase the volume gradually without arriving at a shout long before the
scene is over requires a marvelous technical control of the voice, which is
far beyond the powers of most actresses.

In addition to using ever-increasing animation and ever-increasing volume, it might also be possible to play the entire scene with an increasing
rate of speech, which can be made to fit logically and effectively with
Juliet's thoughts and emotions. Her first supposition, that the potion
might not work at all, could be spoken slowly and deliberately as she pon-
ders the problem:

> What if this mixture do not work at all?
> Shall I be married then to-morrow morning?
> No, no: this shall forbid it: lie thou there.
> (*Laying down her dagger.*)

Her last supposition, that she might go crazy if she woke and found herself
imprisoned in a vault with dead men all about her, would justify a rapid
delivery of the lines, thus giving the impression of a rush and torrent of
words:

> O, if I wake, shall I not be distraught,
> Environed with all these hideous fears?
> And madly play with my forefather's joints?
> And pluck the mangled Tybalt from his shroud?
> And in this rage, with some great kinsman's bone,
> As with a club, dash out my desperate brains?"

These three technical devices—increase in animation, increase in volume, and increase in rate—combine naturally and easily, and by using
them together the actress might hope to convey the emotional frenzy
into which Juliet's imaginings have driven her. Any attempt to use all
three simultaneously throughout the entire scene, however, would result
in a performance of the kind Hamlet was referring to when he said, "O,
it offends me to the soul, to hear a robustious periwig-pated fellow tear a
passion to tatters, to very rags, to split the ears of the groundlings." It
may well be that Juliet is losing control of herself, but the actress playing
the role must never lose control of the scene.

The solution of the problem may well be to use all three techniques in
the scene, but to use them, in a sense, separately—that is, to use an increase
in volume through one section, to maintain that volume through the next
section but to increase the rate, and to maintain the same volume and rate
through the next section but to increase the animation. When played in

this way, the entire scene will seem to grow and develop—that is, to progress—although it will never reach the height which would be attained if all three qualities were increased through each section.

One interesting possibility which suggests itself is to use a sudden contrast for the climax of the scene. If, at the end of the scene, when Juliet thinks she actually sees the ghost of Tybalt, the actress presumes that Juliet is suddenly so frightened that she can scarcely move or speak and that the three lines,

> O, look! methinks I see my cousin's ghost
> Seeking out Romeo, that did spit his body
> Upon a rapier's point: stay, Tybalt, stay!

should be spoken in almost a whisper and in an attitude of motionless horror, an interesting interpretation of Juliet's emotional state may be achieved. To play this last sequence of lines in this manner, however, will be effective only if previous sequences have not been played in the same manner and if the immediately preceding sequence has been played with considerable volume and considerable movement. It is only the contrast which creates the impression of Juliet's extreme terror.

Technical Methods of Achieving Restraint in Acting

Restraint is a term which is frequently used to describe acting in a complimentary way. Shakespeare in his advice to the Players does not use the word *restraint*, but he seems to mean the same thing when he cautions them to "use all gently," and in a "whirlwind of passion" to "acquire and beget a temperance which may give it smoothness"; but he also warns, "Be not too tame neither." Most actors today subscribe to Shakespeare's principle; but there is a great divergence of opinion about how it is to be used.

1. There are those who think that "taste," "temperance," and "restraint" in acting can be achieved by cutting down on the size and the degree of the emotion itself. For these actors, achieving restraint is simply a matter of having Capulet not be angry enough to yell or wave his arms, of having Juliet be less afraid, of having Brutus be more stoical, for with the emotion minimized, there is less need for any large-sized expression of it. In this group are those misguided students who have misunderstood the Stanislavski system. Knowing that every emotion expressed upon the stage should be experienced by the actor and finding themselves incapable of experiencing the desired emotion to the desired degree, they feel justified in playing a particular scene with a lesser degree of emotion. This attitude is manifestly contrary to Shakespeare, who expects a "torrent, tempest, and whirlwind of passion," and to Stanislavski, who devotes much

of his course of study to exercises which may increase an actor's capacity for emotional comprehension but who never suggests that a performance should be limited by the inadequacies of the actor.

2. Actors are frequently given credit for the quality of restraint when they fail to react to the situation indicated in the plot in the manner or to the degree which the audience expects. This kind of acting seems to be popular in motion pictures, and prizes, awards, and Oscars are given to actors and actresses who have acquired an unbelievable degree of composure and stolidity. For this kind of acting to be praised, the story must have been developed in such a way that the audience is keenly aware of the tremendous danger confronting the character, whether it is a maniac with a revolver or an ordinary villain, whether a raging forest fire, a storm at sea, or a horde of charging elephants. Once the audience is convinced that a normal person, faced with these dangers, would show a particular emotion to a particular degree, the actor may elect to give one of those unmoving, stolid, great-stone-face performances, showing none of the emotions which the audience has been led to expect; if he does so, there is plenty of evidence that he has a fair chance of receiving a statue, a peculiarly appropriate gift, as an award for the finest performance of the year.

This kind of acting, although often praised for having restraint, is also frequently used as a legitimate comic device, in which case it is called *underplaying*. When employed in this way, it is usually related to specific lines and concerned with showing a reaction to a much smaller and less serious stimulus than grave danger. In Noel Coward's *Fumed Oak*, for example, Henry Gow's wife, daughter, and mother-in-law wrangle and quarrel all through breakfast in such a way that the audience expects that a normal person would be forced to do something violent, but Henry goes on reading his paper and eating his breakfast as though everything were calm and serene. In the second scene of the same play Henry does take appropriate action and speaks his mind. Here the actor may either show some of the emotions which the audience knows he must feel or play the scene calmly and serenely, even though he is called upon to throw the food on the floor, strike his mother-in-law, and threaten to throw water in her face.

Underplaying—that is, showing an emotion to a lesser degree than expected by the audience, or even showing a different emotion from the one expected—is much more appropriate in comedy than in serious drama because it presents a deviation from a norm. When used in serious drama, it becomes a dangerous device because of its comic potential. In old-fashioned melodramas when the hero or heroine bravely outfaces the villain without cringing or showing fear, the audience, sensing this deviation from an expected norm, often responds with laughter to a scene which was intended to be taken seriously. If some members of the audience find some of the Oscar-winning performances of motion-picture heroes and heroines equally amusing, they are merely confirming the fact that when an actor elects to play a scene showing less emotion than demanded by the situation, or an entirely different emotion, he is constantly in danger of giving a performance in which the contrast between the expected and the unexpected is so great that comedy results.

3. The quality of restraint is best achieved when the actor finds a time, a place, and a technical means of revealing to the audience the full degree of the emotion which the character is experiencing, but then does not continue to reveal the same degree of emotion and does not use the techniques normally associated with the one used for the momentary revelation of the emotion. When this is done, the audience becomes aware of the emotion but assumes, when the actor fails to continue to reveal the emotion in the expected manner, that the character has brought the emotion under control. It is this device that creates a sense of restraint in the performance.

We have seen that certain acting techniques combine naturally; when they are not so combined, the audience tends to believe that the character's emotion necessitated the use of one technique but that his will power denied the use of the others normally associated with it. If, for example, a character raises the volume of his voice in anger, but fails to allow the pitch to rise as it naturally would, both the emotion and the control of the emotion are demonstrated; if a character uses a large and violent gesture, but keeps his voice at a steady volume and pitch, again both the emotion and the control of the emotion are revealed.

There are innumerable possibilities for combining the various techniques in this manner, or perhaps one should say for not combining the techniques in a normal manner, which can be used to reveal the force of the emotion motivating the character without going on to a full statement of that emotion. If the actor gives his voice the variations in pitch and volume usually associated with people who have a desire to cry or who are about to cry but maintains control of his facial muscles, so that none of the facial expressions normally associated with the emotion is allowed to show, or if he allows his facial muscles to move, his lip to quiver, and so on, but keeps his voice at an even pitch and an even level, the contrast between the revelation of the emotion in one way and its concealment in all other ways will suggest a strong emotion which is being restrained by the character. Much the same effect is created when the character begins a gesture which reveals the emotion but then stops the gesture before its completion, as when Capulet raises his arm as though to strike Juliet but does not continue the action.

This method of achieving restraint in acting depends upon an adequate revelation of the emotion to its full degree and intensity, coupled with or immediately followed by a nonrevelation of the same emotion. It differs radically from the other methods of achieving restraint in that the first method involves revealing only a lesser degree of the emotion and the second method consists of not revealing the emotion at all. It can be seen that the first two methods, while frequently confused with restraint, are actually something else—the one involving a different character analysis, in which the character is judged to have a different emotion or a different degree of emotion, and the other requiring that the character's emotions, if he is judged to have any, be concealed rather than expressed. Only when the actor both reveals and conceals the emotion can he be said to have restraint.

Choice of Techniques for Ensemble Playing

In the potion scene, only the actress who is playing Juliet is concerned with the choice of techniques; and in the Capulet scene, it is mainly the actor playing Capulet who must make the decisions, the other actors reacting in an appropriate manner to whatever he does. In many scenes, however, indeed in most scenes, the decisions must be cooperatively made, all the actors agreeing together how the scene should be played and each actor using those techniques which best serve the purposes, not only of his own characterization, but also of all the other characterizations involved in the scene.

The necessity for cooperation between the actors in ensemble playing is the reason why modern productions have come to rely so much upon the director, for he is in a position to dictate to the actors the specific methods each should use; but even if the director makes the decisions and dictates the manner in which each actor should play the scene, it is still essential that the actors be sufficiently trained to be able to play as directed. It is to the actor's advantage, moreover, to understand both the final effect desired and the techniques required to achieve that effect.

In the previous chapter, attention was called to the fact that in the Brutus-Cassius sequence, Act IV, Scene 3, of *Julius Caesar*, Brutus' character denies to the actor playing the role the use of any of the devices usually employed to portray anger—the loud tone, the increased rate of speech, or the sudden violent action; Brutus must, for the most part, use a quiet voice, deliberate speech, and slow, deliberate movements. If this manner of playing the scene is to be effective and is to show the audience the strength and power of Brutus' character, the contrast between the two men must be clearly demonstrated to the audience. The surest way of doing this would be for the actor playing Cassius to use those techniques which are in the sharpest contrast to those used by the actor play-

ing Brutus, and for both actors to contrive the scene so that the contrasting techniques are placed in a nice juxtaposition to each other—that is, if
Cassius speaks loudly, then Brutus responds quietly; if Cassius speaks
quickly, then Brutus speaks deliberately; and if Cassius makes a sudden
and violent movement, then Brutus uses a small and slow movement, or
no movement at all.   If, for example, Brutus is seated and speaking quietly
as he says,

> Let me tell you, Cassius, you yourself
> Are much condemn'd to have an itching palm;
> To sell and mart your offices for gold
> To undeservers.

Cassius might jump to his feet as he replies,

> I an itching palm?

and strike the table angrily with his closed fist as he says:

> You know that you are Brutus that speak this,
> Or, by the Gods, this speech were else your last.

Then Brutus' next speech will be dynamic and powerful, even though
spoken quietly and deliberately as he says,

> The name of Cassius honors this corruption,
> And chastisement does therefore hide his head.

Suppose that the actor playing Cassius chooses to deliver the threat to take
Brutus' life calmly, quietly, and deliberately, speaking the lines slowly,
almost through clenched teeth.   Undeniably, this would be an effective
and powerful manner of playing this particular speech, but then the
other actor would be forced to answer in much the same way, and the
contrast between the two men would be lost.

   The entire scene can be played, and has been played, without violent
action and with neither actor using any considerable movement, the two
men remaining seated across the table from each other.   This manner of
playing the scene is suited to performances in small auditoriums or to
motion-picture productions, in which the camera can be brought in close,
so that the facial expressions of the actors can be seen clearly.   If the scene
is to be performed in this way, the actors will need to be especially careful in selecting specific vocal techniques and in choosing small gestures,
for these will take on the importance of big movements; a mere clenching
of the fist, for example, or a tightening of the muscles around the mouth
can be substituted for pounding on the table.   But whatever type of
production is planned, the performances of the two actors remain interdependent, and neither actor can decide what his reactions should be until
he is familiar with the actions of the other character.

The Effect of Stage Position on Technique

Thus far this discussion of the relative effectiveness of various techniques has concerned itself largely with the vocal techniques and the use of movement because these are the techniques which are most frequently left to the discretion of the actor, while other techniques, such as the use of levels and the pivoting of an actor toward or away from the audience, are more frequently in the province of the director and are dictated by him in the general blocking of the scene. The actor, however, must be fully cognizant of the effect that his position on the stage, whether it has been assigned to him or he himself has chosen it, will have upon his selection of the technical devices by which to convey the desired impression to the audience.

In the exercises for Chapter 5, the scene in which Trigorin describes his life was used to exemplify a situation in which the actor is forced to rely upon facial expressions, small gestures, and vocal techniques to project his interpretation of the character. In one production of *The Sea Gull*, the director arranged the scene so that Trigorin was seated with his face turned three-quarters upstage and away from the audience. His facial expressions, consequently, were invisible to almost the entire audience, but the actress playing the young girl, Nina, sat on the ground at his feet, facing him, and also facing the entire audience. Whenever such an arrangement is used, the actor playing Trigorin obviously cannot depend upon facial expressions at all and must rely exclusively upon vocal techniques and such gestures and changes of bodily position as will be meaningful to an audience even when seen from the back; but the actress playing Nina will find that the slightest change in her facial expression will be observed by the entire audience, sometimes to a degree which detracts attention from Trigorin's speech.

This placement of the characters on the stage is a blatant violation of Goethe's rule 40, which says:

> One must be especially careful never to speak in toward the stage, but always speak out toward the public. For the player must always divide his attention between two objects; that is, between the person to whom he is speaking and his audience. Instead of turning the whole head away, it is better, when necessary, merely to turn the eyes.

Goethe's rule is too arbitrary to meet with favor in contemporary theater, but the actor should remember that whenever he works on the stage with his face turned away from the audience he must rely on devices other than facial expressions to convey the thoughts and emotions of the character he is playing.

The problem of deciding which actors in any scene are to have the privilege of playing faced toward the audience and which are not is a vexing one, and, unfortunately, a frequent cause of contention between the actors.   In most cases the choice of one technique by one actor does not absolutely preclude the possibility that another actor may use the same technique if he so desires—that is, if one actor increases the volume of his speaking, another actor may do the same—but if one actor is faced toward the audience, the other actor or actors, if verisimilitude is to be maintained, are automatically deprived of this particular means of communication to an audience.   Many actors recommend, or at least practice, making a cross toward another actor, not in a natural, direct line, but in a slight arc, approaching the other actor from upstage so that they arrive in a new position faced toward the audience.   They also learn to begin a speech, whenever possible, by shifting their weight to the upstage foot.   In the acting profession, such practices are known as *upstaging*, a term which definitely has unpleasant and egotistical connotations.

As one might expect, Goethe has a rule on the subject:

> It is a cardinal point that when two actors are playing together, the speaker always moves back, and the one who has stopped speaking moves down slightly.   If one makes use of this advantage with understanding, and through practice can go about it without constraint, the best effect arises for the eye as well as for the intelligibility of the speech.   A player who masters this will, with others equally skilled, produce a very fine effect and have the advantage over those who do not observe it.

The trouble with this rule lies in the word "always."   Those who revolted from Goethe's rules and substituted the word "never" for his "always" are equally at fault.   Certainly the skilled actor should be able to move in this manner, always remembering that when he does so he is putting into his performance a movement which is not natural, one which is purely theatrical in its motivation; the actor with taste will use this device only when it is to the advantage of the play as a whole and not exclusively to his personal advantage.   The wording of Goethe's rule dangerously implies that acting is not a group effort but rather a sort of competition between individual actors.

The wise actor, in addition to practicing movements which easily, and seemingly naturally, bring him into a position where his facial expressions may be used for the interpretation of the part, will also try to develop skill in communicating his feelings and emotions to the audience by other techniques, such as bodily pantomime, gestures, and the use of the voice.

In a performance of *The Good Earth* Madame Nazimova played the role of Olan, the Chinese servant girl who is purchased as a wife but who comes to manage her husband's affairs in such a way that the family acquires great wealth and power.   Having completed the purchase of his wife, the husband magnanimously offers to buy his bride some oranges which a peddler is selling three for a penny. Insisting that one should get five for a penny, Olan conducts the bargaining until the peddler gives five. She then picks up her few belongings and starts out after her husband. In playing this scene, Madame Nazimova turned upstage and away from the audience as she made her exit, so that her face was not visible, but as she went out, she gave a little waggle of her head which eloquently expressed her pleasure at having got the best of the bargain and her determination to manage her husband's affairs in this manner in the future. An actress of Madame Nazimova's skill and imagination does not have to rely upon facial expressions to convey the character's emotion to the audience.

Choice of Techniques As a Method of Interpretation

The actor's choice of techniques should always be predicated upon his analysis of the character he is playing in relation to the play as a whole and upon the impression which he, the other actors in the play, and the director have decided is necessary to convey their understanding of the meaning and the quality of the play to the audience. Only after the actor knows what he is trying to do will he be able to make a sensible decision about the best way of doing it. If, for example, the cast and the director of *The Sea Gull* wish to play the Nina-Trigorin scene so that the audience will focus attention primarily on Nina and her reaction to what Trigorin is saying, rather than on Trigorin himself, one of the easiest and simplest devices for doing this would be to place the girl so that her facial expressions will be easily visible and to place Trigorin so that his face will not be seen and the audience will only hear his words. Both actors should know how to play the scene for both sets of values, or for a combination of both sets of values, but neither can decide how he will play the scene until both have agreed together what the total effect of the scene should be. The student of technique should constantly remember that there is no special merit in playing any scene in any particular way but that there is great merit in being able to play any scene in many ways. Only then is he capable of choosing the best way.

EXERCISES

1. Sequence from *Romeo and Juliet*, Act III, Scene 5.
   Divide the Capulet scene into small sections, each dealing with a single thought or emotion, and note where there are or could be changes in the degree of the emotion. Consider each separate section as a progression and assign to each progression a technical device which seems suitable.

CAPULET: How now, wife!
Have you deliver'd to her our decree?

LADY CAP.: Ay, sir; but she will none, she gives you thanks.
I would the fool were married to her grave!

CAPULET: Soft! take me with you, take me with you, wife.
How! will she none? doth she not give us thanks?
Is she not proud? doth she not count her blest,
Unworthy as she is, that we have wrought
So worthy a gentleman to be her bridegroom?

JULIET: Not proud, you have; but thankful, that you have:
Proud can I never be of what I hate:
But thankful even for hate, that is meant love.

CAPULET: How now, how now, chop-logic! What is this?
"Proud," and "I thank you," and "I thank you not";
And yet "not proud": mistress minion, you,
Thank me no thankings, nor proud me no prouds,
But fettle your fine joints 'gainst Thursday next,
To go with Paris to Saint Peter's Church,
Or I will drag thee on a hurdle thither.
Out, you green-sickness carrion! out, you baggage!
You tallow-face!

LADY CAP.: Fie, fie! what, are you mad?

JULIET: Good father, I beseech you on my knees,
Hear me with patience but to speak a word.

CAPULET: Hang thee, young baggage! disobedient wretch!
I tell thee what: get thee to church o' Thursday,
Or never after look me in the face:
Speak not, reply not, do not answer me;
My fingers itch. Wife, we scarce thought us blest
That God had lent us but this only child;
But now I see this one is one too much,
And that we have a curse in having her:
Out on her, hilding!

NURSE: God in heaven bless her!
You are to blame, my lord, to rate her so.

CAPULET: And why, my lady wisdom? hold your tongue.
Good prudence; smatter with your gossips, go.

NURSE: I speak no treason.

CAPULET: O, God ye good-den.

NURSE: May not one speak?

CAPULET: Peace, you mumbling fool!
Utter your gravity o'er a gossip's bowl;
For here we need it not.

LADY CAP.: You are too hot.

CAPULET: God's bread! it makes me mad:
>   Day, night, hour, tide, time, work, play,
>   Alone, in company, still my care hath been
>   To have her match'd: and having now provided
>   A gentleman of noble parentage,
>   Of fair demesnes, youthful, and nobly train'd,
>   Stuff'd, as they say, with honourable parts,
>   Proportion'd as one's thought would wish a man;
>   And then to have a wretched puling fool,
>   A whining mammet, in her fortune's tender,
>   To answer "I'll not wed; I cannot love,
>   I am too young; I pray you, pardon me."
>   But, an you will not wed, I'll pardon you:
>   Graze where you will, you shall not house with me:
>   Look to't, think on't, I do not use to jest.
>   Thursday is near; lay hand on heart, advise:
>   An you be mine, I'll give you to my friend;
>   An you be not, hang, beg, starve, die in the streets,
>   For, by my soul, I'll ne'er acknowledge thee,
>   Nor what is mine shall never do thee good:
>   Trust to't, bethink you; I'll not be forsworn.   (*Exit.*)

a. Rehearse the scene, concentrating on the vocal techniques. Decide which passages seem to require a climax achieved by an increase in volume. Try to find passages which can be played as a progression using an increase or a decrease in rate as a device, rather than an increase in volume.

b. Arrange the vocal techniques in a sequence, so that no two consecutive progressions are developed by the same vocal technique.

c. Rehearse the scene concentrating on the physical techniques. Decide which passages seem to require a climax achieved by using large movements and large gestures.

d. Rehearse the scene so that the largest movements and the largest gestures are used simultaneously with increases in volume.

e. Rehearse the scene trying to avoid using a vocal technique to build a progression if a physical technique is being used.

f. Try to find places where a sudden contrast from loud to soft or from action to inaction can be used effectively.

g. Rehearse the scene trying to rely mainly on a physical technique in the passages that had previously been developed by a vocal technique, and a vocal technique in the passages that had previously been developed by a physical technique.

NOTE: This probably cannot be done satisfactorily, but the attempt will reveal the relative effectiveness of each technique in a specific scene.

The actor will discover that as he gains control of the techniques by which an emotion is to be expressed he also gains control of the emotion itself.

2. Sequence from *Romeo and Juliet*, Act IV, Scene 3.

Divide Juliet's potion scene into small sections, each section dealing with a single thought or emotion, and note where there are or could be changes in the degree of the emotion. Consider each separate section as a progression and assign to each progression a technical device which seems suitable.

a. Rehearse the scene, concentrating on the vocal techniques, avoiding the use of movement and gesture as much as possible. Use a different vocal technique for the playing of each progression, avoiding the use of the same technique in consecutive passages.

b. Attempt to play the sequence from the line, "What if it be poison . . . ," to the end of the scene as a single progression, using a slow increase in volume, rate, and pitch.

c. Rehearse the scene, concentrating on the invention of gestures and using as little movement as possible.

d. Rehearse the scene using as much movement as can be made to seem appropriate. The opening of the scene, when Juliet calls the Nurse, can motivate a full stage cross from the bed to the door and back again. If Juliet imagines a darkened corner of the room on the far side of the stage to be the vault where the bodies and the ghosts are, a long cross toward it and a retreat from it can also be motivated.

e. Rehearse the scene avoiding the use of gestures or movement when the vocal techniques seem adequate, and avoiding vocal techniques when the gestures and movements seem adequate.

f. Search out several places where a sudden contrast in vocal techniques or physical techniques can be used.

NOTE: Perhaps it should be restated that no techniques or combination of techniques will substitute for the emotions of the character. Technique is the method of communicating the emotion, not the emotion itself.

3. Sequence from *The Rivals*, Act II, Scene 1.

Sir Anthony Absolute has just informed his son, Captain Jack Absolute, that he plans to settle an inheritance on him; but when the son learns that with the inheritance comes a wife, he objects on the basis that he already loves another, and refuses to obey his father.

ABS.: I must repeat—in this I cannot obey you.

SIR ANTH.: Now damn me! if I ever call you Jack again while I live.

ABS.: Nay, sir, but hear me.

SIR ANTH.: Sir, I won't hear a word—not a word! not one word! so give me your promise by a nod—and I'll tell you what, Jack—I mean, you dog—if you don't, by—

ABS.: What, sir, promise to link myself to some mass of ugliness! to—

SIR ANTH.: Zounds! sirrah! the lady shall be as ugly as I choose: she shall have a hump on each shoulder; she shall be as crooked as the crescent; her one eye shall roll like the bull's in Cox's Museum; she shall have a skin like a mummy, and the beard of a Jew—she shall be all this, sirrah!—yet I will make you ogle her all day, and sit up all night to write sonnets on her beauty.

ABS.: This is reason and moderation indeed!

SIR ANTH.: None of your sneering, puppy! no grinning, jackanapes!

ABS.: Indeed, sir, I never was in a worse humour for mirth in my life.

SIR ANTH.: 'Tis false, sir. I know you are laughing in your sleeve; I know you'll grin when I am gone, sirrah!

ABS.: Sir, I hope I know my duty better.

SIR ANTH.: None of your passion, sir! none of your violence, if you please!—It won't do with me, I promise you.

ABS.: Indeed, sir, I never was cooler in my life.

SIR ANTH.: 'Tis a confounded lie!—I know you are in a passion in your heart; I know you are, you hypocritical young dog! but it won't do.

ABS.: Nay, sir, upon my word—

SIR ANTH.: So you will fly out! can't you be cool like me? What the devil good can passion do?—Passion is of no service, you impudent, insolent, over-bearing reprobate!—There, you sneer again! don't provoke me!—but you rely upon the mildness of my temper—you do, you dog! you play upon the meekness of my disposition!—Yet take care—the patience of a saint may be overcome at last!—but mark! I give you six hours and a half to consider of this: if you then agree, without any condition, to do everything on earth that I choose, why—confound you! I may in time forgive you.—If not, zounds! don't enter the same hemisphere with me! don't dare to breathe the same air, or use the same light with me; but get an atmosphere and a sun of your own! I'll strip you of your commission; I'll lodge a five- and threepence in the hands of trustees and you shall live on the interest.—I'll dis-own you, I'll disinherit you, I'll unget you! and damn me! if I ever call you Jack again! (*Exit Sir Anthony.*)

NOTE: This scene is very similar to the Capulet scene in that a father has arranged a marriage which has been refused, but the scene is comic, rather than serious; the virtues of the intended are extolled in a comic reversal, and the scene ends with a threat of disinheritance. The actor playing Sir Anthony will get little help from the other actor in building the climax, except in so far as the contrast provided by the other character helps to point Sir Anthony's reactions.

a. Divide the scene into sections, each dealing with a separate thought or degree of emotion.

b. Rehearse the scene concentrating on the vocal techniques of change of volume, rate, and pitch, assigning a separate technique as the basis of building the progression in each section of the scene.

c. Rehearse the scene concentrating on the physical techniques, using gestures and movements to build each progression.

d. Rehearse the scene so that the largest gestures and the largest movements coincide with the vocal climaxes—that is, the largest volume and the fastest rate.

e. Rehearse the scene, avoiding the coincidence of a large movement or gesture with a large volume.

NOTE: This scene will be discussed again in the chapters on timing and pointing.

4. Sequence from Act I of *Death of a Salesman.*[1]

This scene is complicated by the fact that there are several overlapping emotional progressions. Each actor, therefore, must work out the techniques necessary for his own progression in such a way that they will coincide with the demands of the scene as a whole. First, there is the climax of the enthusiasm for the business plan; second, there is the conflict between Biff and Willy and their mounting anger, which is interrupted and delayed by their enthusiasm for the scheme; third, there is Linda's desire to have Biff and Willy understand each other; fourth, there is Willy's irritation because of Linda's participation in the scene; and fifth, there is the return of Biff's anger, caused by Willy's treatment of Linda.

The scene begins as Willy enters from the yard, having overheard Biff's remarks.

BIFF: I don't care what they think! They've laughed at Dad for years, and you know why? Because we don't belong in this nut-house of a city! We should be mixing cement on some open plain, or—or carpenters. A carpenter is allowed to whistle!

(*Willy walks in from the entrance of the house, at left.*)

WILLY: Even your grandfather was better than a carpenter. (*Pause. They watch him.*) You never grow up. Bernard does not whistle in the elevator, I assure you.

BIFF: (*As though to laugh Willy out of it*) Yeah, but you do, Pop.

WILLY: I never in my life whistled in an elevator! And who in the business world thinks I'm crazy?

[1] Copyright by Arthur Miller.

BIFF: I didn't mean it like that, Pop. Now don't make a whole thing out of it, will ya?

WILLY: Go back to the West! Be a carpenter, a cowboy, enjoy yourself!

LINDA: Willy, he was just saying—

WILLY: I heard what he said!

HAPPY: (*Trying to quiet Willy.*) Hey, Pop, come on now. . . .

WILLY: (*Continuing over Happy's line.*) They laugh at me, heh? Go to Filene's, go to the Hub, go to Slattery's, Boston. Call out the name Willy Loman and see what happens! Big shot.

BIFF: All right, Pop.

WILLY: Big!

BIFF: All right!

WILLY: Why do you always insult me?

BIFF: I didn't say a word. (*To Linda*) Did I say a word?

LINDA: He didn't say anything, Willy.

WILLY: (*Going to the doorway of the living room.*) All right, good night, good night.

LINDA: Willy, dear, he just decided. . . .

WILLY: (*to Biff*) If you get tired hanging around tomorrow, paint the ceiling I put up in the living-room.

BIFF: I'm leaving early tomorrow.

HAPPY: He's going to see Bill Oliver, Pop.

WILLY: (*interestedly*) Oliver? For what?

BIFF: (*with reserve, but trying, trying*) He always said he'd stake me. I'd like to go into business, so maybe I can take him up on it.

LINDA: Isn't that wonderful?

WILLY: Don't interrupt. What's wonderful about it? There's fifty men in the City of New York who'd stake him. (*To Biff*) Sporting goods?

BIFF: I guess so. I know something about it and—

WILLY: He knows something about it! You know sporting goods better than Spalding, for God's sake! How much is he giving you?

BIFF: I don't know. I didn't even see him yet, but—

WILLY: Then what're you talkin' about?

BIFF: (*getting angry*) Well, all I said was I'm gonna see him, that's all.

WILLY: (*turning away*) Ah, you're counting your chickens again.

BIFF: (*starting left for the stairs*) Oh, Jesus, I'm going to sleep!

WILLY: (*calling after him*) Don't curse in this house!

BIFF: (*turning*) Since when did you get so clean?

HAPPY: (*trying to stop them*) Wait a. . . .

WILLY: Don't use that language to me! I won't have it!

HAPPY: (*grabbing Biff, shouts*) Wait a minute! I got an idea. I got a feasible idea. Come here, Biff, lets talk this over now, lets talk some sense here. When I was down in Florida last time, I thought of a great idea to sell sporting goods. It just came back to me. You and I, Biff—we have a line, the Loman Line. We train a couple of weeks, and put on a couple of exhibitions, see?

WILLY: That's an idea!

HAPPY: Wait! We form two basketball teams, see? Two water-polo teams. We play each other. It's a million dollars' worth of publicity. Two brothers, See? The Loman Brothers. Displays in the Royal Palms—all the hotels. And banners over the ring and the basketball court: "Loman Brothers." Baby, we could sell sporting goods!

WILLY: This is a one-million-dollar idea!

LINDA: Marvelous!

BIFF: I'm in great shape as far as that's concerned.

HAPPY: And the beauty of it is, Biff, it wouldn't be like a business. We'd be out playin' ball again. . . .

BIFF: (*enthused*) Yeah, that's. . . .

WILLY: Million-dollar. . . .

HAPPY: And you wouldn't get fed up with it, Biff. It'd be the family again. There'd be the old honor, and comradeship, and if you wanted to go off for a swim or somethin'—well, you'd do it! Without some smart cooky gettin' up ahead of you!

WILLY: Lick the world! You guys together could absolutely lick the civilized world.

BIFF: I'll see Oliver tomorrow. Hap, if we could work that out. . . .

LINDA: Maybe things are beginning to—

WILLY: (*wildly enthused, to Linda*) Stop interrupting! (*To Biff*) But don't wear a sport jacket and slacks when you see Oliver.

BIFF: No, I'll—

WILLY: A business suit, and talk as little as possible, and don't crack any jokes.

BIFF: He did like me. Always liked me.

LINDA: He loved you!

WILLY: (*to Linda*) Will you stop! (*To Biff*) Walk in very serious. You are not applying for a boy's job. Money is to pass. Be quiet, fine, and serious. Everybody likes a kidder, but nobody lends him money.

HAPPY: I'll try to get some myself, Biff. I'm sure I can.

WILLY: I see great things for you kids, I think your troubles are over. But remember, start big and you'll end big. Ask for fifteen. How much you gonna ask for?

BIFF: Gee, I don't know—

WILLY: And don't say "Gee." "Gee" is a boy's word. A man walking in for fifteen thousand dollars does not say "Gee!"

BIFF: Ten, I think, would be top though.

WILLY: Don't be so modest. You always started too low. Walk in with a big laugh. Don't look worried. Start off with a couple of your good stories to lighten things up.   It's not what you say, it's how you say it—because personality always wins the day.

LINDA: Oliver always thought the highest of him—

WILLY: Will you let me talk?

BIFF: Don't yell at her, Pop, will ya?

WILLY: (*angrily*) I was talking, wasn't I?

BIFF: I don't like you yelling at her all the time, and I'm tellin' you, that's all.

WILLY: What're you, takin' over this house?

LINDA: Willy—

WILLY: (*turning on her*) Don't take his side all the time, goddammit.

BIFF: (*furiously*) Stop yelling at her!

WILLY: (*suddenly pulling on his cheek, beaten down, guilt ridden*) Give my best to Bill Oliver—he may remember me.   (*He exits through the living-room doorway.*)

TECHNICAL ANALYSIS: (1) Willy's three speeches in resentment to Biff's remark. (2) The first of Linda's interruptions which annoy Willy. (3) Three speeches by Biff to pacify his father and three speeches in which Willy brags. (4) The second Linda interruption. (5) Biff and Happy's introduction of the Oliver proposition and Willy's three speeches in response. (6) Another Linda interruption, breaking the preceding sequence. (7) Three speeches in which Biff and Willy quarrel. (8) Happy's enthusiasm about the idea of a sporting-goods business, and the others' response. This sequence is longer than most and perhaps should be divided. (9) The third Linda interruption. (10) Willy's advice to Biff. (11) The fourth Linda interruption, breaking the preceding sequence. (12) Willy's advice to Biff on the subject of the money to be requested. (13) The next Linda interruption. (14) Biff's defense of his mother. (15) The last Linda interruption, breaking the previous sequence. (16) Willy's final line, showing his defeat.

a. Attempt to play the scene with everyone using an increase in volume and rate.

b. Rehearse the scene with Willy using an increase in volume on all of his replies to Linda's interruptions and search out other techniques for the other sequences.   In sequence 7 when Willy and Biff quarrel, the author has suggested movement as a technical device.   The same thing is true at the end of sequence 3.

c. Experiment with an increase in rate, but not in volume, and an increase in gesture in the Happy sequence 8.

d. Work on the invention of action and the use of pauses in Willy's last speech so that Willy's new emotional state may be adequately projected before his exit.

Chapter 7. TIMING

In chapter 6, the use of movement, one of the chief creative contributions of the actor, was discussed as a device by which the actor may make clear the thought and emotional patterns of the character he is playing. A considerable portion of that chapter is devoted to explaining the method by which the actor considers each thought or emotional state as a separate unit, devises the best technical means for its expression, and then combines the units into a sequence which has coherence and a logical continuity, making a new and larger unit out of the component parts. Before going on to a consideration of how these larger units are combined to make an artistic unit of an entire act and the whole play, it is necessary to consider the relationship between the action invented by the actor and the words of the author in the smallest and most precise detail possible. This is the relation of action, not to the scene as a whole, not to the thought sequences which make up the scene, but to the individual sentences, the phrases which make up those sentences, the words which make the phrases, and even to the syllables which combine to make the words.

Walter Kerr, in his review of Lloyd Nolan's performance in *The Caine Mutiny Court Martial*, said, "Through the evening Mr. Nolan must work cagily against the lines, offering what seem to be casually reasonable statements of fact and at the same time betraying the sick fear which lurks hauntingly behind every word, every affable wave of his hand, every studied crossing of his legs." In the same review, speaking of the work of the director, or directors, he said, "In the staging, Charles Laughton (succeeding Dick Powell) has infused the minutest movement with aching suspense." Too few critics have shown this kind of insight into the work of actors and directors, an insight which reveals a knowledge that the total effect of any performance is composed of the smallest and most minute and most carefully worked out details.

In many ways an acting performance is like a mosaic; the total effect, no matter how large and how impressive, is achieved by the careful selection of tiny bits which are skillfully combined, so that each particle makes its contribution to the complete picture. Perhaps it is inevitable that even actors and directors, as well as critics and audiences, should be

unaware of the importance and the significance of the small details of
a performance and the techniques and artifices by which these details are
incorporated into a performance, since actors, much more than artists
in other fields, are striving to conceal their techniques, and the final effect they are trying to create is that every little action is natural, inevitable, and accidental. One presumes that when Mr. Kerr spoke of the
"studied" crossing of the legs he meant that he, as a critic, was aware
that the action was the result of careful study on the part of the actor,
not that the final effect seemed calculated and studied to the audience.

A Definition of Timing

In many discussions of the art and the technique of acting, one hears
the term *timing*, which most actors seem to understand but few can define. In fact, there is no generally accepted definition of timing, although it is generally known that timing is an element of the actor's technique and that some actors employ it with greater effectiveness than do
others.

For the purposes of the study of the technique of acting, the student
might use the following definition: timing is the exact and precise time
relationship between a physical action of relatively short duration and
the spoken word or words with which it is associated. It should be understood that the words are not necessarily spoken by the actor who
performs the action, although the term is most frequently used that way.
It should also be understood that the rate or speed with which the action is performed and the word is spoken has nothing to do with timing,
just as a waltz may be played slowly or fast and still be a waltz as long
as the time relationship of the individual notes within the measure remains relatively the same. In a broader sense, adjusting the duration of an
action or gesture to the duration of a speech or thought, is also timing;
but it is the precision of the simultaneous beginning and ending which
creates the effect of good timing.

There is a prevalent misconception that timing is an element of technique which is present only in comedy and is not employed in playing
serious drama or tragedy. This misconception has arisen because skill
or lack of skill in timing is more apparent in comedy than in other forms
of drama, but it is absolutely impossible to give any acting performance
without using timing, since there is, of necessity, some time relationship
between the actions and the words. There is correct timing and incor-
rect timing, effective timing and ineffective timing, obvious timing and
timing which is performed with such skill and ease that only the most
trained observers are aware of it; but there is always timing.

The Three Time Relationships

There are only three possible time relationships between an action and the words with which it is associated. The action may be performed before the words are spoken, while the words are being spoken, or after the words are spoken. It sometimes appears that an action is performed in the middle of a line, but this simply means that the action is performed after certain phrases or words and before others; the confusion arises because the actor is thinking of a whole sentence rather than of the phrases and words which compose the sentence.

A simple line like, "Go. Get out," which might well appear in hundreds of different situations in hundreds of different plays, will serve to illustrate the technique of timing. The action to be associated with these words may be the obvious one of raising the right arm from a relaxed position at the speaker's side and extending it fully at shoulder height, with the finger pointing toward the exit. If the actor elects to use the first time relationship, the gesture may be completed before the words are spoken, the speech beginning at the exact moment that the gesture is completed and the gesture being sustained until the speech has been completed. It will be noted that if the spoken words are delayed for a second or two, the effect created is that the character had considered the gesture a sufficient command and that he gave the spoken command only because the gesture had not brought the desired response. In a sense, the delay in the speech, if there is an appreciable moment between the completion of the gesture and the beginning of the speech, has created two thoughts in the place of one, or at least a reiteration of the one thought. There is no particular reason why the actor should not choose either of these methods of delivering the gesture and line, provided that he is aware of the difference in implication, slight though it may be, and provided that the effect created is in accordance with his interpretation of the character in the particular situation.

Second, the gesture may be begun at the precise moment that the actor speaks and executed in such a way that it is completed at the exact moment that the speech is completed. If the sentence used by the author to express the thought happens to be slightly longer than the one used here for purposes of illustration, the actor will find that he is forced to perform the gesture more deliberately in order to make it coincide exactly with the line; if, for example, the words were, "Go. Leave this house at once," a five-syllable line in place of the simple two-syllable order, "Get out," the gesture may also be completed while saying either, "Go," or, "Get out." In either case the speech seems to have become two speeches with two thoughts, or at least a reiteration of the same thought. As a further possibility, the gesture may be performed after saying, "Go," and before saying, "Get out." Again the line has been divided into two thoughts, and whether the gesture is considered as coming after the first speech or before the second one, the whole sequence now suggests a triple repetition of the thought expressed in the words and the gesture.

Third, the gesture may be begun at the precise moment that the speaking stops. Again it should be noted that any appreciable delay between the end of the speaking and the beginning of the gesture creates the impression of two thoughts or a reiteration of the same thought.

Syncopated Timing

The actor should also experiment with combinations of the gesture and the line in which the gesture does not exactly coincide with the words. This device is analogous to syncopation in music, in which a tone is begun on an unaccented beat and sustained through the next accented beat, or begun on the last half of a beat and sustained through the first half of the next beat. The actor may begin the gesture on "Go" and complete it on "Get," leaving the word "out" dangling at the end. He may also begin and finish the gesture on the word "out," or begin the gesture on the word "out," completing it only after the speech is finished. Many more interesting variations can be devised if the longer sentence, "Leave this house at once," is used.

The beginning actor is likely to find syncopated timing much more difficult to perform than other types because it will seem illogical, uncoordinated, and therefore unnatural. This does not mean that the actor should not use the device, however, any more than it means that a musician should not use syncopation. There are many occasions when the actor will wish to create the impression that the character he is playing is, for some reason, behaving illogically and unnaturally. One of the most useful devices for creating this effect is to combine the character's actions and speeches in such a way that they seem uncoordinated. To do this, however, the actor must actually have more control and coordination than he would need if he were using a more natural and normal relationship between actions and words.

Much of the fault with Goethe's rules for actors lies in their dogmatism; he said "always" do this and "never" do that. For the modern actor there is probably only one dogmatic rule: Never do anything without knowing that you are doing it and why you are doing it and always consciously choose the method of playing a scene which you consider best adapted to the effect you wish to create. In recent years there has been so much talk among actors about the subconscious that many of them seem to be striving for an unconscious method of playing. If a performance is accidental, it is not art, by the very definition of the word. Art, no matter how lifelike it is striving to be, must always be planned and contrived with the purpose of making the beholder respond to it in the particular way desired.

The Competition between Actions and Lines

Of all the devices which an actor may use to emphasize a selected line which expresses a thought, reveals a facet of the character, or conveys an emotional state, movement is unquestionably the most dynamic and powerful. In addition, the pantomimic action of a play is in itself capable, upon occasion, of expressing thoughts and emotions and revealing character with as much clarity and force as the spoken word. The actor must never forget the adage that actions speak louder than words.

It frequently happens that the actions which are largely the invention and the creation of the actor seem to be in direct competition with the words of the author; to avoid this possibility, the actor must exercise the greatest care in coordinating the actions with the words. There is always the danger that since the pantomimic action of the role is the child of the actor's brain and the words are the author's creation, the actor will, either consciously or unconsciously, like a fond parent, favor his own inventions above those of the author. If the invented actions express exactly the same meaning as the words, there is less danger of conflict; but frequently the actor deliberately invents pantomime to suggest a slight change of meaning. Then he must be doubly careful.

The possibility of competition between words and actions is so great, especially when the actions are performed by one actor while the words are being spoken by another, that the beginning actor might well study how and when not to move rather than how and when to include movement. One actor moving on another actor's lines has been the cause of much dissension in rehearsals and performances. Not to do this is one of the first things that the inexperienced actor learns from the more experienced actor. Failure to learn this lesson has often been the cause of a young actor's dismissal from a cast during rehearsals, and to err in this matter during a performance is to court disaster and the loss of one's job.

To comprehend the dynamic power of even the slightest movement, and the significance of the problem that arises when movement is not carefully correlated with the words, one need only remember that hundreds in the audience at an oratorio concert will momentarily have their attention diverted from the soloist if any member of the chorus cleans his glasses or, failing to resist an itching nose, dares to scratch while the soloist is singing.

The Danger of Combining the Action of
One Character with the Speeches of Another

While many actors quickly learn the dangers inherent in moving while
another actor is speaking (they learn it because experienced actors will
not tolerate any uncorrelated action), it is more difficult for them to
learn that their own actions, even when they are well thought out and
meaningful actions, tend to set up the same kind of competition with
what they themselves are saying, unless their movements are incorporated
into the performance with careful timing.

In order to prove the dynamic quality of movement and the tendency
for movement to attract attention to itself, the student-actor might do
well to rehearse some scenes as they should never be played. In the
Capulet scene in Act III, Scene 5, of *Romeo and Juliet*, which was
analyzed in a previous chapter, let Lady Capulet pace up and down the
room in agitation, as she well might do if she were fearful of the outcome of the quarrel between Juliet and her father. One will soon see
that the attention of the audience is likely to be distracted from the words
that Capulet is speaking and that their sense and meaning are lost because
it is almost impossible for an audience to watch one actor and listen to
another. There is no question that Capulet will be heard, but with the
audience watching Lady Capulet there is little hope that what he says
will communicate anything except the fact that he is angry. Certainly
the actor playing Capulet will find it impossible to impress upon the audience any nuances of meaning.

For a more bizarre and fantastic example of the competitive quality of
movement, suppose that among the citizens who have come into the
Forum to hear Brutus speak, in Act III, Scene 2, of *Julius Caesar*, there
is one who is not particularly interested in the proceedings, as there well
might be, one who has come with the crowd because the crowd was
coming that way, but who thinks that Brutus is only another politician
striving to sway the mob with words, words which this imagined citizen
knows will have little effect upon his life. While Brutus delivers his
oration, let the citizen sit in some place which is visible to the audience
and swing his legs idly while the speech goes on. The actor playing
Brutus could not be blamed if he demanded that the management get rid
of the actor who was playing the cynical citizen.

If movement has the power to attract and, therefore, to distract the
attention of the audience, it would seem advisable to have whatever movement is on the stage closely associated with the spoken lines whenever
it is the aim of the actors and the director to have the audience focus
their attention upon the speaker and the speech. Naturally, since it is

the purpose of the actor to interpret the author, and since the author's thoughts and ideas are for the most part expressed in the speeches he has written for the characters, the actors will almost always be trying to use movement in such a way that it draws attention to the speech, rather than away from it.   This does not mean that it is necessary for the speaking actor to stay in constant motion.   Often there is no movement at all upon the stage, and when there is no distracting movement, there is no necessity to use movement to attract attention, for under these circumstances the attention of the audience will quite naturally follow the sound and go to the speaker.

In the first scene of *Richard II*, when Mowbray and Bolingbroke are making their charges and countercharges before King Richard, and in Act I, Scene 3, where the quarrel is continued (in modern productions these scenes are frequently joined together and played continuously), it may well be that the strongest dramatic values are not in having the audience pay strict attention to the argument but in having the audience note that Richard himself, instead of paying serious attention so that he will be able to decide the issue justly, maintains a supercilious attitude, thus indicating that his decision will be based upon whim or expediency and selfish interests, rather than upon the merits of the case.

To play the scene for these values, Richard might walk away from the contestants, straighten his flowing sleeve, pour himself a glass of wine, or perform some other action which would connote his attitude toward the speakers.   This would distract the attention of the audience from the speakers and their speeches, but in this case, it would be justifiable, particularly if it were done during one of Mowbray's speeches, since he is a minor character and holds little interest for the audience.

Combining Action and Words for Emphasis

There are many occasions when the actor will wish to use movement to focus the attention of the audience on himself just before he speaks. In these cases the actor makes a movement, not while another actor is speaking, but just after he has spoken.

In Act I, Scene 2, of *Hamlet*, the King has been conducting the affairs of state and has just granted Laertes permission to return to France; Hamlet has been present during these proceedings but has not participated in the scene.   Throughout the first sixty-three lines of the scene, any movement on the part of Hamlet would be distracting; he should be on the scene, but not in the scene.   Now the King turns his attention to Hamlet and says, "But now, my cousin Hamlet, and my son," and Hamlet speaks for the first time, saying, "A little more than kin, and less than kind."   Here some movement such as a turning of the head, or a cross-

ing of the legs, or any other move which the actor deems appropriate
to Hamlet's character and emotional state will help to shift the attention
from the King to Hamlet.

There are two important factors which affect the decision as to whether
or not it is necessary for Hamlet to make a slight move in order to catch
the attention of the audience. The first of these is the actions of the
King and the rest of the court; if the King turns directly to Hamlet and,
with some gesture, points out where Hamlet is sitting and waits for
Hamlet to speak, or if the stage is so arranged that Hamlet is sitting near
the King and is already part of the picture, it will not be necessary for
the actor playing Hamlet to make any move, unless he chooses to do so.
But if the actor playing the King chooses to turn and look fondly at
the Queen as he says, "And my son," a gesture which could easily be
justified in terms of the King's character and his emotional state, or if
the play is being performed on a large stage and the director has arranged for Hamlet to be sitting at some distance from the King, a movement on the part of Hamlet becomes obligatory, provided that it is
considered desirable for the attention of the audience to be fully focused
upon Hamlet as he speaks. It can be seen, at least in this instance, that
using movement in this way, directly preceding a line, brings emphasis
to the speech.

It is also possible for the action to be performed while the line is being
said, the movement beginning as the line begins and ending as the line
ends. Suppose, for purposes of illustration, that the movement selected
is for Hamlet, who has been looking down and paying little attention to
the scene, to raise his head to look at the King or, if he has been watching
the King during the early part of the scene, to turn away. There is
no question that the attention of the audience will quickly shift to Hamlet if it is not already there, but the action will, in a sense, detract from
the line itself. The attention will be both upon the line and the action
and, therefore, divided between them. The emphasis will be on Hamlet,
but not so much on what he says, or on what he does, as on the emotional
state which motivated both the speech and the movement.

In order to contrast the different dramatic values that result from different technical ways of playing a scene, suppose that the placement of
the characters on the stage and the performance of the King are such
that the attention of the audience is surely upon Hamlet before he speaks,
so that there is no compulsion for the actor to do anything to attract
attention. If the speech is delivered with no movement at all, save what
facial expression is necessary for the actual speaking of the lines, the
scorn, the irony, and the sarcasm of the speech will become evident to
the audience; if the speech is delivered with a body movement, as has
been suggested, the speech will seem to lose some of its force and vigor,

but Hamlet's emotional reaction to the scene, and to the King, will be more clearly stated to the audience.

In this situation the actor cannot possibly accomplish both effects to the same degree; the line will always seem more powerful if it is delivered with a minimum of action, provided that the attention is already upon Hamlet. One may deduce from this example that action performed while the line is being spoken brings emphasis to the character, but more to his emotional state than to the actual words he is speaking.

If the action is combined with the line but the line is considered as two lines rather than as one, still another effect will be created. In this instance the action may be performed on the words, "A little more than kin," leaving the rest of the line, "And less than kind," to be spoken without action; or the first half of the line may be spoken without action, and the movement performed while speaking the last half of the line. The first thing to notice in using either of these methods is that the two halves of the thought, though presented separately, have a close cause-and-effect relationship. Performing the action on the first half of the line suggests that Hamlet's emotional state has motivated the thought in the second half of the speech and thus places great emphasis upon this half, so that the "And less than kind" becomes more bitter and more antagonistic. If the method is reversed, the thought in the first half of the speech seems to motivate the emotional reaction expressed by the action performed on the last half of the speech.

A similar effect may be achieved by performing the action, not on either half of the speech, but between the two halves. This seems to divide the sequence into three parts: the first thought, the emotional reaction caused by this thought and expressed in pantomimic action, and the following thought, which seems to have been motivated by the emotion.

The next possible variant in methods of playing the scene is one which no actor would wish to use unless he wanted to play the role so that Hamlet would seem already mentally deranged in his first speech. This method would be to use syncopated timing—to begin the speech without movement, start the action after saying, "A little more," and complete it on the words, "And less," speaking the last two words, "Than kind," without any action. The student-actor will find this method of playing the scene very difficult, for it will seem unnatural.

The final possibility, still assuming that the attention is already upon Hamlet, is for the actor to speak the entire line without movement and to begin the movement directly after the line. When this method is used, the entire line seems to become a motivation for Hamlet's emotional reaction, which is expressed in the pantomimic action, and since the attention of the audience is shifted immediately from the thought of the line to the action which follows, the action will tend to have the greater emphasis. Certainly the action will receive more attention here than it would in any of the other possible time relationships discussed. It should be noted that in this last method of timing the scene, the actor playing Hamlet must rely on the cooperation of the actor playing the King, for if the King speaks immediately on cue following Hamlet's first line, he will be speaking while Hamlet is performing the action, so that the King's speech and Hamlet's action will come into undesirable competition with each other.

Remembering that the whole subject of movement might well be studied to discover when not to move rather than when to use movement, imagine what this scene would be like if the player in the King's role elected to rise as he said, "But now, my cousin Hamlet, and my son," and began to move toward Hamlet, continuing to walk throughout Hamlet's line and through his own next line, "How is it that the clouds still hang on you?" finishing the walk with his hand on Hamlet's shoulder just as he completes the latter line. This would be effective and emphatic business for the King, but it would make it extremely difficult for the actor playing Hamlet to make any impression at all with his speech.

If this discussion of all the possible ways that a single line may be played has seemed overly long and ponderous for such a minute problem, the student may console himself with the thought that one definition of genius is that it is "the infinite capacity for taking pains." No actor would ever sit down to study a script and puzzle out all the possible variations in timing every sentence, every phrase, and every word of a part, because the right way, or at least a plausible way, will readily suggest itself for many of the lines; but the actor should always be aware of all the other possibilities. Then, when he is dissatisfied with his performance in any particular passage, he will know what other ways of playing the scene are available to him, and as he begins the process of trial and error he will have some advance knowledge of what to try.

The Effect of Timing on Emphasis

In the analysis of the techniques of timing as applied to Hamlet's first line, several principles are apparent:

1. When movement is closely related to a spoken line, the movement tends to bring emphasis to the line.

2. When the movement is performed as the line is spoken, the character and his emotional state receive emphasis above other characters on the stage, but the movement tends to compete with the thought of the

line, and the effectiveness of both the action and the line is diminished.

3. When the movement and the line are in a close time relationship but one precedes the other, that which comes first tends to throw greater emphasis on that which follows, and also to become the motivation for that which follows.

Whether or not these principles are universal and may be applied to all characters in all situations can only be determined by testing the theory in as many instances as possible. If the principles are valid, it remains for the actor to decide when he wishes to use movement for emphasis. He must also decide whether he wishes to use the movement to bring emphasis to the line or whether he desires the movement itself to receive emphasis. Such decisions are matters of taste and interpretation and are not properly part of the subject of technique, which concerns itself with methods of achieving results, not with the results themselves.

Since movement is such a powerful and dynamic force on the stage and since it is such a competitive force, particularly in the interrelationship of several characters on the stage, the actor must learn to use it with care and discretion, reserving it as an emphatic device for those situations where it is necessary. In Act I, Scene 2, of *Hamlet*, the Queen, Hamlet himself, and all others on the stage who are not directly involved in the proceedings will wish to avoid movement lest it detract from the main business of the scene between the King and Laertes. If the actors playing these two roles already have the attention of the audience, they, in turn, will use movement only as it assists in clarifying the meaning of the scene. In the Trigorin-Nina scene from *The Sea Gull*, the actress playing Nina will be chary of using movement lest it distract from the speech of Trigorin, unless the actors have agreed to place the greater emphasis upon the listening figure, in which case the actress will search out meaningful and appropriate movements to assist in this interpretation of the scene.

When the movement of the scene is to be performed by the speaker himself, equal care must be taken that the action does not distract from the speech when it is not intended to do so. When Aline MacMahon was rehearsing for a production of Daudet's *L'Arlesienne*, she wanted to create the impression that the character she was playing was a busy, hardworking peasant woman. In playing her first scene, in which the character is called to the door of the farmhouse, Miss MacMahon appeared with a glass and a dish towel in her hand and, as she spoke, finished wiping and polishing the glass, thus suggesting a woman who was too busy to stop her work to talk and a housewife who took pride in her housekeeping.

In another scene, when preparations are being made to attend a village fair or festival, Miss MacMahon brought with her some jewelry, includ-

ing earrings, which she put on while she was talking.   Although this action definitely suggested that the woman had had too many things to do
in the house to have time to get ready for the celebration, the audience
became far too fascinated watching Miss MacMahon attach the earrings
to pay very much attention to what was being said, and the action had
to be cut out of the scene.

To light a cigarette on the stage becomes a hazard, for the actor must
find time to get the cigarette, get the match, light the match, light the
cigarette, extinguish the match, and take the first puff without having any
of these actions detract from important or significant lines.   A lady's fan
in a Restoration play, a meal to be eaten on the stage, cocktails to be
shaken, or clothes to be put on or taken off, all involve action which gives
the actor an opportunity to create emphasis on his character and on his
speeches but also presents him with a problem, for he must perform the
action without allowing it to become the most important thing in the
performance.   Many ingenues, when playing animated and vivacious
young ladies, fall into the habit of expressing that animation by a constant shaking of the head while they are speaking.   This definitely creates
the impression that they are animated and enthusiastic, but it makes it
difficult for the audience to know what they are being enthusiastic about.

Sometimes action of this kind is inherent in the scene and inevitable.
Sometimes it is invented by the actor for the express purpose of revealing character.   At other times action is created for a scene by the director
or the actors solely to add interest and variety when it is thought that the
attention of the audience could not be sustained by the words alone.   In
the New York production of *The Cocktail Party*, the characters were frequently getting up and looking for cigarettes and putting them out again,
crossing to sit in a different chair, or having another cocktail for no apparent reason, except that they seemed to fear that the audience would
be getting bored with the talk and needed a distraction.   Or perhaps the
characters or the actors had themselves become too bored to sit still another moment.   Whether or not Mr. Eliot's dialogue is of sufficient
interest to hold the attention of the audience without the introduction of
extraneous action is a matter for the critics to decide.

The Charles Laughton reading of *Don Juan in Hell* took the other tack
and included as little movement as possible, making what movement there
was serve the purpose of bringing greater emphasis to particular and selected lines.   Both performances were skillful, and the fact that the
actors in each production had chosen to use movement to a different degree and for a different purpose does not mean that one method was right
and the other wrong; it may well be that the best solution was found for
each problem.

Timing As a Device to Suggest Motivation

When a specific action is to be performed in relation to a specific line, but not while the line is being spoken, the actor must decide which is to come first, the line or the action. Since that which comes first appears to be the motivation for that which follows, there is often a logical basis for deciding the matter. If a character is invited to go on a picnic and replies by saying, "I think it is going to rain," and then goes to the window to look out at the weather, the audience will understand, since he performs the action after the line, that he knows the state of the weather and looks outside merely to verify his opinion. Using action to suggest motivation, while it automatically provides emphasis, is very different from inventing and performing action for the sole purpose of achieving emphasis.

Since the technique of timing involves a decision as to the appropriate chronological order of lines and actions and since the chronological order invariably suggests to an audience a cause-and-effect relationship, it can be seen that timing is a most important device in clarifying a character's motivation. This matter is close to the very center of the actor's problem, for his chief aim must always be to make the character he is playing understandable to the audience. The author has decreed what the character must say; the director, the author, and the actor himself have decided what he must do; but the actor alone is concerned with the problem of explaining to the audience why the character says what he says and does what he does.

If an actor finds that the motivation for one of his lines is not obvious to the audience, he may search for an action which will convey the emotion which is the true motivation and then perform the action directly before he speaks the line. The action may be nothing more than a change in facial expression, showing surprise, shock, hate, love, fear, or whatever emotion the actor considers the motivation for the speech. If, on the other hand, the actor is required to perform an action, which is motivated by one of his lines, he should take care that the line precedes the action and should search out some technique of emphasis so that the line will have the attention of the audience when he speaks it.

Frequently the actor will find a required action which is not explained by any immediate line and which can be satisfactorily motivated only by another action directly preceding the action in question. If, for instance, one character is required to strike another character in response to a line the other character has spoken, it may be desirable for the actor first to show that the stimulus has aroused an emotion which, in turn, motivates the action. The emotion may be expressed in a change of facial expression, which must be performed directly before the major action of striking. Performing the two actions together would suggest that the striking action is impulsive, almost an involuntary reflex.

Let us assume, for purposes of illustration, that one character has the line, "I hate you," and the action of striking the other character across the face. The actor could either say the line and then perform the action, in which case the line would explain the action, or perform the action and then say the line, in which case the action would seem impulsive and the line a delayed explanation. It would also be possible to deliver the line and perform the action simultaneously, in which case both would seem impulsive and without motivation, except as earlier passages in the scene may have made the emotional motivation clear. If the actor elects this method of timing, he may wish to include an additional action, such as a sudden look of hate, to precede both the line and the action which are to be performed simultaneously. It will be seen that each of these variations in timing suggests a slightly different kind of person reacting to the situation in a slightly different way.

The Danger of Using Timing for Motivation Too Frequently

While the use of action preceding a line to suggest the emotional motivation of the line is something every actor must learn, it is also something which he must learn to use sparingly. One of the most frequent faults of the untrained actor is the habit of using a brief moment of pantomimic action, usually a facial expression, before every line he speaks. Many actors, unfortunately not all of them beginners, seem to experience great personal satisfaction from this kind of acting, even though the effect is often to surfeit the audience with emotion.

It is easy for the untrained actor to acquire this habit; he spends weeks of study and many hours of rehearsal time trying to stimulate himself to experience the desired emotion or a reasonable facsimile of it, and having convinced himself that he has engendered the emotion, he feels compelled to give it some expression. The actor must study his part carefully to discover whether the expression of the emotion by pantomimic action is absolutely essential to the audience's understanding of the lines and the character. He must remember that most people in real life, even when they are acting under the impulse of a strong emotion, make some effort to control the emotion and to avoid betraying their feelings to the casual observer. The actor, on the other hand, has deliberately evoked the emotion; he has done so with the purpose of revealing it to the audience; not to reveal the emotion at every opportunity seems to him not to be acting.

This overstatement of the emotions—not to be confused with exaggeration of the emotions—most frequently shows itself in the repetition of pantomimic actions directly preceding the lines. If the action is considered essential, the actor should strive to perform it while he is speaking the line, thus reinforcing the line. Only when the action adds something new to the characterization or is essential to clarify and explain the line should the actor use the device of having the action precede the line. Used sparingly, it is one of the most effective techniques available to the actor.

Cooperative Timing for Ensemble Acting

Timing emotional reactions to the speeches of another character is infinitely more complicated than timing them to one's own speeches. It is no longer possible to perform the action with the speech, since when the speech is delivered by one character and the action performed by another, the immediate result is a division of interest on the part of the audience, which is usually undesirable.

Since the action is usually an emotional reaction to what is said, it would not be logical to perform the action prior to the speech. It must be confessed that actors frequently fall into this habit of reacting to a speech before it has been given, or at least before it has been completed. The actor has read the play, whereas the audience, one assumes, has not; he has planned his reactions and knows what is coming next; as a result, he often unconsciously reacts a moment too soon, thus destroying the illusion that the events of the play are happening for the first time and that the reactions are spontaneous.

To counteract this tendency, the Stanislavski system recommends exercises in concentration and relaxation in the hope that during the rehearsals, the actor will be able to train himself to think only the thoughts of the character and school himself to respond to the events of the play with a sort of conditioned reflex. The technical solution to the problem is carefully to select reactions which seem relevant and necessary and to choose the exact words or actions which are to be the immediate stimuli. The scene must then be rehearsed with the speaking actor making the pauses in his lines necessary to allow the listening actor's reactions to be inserted into the scene. This process is often best accomplished with the aid of the director, for the actors are likely to have conflicting opinions about the importance and the relevance of the proposed reactions.

Beginning actors often complain that such careful attention to details hampers their ability to "feel" a scene and makes the scene contrived and artificial, forgetting that in art everything must be contrived and artificial and that it is the business of the actor to make it seem real and natural and spontaneous. When the emotion of the listening character is expressed in the words of the script, both actors accept it as necessary to the scene; it is only the fact that the reaction is to be expressed in a pantomimic action invented by the actor that invites rebellion.

Ever since the founding of the Saxe-Meiningen company, the acting profession has devoted much time and effort to achieving true ensemble playing. The Moscow Art Theatre, the theaters of Antoine and Copeau in France, the Manchester Repertory and other companies in England, The Abbey Players, and in this country the numerous efforts of The Theatre Guild and others to establish permanent acting companies, such as The Civic Repertory Theatre of Eva Le Gallienne, Walter Hampden's company, and The Group Theatre, have all been inspired by the ideal of perfect ensemble playing. In most instances their method of attempting to achieve the ideal was to assemble a group of actors and let them work together over a period of years, so that they might acquire a mutual respect for one another, an understanding of the methods employed by each actor, and a sensitivity to the abilities and personalities of every member of the company. In technical terms what these groups were trying to accomplish, at least in part, was the proper timing of the actions of the actors who were not speaking at a particular moment to the lines of the speaking actor.

There can be no doubt that close association and experience in working together on many plays are helpful, and possibly essential, to a group of actors if they are to achieve true ensemble playing; just as two expert tennis players do not make successful partners until they have played a few games together and each has learned to take advantage of the particular skills and to compensate for the special weaknesses of the other. Even with the opportunity for close association, however, an acting ensemble will never achieve perfect timing unless all of the actors understand the craft of timing, not only as it relates to their own parts, but also as it relates to the performances of the others.

Timing to Achieve Emphasis

The actor who uses movement as a device for emphasis must make his timing decision on the basis of the relative importance and eloquence of the line and the movement. When the gesture is thought to be the more forceful and expressive statement of the idea, it should come after the line; and when the line is considered the more eloquent and meaningful expression, it should come after the gesture.

In the third act of *Arms and the Man*, when Raina, who has tried to maintain her romantic, noble, and idealistic attitude toward life, is told by the practical Bluntschli that he does not believe that she has told only two lies in her whole life, she is insulted, and the following dialogue takes place:

RAINA: (*staring haughtily at him*) Do you know, sir, that you are insulting me?

BLUNTSCHLI: I can't help it. When you get into that noble attitude and speak in that thrilling voice, I admire you; but I find it impossible to believe a single word you say.

RAINA: (*superbly*) Captain Bluntschli!

BLUNTSCHLI: (*unmoved*) Yes?

RAINA: (*coming a little towards him, as if she could not believe her senses*) Do you mean what you said just now? Do you know what you said just now?

BLUNTSCHLI: I do.

RAINA: (*gasping*). I! I!!! (*She points to herself incredulously, meaning "I, Raina Petkoff, tell lies!" He meets her gaze unflinchingly. She suddenly sits down beside him, and adds, with a complete change of manner from the heroic to the familiar*) How did you find me out?

Since this is the exact climax and turning point of the relationship between Raina and Bluntschli, it is quite appropriate that considerable action should be included in the scene.

In his stage directions, Shaw instructs the actress playing Raina to perform two separate actions in immediate succession without an intervening line. She is to point to herself incredulously, and then she is to sit down. The first action is in relation to her saying, "I! I!!!" and carries on that emotional state in pantomime, which cannot be as adequately expressed in words. Her second action is to sit down, thus showing that her romantic bubble has burst, and this action is related to the line that follows, "How did you find me out?" The spoken line which reveals that she, too, has known that her romanticism and idealism were only an attitude is therefore of much greater interest than the action which expresses the same idea, but not as fully or as eloquently. To convince herself that Shaw's sense of timing is correct, the actress should experiment with reversing the order of the action and the lines, making the gesture of incredulity before she says, "I! I!!!" and sitting down after she says, "How did you find me out?"

It is interesting to note that Shaw has taken care to instruct the actor playing Bluntschli not to use movement which would compete with the actions and speeches of Raina by inserting the stage direction "unmoved." To test the validity of this direction, the actor playing Bluntschli might try inventing some action to show his indifference and lack of concern, such as turning away and sitting down. Such an action would effectively destroy the force of Raina's actions, and the meaning of the scene would be lost to the audience. Shaw has also suggested Raina's cross toward Bluntschli one line earlier to provide emphasis on the climax of the scene.

Timing versus Phrasing

Frequently the desirability of using movement to emphasize a specific line or phrase comes into conflict with the use of movement to indicate the beginning and end of thoughts and emotions sustained for a longer duration, as discussed in a previous chapter.

In a television performance of *Richard II*, Maurice Evans, in Act III, Scene 2, began the following passage with the gesture of pointing his finger to his head:

> for within the hollow crown
> That rounds the mortal temples of a king
> Keeps Death his court and there the antic sits,
> Scoffing his state and grinning at his pomp,
> Allowing him a breath, a little scene,
> To monarchize, be fear'd and kill with looks,
> Infusing him with self and vain conceit,
> As if this flesh which walls about our life
> Were brass impregnable, and humour'd thus
> Comes at the last and with a little pin
> Bores through this castle wall, and farewell king!

Instead of sustaining the gesture throughout the entire passage, which is obviously one continuous thought (Richard could not have begun the speech if he had not already thought of the end), Mr. Evans elected to bring his arm down to his side as he spoke. But on the last lines,

> Comes at the last and with a little pin
> Bores through the castle wall, and farewell king!

he indicated a small circle with the thumb and forefinger of his left hand and, with the forefinger of his right hand, pantomimically demonstrated how the "little pin bores through his castle wall." Mr. Evans brought his hands into position precisely on the word "pin," moved his right forefinger toward his left hand on "bores," sustained this gesture without movement as he said, "Through this castle wall," and then opened the fingers of both hands in a movement of futility, completing this gesture before he said, "And farewell king."

This is precise and careful timing, part of the gesture being performed while the lines are spoken and the final part being completed without lines but directly before the last phrase. Appropriately, this gesture was reserved for the end of the entire speech to help give a sense of climax; but by abandoning the first gesture of the finger pointed toward his own head, which was used at the beginning of the speech, Mr. Evans abandoned the

possibility of using the sustained gesture to indicate the length and duration of the thought in favor of using gesture to bring special emphasis to
a smaller portion of this thought.   One technical solution is not superior to
the other, but the two cannot be used simultaneously, and the actor is
forced to choose between using movement to emphasize a phrase and
using it to indicate the beginning and the end of a longer thought sequence.

In Act I, Scene 2, of *The Merchant of Venice*, Nerissa names six of
Portia's suitors, and Portia gives her impression and opinion of each as he is
named.   It seems unlikely that the scene can be played without considerable use of movement and still sustain the interest of the audience.   On
the other hand, if the actress playing Portia prances about the stage and
acts out all her impersonations, the wit of some of the lines will be lost,
and the scene will become boring for a different reason.

The first task for the actress playing Portia is to invent all the possible
actions which might be appropriate to every sentence and phrase in the
scene and, where several different pantomimic ideas or gestures suggest
themselves for the same sentence or phrase, to select the one that seems
most interesting.   Next, she must decide which of the speeches are most
in need of pantomimic elaboration in order to make them interesting to
an audience.   The next step is to select those sentences or phrases which
are of special interest, because of their wit, their revelation of Portia's
character, or some other reason; and which can best be served by having
some movement related to them to give them special emphasis.

Now all of the invented business must be examined to see which actions
are of sufficient interest to have emphasis given to them by the lines.   In
speaking of Monsieur Le Bon, for instance, Portia says, "If a throstle sing,
he falls straight a capering," in reference to Falconbridge, she says, "Who
can converse with a dumb-show?" and of the Duke of Saxony's nephew she
says that she likes him "most vilely, in the afternoon, when he is drunk";
Portia might give a pantomimic impersonation of each gentleman, one
capering, one conversing in dumb show, and one drunk.   Whether or not
each of these pantomimic actions is of sufficient interest to be included in
the final performance will depend upon the actress' abilities and invention;
whether, even if all three are excellent, all should be included is a matter
of taste.   Whatever actions are to be left in, however, must be timed with
the words, being performed either while the words are spoken or directly
before or after the words, according to the actress' judgment as to the
relative value of the words and the actions.

Another scene which requires the same kind of invention of business
and careful attention to timing, but to a far greater degree, is the famous
speech from *Cyrano de Bergerac* in which Cyrano demonstrates for Valvert all the insulting things which Valvert might have said about Cyrano's

nose if Valvert had had "some tinge of letters, or of wit." Cyrano lists twenty different kinds of insults and gives an example of each. This is bravura writing, and it calls for bravura action. For each of the insults the actor will need to invent an appropriate physical attitude which may be sustained throughout the particular insult, or a pantomimic action which clarifies the imagery of the speech and which may be performed before, during, or after the speech, according to the relative merits of the action and the speech.

With each separate bit of the speech being performed for its own specific value, the actor will have to find some way of unifying the entire speech and holding it together. One solution might be for the actor to assume an attitude in a particular place on the stage as he begins the speech,

> Ah, no, young sir!
> You are too simple. Why, you might have said—
> Oh, a great many things!

thereafter moving to any part of the stage which seems convenient and suitable as he continues the speech, but returning to the identical attitude and the identical place on the stage as the passage is finished, "These, my dear sir, are things you might have said."

In these two scenes, for Portia and Cyrano respectively, the importance and necessity of expert timing are particularly obvious, but the actor who has mastered the technique of timing will find that he will use his ability in every scene of every role.

EXERCISES

1. Combine the line, "Go, get out," with the action of raising the arm to shoulder height, the index finger extended and pointing toward the exit.

   a. Perform the action and begin to speak at the precise moment when the action has been completed. Sustain the gesture until the end of the line.

   b. Perform the action but delay the beginning of the speech for an appreciable moment.

   NOTE: In a there seems to be one statement of the thought, while in b the same thought seems to be repeated for emphasis.

   c. Perform the exercise as in b, but be looking toward the exit as the action is performed and in the moment before speaking turn to look back at the person to whom the speech is delivered.

   NOTE: The effect of reiteration for emphasis is increased.

   d. Begin the action at the beginning of the speech and complete it at the exact moment that the speech is completed.

   e. Perform the entire action while saying, "Go," and sustain the gesture while saying, "Get out."

   f. Say, "Go," without any action, but begin the action on "Get out," completing the action as the line is finished.

   g. Substitute the words, "Leave this house at once," for "Get out" and perform the exercise as in *d, e,* and *f.*

   h. Use the line, "Go. Leave this house at once," and perform the action after saying, "House," and before saying, "At once."

   i. Delay the action until after saying, "House," but complete the action while saying, "At once."

   NOTE: With the action delayed until toward the end of the line, as in *h* and *i,* an effect of climax is created.

   j. Speak the line, "Go. Get out," and begin the action immediately after the line has been spoken.

   k. Speak the line, "Go. Leave this house at once," and begin the action immediately after the line has been spoken.

   NOTE: An effect of exasperation and frustration is created in both *j* and and *k,* but more so in *k* because the increased length of the line seems to delay the action further.

   l. Syncopate the action, using the longer line and beginning the action at some illogical place, such as after the saying, "This."

   NOTE: Syncopating the action makes it seem that the character has less control of his emotions.

   m. Perform the action, but include in the action the return of the gesturing arm to the position it was in before the action was begun. Try the business of relaxing the gesture in all the timing arrangements suggested above.

   NOTE: The relaxing of the gesture tends to create an impression of futility.

It can never be stated too frequently that there is no particular virtue in using any specific technique, but that there is great virtue in being capable of all of the techniques, so that the one which is most suitable for a particular character in a particular scene may be used at the discretion of the actor.

2. Capulet's scene from *Romeo and Juliet,* Act III, Scene 5.

   a. Perform the scene as it should never be played, with all the characters inventing as much action as possible, both in relation to their own lines and during the lines of the others. Let Lady Capulet walk up and down in nervous excitement. Let Juliet weep, stamp her foot, shake her head in denial of Capulet's accusations, and walk away from him in anger. Let the Nurse comfort Juliet, sit and fan herself in angered irritation, etc.

   NOTE: The resulting bedlam should convince the actors that action during one's own lines or the lines of another is a dangerous thing and that while all the invented actions may be true to life and in character for each player, art will not permit such a degree of realism.

3. Sequence from *Hamlet*, Act I, Scene 2.

KING: But now, my cousin Hamlet, and my son,—
HAMLET: (*Aside.*) A little more than kin, and less than kind.
KING: How is it that the clouds still hang on you?
HAMLET: Not so, my lord; I am too much i' th' sun.

Suppose that the action for the King is to turn toward Hamlet on the first line and remain facing him for the duration of the four lines. Suppose that Hamlet has been sitting, watching the scene, and that his action is to turn away from both the King and the scene.

a. Let Hamlet perform his action before he speaks his first line.
b. Let Hamlet perform the action while he says, "A little more than kin."
c. Let Hamlet perform the action while he says, "And less than kind."
d. Let Hamlet perform the action after he says, "A little more than kin," and before he says the remainder of the line.
e. Let Hamlet perform the action after speaking the line.
f. Let Hamlet remain in his original position as he speaks his first line and perform the action just before the second line.
g. Let Hamlet perform the action while he says, "Not so, my lord."
h. Let Hamlet perform the action while he says, "I am too much i' th' sun."
i. Let Hamlet perform the action after saying, "Not so, my lord," and before saying, "I am too much i' th' sun."
j. Let Hamlet perform the action after the line has been spoken. Now suppose that Hamlet is sitting some distance apart from the other characters and that the action of the King is to rise as he speaks his first line and, just as he finishes the line, to start to cross toward Hamlet, continuing to cross as Hamlet speaks, arriving in his new position as Hamlet finishes his first line.
k. Combine the King's action as in *k* with Hamlet's action in exercises *a*, *b*, *c*, *d*, and *e*.
l. Place the King's action in relation to his line, "How is it that the clouds still hang on you?" and continue the action through Hamlet's next speech.
m. Combine this timing of the King's action with Hamlet's action as in exercises *f*, *g*, *h*, *i*, and *j*.
    NOTE: In the exercises in which the King is performing an action while Hamlet is either speaking or performing an action, the competition for the attention of the audience will be apparent.
Suppose that Hamlet was looking away before the sequence begins and that his action in relation to the first speech is to look up and toward the King

and that his action in relation to his second speech is to rise and turn away from the King; and suppose that the King has a rise, a turn toward Hamlet, and a cross to Hamlet in relation to his first line, and an action of putting a friendly hand on Hamlet's shoulder in relation to his second speech.

n. Work out all the possible timing combinations of each of these actions with the lines.

NOTE: Any timing of this much action with these few words is likely to create a confusing effect, and the scene will tend to lose its effectiveness.

o. Before leaving this scene, just for fun work out several versions in which either the King or Hamlet or both use syncopated timing.

4. Test the theory of timing as a device for motivation by performing the action of going to look out the window in relation to the line, "I think it is going to rain." Perform the action before the line, during the line, and after the line. Use the line, "Let's go on a picnic," as a cue.

5. Work out the possible timing variations of the line, "I hate you," and the action of striking the other actor. Observe the variations in the meaning of the scene and the emotional connotations of each variant.

FIRST ACTOR: Don't! (*Meaning! "Don't touch that," or, "Don't do that"*)
SECOND ACTOR: I hate you. (*Action of striking the First Actor*)

a. Perform the action before the line.
b. Perform the action during the line.
c. Perform the action after the line.

6. Sequence from *Arms and the Man*,[1] Act III.

BLUNTSCHLI: (*dubiously*) There's reason in everything. You said you'd told only two lies in your whole life. Dear young lady: isn't that rather a short allowance? I'm quite a straightforward man myself; but it wouldn't last me a whole morning.
RAINA: (*Staring haughtily at him*) Do you know, sir, that you are insulting me?
BLUNTSCHLI: I can't help it. When you get into that noble attitude and speak in that thrilling voice, I admire you; but I find it impossible to believe a single word you say.
RAINA: (*superbly*) Captain Bluntschli!
BLUNTSCHLI: (*unmoved*) Yes?
RAINA: (*coming a little towards him, as if she could not believe her senses*) Do you mean what you said just now? Do you know what you said just now?
BLUNTSCHLI: I do.
RAINA: (*gasping*) I! I!!! (*She points to herself incredulously, meaning "I,*

[1] Copyright by The Public Trustee and The Society of Authors.

*Raina Petkoff, tell lies." He meets her gaze unflinchingly. She suddenly sits
down beside him, and adds, with a complete change of manner from the heroic
to the familiar*) How did you find me out?

    a. Rehearse the scene, carefully following Shaw's indication of action.

    NOTE: Shaw establishes the change in Raina's character with a "complete
    change of manner" directly before the line which expresses the change.

    b. Rehearse the scene with new action and different timing. Let Bluntschli
    rise as he says, "Yes." Let Raina remain in her position on her next line.
    Let Bluntschli walk away as he says, "I do." Place Raina's pointing
    action before the "I! I!!!" and let her sit after she says, "How did you find
    me out?"

    NOTE: This timing and these actions should effectively destroy the quality
    of the scene.

7. Sequence from Act I, Scene 2, of *The Merchant of Venice.*

NERISSA: But what warmth is there in your affection towards any of these
princely suitors that are already come?

PORTIA: I pray thee, over-name them; and as thou namest them, I will describe them; and, according to my description, level at my affection.

NERISSA: First, there is the Neopolitan prince.

PORTIA: Ay, that's a colt indeed, for he doth nothing but talk of his horse;
and he makes it a great appropriation to his own good parts, that he can shoe
him himself. I am much afeard my lady his mother played false with a smith.

NERISSA: Then there is the County Palatine.

PORTIA: He doth nothing but frown, as who should say "An you will not
have me, choose:" he hears merry tales and smiles not: I fear he will prove the
weeping philosopher when he grows old, being so full of unmannerly sadness in
his youth. I had rather be married to a death's-head with a bone in his mouth
than to either of these. God defend me from these two.

NERISSA: How say you to the French lord, Monsieur Le Bon?

PORTIA: God made him, and therefore let him pass for a man. In truth, I
know it is a sin to be a mocker: but he! why, he hath a horse better than the
Neopolitan's, a better bad habit of frowning than the Count Palatine; he is every
man in no man; if a throstle sing, he falls straight a capering; he will fence with
his own shadow: if I should marry him, I should marry twenty husbands. If
he would despise me, I would forgive him, for if he loves me to madness, I shall
never requite him.

NERISSA: What say you, then, to Falconbridge, the young baron of England?

PORTIA: You know I say nothing to him, for he understands not me, nor I
him: he hath neither Latin, French, nor Italian, and you will come into the
court and swear that I have a poor pennyworth in the English. He is a proper
man's picture, but, alas, who can converse with a dumb-show? How oddly

he is suited!   I think he bought his doublet in Italy, his round hose in France, his bonnet in Germany and his behaviour every where.

NERISSA: What think you of the Scottish lord, his neighbour?

PORTIA: That he hath a neighbourly charity in him, for he borrowed a box of the ear of the Englishman and swore he would pay him again when he was able: I think the Frenchman became his surety and sealed under for another.

NERISSA: How like you the young German, the Duke of Saxony's nephew?

PORTIA: Very vilely in the morning, when he is sober, and most vilely in the afternoon, when he is drunk: when he is best, he is a little worse than a man, and when he is worst, he is little better than a beast: an the worst fall that ever fell, I hope I shall make shift to go without him.

NERISSA: If he should offer to choose, and choose the right casket, you should refuse to perform your father's will, if you should refuse to accept him.

PORTIA: Therefore, for fear of the worst, I pray thee, set a deep glass of rhenish wine on the contrary casket, for if the devil be within and that temptation without, I know he will choose it.   I will do anything, Nerissa, ere I'll be married to a sponge.

NERISSA: You need not fear, lady, the having any of these lords: they have acquainted me with their determinations; which is, indeed, to return to their home and to trouble you with no more suit, unless you may be won by some other sort than your father's imposition depending on the caskets.

PORTIA: If I live to be as old as Sibylla, I will die as chaste as Diana, unless I be obtained by the manner of my father's will.   I am glad this parcel of wooers are so reasonable, for there is not one among them but I dote on his absence, and I pray God grant then a fair departure.

NERISSA: Do you not remember, lady, in your father's time, a Venetian, a scholar and a soldier, that came hither in company of the Marquis of Montferrat?

PORTIA: Yes, yes, it was Bassanio; as I think, he was so called.

NERISSA: True, madam: he, of all the men that ever my foolish eyes looked upon, was the best deserving a fair lady.

PORTIA: I remember him well, and I remember him worthy of thy praise.

a. Invent actions for Portia which will help the audience to visualize the various suitors.   Having selected the pantomimic actions, work out the timing which seems most appropriate, performing some actions before the line, some during the line, and some after the line.

NOTE: If the same timing is used for all the speeches, the scene becomes monotonous.

b. Let Nerissa work out pantomimic impersonations of the men she mentions and the timing methods that seem most suitable.

NOTE: This version will tend to let Nerissa "steal" the scene from Portia and would not be appropriate in actual performance.

c. Let the two actresses decide which of the pantomimic inventions that either has invented would be the most interesting and the most entertaining to an audience. Work out the scene so that Portia uses some of her pantomimes and Nerissa uses some of hers.

NOTE: Portia's reaction to the mention of Bassanio calls for a sudden change in attitude which is very similar to Raina's change of attitude in exercise 7. It is possible that Nerissa might also use a sudden change of attitude as she first mentions Bassanio. This is helpful, on the one hand, because it foreshadows Portia's reaction, but it is harmful in that it detracts from Portia's reaction. The two actresses and the director must make a decision as to which is the more interesting and effective way to play the scene.

8. Sequence from *Cyrano de Bergerac*,[2] Act I.

Valvert has just insultingly remarked that Cyrano's nose is rather large. Cyrano responds:

Ah, no, young sir!
You are too simple. Why, you might have said—
Oh, a great many things! Mon dieu, why waste
Your opportunity? For example, thus:—
Aggressive: I, sir, if that nose were mine,
I'd have it amputated—on the spot!
Friendly: How do you drink with such a nose?
You ought to have a cup made specially.
Descriptive: 'Tis a rock—a crag—a cape—
A cape? say rather, a peninsula!
Inquisitive: What is that receptacle—
A razor-case or a portfolio?
Kindly: Ah, do you love the little birds
So much that when they come and sing to you
You give them this to perch on?
Insolent: Sir, when you smoke, the neighbors must suppose
Your chimney is on fire.
Cautious: Take care—
A weight like that might make you top-heavy.
Thoughtful: Somebody fetch my parasol—
Those delicate colors fade so in the sun!
Pedantic: Does not Aristophanes
Mention a mythologic monster called
Hippocampelephantocamelos?
Surely we have here the original!
Familiar: Well, old torchlight! Hang your hat

[2] Copyright by Henry Holt and Company, Inc.

Over that chandelier—it hurts my eyes.
Eloquent: When it blows, the typhoon howls,
And the clouds darken.
Dramatic: When it bleeds—
The Red sea!
Enterprising: What a sign
For some perfumer!
Lyric: Hark—the horn
Of Roland calls so summon Charlemagne!
Simple: When do they unveil the monument?
Respectful: Sir, I recognize in you
A man of parts, a man of prominence—
Rustic: Hey? What? Call that a nose? Na, na—
I be no fool like what you think I be—
That there's a blue cucumber!
Military: Point against cavalry!
Practical: Why not
A lottery with this for the grand prize?
Or—parodying Faustus in the play—
"Was this the nose that launched a thousand ships
And burned the topless towers of Illium?"
These, my dear sir, are things you might have said
Had you some tinge of letters, or of wit
To color your discourse. But wit,—not so,
You never had an atom—and of letters,
You need but three to write you down—an Ass.
Moreover,—if you had the invention, here
Before these folk to make a jest of me—
Be sure you would not then articulate
The twentieth part of half a syllable
Of the beginning! For I say these things
Lightly enough myself, about myself,
But I allow none else to utter them.

a. Invent the pantomimic action which seems most appropriate for each of
the descriptive phrases. Select the timing device—before, during, or
after the speech—which seems most suitable.
NOTE: At the end of the speech Cyrano seems to become serious and, to a
certain extent, drops his comic manner. This shift in attitude is similar
to Raina's in exercise 7 and Portia's in exercise 8.

Chapter 8. THE SIZE OF A PERFORMANCE

F REQUENT REFERENCE has been made in the preceding chapters to the relative sizes of performances, but there has been no previous opportunity to discuss the problem as a whole. The size of a performance is a matter of vital importance to the actor, particularly today when performances are given in so many different types of theaters, such as conventional proscenium-arch theaters of all sizes and the newer "arena" or "in-the-round" theaters, as well as in motion pictures, on the radio, and on television.

The actor will need to develop his techniques so that he will be able to adapt them readily to the conditions under which a particular performance is to be given. Many a skilled player who has had most of his training in small theaters seating less than 500 persons has found that he is much less effective when he is called upon to play in larger theaters; and many actors with most, or all, of their experience playing in large theaters have found themselves at a disadvantage when working in such media as motion pictures and television, where the camera, and therefore the audience, is frequently within a few feet of them. The size of a performance is of tremendous importance to the motion-picture actor because the techniques of a performance to be filmed as a long shot are different from those to be used in a close-up.

Size in Relation to the Play

Many factors besides the size of the auditorium or of the particular medium in which a performance is to be given have an effect upon the size of a performance. The most important of these is the quality of the play itself. Some plays, because of their subject material and the author's treatment of that material, are more suitable for large performances in large theaters, while other plays require smaller performances and demand more intimate contact with the audience.

Frequently the quality of a play which determines the size of the performance was derived from the theaters and auditoriums with which the author was familiar and for which he wrote the play. The Greek dramas, which were originally conceived for performances on huge outdoor

150

stages, are very difficult to adapt to a more intimate performance; the plays
of Chekhov would be most ineffective if produced in an outdoor amphitheater.

A small-sized performance of a play which was designed for performance
in a large theater—a play which is concerned with large emotions and
written in language intended to impress and emotionally move large audiences—calls for a shift in the techniques of the actors which will almost
certainly alter the original values of the play. Adapting such a play
for a small performance is like reducing a symphony which has been
scored for sixty or seventy instruments to a piano score. Different techniques will have to be used. Inevitably new values will be substituted,
and while the two compositions will deal with the same musical ideas and
will strive to express the same emotions, they will be different compositions.
If they are to succeed in adequately expressing the same emotions to the
same degree, they must rely on different methods of conveying those
emotions.

All plays are, of necessity, an intensification of life, if only because they
are a concentration of life. Even in the Greek plays, which took a whole
day to perform, or in Shaw's *Back to Methusalah*, which was written to
be played on three consecutive evenings, or in O'Neill's *Mourning Becomes Electra*, which takes five hours to perform, there is still a time
limitation within which the lives of the characters must be compressed
and, in being compressed, become concentrated and intensified. The
entire action of *Romeo and Juliet* is supposed to take place in approximately
four days, but Shakespeare has compressed the events of those four days
into what he calls, with some poetic license, "the two hours' traffic of our
stage."

The writers of realistic and naturalistic plays have not been able to
escape from the time limitation of drama, and while their characters may
be ordinary and unimportant people and the events depicted may be everyday events which might happen to anyone, the characters and events,
however trivial, have been selected, and the mere act of selection has given
them an importance and a significance. Realistic drama and naturalistic
drama tend to examine the lives of "little" people and the minutiae of human experience, but the examination is conducted under the microscope
of the theater, and the concentrated attention of the audience gives to
these insignificant people and the unimportant events of their lives a size
and a magnitude. Arthur Miller in *Death of a Salesman* has Linda say of
her husband:

> I don't say he's a great man. Willy Loman never made a lot of money.
> His name was never in the paper. He's not the finest character that ever
> lived. But he's a human being, and a terrible thing is happening to him.

So attention must be paid. He's not to be allowed to fall into his grave like an old dog. Attention, attention must be finally paid to such a person.

Willy Loman is a little person, an unimportant person—a salesman who is ambitious to be popular and successful and to have his sons successful. Ambition and its power to destroy human character have been a favorite theme of playwrights of many periods of dramatic literature. According to Brutus, Caesar was ambitious; and Macbeth was ambitious. But Shakespeare's characters are superior beings; they are emperors and generals and kings, while Mr. Miller's character is an ordinary human being.

The task for the actor is, in the one case, to show that the emotion of ambition, as revealed by emperors, generals, and kings, is common to many men and, in the other, to show that the same emotion, as revealed by an insignificant person participating in unimportant and commonplace events, has a significance and importance beyond the character and the episodes. The problem for the actor is to express the same emotion in characters diametrically opposed and in plays of such different qualities that they almost represent different media. Whether the destruction of a "noble" character by false ambition makes true tragedy and the obliteration of a "little" character by the same emotion makes only pathos is a distinction which can be left to the critics and the philosophers.

Volume as a Device to Alter Size

It is extremely difficult to alter the size of the vocal techniques without changing the qualities which they express. The loud tone tends to indicate to an audience a larger emotion and a much more extroverted personality than does a quiet tone, which tends to indicate an intimate relationship between the speaker and the listener. This tendency (and it is only a tendency, as there are many exceptions) may be illustrated by practicing the simple command, "Come here." Spoken quietly it has the quality of a friendly invitation, perhaps with a hint of pleading; spoken louder it becomes a command; spoken even louder it is a command given in anger. Spoken softly, it may be made to have some of the qualities of the angry command if no change in pitch is permitted, and if the rate is considerably slowed; but it will still differ in quality from the loud, angry command because the anger will seem controlled and suppressed.

Unfortunately, the volume cannot be decided solely on the basis of the character, the situation, and the emotions involved, because the size of the auditorium indicates a volume level below which the speech must not fall. In the first act of A Doll's House Nora has renewed her friendship with Mrs. Linden, and they have told each other of the events of their lives since they have been separated. Then Nora is about to reveal her great secret. Until this time, in spite of the size of the auditorium, the conversation must seem to have been carried on in normal tones appropriate to two women speaking together in a room. But now Nora says:

> NORA: Hush! Not so loud. Only to think, if Torvald were to hear! He musn't—not for worlds! No one must know about it, Christina—no one but you.
>
> MRS. LINDEN: Why, what can it be?
>
> NORA: Come, over here. (*Draws her down beside her on the sofa*) Yes, Christina, I, too, have something to be proud and glad of. I saved Torvald's life.

And now Nora tells how she obtained the money with which to finance a health tour for her husband, and she must tell it so that only Christina, and the entire audience, may hear—not her husband, who is only in the next room and who has already talked with his wife through the closed door. Here the actor is forced to attempt to make believable and natural something which is obviously an artificial convention of the theater.

There are several things which the actresses may do to achieve the effect. First, they may play the lines immediately preceding this sequence in relatively loud tones so that the volume may be noticeably lowered for the hushed conversation and still be sufficient to be heard in the auditorium. The tone may be made to seem quiet, by the simple device of making it quieter than what has immediately preceded it. Second, the illusion of a quiet tone may be created by lowering the pitch without lowering the volume. Third, as instructed in the stage directions, the actresses may put themselves in physical attitudes which suggest that they are speaking confidentially to each other, for if they look as though they are speaking quietly, the audience will be willing to believe that they are speaking quietly.

Rate as a Device to Alter Size

The rate of speech is much less closely connected with the size of a performance than is the volume. The student will quickly discover that it is difficult to speak rapidly and loudly at the same time and that there is a natural tendency to slow the rate with any considerable increase in volume. The actor can well follow his natural tendencies in this matter as far as adjusting the size of his performance to the size of the auditorium and stage is concerned.

There is a time element involved in the audience's comprehension of what is being said on the stage; the farther spectators sit from the stage, the longer it will take them to understand a thought or an idea. Many times a speech is entirely audible, but not understandable, because the rate of speaking is too fast.   The primary importance of the rate of speech in relation to the size of a performance, however, lies in the fact that a slower rate seems to lend importance and significance to what is being said.   In certain instances, therefore, it can be substituted for an increase in volume.

Pinging and Ponging

In practicing the technique of slowing the rate of speech to give the lines importance and significance, the actor should note that this effect can be accomplished in two ways.   He may either leave slight pauses between each word or between phrases or prolong the words themselves by sustaining the vowels.   English actors have two words to describe the different methods.   They say that a line is to be "pinged" when they mean that it should be spoken with force and emphasis, but not prolonged, and that it should be "ponged" when a similar effect is to be achieved by prolonging the actual word itself.

Too much of either pinging or ponging will create an unpleasant effect. The actor should practice these technical devices so that he can use either of them whenever he thinks it will help his performance, but he must use them with discretion.   When poetic drama is read so that it begins to sound as though it were being sung or intoned, there has been too much ponging. When the same poetic drama has been read naturally and colloquially, so that it no longer sounds like poetry and is brought down to the level of natural speech, there has been little of either pinging or ponging.

Pitch and Timbre in Relation to Size

The pitch and the timbre of the voice have almost nothing to do with the size of a performance, beyond the fact that using contrasts in pitch and timbre in speaking consecutive passages often produces a strong emphasis which can contribute to a larger performance and avoiding such contrasts tends to make for a smaller performance.

Size of Performance in Rehearsal

Because each change in the size of the vocal techniques used tends to change the interpretation of the lines and the characterization of the speaker and to necessitate a change in the emotional motivation to be supplied by the actor, it is very dangerous to rehearse a scene for any considerable number of times in a different size from that in which the actual performance is to be given.   Many casts, however, both professional and nonprofessional, are forced by economic necessity to rehearse in rooms, halls, and auditoriums which differ in size from the theater in which the actual performance is to be given.

Since there is a natural tendency for the actor, particularly for the experienced player, to adjust the size of his performance to the size of the room in which he rehearses, he is in danger of working out ways to play the scenes, and of choosing certain techniques, which create the desired effect in the rehearsal hall but which create a different effect when used on the stage. Thus he risks the possibility of spending his rehearsal time building a characterization and evolving emotional motivations for the wrong performance. It has been noted that actors with a great amount of experience in motion pictures or radio often find it difficult to be equally effective on the stage and vice versa; many actors also find it difficult to shift from the rehearsal hall to the stage, because they have not learned to rehearse with the size of the finished performance clearly in mind.

It is equally dangerous, especially for the inexperienced player, to rehearse a play in the final size of the performance too soon, before he knows exactly which emotions he wants to reveal, at what moment, and at what intensity. Without a clear concept of the character and the final effect to be achieved, the actor is likely to fall into the trap of rehearsing the techniques, without rehearsing the emotions which are to be expressed by the techniques. The emotionally immature person who forces himself into a large statement of an emotion before he is fully aware of what that emotion is will probably give a performance which is all sound and no fury.

The emotions and the techniques which are to express those emotions must be evolved together, the final performance being created from appropriate emotions which are capable of being expressed by the techniques available to the actor. The worst habit an actor can get into is that of telling himself and the director that he "will do it in the performance" without ever having rehearsed "it." The chances are that he will not do it very well.

One exercise which is especially valuable in aiding the actor to become aware of the various sizes of vocal techniques is to rehearse a chorus from one of the Greek plays in which individual speeches are assigned to individual members of the chorus. Naturally these must be rehearsed with accompanying actions, but for practice purposes the actors may concentrate on the vocal techniques. The actors will discover that each member of the group must become aware of the volume, pitch, rate, and timbre of all of the other actors and that he must play in size with the other actors. If some actors tend to get stress and emphasis by pinging words while others pong the words, the difference can be clearly heard.

In some Greek choruses, including the one from *Agamemnon* and the one from *The Trojan Women* which are given as exercises at the end of this chapter, it is quite possible to use simple, natural speech suitable for an intimate, realistic performance. Even though the plays were originally written for large amphitheaters and it would probably not be possible to speak the choruses in small size in actual performance, the actors would do well to rehearse the choruses, inventing individual characterizations for each member of the chorus, in as simple and as unenlarged a performance as possible and then gradually increase the size of the performance, noting the changes in values and in emotions which evolve as the size is increased.

One error which inexperienced actors frequently make is to enter a scene which has been in progress for some time without being aware of the size of the performances which the other actors are giving. This is quite natural. The actor has been back stage; if he has conversed at all, it has been in whispers; his movements have been confined and restrained. In a sense, he has had no opportunity to warm up, as an athlete might do before entering a game. The result is that for a few moments his performance, while it might have been completely adequate had it been given earlier in the play, is below the level of performance of the other actors, and therefore seems inadequate.

The Stanislavski system suggests that to overcome this tendency, the actor, while off stage, should concentrate on his character and his emotions and "think" himself into the situation. It will also help if he has trained himself to be aware of the techniques being used by other actors and if he listens to their performances before he enters. Concentration on the emotions and feelings of the character he is about to play is not always the solution to the problem. The actress playing a maid who enters at the end of the second act, when the family is having a heated argument, and announces that dinner is served would be fired as a maid if she ever announced dinner as loudly as she must in the play, but she will be fired as an actress if she doesn't.

Facial Expressions as a Device to Alter Size

The physical techniques are much more capable of being varied in size than are the vocal techniques. Facial expressions, however, are a possible exception to this generalization, for they are effective only when the audience is close enough to the stage to see the expressions clearly. The Greeks, producing their plays in huge outdoor theaters, resorted to masks which enlarged the features and made them visible at a greater distance, but which obviously prohibited any mobility of expression. Even in intimate theaters facial expressions are useful as a technical device only if the actor is in such a position on the stage that his face is visible.

Most actors are unaware of their own facial expressions, depending upon their thoughts and emotions to exercise an unconscious control of the intricate muscles of the face to form the appropriate expression. Many actors have used mirror studies in order to become aware of their own facial expressions, but this method is not entirely satisfactory, since the mere fact of looking into the mirror alters the expression. Woodrow Wilson's jingle concerning his own face has some significance for the actor:

> My face, I don't mind it,
> 'Cause I am behind it.
> The fellow in front gets the jar

There are no known exercises to develop control of the facial muscles. The best an actor can do is to study his own face, get to know its potentialities for variety of expression, and then make the best of it.

Any effort to enlarge a facial expression is likely to result in distortion, which will alter the original meaning of the expression. A twinkle in the eye cannot be seen at any distance; enlarged, it becomes a smile; further enlarged, it becomes a grin; and then it becomes a leer. To a certain extent make-up can help the actor by emphasizing certain features, accenting certain lines, and sometimes actually altering features by adding putty or other materials to the face; but using make-up to alter the face is a separate technique and should be studied separately by the actor. It is not actually a part of the technique of acting.

Usually, the actor who finds that the facial expressions of which he is capable are not adequate to convey the particular emotion, either because of the size of the auditorium or his position on the stage, would do well to search for some gesture or physical attitude which will convey the same emotion. To attempt to enlarge the facial expressions themselves is likely to result in what is known in the acting profession as "mugging." Since every facial expression must be emotionally motivated and appropriate to the character and since most people do not normally use large facial expressions, any effort on the actor's part to use large facial expressions will probably lead to a distortion of the characterization, or to unmotivated actions which will seem false to the audience.

The uncomplimentary term "mugging" is applied to the use of too many facial expressions as well as to the use of overly large expressions. In this case the actor, usually to convey animation and interest, changes quickly and frequently from one facial expression to another. It is a fault common to young actors who are playing spirited and animated characters and who persist in "making faces," often during their own speeches, but especially when they are listening to other characters. In the scene from *The Sea Gull* which was used as an exercise in Chapter 5, the girl who plays Nina must be particularly careful, in expressing her interest in Trigorin and what he is saying, not to use more facial expressions than would be appropriate to the character.

Gestures as a Device to Alter Size

Hand and arm gestures can be varied in size in three different ways: the actual size of the gesture can be altered; the specific gesture may be sustained for a longer or shorter duration of time, so that its size seems to have been changed; and the number of gestures performed during a specific period of time may be increased or decreased, again giving an impression of a change in size.

If the gesture to be used with the command, "Come here," is to indicate the person to whom the command is addressed and then the place to which he should come, the smallest possible gesture would probably be just a movement of the eyes, the actor looking first at one place and then at another. This device would probably be effective only in motion pictures or in television, where a close-up is possible, and only when the line is intended more as an invitation than a command—although if the line is delivered with a firm, deliberate, slow rate of speech, the effect of a command can be retained.

The next size of gesture would be a movement of the eyes together with a slight movement of the head. If the actor is working in a medium in which the close-up is not possible and he still wishes to create the effect of a command without including more than a slight gesture, using a head turn with the eye movement would probably be the best solution. It should be noted that whether the actor is smiling or not smiling as he delivers the line will have considerable effect upon the interpretation, making it either a command or an invitation.

The next largest size might be a small finger point, with the arm, and possibly even the hand, being held still, while the forefinger performs the gesture. Whether or not the actor also uses the eye and head movement with the finger gesture is optional, for the meaning will be clear in either case.

Now the gesture itself can be gradually increased, more and more of the arm being used, until—in the largest possible gesture—the whole arm, with the hand pointing, is extended as far as possible in the direction of the person to whom the command is given and then to the place to which he is to come. If the quality of an invitation rather than a command is desired, then instead of using a finger point, the actor should cup his

THREE HAMLETS

John Gielgud VANDAMM

Leslie Howard VANDAMM

Maurice Evans VANDAMM

Each actor in these photographs relies chiefly upon the facial expression to convey the sense of the character. Leslie Howard uses a gesture which is dynamic enough and has enough emphasis to share equally with the facial expression. John Gielgud's left hand suggests a physical tension in addition to the character revealed in the face. Maurice Evans is less selective, his facial expression, both hands, and his physical attitude all being used to contribute to the total effectiveness of the character, but all in competition with each other.

HAMLET AND
THE QUEEN

Leslie Howard and Mary Servoss have used gesture, physical attitude, and a space relationship to suggest the character relationship. Note how the emphasis on gesture takes away from the emphasis on facial expression. Maurice Evans and Mady Christians have used gesture to bring emphasis to the facial expression. The nearness of the two actors suggests a different character relation from that shown in the Howard-Servoss picture. John Gielgud and Judith Anderson have used gesture and physical attitude to suggest a much closer character relationship. The emphasis is largely upon the facial expressions, but Hamlet's clutched hand on the sword reminds the audience that this is a revenge play.

Leslie Howard and Mary Servoss   VANDAMM

VANDAMM

Maurice Evans and Mady Christians
VANDAMM

John Gielgud and Judith Anderson

KATHARINE
CORNELL

In each photograph, Miss Cornell has used a gesture to suggest the character. The facial expressions are obviously her own, adapted to the character. In *Wingless Victory* there is a slight use of makeup to alter the appearance of her eyes. In all four pictures the costumer has been of great assistance to help suggest the simplicity of Juliet, the open frankness of Candida, the sophistication of Mrs. Dubedat in *The Doctor's Dilemma*, and the sultry passion in *Wingless Victory*.

as Candida
VANDAMM

in *The Doctor's Dilemma*
VANDAMM

in *Wingless Victory*   VANDAMM

as Juliet   VANDAMM

in *Harriet*
VANDAMM

in *The Wisteria Trees*
VANDAMM

in *Victoria Regina*

VANDAMM

HELEN
HAYES

In all four plays Miss Hayes was called upon to play variations on the theme that the woman must make the man think that he is wise and strong. The four poses provide an interesting study of physical attitudes and gestures to suggest variations of the same character relationship.

in *What Every Woman Knows*   VANDAMM

In *The Fourposter* the two leading characters are required to portray an age range from youth to old age. The actors made surprisingly little use of make-up, or even physical attitudes, but relied rather upon a mental and emotional characterization. The last picture, showing the final exit, depends, of course, upon a physical attitude.

the beginning   VALENTE

JESSICA
TANDY
AND
HUME
CRONYN

the middle

FEHL

the end   FEHL

VALENTE

in *The Confidential Clerk*   in *The Eddie Cantor Story*

in *The Guest in the House*
HOMMEL

Only in *The Confidential Clerk* does Miss MacMahon play a role which is close to herself in physical appearance, but only in *The Eddie Cantor Story* does she rely upon make-up to help achieve the effect. In the other photographs the characterization is realized by a change in the facial expression, motivated by the thoughts and feelings of the character. Note the expressive use of the hands.

in *The Eve of St. Mark*   FEHL

ALINE
MACMAHON

in *Dragon Seed*

ALFRED LUNT AND LYNN FONTANNE

These photographs illustrate the versatility of the Lunts and their ability to adapt their personalities to farce, serious drama, and high comedy. It is interesting to compare the size of gesture and physical attitude in *The Taming of the Shrew* and *Quadrille* with that in *There Shall Be No Night*.

in *There Shall Be No Night*

VANDAMM

in *The Taming of the Shrew*

VANDAMM

in *Quadrille*

VANDAMM

VANDAMM

in *Amphytrion*

JUDITH ANDERSON

Miss Anderson, usually appearing in roles of emotional intensity and tragic power, relies tremendously upon vocal techniques and seldom upon physical details of characterization. Note the expressive use of the hands.

in *Family Portrait*   VANDAMM

in *Macbeth*   VANDAMM

in *The Old Maid*
with Helen Menken   VANDAMM

hand slightly, with his fingers held together in the natural position of the hand, and—in a sense—scoop or wave the person toward the place.

As with all technical devices, there is no special virtue in using a gesture of any particular size, except in so far as that size is suited to the character, the situation, the quality of the play, the size of the place in which the performance is being given, and the techniques being used by the other players. When Ernest Truex was acting in a play produced by the Shuberts, one of the producers said to him, after a few tryout performances, "In that place where you jump a little bit and the audiences laugh a little bit, jump a lot and they'll laugh a lot." Mr. Truex had to explain that to show his anger, he had jumped a little but that a bigger jump would have been untrue to the character, who was supposed to be a little, petulant, and inhibited man. A large jump would have indicated uninhibited anger, and uninhibited anger would never be expressed with a jump. In this case, the little jump was the largest possible expression of character in the situation, and a change in size would have completely changed the meaning of the gesture.

The student should remember that, in practicing gestures of varying sizes, he is looking for larger or smaller statements of the same characterization and the same emotional state. If the larger or smaller gesture seems to shift the meaning, then he should be ready to shift the technical device he is using, substituting vocal techniques or facial expressions for gestures as he strives for a smaller technical device and substituting movements for gestures as he works toward a larger performance.

Duration of the Gesture as a Device to Alter Size

The duration of a gesture has already been discussed in the chapters on phrasing and progressions. It should be noted, however, that as a device for changing the size of a performance, sustaining a large gesture for a considerable time seems to increase the size of the gesture itself. Greek and Elizabethan drama, in fact any poetic drama, tends to include passages in which a single thought and a single emotion are sustained and developed by the poetry and which demand that the actor be able to sustain the gesture for the same length of time. The actor should be cautioned that, when he is required to do this, he must take care to motivate the gesture emotionally for the same length of time; merely holding a pose without also holding the emotion which motivates the pose will make the actor seem like an exhibit in the hall of statuary of some museum.

One of the best ways to attain size through prolonging the duration of a gesture is to combine several gestures into one, keeping the gesture flowing from one to the other without break and without pause. In

Bulwer-Lytton's *Richelieu* there is a passage in which Cardinal Richelieu
warns his enemies that they are not to harm his young ward, Julie:

> Lo, where she stands,
> Around her form I draw the awful circle of our holy church;
> Step but one foot within that circle,
> And on thy head, yea, though it wore a crown,
> I launch the curse of Rome.

On the first line the Cardinal could point to Julie, continuing this gesture
through the second line.   On the third line, he could draw the imaginary
circle, and starting on the fourth line and continuing through the fifth
line, he could gradually raise the pointing finger until it points toward
heaven as he calls on the powers of the Church.   There are actually four
gestures, but because each is made to flow continuously into the next,
they become like one gesture which has been sustained through the four
lines.

The same principle of extending one gesture into the next in a continuous flow in order to create the effect of a single sustained gesture may be
applied to Hecuba's first speech in *The Trojan Women*.   Here the entire gesture consists of Hecuba's raising herself from a position of lying
on the ground to a full standing position.   The separate gestures of rubbing her aching back, feeling the stiffness in her limbs, sitting up, kneel-
ing, and finally standing erect may be made to seem like one gesture if
a continuous flow is maintained.

Passages requiring sustained gestures occur infrequently in twentieth-
century drama, for contemporary playwrights have generally used more
colloquial speech, which calls for more colloquial gestures.   One reason
why actors who have received much of their training and experience in
Shakespearean drama seem out of place in a contemporary realistic play
is that they have learned the technique of sustaining gestures and persist
in using it in a play where it is inappropriate.   The reverse is also true,
actors who have trained themselves in colloquial plays often seem ill at
ease and inadequate in poetic dramas because they persist in using small
and unsustained gestures when the play demands larger gestures which
can be sustained for the longer duration of the poetically extended
thoughts and emotions.

In most instances, an increase in the number of gestures will tend to
decrease the size of a performance.   For one thing, when there are more
gestures, it is probable that the gestures themselves will need to be smaller.
In some instances, however, it is possible to build a large performance out
of an accumulation of small details.   Acting in this manner is like painting with many small brush strokes, each of which adds one more detail

to the picture, but which, when viewed from a little distance, blend together to create the total effect. Naturally to be fully appreciated, the picture must also be viewed close up. It sometimes seems that Franz Hals, an artist noted for this technique, painted every thread in a lace collar; the fineness of his work, like that of an actual piece of lace, can only be fully appreciated when examined closely, but viewed from some distance the painting retains its delicate quality, even though the details have become invisible.

As has been noted, the drama of the twentieth century, which strives for verisimilitude, usually requires many small gestures rather than fewer and more sustained gestures. The dramas of Ibsen have many passages which the actor may well treat in this manner. In the second act of *A Doll's House*, for example, when Nora watches Krogstad place the fatal letter in the mail box, almost every line and every phrase of every line can be played with a separate and distinct gesture, each helping to build the larger picture of Nora's terror. Krogstad goes out through the hall door. Nora hurries to the door, opens it a little, and listens. She says:

> He's going. He's not putting the letter into the box. No, no, it would be impossible! (*Opens the door further and further.*) What's that. He's standing still; not going down stairs. Has he changed his mind? Is he—? (*A letter falls into the box. Krogstad's footsteps are heard gradually receding down the stair. Nora utters a suppressed shriek, and rushes forward towards the sofa-table; pause.*) In the letter-box! (*Slips shrinkingly up to the hall door.*) There it lies. Torvald, Torvald—now we are lost!

The entire next short scene between Nora and Mrs. Linden will be most effectively played if both actresses use a great many short, quick gestures, just as the lines are short and should be read rapidly to give the scene the quality of excitement and terror which it should have.

Movement as a Device to Alter Size

Hand and arm gestures can be increased only up to a point. Beyond that, to increase the size of a performance the actor must begin to use physical movement from one place on the stage to another. The "Hello. How are you?" exercise, which was included in an earlier chapter to demonstrate movement as a means of communicating thought and emotion, is also an exercise in varying the size of a performance. To play this greeting scene in its smallest size, the actor would use only a facial expression; but playing the scene in its next size would involve walking several steps toward the person being greeted.

Working on large stages in large auditoriums, the actor will seek to motivate as much meaningful movement as the character and the play will allow, and whenever possible he will add movement to his facial expressions and gestures in order to convey his thoughts and emotions to the back rows. Working in more confined spaces, as on a television set or on the small stage of an intimate theater, he will strive to find means of conveying his thought with as little movement from one place to another as is possible.

Many actors find it extremely difficult to motivate movement of any size when it is not specifically called for in the plot and when it is needed only to express an emotion. Several of the scenes which have already been used to illustrate other technical problems may also be used to illustrate this problem. In the potion scene, for example, the actress playing Juliet may deliver the entire speech without leaving the bed, or she may, as Juliet imagines the horrors of the tomb, move in fascinated horror toward where she thinks she sees the ghosts or move in terror away from them. The Portia-Nerissa scene, in which the two characters discuss Portia's suitors, may be played all in one place or with one or both of the characters motivated to move around the stage.

One of the reasons that inexperienced actors find it difficult to move in scenes that may be played without movement is that the movement seems unnatural. The actor must learn that the compulsion to move does not always come from the character, that it is often the size of the stage and the size of the performance which dictate the need for movement, and that it is the actor's task to make such movement seem natural. To play Juliet's potion scene on a large stage in a large auditorium, where facial expressions will not be very effective, without moving from one place is to run the risk of having the character seem small and inconsequential. The actress will find it difficult to dominate the stage.

Ham Acting

There are several adjectives that are frequently applied to actors which are loosely used and often misunderstood and which seem to be mainly concerned with the size of a performance. One of these is "ham," which seems to be a term of opprobrium applied to actors who are thought to be doing too much, to be overplaying or giving too large a performance, whether or not the play and the physical production make a large performance either necessary or appropriate.

Many self-appointed critics, and even some critics who are hired to pass judgment on theatrical performances, fail to differentiate between the character analysis and the techniques by which the results of that analysis are made evident to an audience. Whether or not a character would experience a certain emotion with a certain degree of intensity is a problem of analysis; what means should be used to express that emotion in a particular production is a problem of technique.

We have seen that enlarging the techniques used to achieve a larger performance is likely to change the quality of a performance. Too few actors are capable of giving a large performance of a small emotion. Mere size in itself is neither a virtue nor a fault, but the actor must take great care to discover those techniques which he personally can use in varying degrees of size without altering the characterization which he is presenting. Properly understood, the term "ham," if used in a derogatory sense, should be reserved for the actor who does more than is necessary to give an effective performance in the particular type of production in which he is appearing, or who cannot give an effective performance without distorting the character that he is playing.

Obvious Acting

Another adjective which is frequently used to describe actors and acting is *obvious*. Properly understood, the term *obvious*, as applied to acting, should be considered a compliment, although it is seldom used this way. In most instances it seems to be used as a near synonym to *ham*. Actually, it means that the actor has done those things that are necessary to make the meaning of his character plain to the entire audience, that he has achieved what should have been his aim and object when he began work on the part. Unless the spectators sitting in the last rows are going to understand the play as well as those sitting in the first rows, no one should be surprised if the last rows are empty.

In its uncomplimentary sense, *obvious* seems to mean *redundant* or *repetitive*, for it is applied to an actor who has made a thought or an emotion clear to an entire audience but who continues to restate the same thought or emotion, without any growth or development or change. Here the actor has neglected to observe the progressions discussed in a previous chapter, or he has begun a performance in a size that he is incapable of varying. What the actor should strive for is skill in making shades and tones and degrees of thought and emotion obvious. It is not a virtue to be less clear, but it is a great virtue to be able to be clear in the little facets of a role, as well as in the main facets.

Subtle Acting

The third adjective to be considered is *subtle*, which is usually meant as a compliment and should usually be accepted as such. In one sense, however, the word *subtle* is uncomplimentary, for one definition of the word listed in the dictionary is "intricate; abstruse; evasive; hard to understand." These are all qualities which should not exist in the art of acting. Lest they appear in a performance, the actor should take care that, however small and delicate the nuances of his role, the techniques he uses to express those nuances are sufficiently effective to make them obvious.

EXERCISES

1. Use the line, "Come here," and some pantomimic action which will indicate the place from which the person being spoken to should come and the place to which he should come.

a. Using the line as a command, not as an invitation, speak it quietly.

b. Still using the line as a command, speak it more loudly.

c. Now speak the line still more loudly.

NOTE: In order to keep the meaning of a firm command, exercise a will depend upon facial expression, a deliberate rate, and an even, unchanging pitch. Exercise c will depend more upon the volume to establish the effect. Try to perform exercises a, b, and c without changing the meaning or the degree of the emotion, merely adapting the line to various-sized theaters.

d. Using the line as an invitation, rather than as a command, speak it quietly.

e. Still using the line as an invitation, speak it more loudly.

f. Now speak the line still more loudly.

NOTE: The quiet tone seems more suitable as an invitation than as a command, and the loudest tone seems more suitable as a command than as an invitation. Try to perform exercises d, e, and f without changing the meaning or the degree of the emotion.

g. Try to match an appropriate facial expression to the readings in exercises a, b, and c.

h. Try to match an appropriate facial expression to the readings in exercises d, e, and f.

i. Add a small hand gesture which would be appropriate to a, b, and c.

j. Add a small hand gesture which would be appropriate to d, e, and f.

k. Enlarge the small hand gesture of i and j, so that it can be performed in at least three sizes—small, larger, and largest.

NOTE: In all of these exercises try not to change the meaning or the degree of the emotion. Merely change the size of the statement.

l. Now attempt to include movement from one part of the stage to another when the line is used as a command and when it is used as an invitation.

m. Try combining the loudest voice with the smallest gesture and the most quiet reading with the largest gestures.

NOTE: This arrangement of a large technical device combined with a small technical device tends to create the effect of emotional restraint.

2. Sequence from *A Doll's House*,[1] Act I.

NORA: But now let me tell you, Christina—I, too, have something to be proud and glad of.

MRS. LINDEN: I don't doubt it. But what do you mean?

NORA: Hush! Not so loud. Only think, if Torvald were to hear! He mustn't—not for worlds! No one must know about it, Christina—no one but you.

MRS. L.: Why, what can it be?

NORA: Come over here. (*Draws her down beside her on the sofa.*) Yes, Christina—I, too, have something to be proud and glad of. I saved Torvald's life.

MRS. L.: Saved his life? How?

NORA: I told you about our going to Italy. Torvald would have died but for that.

MRS. L.: Well—and your father gave you the money.

NORA: (*Smiling.*) Yes, so Torvald and everyone believes; but—

MRS. L.: But——?

NORA: Papa didn't give us one penny. It was *I* that found the money.

MRS. L.: You? All that money?

NORA: Twelve hundred dollars. Four thousand eight hundred crowns. What do you say to that?

MRS. L.: My dear Nora, how did you manage it? Did you win it in a lottery?

NORA: (*Contemptuously.*) In the lottery? Pooh! Anyone could have done that!

MRS. L.: Then wherever did you get from?

NORA: (*Hums and smiles mysteriously.*) H'm; tra-la-la-la.

MRS. L.: Of course you couldn't borrow it.

NORA: No? Why not?

MRS. L.: Why, a wife can't borrow without her husband's consent.

NORA: (*Tossing her head.*) Oh! when the wife has some idea of business, and knows how to set about things—

MRS. L.: But, Nora, I don't understand—

NORA: Well, you needn't. I never said I borrowed the money. There are many ways I may have got it. (*Throws herself back on the sofa.*) I may have got it from some admirer. When one is so—attractive as I am—

MRS. L.: You're too silly, Nora.

NORA: Now I'm sure you're dying of curiosity, Christina—

MRS. L.: Listen to me, Nora dear: haven't you been a little rash?

NORA: (*Sitting upright again.*) Is it rash to save one's husband's life?

MRS. L.: I think it was rash of you, without his knowledge—

NORA: But it would have been fatal for him to know! Can't you under-

[1] Copyright by Charles Scribner's Sons.

stand that? He wasn't even to suspect how ill he was. The doctors came to me privately and told me his life was in danger—that nothing could save him but a winter in the South. Do you think I didn't try diplomacy first? I told him how I longed to have a trip abroad, like other young wives; I wept and prayed; I said he ought to think of my condition, and not to thwart me; and then I hinted that he could borrow the money. But then, Christina, he got almost angry. He said I was frivolous, and that it was his duty as a husband not to yield to my whims and fancies—so he called them. Very well, thought I, but saved you must be; and then I found the way to do it.

Mrs. L.: And did your husband never learn from your father that the money was not from him?

Nora: No; never. Papa died at that very time. I meant to have told him all about it, and begged him to say nothing. But he was so ill—unhappily, it wasn't necessary.

Mrs. L.: And you have never confessed to your husband?

Nora: Good heavens! What can you be thinking of? Tell him, when he has such a loathing of debt! And besides—how painful and humiliating it would be for Torvald, with his manly self-respect, to know that he owed anything to me! It would utterly upset the relation between us; our beautiful, happy home would never again be what it is.

Mrs. L.: Will you never tell him?

Nora: (*Thoughtfully, half-smiling*) Yes, sometime perhaps—many, many years hence, when I'm—not so pretty. You mustn't laugh at me! Of course I mean when Torvald is not so much in love with me as he is now; when it doesn't amuse him any longer to see me dancing about, and dressing up and acting. Then it might be well to have something in reserve. (*Breaking off.*) Nonsense! Nonsense! That time will never come. Now, what do you say to my grand secret, Christina?

a. Rehearse the scene as quietly as it would be in real life if two women were talking together on a sofa and were afraid they would be heard by someone in the next room.

b. Rehearse the scene as loud as it must be to be heard in a moderately large theater.

c. Rehearse the scene as loud as it must be in a very large theater.
   NOTE: If the actresses are in physical attitudes which suggest that they are speaking confidentially, the effect of a quiet scene can be maintained without actually being quiet.

d. Experiment with using larger actions than those suggested in the script. Put in hand gestures wherever possible. In the speech beginning, "But it would have been fatal . . . ," let Nora go back near the door to Torvald's room to listen and then return to the sofa. Let Nora add a swinging foot in the place where the directions say she "hums and smiles mysteriously."

3. Chorus from *Agamemnon*.[2]

This passage was written to be spoken simultaneously by the chorus of old men. The division of the speeches between the individuals of the chorus is entirely arbitrary.

FIRST SPEAKER:	The tenth year is this from the time Priam's foe,
SECOND SPEAKER:	The great adversary,
THIRD SPEAKER:	Agamemnon and Prince Menelaus,
FIRST SPEAKER:	with honor of scepter and honor of throne,
THIRD SPEAKER:	strong men,
SECOND SPEAKER:	yoked together and brothers,
FIRST SPEAKER:	launched a thousand ships from this Argive land, a warrior band to carry help,
THIRD SPEAKER:	and they shouted a great shout,
FIRST, SECOND, AND THIRD SPEAKERS:	War!
FOURTH SPEAKER:	So eagles scream as they circle aloft on their feathered oars,
FIFTH SPEAKER:	high over their nest on a lonely crag,
FOURTH SPEAKER:	when the eaglets are stolen away.
FIFTH SPEAKER:	And they grieve for their young and the nest never more to be tended.
SIXTH SPEAKER:	But in heaven above there is one who hears,
SEVENTH SPEAKER:	or Pan or Zeus or Apollo,
SIXTH SPEAKER:	Hears the shrill, screaming cry of the dwellers in air,
EIGHTH SPEAKER:	and slow-footed vengeance he sends to those that transgress.
FOURTH SPEAKER:	Even thus the Almighty who guards guest and host, sent the children of Atreus to Paris,
FIFTH SPEAKER:	for a woman wooed of many men.
SECOND SPEAKER:	And many a struggle that weighs down the limbs,
FIRST SPEAKER:	when the knee is bowed in the dust,
THIRD SPEAKER:	when the spear-shaft is shivered in the prelude of the fight,
SECOND SPEAKER:	he has sent to the Greek and the Trojan.
SIXTH SPEAKER:	It is as it is.
EIGHTH SPEAKER:	It shall end as it must.
SEVENTH SPEAKER:	Not by secret grief,
FOURTH SPEAKER:	not by secret gifts,
FIFTH SPEAKER:	not by tears,

SEVENTH SPEAKER:	can one make atonement for altars without fire and stubborn wrath of God.
THIRD SPEAKER:	But we, all unhonored for that we are old,
SECOND SPEAKER:	Left behind when the host sailed to help,
FIRST SPEAKER:	weak as a child, we lean on our staves.
FIRST, SECOND, AND THIRD SPEAKERS:	We are waiting.
EIGHTH SPEAKER:	When the marrow in the bones is young,
SEVENTH SPEAKER	when a child's heart is lord within the breast, war is far away—
SIXTH SPEAKER:	the aged are like children.
FOURTH SPEAKER:	He that is exceeding old, when the leaf is withered, walks the roads on three feet with his staff.
FIFTH SPEAKER:	No better than a child, he wanders, a dream—at noonday.

a. Rehearse the scene with each actor trying to achieve individuality, each actor inventing small individual actions to set himself apart from the others. All are old men, and all have been aroused in the night by the cry of the Watchman who has proclaimed the end of the war.

Let the First, Second, and Third Speakers enter from up left, two carrying staves which they use to help them walk, one carrying a lantern. Let them speak as they enter and cross down right to the steps of the palace, where they will sit during the first speeches of the Sixth, Seventh, and Eighth Speakers.

Let the Fourth and Fifth Speakers, one carrying a torch, enter from down right and come to a position to the right of the palace steps, where they are met by the First, Second, and Third Speakers. On the third speech of the Fourth Speaker, let the Fourth and Fifth Speakers cross toward the center, the First, Second, and Third Speakers having sat on the steps by this time.

Let the Sixth, Seventh, and Eighth Speakers enter from up right as the Fourth Speaker speaks for the first time, and crossing behind the others come to the altar, which is downstage and left of the center of the stage. Let one carry a stave and one a lantern. The Eighth and Sixth Speakers remain near the altar, but the Seventh Speaker crosses on his line, "Can one make atonement . . . ," in front of the Fourth and Fifth Speakers to come near the Third Speaker, who is sitting on the steps.

The first nine speeches are one thought sequence, each speaker picking up the cue as though he too knew the story and wanted to get in his word. This sequence builds to a vocal climax. The next four speeches are another thought, more lyrical than the first sequence. It should go down from the vocal volume of the climax of the first sequence, beginning loud and ending less loud. The next four lines should be spoken firmly and with power, filled with awe. These lines should be ponged more than the others.

With the vocal techniques established in the scene by each individual actor, continue the scene so that the contrasts in the methods of speaking make interesting patterns. Be careful to observe the thought sequence, each actor continuing a thought begun by another or beginning a new thought as the case may be.

b. Rehearse the scene with all eight actors speaking the lines in unison. Work for variety of volume, pitch, and rate. Work out unison action for all eight, making use of the duration or continuity of gesture to help clarify the thoughts for the audience.

4. Sequence from *The Trojan Women*.[3]

Hecuba, the aged queen of Troy, is lying on the ground. As she starts to move, she speaks:

> Up from the ground—O weary head, O breaking neck.
> This is no longer Troy. And we are not
> the lords of Troy.
> Endure. The ways of fate are the ways of the wind.
> Drift with the stream—drift with fate.
> No use to turn the prow to breast the waves.
> Let the boat go as it chances.
> Sorrow, my sorrow.
> What sorrow is there that is not mine,
> grief to weep for.
> Country lost and children and husband.
> Glory of all my house brought low.
> All was nothing—nothing, always.
> Keep silent? Speak?
> Weep then? Why? For what?
> (*She begins to get up.*)
> Oh, this aching body—this bed—
> it is very hard. My back pressed to it—
> oh, my side, my brow, my temples.
> Up! Quick, quick. I must move.
> Oh, I'll rock myself this way, that way
> to the sound of weeping, the song of tears,
> dropping down forever.
> The song no feet will dance to ever,
> for the wretched, the ruined.

O ships, O prows, swift oars
out from the fair Greek bays and harbors,
over the dark shining sea,
you found your way to our holy city,
and the fearful music of war was heard,
the war song sung to flute and pipe,
as you cast on the shore your cables,
ropes the Nile dwellers twisted and coiled,
and you swung, oh, my grief, in Troy's waters.

What did you come for?   A woman?
A thing of loathing, of shame,
to husband, to brother, to home.
She slew Priam, the king,
father of fifty sons,
she wrecked me upon
the reef of destruction.

What am I that I wait
here at a Greek king's door?
A slave that men drive on,
an old gray woman that has no home.
Shaven head brought low in dishonor.
O wives of the bronze-armored men who fought,
and maidens, sorrowing maidens,
plighted to shame,
see—only smoke left where was Troy.
Let us weep for her.
As a mother bird cries to her feathered brood,
so will I cry.
Once another song I sang
when I leaned on Priam's scepter,
and the beat of dancing feet
marked the music's measure.
Up to the gods
the song of Troy rose at my signal.

a. Speak the speech as naturally as possible, using only normal and natural
volume. Use small gestures, natural to an old woman. Begin to rise at
the place indicated and be standing nine lines later. Turn to the right in
the direction of the harbor as Hecuba speaks of the ships. Turn away
from right in disgust when she says, "What did you come for? a woman?"
Move a few steps to the left on, "What am I that I wait. . . ." Go farther

left to call to the women on the lines, "O wives of the bronze-armored men. . . ."

b. Enlarge the volume of the speech and practice prolonging some of the vowels. Use larger gestures and practice prolonging the gestures through three or four lines. For instance, as Hecuba speaks of the ships let her move to the right and extend her arm and hand in the direction of the ships through at least four lines. Find another gesture, perhaps clenching the fist with the arm raised and the elbow bent on the next four lines. Continue to search for large gestures that are expressive of the emotions and thoughts and which can be sustained as long as the words continue to express the same thought and emotion. Use longer crosses. See the ships at the extreme right, and cross to the extreme left to call the women, then back to the right on "see—only smoke left where was Troy."

5. Sequence from *The Trojan Women.*[4]

This is a direct continuation of the scene above. The door of one of the huts opens and a woman steals out, then another, and another.

FIRST WOMAN: Your cry, O Hecuba—oh, such a cry—
What does it mean? There in the tent
we heard you call so piteously,
and through our hearts flashed fear.
In the tent we were weeping, too,
for we are slaves.

HECUBA: Look, child, there where the Greek ships lie—

ANOTHER WOMAN: They are moving. The men hold oars.

ANOTHER: O God, what will they do? Carry me off over
the sea in a ship far from home?

HECUBA: You ask and I know nothing,
but I think ruin is here.

ANOTHER WOMAN: Oh, we are wretched. We shall hear the summons.
Women of Troy, go forth from your home,
for the Greeks set sail.

HECUBA: But not Cassandra, oh, not her.
She is mad—she has been driven mad. Leave
her within.
Not shamed before the Greeks—not that grief too.
I have enough.
O Troy, unhappy Troy, you are gone
and we, the unhappy, leave you,
we who are living and we who are dead.

(*More women now come out from a second hut.*)

4 Copyright by W. W. Norton & Company, Inc.

A WOMAN: Out of the Greek king's tent
Trembling I come, O Queen,
to hear my fate from you.
Not death— They would not think of death
for a poor woman.

ANOTHER: The sailors—they are standing on the prow.
Already they are running out the oars.

(*Still another woman comes out of a third hut and several follow her.*)

ANOTHER: It is so early—but a terror woke me.
My heart beats so.

ANOTHER: Has a herald come from the Greek camp?
Whose slave shall I be?   I—bear that?

HECUBA: Wait for the lot drawing.   It is near.

ANOTHER: Argos shall it be, or Phthia?
Or an island of the sea?
A Greek soldier lead me there,
far, far from Troy?

HECUBA: And I a slave—to whom—where—how?
You old gray woman, patient to endure,
you bee without a sting,
only an image of what was alive
or the ghost of one dead.
I watch a master's door?
I nurse his children?
Once I was queen of Troy.

ONE WOMAN
TO ANOTHER: Poor thing.   What are your tears
to the shame before you?

THE OTHER: The shuttle will still pass through my hands,
but the loom will not be in Troy.

ANOTHER: My dead sons.   I would look at them once more.
Never again.

ANOTHER: Worse to come.
A Greek's bed—and I

ANOTHER: A night like that?   Oh, never—
oh, no—not that for me.

ANOTHER: I see myself a water carrier,
dipping my pitcher in the great Pierian spring.

ANOTHER: The land of Theseus, Athens, it is known
to be a happy place.   I wish I could go there.

ANOTHER: But not to Eurotas, hateful river,
where Helen lived.   Not there, to be a slave
to Menelaus who sacked Troy.

ANOTHER: Oh, look. A man from the Greek army—
a herald. Something strange has happened,
he comes so fast. To tell us—what?
What will he say? Only Greek slaves are here,
waiting for orders.

a. Assign the speeches to individual actors, taking care that each actor has lines of a similar quality. Let each actor plan natural actions, some hurried and fearful, some sleepy and yawning, some angry and resentful, some proud and restrained. Rehearse the scene so that the scene itself has vocal climaxes and action climaxes, each individual actor playing so that each individual part contributes to the volume, rate, and pitch of the vocal pattern of the scene and so that the individual actions combine to make a visual pattern for the entire scene.

b. Let the chorus enter in groups of three, each group performing the same movements in unison, the nonspeaking actors sustaining the movements and gestures on the speeches of others as well as on their own speeches. Again make the scene fit an over-all vocal and visual pattern.

6. Sequence from *A Doll's House,*[5] Act II.

Krogstad goes out through the hall. Nora hurries to the door, opens it a little, and listens.

NORA: He's going. He's not putting the letter into the box. No, no, it would be impossible! (*Opens the door further and further.*) What's that? He's standing still; not going down stairs. Has he changed his mind? Is he—? (*A letter falls into the box. Krogstad's footsteps are heard gradually receding down the stair. Nora utters a suppressed shriek, and rushes forward towards the sofa-table; pause.*) In the letter-box! (*Slips shrinkingly up to the hall door.*) There it lies. Torvald, Torvald—now we are lost!
(*Mrs. Linden enters from the left with the costume.*)
MRS. L.: There, I think it's all right now. Shall we try it on?
NORA: (*Hoarsely and softly*) Christina, come here.
MRS. L.: (*Throws down the dress on the sofa.*) What's the matter? You look quite distracted.
NORA: Come here. Do you see that letter? There, see through the glass of the letter-box.
MRS. L.: Yes, yes, I see it.
NORA: That letter is from Krogstad——
MRS. L.: Nora—it was Krogstad who lent you the money?
NORA: Yes; and now Torvald will know everything.
MRS. L.: Believe me, Nora, it's the best thing for both of you.
NORA: You don't know all yet. I have forged a name—

[5] Copyright by Charles Scribner's Sons.

Mrs. L.: Good heavens!

Nora: Now, listen to me, Christina; you shall bear witness—

Mrs. L.: How "witness"?   What am I to——

Nora: If I should go out of my mind—it might easily happen—

Mrs. L.: Nora!

Nora: Or if anything else should happen to me—so that I couldn't be here—

Mrs. L.: Nora, Nora, you're quite beside yourself!

Nora: In case any one wanted to take it all upon himself—the whole blame —you understand—

Mrs. L.: Yes, yes; but how can you think—?

Nora: You shall bear witness that it's not true, Christina.   I'm not out of my mind at all; I know quite well what I'm saying; and I tell you nobody else knew anything about it; I did the whole thing, I myself.   Remember that.

Mrs. L.: I shall remember.   But I don't understand what you mean—

Nora: Oh, how should you?   It's the miracle coming to pass.

Mrs. L.: The miracle?

Nora: Yes, the miracle.   But it's so terrible, Christina; it mustn't happen for all the world.

   a. Play the scene using as many short, quick actions as possible.   Work for variety by using different timings, sometimes having the action before the line, sometimes during, and sometimes after the line.

7. It would be beneficial to rerehearse any of the scenes used as exercises in previous chapters, changing the size and duration and amount of action used in the scenes.

Chapter 9. POINTING

Most actors refer to pointing as though it were a separate technique, when actually it is a combination of all the techniques. It is closely related to the problem of the size of a performance in that it involves the use of techniques in relation to a single line, to a short phrase which is part of a line, or even to a single word. Pointing is frequently confused with timing because it often uses a physical action in a nice time relationship with the word or phrase which is being pointed, but it differs from timing in some respects because it can sometimes be done with the vocal techniques alone and sometimes with only the physical techniques.

Definition of Pointing

Pointing is the use of any technical device to bring special emphasis to a thought or an emotion which is expressed by some relatively brief phrase or action. It is, in a sense, the smallest possible unit of acting; but the sum of all the things which an actor chooses to emphasize, plus the skill with which he achieves that emphasis, adds up to the interpretation of the role. Pointing is to acting as the use of highlight and shadow is to painting; it gives the performance roundness and fullness. The actor's understanding and grasp of the character, and therefore his stature as an artist, will be revealed by the things which he selects to receive special emphasis, and his skill will be revealed by the facility with which he is able to point the passages he has selected.

The Uses of Pointing

When Hamlet, in Act III, Scene 3, has the opportunity to kill the King as he comes upon him while the King is praying, he does not seize the opportunity, lest the King should go to Heaven.

> Now might I do it, pat, now he is praying;
> And now I'll do't:—and so he goes to Heaven;
> And so am I revenged?   That would be scann'd:

175

> A villain kills my father; and for that,
> I, his sole son, do this same villain send
> To Heaven.

This action, or failure to take action, is based upon Hamlet's religious beliefs, beliefs which were for the most part shared by Shakespeare's audiences. Since these beliefs were understood and shared by the audience, there was no need for Shakespeare to expound or to explain them; but the same beliefs would not be held by everyone in an audience today, and so in a contemporary production it might be considered necessary to show Hamlet as a religious man in order to make his action understandable.

There are several scenes in the first two acts of the play where Hamlet's piety might be established. In Act I, Scene 2, he says:

> O, that this too, too solid flesh would melt,
> Thaw, and resolve itself into dew;
> Or that the Everlasting had not fix'd
> His canon 'gainst self-slaughter.

And when Hamlet first sees the Ghost, he says:

> Angels and ministers of grace defend us!

The Ghost in Act I, Scene 5, also sheds some light on the religious beliefs of the time when he explains that he is:

> Doom'd for a certain term to walk the night,
> And for the day confin'd to fast in fires,
> Till the foul crimes, done in my days of nature,
> Are burnt and purg'd away.

These are the main passages which explain Hamlet's religious beliefs. In addition, there are several oaths, imprecations, and references to God, the Devil, Heaven, and Hell. There is also the episode in which Hamlet swears his friends to secrecy by having them kiss the hilt of his sword, the handle of which may be held in such a way that it appears as a cross and a religious symbol. If the actor thinks that Hamlet's failure to kill the King while he is praying needs preparation in order to be understandable, these are lines which must be pointed. The actor may also discover places where actions which reveal Hamlet to be a religious man may be included in the performance, and these actions will also need to be pointed, or specifically called to the attention of the audience. Skill in the ability to highlight, or point, such passages and actions enables the actor to communicate to the audience the nuances of the character and the subtleties of his interpretation.

The Method of Pointing

The method by which an actor calls attention to a particular line or action is to select any one, or any combination, of those techniques which may be used to achieve emphasis and which are appropriate to the specific line or action, and then apply those techniques to bring emphasis to the concepts which he wants to point. Thus, it can be seen that pointing is not a technique in itself but rather an effect which may be accomplished by the use of techniques. The techniques involved are all those that have already been discussed: the vocal techniques—change of volume, rate, pitch, or quality—and the physical techniques—facial expressions, hand or arm gestures, body turns, changes in elevation, and larger movements from one place to another on the stage.

Vocal Techniques in Pointing

When using vocal techniques to point a particular line, the actor will discover that providing a contrast with what has immediately preceded the line in question is the most effective way of accomplishing the emphasis. If, for example, the actor wishes to point the lines,

> Or that the Everlasting had not fix'd
> His canon 'gainst self-slaughter,

the best reading will be determined by what has been done with the preceding lines,

> O, that this too, too solid flesh would melt,
> Thaw, and resolve itself into dew.

If the first two lines are read rapidly, then the next two will be more effective if they are read at a slower rate; if the beginning lines are read loudly, then the second two lines will have more emphasis if they are read less loudly. It can readily be seen that while an increase in the rate of speaking is an excellent way to develop a progression and to build a climax, it is less useful as a device to give special emphasis to a specific line or word, because it directs attention to the specific line for a shorter time, so that the audience will tend to pay less attention to the thought being expressed in the line.

If the actor elects to read all four of these lines with the same volume, the same rate, the same pitch, and the same quality of voice, he will have failed to use vocal techniques to differentiate the thoughts in the lines and will not have vocally stressed the concept that Hamlet is religious to the extent of believing that suicide is forbidden, a concept which has some bearing upon his later decision to forego revenge lest killing the King while he is in prayer send the King's soul to Heaven rather than to Hell.

Physical Techniques in Pointing

The physical techniques are usually a much more dynamic means of pointing than are the voice techniques. If Hamlet wears a crucifix throughout the performance, he will be marked as a religious person. If, at certain moments in the play, he fingers the crucifix, the audience will understand that at those moments he is remembering his religious conviction. When such an action is combined with lines which also have possible religious connotations, the concept of Hamlet as a man with strong religious convictions will be forcefully presented to the audience.

If the actor did not wish to make the point so strongly, he might contrive the scene so that he could use a body turn toward the audience just before or during the lines to be pointed. A change of level could be used in the same way. If he were sitting with his head in his hands as he began to speak, he might raise his head as he came to the lines or words to be pointed. The particular lines cited here as evidence of Hamlet's religious beliefs do not lend themselves to the use of any large gestures or movements, but some of the other lines which might be used to show Hamlet's religious nature could be pointed by larger movements.

Pointing in A Doll's House

In almost every play in which the characters are written as three-dimensional figures, with several facets to their personalities, the actor will find instances where the author has provided a few brief lines which illustrate one of these facets of the character but which need to be pointed if the audience is to grasp the full significance of the lines. All through the first act of *A Doll's House*, for example, the actress playing Nora must seem to be the gay, frivolous, and irresponsible wife her husband thinks her to be, but she must also show the audience that there is a more serious and responsible side to her nature; otherwise her actions in the last act will come as a surprise, not only to her husband, but also to the audience, and will seem to be contrary to her character.

In the scene from this play which was used as an exercise in the preceding chapter, Nora speaks of the miracle which will happen. Ibsen has taken pains to repeat the word *miracle* three times, but the actress should also look for some way to point the lines in which the word appears:

> MRS. LINDEN: But I don't understand what you mean—
> NORA: Oh, how should you? It's the miracle coming to pass.

> MRS. LINDEN: The miracle?
> NORA: Yes, the miracle.

In the last act the entire structure of the play is dependent upon this concept of the miracle which Nora expected to happen.

> HELMER: And can you also make clear to me how I have forfeited your love?
> NORA: Yes, I can. It was this evening, when the miracle did not happen; for then I saw you were not the man I had imagined.
> HELMER: Explain yourself more clearly; I don't understand.
> NORA: I have waited so patiently all these eight years; for of course I saw clearly enough that miracles don't happen every day. When this crushing blow threatened me, I said to myself so confidently, "Now comes the miracle!" When Krogstad's letter lay in the box, it never for a moment occurred to me that you would think of submitting to that man's conditions. I was convinced that you would say to him, "Make it known to all the world"; and that then—
> HELMER: Well? When I had given my own wife's name up to disgrace and shame—?
> NORA: Then I firmly believed that you would come forward, take everything upon yourself, and say, "I am the guilty one."
> HELMER: Nora——!
> NORA: You mean I would never have accepted such a sacrifice? No, certainly not! But what would my assertions have been worth in opposition to yours?—That was the miracle that I hoped for and dreaded.

Lest the second-act reference to the expected miracle should be lost or absorbed into the excitement of the scene as a whole, even with Ibsen's repetition of the word, the actress will want to give some special emphasis to the lines, and this can be done only by the use of one or more of the techniques already discussed.

Size of Pointing Techniques

Because pointing is concerned with bringing special emphasis to a brief section of the play, one must not think of the techniques involved as necessarily being used in a small way. In any performance, what is needed to bring special emphasis to a line or an action will be determined by the size of the entire performance. In a small, intimate production, all that may be needed to point a particular passage may be a slight variation in the vocal techniques, or a turn of the head or the body, or a change in the facial expression. In larger productions, larger physical actions will be required. To use too large a technical device to make a point is one

of the surest ways of being classed as a ham actor, and to use too small
a device is to risk failing to make the point entirely.

Pointing to Clarify Plot

Thus far, the examples given of the actor's need of skill in pointing
have been concerned with the development and the presentation of characterization. Sometimes, however, the actor must use this same skill to
make sure that the audience understands the plot clearly. In Act IV,
Scene 7, of *Hamlet*, the King and Laertes plot that Laertes shall duel
with Hamlet, using a poisoned rapier, and that the King shall prepare a
poisoned drink, so that if Hamlet escapes Laertes' sword, his murder
may still be accomplished.

In Act V, Scene 2, there are only two lines to be delivered while
Laertes and Hamlet choose their weapons:

> LAERTES: This is too heavy; let me see another.
> HAMLET: This likes me well. These foils have all a length?

In this brief moment the actor playing Laertes must make it clear to
the audience that he has been successful in selecting the poisoned weapon.
Since there is no line to help him, he must convey his success by inventing
and carefully pointing some appropriate action. Possibly he might choose
the foil, then turn away from Hamlet—but toward the King and also
toward the audience—and carefully examine the point of the foil to see
whether he has the right one. Perhaps the actor playing Hamlet will
wish to do something on his line to suggest that, contrary to the King's
expectations, his suspicions are aroused as he asks, "These foils have all
a length?"

Later in the scene there is the stage direction, "Laertes wounds Hamlet; then, in the scuffling they change rapiers, and Hamlet wounds
Laertes." If this action is to appear to the audience as anything more
than scuffling, it must be performed with great care and dexterity, with
each separate part worked out in meaningful pantomime. First, Laertes
must be seen to wound Hamlet, and Hamlet must be seen to be wounded
—a pantomime which involves two separate actions. Second, the dropping of the rapiers must be managed in a way which seems natural and inevitable. Third, Hamlet must be seen to pick up Laertes' sword, and
Laertes must be seen to recognize what has happened. The actor playing the King could help in this, as his pantomime when the swords are
changed might be used to point out to the audience what has happened.
Fourth, Hamlet must be seen to wound Laertes with the poisoned foil,
and Laertes must be seen to be wounded, and he and the audience must be
aware that the wound is fatal because of the poison.

Interspersed with the dueling, which precedes the fatal wounding of both Hamlet and Laertes, is the business of the poisoned drink; if the duel is allowed to continue through the time when the Queen drinks, the larger movements of the fighting will pull the emphasis away from the Queen and what she is doing. When the King says,

> Stay; give me drink. Hamlet, this pearl is thine;
> Here's to thy health.—Give him the cup,

the King's first word must stop the fighting. If the cups are brought by a servant from some distance, this movement will help to focus audience attention on what the King is about to do. The dropping of the pearl into the wine must be performed so that the audience knows that it is by this means that the King places the poison in Hamlet's goblet. Again, when the King orders the cup to be given to Hamlet, it will be desirable if the servant who offers it has to take a few steps toward Hamlet, so that there will be a larger movement to help point the action. When Hamlet refuses the drink, saying, "I'll play this bout first; set it by a while," the cup must be obviously placed near the Queen. Only after this action has been completed is it safe to resume the fighting.

It is only three lines later that the fighting must again be stopped as the Queen suggests that Hamlet wipe his brow:

> Here, Hamlet, take my napkin, rub thy brows:
> The Queen carouses to thy fortune, Hamlet.

Whatever action is invented to go with the offer of the napkin and the wiping of the brows should be minimized, since it has no significance in the plot; but the King, Laertes, and the audience must be aware that the Queen holds the poisoned cup. Apparently Shakespeare feared that the Queen's drinking of the poison might be missed because he has written an aside for the King which is little more than a stage direction: "It is the poisoned cup! It is too late."

The next few moments must be managed with much care, for the audience is aware that the Queen is poisoned and dying while the duel is resumed, and the Queen's actions must not detract from the wounding of Hamlet and Laertes. Unless the entire cast plays this scene with each member fully aware which point is being made at which moment and unless every actor uses the utmost skill in focusing attention on that part of the action which is momentarily the most significant, there is danger that the whole play will end in confusion. The techniques most useful for pointing these brief episodes will be large gestures and large movements. Complicated scenes like this, which have so many significant actions and so few speeches to explain those actions, require great skill in pointing.

Pointing in Poetic Drama

In addition to using pointing to aid in presenting various facets of a character and to make clear the intricacies of a plot, the actor may also wish to use it to call the attention of the audience to the force and vigor or to the special beauty that lies in the author's choice of words. The actor must remember that the author, too, is an artist and that, as such, he has carefully selected every word he has used.

This particular need for pointing most frequently occurs in plays that have a poetic quality, whether or not they are written in any verse form. The poet chooses his words with care for their exact and precise meaning, for their imagery, and for the emotional values which are theirs by association. Juliet's potion scene, which has already been suggested as an exercise for another purpose, is an excellent example of a speech in which the actor must take care that the vigor and the imagery which come from the choice of words are conveyed to the audience.

An obvious example of the use of words that have emotional value through association is the passage in Act V, Scene 5, of *Richard II* in which Richard quotes from the Bible:

> The better sort,
> As thoughts of things divine, are intermix'd
> With scruples and do set the word itself
> Against the word:
> As thus, "Come, little ones," and then again,
> "It is as hard to come as for a camel
> To thread the postern of a small needle's eye."

In any Christian country these quoted words have special meaning and significance and thus should be stressed. In addition to this, Shakespeare has placed in juxtaposition two contrasting thoughts, which, to be appreciated by the audience, must be delivered with some special emphasis upon the word, "Come," and the phrase, "Hard to come." It is unlikely that the actor, to make the thought clear to the audience, will need to use anything but the vocal techniques, stressing the words slightly by change of volume, rate, and pitch. In order to see how wrong pointing can destroy the meaning of a passage, the actor should try placing the emphasis on "little" instead of upon "come."

Some of Maxwell Anderson's poetic dramas provide interesting examples of passages which require careful pointing to make their meaning clear. In the closing speeches of *High Tor*, the Indian sums up his and, one must suppose, also the author's philosophy. Van has valiantly opposed the encroachment of civilization upon the last wildernesses, but he has had to give way, and the steam shovels have moved in on his own particular piece of wilderness. The Indian offers his words of comfort:

THE INDIAN: And there's one comfort.
I heard the wise Iachim, looking down
when the railroad cut was fresh, and the bleeding earth
offended us. There is nothing made, he said,
and will be nothing made by these new men,
high tower, or cut, or buildings by a lake
that will not make good ruins.
JUDITH: Ruins? This?
THE INDIAN: Why, when the race is gone, or looks aside
only a little while, the white stone darkens,
the wounds close, and the roofs fall, and the walls
give way to rains. Nothing is made by men
but makes, in the end, good ruins.
VAN: Well, that's something.
But I can hardly wait.

If in The Indian's last speech the words, "white stone," "wounds," "roofs," and "walls" are given special emphasis in one reading, and the words, "darkens," "close," "fall," and "give way to rains" are pointed in another reading, the difference in the effectiveness of the speech may be clearly heard.

Much of the special quality of a play which marks it with the individuality and personality of the author lies in the playwright's choice of words, the language in which the thoughts and emotions of the characters are revealed. In the same way, much of the individuality of the actor lies in his understanding and appreciation of the language, as revealed to the audience through his selection of the words which are to receive some special degree of emphasis and of the techniques by which this emphasis is to be achieved. The actor should be warned, however, that there are very few characters who talk because they like to hear themselves talk; the performance he must give is not one in which the character shows how much he appreciates the beauty of his own conversation but rather one in which he speaks the words in a way that enables the audience to appreciate the author's use of language.

There can be no question that Shakespeare has given many of his characters, such as Romeo, his own eloquence. When Romeo says,

Night's candles are burnt out, and jocund day
Stands tiptoe on the misty mountain tops,

he is given a power of expression to describe what he sees and to express what he feels which is not common. One definition of poetry is that it is the ability to say "what is often thought, but ne'er so well expressed." Certainly Romeo has this ability. But while the actor must be conscious of the beauty of the speech, and must seek to make the audience conscious of it, Romeo himself is only striving to communicate to Juliet what he sees and feels.

The difference between a performance in which the actor reveals to the audience his own awareness of Romeo's eloquence and a performance in which he makes Romeo himself aware of his eloquence is slight, but tremendously important. The pointing in both performances would tend to be identical, the same words being selected for emphasis, but the facial expressions and the quality of the voice would be different. Actors who give performances that they themselves enjoy instead of performances that audiences may enjoy tend to look toward, but not at, the person to whom they are speaking, to use a facial expression which suggests that they are listening to beautiful music, rather than that they are trying to explain something to someone, and to form the sounds of the words inside their mouths rather than to speak them "trippingly on the tongue."

Pointing in Comedy

Thus far, pointing has been discussed without any consideration of whether it is to be used in a serious play or in a comedy; and yet pointing is often spoken of as being necessary only in playing comedy. It may well be that the term *pointing* derives directly from the "point" of a joke or story. One of the reasons why actors are especially aware of the need for pointing when playing comedy is that they can easily tell from the reactions of the audience whether they have been right or wrong in their method of playing a comic line; if the audience laughs, the point has been made; if not, something is wrong. There is no such absolute test in serious drama.

The first requisite for the actor playing comedy is that he himself recognize the joke and see the point, but the actor's awareness of the humor of a situation or a line must not be confused with the character's awareness. In most instances the audience will consider a character funnier if he himself is unaware that what he says or what he does, or what he is, is in the least degree comic; and yet the actor must know exactly what is comic about what is being said or done, so that he will know what to point. Most philosophers who have seriously considered the subject of comedy have placed great emphasis upon the need for the observers to understand that what is being said and done is performed with the intention of appealing to the comic spirit; but in the theater, it is usually only the actor, and not the character he is playing, who must see the point.

If a child does something which makes people laugh at him, he may repeat it; but the chances are that the repetition will be unfunny for the simple reason that he is now conscious of the humor and intends to be funny. Naturally, if he is skillful enough to be able to perform the repetition exactly as he did the original act, duplicating his own unawareness of the humor he caused, the repetition will also be funny. He will then have confined the awareness of the comedy to the performer and denied it to the character, just as any successful comic actor must do. This principle is identical with the one discussed in connection with poetic drama—that the actor who wishes the audience to be aware of the particular beauty or force of a line must not allow the character to seem aware of his own eloquence. Whether serious or comic, an actor should avoid showing that he enjoys his own performance.

Plot Comedy

This is not the place for a study and analysis of humor, but it is useful for the actor to consider that there are different kinds of humor according to the source from which the humor arises. He must understand the source of the particular type of humor he is trying to convey so that he will know what he should point. The least difficult type, as far as the technique of acting is concerned, arises from the plot and the comic situation. Shakespeare's many mistaken identity situations are examples of this kind of humor, and it is essential only that the actors carefully point the details of the plot, making sure that the audience knows who the characters really are and for whom they are mistaken. The author will do most of the remaining work.

In the first act of *Saturday's Children*, the proposal scene, which immediately follows the scene which has already been used as an exercise, might be considered as fundamentally a comic scene based upon the plot, although character comedy is also involved. Florrie has already predicted what the boy will say and do in response to what Bobby says. Bobby must carefully point the action so that the audience knows when she is reading from her sister's instructions and when she is not. The actor playing Rims must know when he is following Florrie's predictions exactly and when he is not, but the author has so carefully prepared the audience that the actor needs only to speak the lines and they will be funny.

Those who hold to the theory that comedy is always based on a deviation from a norm would do well to study this scene, for Rims is presented as a normal young man in a common situation, his reaction to which is, as predicted, entirely normal, and the spectators' enjoyment of the scene is based upon their recognition that the scene corresponds to their own experiences and fundamentally represents the truth. It can be regarded as a deviation from a norm only if one is willing to believe that normally Rims makes his own decisions, or that normally a young man proposes marriage prompted only by his own desires and wishes, without assistance from the girl in question.

It is interesting to note that Bobby, the audience, and the actor playing Rims are all aware of the plot and the situation and that only Rims himself does not know what is happening. Actually most of the laughs in this scene will come in response to the speeches of Bobby, who is doing what most of the women in the audience think that most girls would do in a similar situation. The actors will find that there is little need for pointing in this scene, since the author, by prequoting the speeches in an earlier scene, has done all the pointing that is needed, and the actress who adds extra emphasis will run the risk of doing too much and will seem to be overacting, or giving a ham performance.

Character Comedy

Comedy which arises out of character is much more the province and the concern of the actors than is plot comedy. In character comedy the principle of the deviation from the norm is most frequently the key to both the understanding of the humor and the method of playing the scene, and the actor's first care will be to discover the norm from which the character deviates. There are two places where the actor may look for the norm: within his own characterization or outside his own characterization and in the performance of some other character in the play, or even in the minds of the audience, although usually the skillful playwright will take care to present a character in the play whom the audience will accept as the norm.

Katherine in *The Taming of the Shrew* has both kinds of norms. First, there is her sister, who is the exemplification of the sweet, modest, submissive girl that all daughters should be. All of Katherine's violence and shrewishness are seen in comic contrast to the model behavior of her sister, Bianca. But at the end of the play, when Katherine has been tamed, the humor arises because she is now deviating from her own norm; her actions become funny because they are in contrast to her own previous behavior.

In playing the first kind of comedy, both actors must take care to point, or give special emphasis, to those speeches and actions which are to be seen in contrast to each other; while in the second kind of comedy, in the early part of the play the actor must point the qualities of the character from which there is to be a later deviation.

In addition to finding the established norm, the actor must understand the nature and the degree of the deviation. Since this kind of comedy is based upon characterization and since characterization may be developed on several levels—on the physical level, or how one appears; on the level of habit and bent, or how one thinks and feels according to habit and custom; and finally on the level of thought and emotion, or how one consciously makes decisions. The actor may expect to find the comic deviations on all of these levels.

Character Comedy on the Physical Level

Deviation from a norm on the physical level rarely requires the actor to use his techniques for the purpose of pointing that deviation, for it exists in his own physical personality and is thus constantly visible to the audience. If one is too fat or too thin, too tall or too short, one deviates and is therefore comic, provided, of course, that the deviation is presented in a nonserious and comic manner. But the actor who is fortunate enough to have, or to seem to have, physical characteristics which are comic deviations may enhance the audience's enjoyment by devising actions which emphasize those characteristics.

Joe E. Brown and Martha Raye, who have mouths that are too big, may use make-up which will make the mouth appear even larger and then use facial expressions to emphasize the size of the mouth. The actor who has funny legs—too thin, too muscular, or too knobby—and who plays Malvolio can devise action which will call the attention of the audience to his legs, particularly in the cross-gartered scene. The actor playing Cyrano wears a large false nose and plans his performance to emphasize the nose in certain scenes, possibly playing in profile more than he would normally do, so that the outline of the nose may be clearly visible. The actor playing Falstaff, whether he is actually fat or is wearing padding to appear fat, should learn to waddle like a fat man and then use the waddle in places where emphasis will be placed upon it.

This kind of pointing of a comic deviation, if continued throughout an entire performance, is ultimately likely to bore the audience. The actor, therefore, should not use this device in every scene but should search out those places where it will be most effective. It will be advantageous if he can find opportunities to point the deviation in close juxtaposition to a pointing of the norm, so that the two points can be made almost simultaneously. The simplest way of presenting physical deviations in visible relationship to their norms, or even to a contrasting deviation, is to let a fat man stand near to a thin woman or to cast a tall

wife with a short husband.   These methods are largely in the province of
the director or the casting director, but it remains for the actor to be
aware of the opportunities for comedy which are presented to him and
to devise actions which will take advantage of those opportunities.

Much more interesting, however, are the opportunities an actor has
to present both the deviation and the norm within his own performance.
Rostand in *Cyrano de Bergerac* does in a line what the actor must frequently do in his performance, if he is to take full advantage of the comic
possibilities of his tremendous nose.   In telling his friend that he has
fallen in love with the most beautiful woman in Paris, Cyrano says, "My
poor big devil of a nose inhales April," thus putting together the concepts
of the ugly man and the romantic lover.   The speech goes on:

> · and so I follow with my eyes
> Where some boy, with a girl upon his arm,
> Passes a patch of silver——and I feel
> Somehow, I wish I had a woman too,
> Walking with little steps under the moon,
> And holding my arm so, and smiling.   Then
> I dream—and I forget——
> And then I see
> The shadow of my profile on the wall!

To read, "My poor big devil of a nose inhales April," without using
a change in the rate of speaking and in the pitch and quality of the voice
to differentiate "inhales April" from the rest of the speech is to sacrifice
the comic possibilities of the line.   For extra emphasis, the actor might
well put a pause before "inhales April," during which he could assume
a posture which would both suggest the romantic lover and make the
nasal protuberance particularly noticeable.   The same kind of thing
might be done on the next passage, but in reverse order—the actor assuming a romantic attitude through most of the speech but pausing to
change his bodily attitude to one of dejection, again keeping the nose
prominent, just before he says, "And then I see the shadow of my profile
on the wall."   There are several more instances in the remainder of the
scene where this kind of pointing is needed.

George Bernard Shaw in *Candida* explicitly instructs the actress playing Prossy to pantomime both the deviation and the norm in immediate
juxtaposition.   Prossy, throughout the play, should be played as a most
prim and proper and dignified woman.   Just before the third act she
deviates from her norm by having a little too much champagne.   Shaw's
stage direction says:

> *Miss Garnett* [Prossy], *with her smartest hat and jacket on, follows them;
> but though her eyes are brighter than before, she is evidently a prey to*

misgiving. She places herself with her back to her typewriting table, with one hand on it to rest herself, passes the other across her forehead as if she were a little tired and giddy.

Here the one hand on the table to steady herself and maintain her dignity, reminds the audience of the norm, while the other hand indicates her present state.

Shaw's instructions for Prossy's exit are also illuminating. Lexy has offered to take Miss Garnett home, but she declines the offer and "walks straight out." There is a lesson in that instruction for all actors who play drunk scenes. There is nothing funny in the drunk who staggers and falls when the actor playing him is trying to stagger and fall. The comedy can come only from the desire to stand up and walk straight, contrasted with the inability to do so. The actor must point both the norm and the deviation. Unless the audience is constantly reminded of the norm, the deviation itself will become a norm for the character and will lose its comic qualities. Falstaff is funnier if he tries to be dignified or romantic in spite of his fatness, and Malvolio should be proud of his knobby legs.

Character Comedy on the Habit Level

For the most part, the comedy which arises from the habit and bent of a character is too broadly stated to be in need of special pointing. The problem in this kind of comedy is much more one of size and degree than one of devising special emphasis for phrases or inventing little bits of pantomimic action. When an author builds an entire characterization upon a single habit of thought or emotion, sometimes even naming the character after this habit—as was often the case in Restoration drama, where such names as Slander, Sneerwell, and Languish are frequently found—the selection has already been so exclusively made by the playwright, and the emphasis is so persistent, that the actor needs only to decide on the degree of exaggeration which is appropriate to the particular character and production.

In these plays the norms are usually clearly stated in other characters or are assumed to be present in the minds of the audience. Frequently an author will place two characters with strongly contrasting habits of thought and emotion in the same situation, so that the audience may have the fun of watching their different reactions to the same stimuli. In *Arms and the Man*, for example, Raina's romanticism is placed in contrast to Bluntschli's practical and mundane attitude toward war and love. Fundamentally, the comedy rests upon the total characterization, but the actors must take care that, in moments when they are called upon to react to a specific stimulus, their reactions are typical of their characterization and special emphasis is given to either a line or an action which clearly reveals their habits of thought and emotional response.

After the officers have searched the room in which Raina has successfully concealed Bluntschli, she discovers that the pistol was out in plain view all the time; Shaw's stage directions say that when she sees the pistol she utters an irrepressible cry of alarm, while Bluntschli "shies like a frightened horse." Whatever the actors do at this moment will be sufficiently pointed; the only question involves the size of the reactions and the appropriateness of the reactions in terms of the basic characterizations.

Character Comedy at the Level of Thought

When a characterization is developed at the level of conscious thought, so that the character is given the power to choose his actions, his thoughts, and feelings and is not motivated by his already formed habits of thought and feeling, he tends to become a serious character, and therefore noncomic. There are, however, some borderline cases where whether or not a character remains comic depends upon the audience's reaction.

In *Born Yesterday*, the uneducated and unintelligent paramour of the grasping junk dealer begins to read books and begins to think; to the extent that the audience accepts her as a thinking person capable of making decisions, she becomes noncomic; to the extent that the audience regards her first efforts at thinking as a deviation from her established norm, she remains comic; in any case, the junk dealer's reactions to her new capabilities are comic because his norm has been violently upset.

In many other comedies which follow a similar structure, some of the characters clearly change, but change only their habits, and do so under emotional stress and without conscious thought or deliberate choice. Perhaps the largest group of plays in this category are the ones in which the henpecked husband finally asserts himself. In playing such comedies, the actor must point, in the first part of the play, the specific habits from which he is to deviate in the last act. If, for instance, the wife will not allow the husband to smoke and one sign of his assertion of independence is to be the fact that he does smoke, the lines or actions early in the play which reflect his desire to smoke and his fear of doing so must be called to the audience's attention, and later in the play the lines or actions associated with his smoking must also be pointed. Even then, most of the comic effect is likely to derive from the wife's reactions, rather than from those of the husband.

Some actors refer to the pointing of an early action which is to become the basis of a later comic action as "planting" for comic effect. In Act

II, Scene 1, of *The Rivals*, Captain Absolute refuses to accept his father's choice of a wife for him. The father, Sir Anthony Absolute, upbraids him for his defiance of paternal authority, finishing his tirade by saying, "I'll disown you, I'll disinherit you, I'll unget you! and damn me! if ever I call you Jack again." In Act III, Scene 1, the young man has discovered that the girl his father wants to force him to marry is the very girl with whom he is in love, and he resolves to appear in a penitential mood. At first Sir Anthony can scarcely believe his ears, but when he becomes convinced that his son has actually submitted to his will, he says, "Why now you talk sense—absolute sense—I never heard anything more sensible in my life. Confound you! you shall be Jack again." Obviously the humor of the second speech is directly dependent upon the audience's awareness of the first speech.

The actor should also note the parallel structure of the two speeches. The first has a series of three verbs which make a progression, "disown, disinherit and unget," followed by an oath, and then one sentence on the subject of calling his son Jack. The second speech also has a threesome progression, this time on the subject of the son being sensible, followed by an oath, followed by one sentence on the subject of calling him Jack. Since action preceding a line is one of the strongest devices for emphasis and since the two "Jack" lines are in direct contrast to each other, it would seem appropriate if the actor invented two contrasting actions to precede each of the lines. On the first speech he might, for example, stride away from Jack and toward the exit, turning to face Jack, and also the audience, just before he says, "If ever I call you Jack again"; and in the next scene he might stride toward Jack and clasp his hand, or clap him on the shoulder, before he says, "You shall be Jack again." This special emphasis upon a single phrase, particularly when the emphasis is achieved by a careful timing of action with speaking, is a use of technique which many actors refer to as pointing.

Pointing Both the Norm and the Deviation

The most common use of the term *pointing*, however, is in reference to the performance of lines in which both the norm and the deviation from the norm can be expressed in the same short sentence or phrase. The examples so far given have dealt mostly with the establishment of the norm at some time prior to the statement of the deviation; while this requires the use of carefully selected methods of achieving emphasis, it does not require the nice precision that is necessary when both the norm and the deviation must be emphasized in the same sentence, and it is therefore less difficult to do.

Mrs. Malaprop's lines in *The Rivals* include many examples of this

kind of comedy, and this is one reason why the role has come to be accepted as a test of the art of a comedienne.   In Act I, Scene 2, Mrs.
Malaprop lists the elements which she considers essential to the education
of a woman.   Among other things, she says a young lady should be
"instructed in geometry, that she might know something of the contagious countries."   This is a very complex joke because it is composed
of three separate jokes.   First, Mrs. Malaprop is proud of her own learning, and this display of her ignorance is a deviation from the norm repre-
sented by what the audience would usually consider an educated woman;
second, the word "geometry" is seen to be a deviation from the word
"geography," but this does not become obvious until the actress gets to the
word "countries"; third, the word "contagious" is seen to be a deviation
from the word "contiguous," a fact which also becomes obvious when the
audience hears the next word, "countries."

Mrs. Malaprop's pride will, of course, be previously established, but
during this speech, her whole bearing, facial expression, and manner
of speech must be that of a woman who considers herself well bred,
well educated, and generally superior.   The actress must also find
technical devices to give special emphasis to the three key words—
"geometry," "contagious," and "countries"—but to avoid the charge of
overacting, she must select devices that will make the humor obvious without seeming to do so.

Possibly mere vocal stress on the key words, or an increase in volume,
would accomplish the desired result; but the sentence occurs in a speech
which has many other similar abuses of the language, and the entire
characterization of Mrs. Malaprop is based upon the use of "her oracular
tongue, and a nice derangement of epitaphs!"   If the actress playing the
role has no more technical facility than to make the emphasis by a vocal
stress, the entire performance is likely to sound like a steam engine chug-
ging up a steep grade.

Perhaps the next most useful device would be a change of rate, which
can even include a pause directly before the word or phrase which needs
pointing.   It might also be effective for the actress to turn her head or
body so that she faces the audience on the specific word.   Such a turn,
however, must have some motivation other than the actress' desire to
emphasize a word.   Another possibility is to associate the word with
an action, which could be performed either directly on the word or in
the pause which might precede it.

Actors who excel in the playing of comedy learn to achieve emphasis in
a variety of ways, seldom using the same technique on a succession of
comedy lines.   Part of the art of the comedian is to become so technically
skilled that an audience will be unaware of his methods, for part of
the pleasure for an audience is the sense of having caught on to the joke

without being aware that the joke has been pointed; but the greatest possible fault that a comedian can commit is to play a scene with such restraint and subtlety that the audience does not get the joke at all. The goal is to play the scene so that every member of the audience thinks he has been particularly clever to have seen the joke and fails to notice that all the others in the audience are as clever as he.

When the actor decides to use some action as a means of pointing a word or a phrase, he frequently has several alternative sources for that action. First, he may invent a gesture which will remind the audience of that facet of his characterization from which the line to be spoken is a deviation. In the case of Mrs. Malaprop this would be a gesture or facial expression which would show that she considers herself a well-educated, elegant, and proud lady. Second, it may be possible to invent an action which would remind the audience of the expected meaning from which the word to be spoken is a deviation. Third, the invented action may be related to the deviation itself, rather than to the concept from which it deviates.

In Act V, Scene 1, Mrs. Malaprop says, "Come, sir, you're our envoy —lead the way, and we'll precede." This line has been played with the actress pointing in the direction Fag should go and dropping a curtsy to suggest that she really means Fag to go first, so that the word "precede" becomes the deviation. It has also been played with Mrs. Malaprop throwing her cape about her and starting toward the exit directly before the word "precede." Either action is defensible; either will point the comedy of the line; but each gives a pantomimic dramatization of an entirely different concept.

Pointing by Two Characters

Special care must be taken when the joke is cracked by two people. Frequently the word which carries the thought that is the basis for the joke is placed in the speech of one character while the reversal that makes the joke is in the following speech of another character. The same principle of pointing the words which carry the comic thought must be followed, but one actor must point one word for the sake of the other actor, who must crack the joke.

Often comedy which is played between two or more persons is based upon the reaction of one character to what has been said or done by another character. When this kind of comedy is based solely on physical action, it is frequently referred to as "custard pie" comedy, the humor lying in some injurious, or at least unpleasant, action that is done to one character by another character. The actor should remember that throwing a custard pie is not funny; it is being hit by a custard pie which is comic. In other words, the reaction to the action is the source of the comedy, rather than the action itself.

There are also verbal custard pies, jokes in which what is said by one character becomes an unpleasant surprise and shock to another character. Here again, it is the reaction which is comic, not the speech itself. In Act II, Scene 1, of *The Rivals*, Sir Anthony tells his son that plans have been made for the son to have an independent income and large estates. Naturally Captain Absolute is pleased at this prospect, and there is a sequence of several lines in which the actor can build a progression of pleasure and enthusiasm:

> CAPT. ABSOLUTE: Let my future life, sir, speak my gratitude; I cannot express the sense I have of your munificence.—Yet, sir, I presume you would not wish me to quit the army?
> SIR ANTHONY: Oh, that shall be as your wife chooses.
> CAPT. ABSOLUTE: My wife, sir!

The joke lies in the son's surprise and shock that his promised wealth and independence includes having a wife. It is quite possible that an audience will laugh when Sir Anthony first mentions a wife, but if so, it will be because the son's reaction is anticipated.

EXERCISES

1. Religious passages from *Hamlet*.

   Assuming that the actor playing Hamlet believes that it is essential to present Hamlet as a man of deep religious convictions, in order to make clear his failure to kill the King when he comes upon him praying, carefully study the first two acts and the first three scenes of Act III to discover every line which can be construed to show this facet of Hamlet's character.

   a. Select the lines which clearly relate to this concept of character.

   b. Assuming that Hamlet wears a crucifix, select those lines which can be made to have a religious connotation if Hamlet touches the crucifix as he says the lines.

   c. Assume that Hamlet uses the handle of his sword as a sign of the cross, look for lines, especially in Scenes 4 and 5 of Act I, where this action may be used to indicate Hamlet's convictions. *Example:* On Hamlet's last line in Scene 4, "I say, away!—Go on, I'll follow thee," let Hamlet raise the sword as the sign of the cross in the pause before "go on," and exit, holding the sword as a guard between him and the Ghost.

   d. Study the speeches of the Ghost in Scene 5 and work out devices for bringing special emphasis to those lines in which he explains that a man who is killed without having a chance to confess his sins is doomed to expiate those sins. Rehearse the sequence between Hamlet and the Ghost in this scene.

2. Sequence from *A Doll's House*,[1] Act III.

HELMER: Can you also make clear to me how I have forfeited your love?
NORA: Yes, I can. It was this evening, when the miracle did not happen; for then I saw you were not the man I had imagined.

> *a.* Read Nora's line, using vocal techniques for emphasis, so that the words "miracle" and "man" are pointed.
> *b.* Read the line so that the word "not" is pointed both times it occurs.
> *c.* Read the line so that the words "happen" and "imagined" are pointed.

HELMER: Explain yourself more clearly; I don't understand.
NORA: I have waited so patiently all these eight years; for of course I saw clearly enough that miracles don't happen every day. When this crushing blow threatened me, I said to myself so confidently, "Now comes the miracle!" When Krogstad's letter lay in the box, it never for a moment occurred to me that you would think of submitting to that man's conditions. I was convinced that you would say to him, "Make it known to all the world"; and then—
HELMER: Well? When I had given my own wife's name up to disgrace and shame—?
NORA: Then I firmly believed that you would come forward, take everything upon yourself, and say, "I am the guilty one."
HELMER: Nora——!
NORA: You mean I would never have accepted such a sacrifice? No, certainly not! But what would my assertions have been worth in opposition to yours?—That was the miracle that I hoped for and dreaded.

> *d.* Examine each of Nora's sentences carefully and decide which words might have special pointing by using vocal techniques.
> *e.* Select a different set of words to be pointed and note the changes that might result in Nora's character and emotions. *Example:* In the sentence, "I have waited so patiently all these eight years," it is possible to give special stress to "waited," "so," and "patiently," "all," and "eight." Each change of vocal emphasis will make a slight change in the thought and feeling of Nora.
> NOTE: A role has not been completely studied until the implications of every minute shift in emphasis have been considered. One hopes that the readings instinctively arrived at in rehearsals will be the right readings, but the final decision should not be left to either accident or chance.
> *f.* Try to invent small hand gestures and changes of facial expression which

1 Copyright by Charles Scribner's Sons.

could be used for pointing selected words in order to relieve the monotony of constantly using vocal techniques.

NOTE: This sequence is fundamentally one single continuous thought. Be careful that the pointing of individual words does not destroy the continuity of the sequence.

3. Sequence from *Hamlet*, Act V, Scene 2.

HAMLET: Give us the foils; come on.
LAERTES: Come; one for me.
HAMLET: I'll be your foil, Laertes: in mine ignorance
              Your skill shall, like a star i' th' darkest night,
              Stick fiery off indeed.
LAERTES: You mock me, sir.
HAMLET: No, by this hand.
OSRIC: Give them the foils, young Osric.—Cousin Hamlet,
              You know the wager?
HAMLET: Very well, my lord;
              Your Grace hath laid the odds o' th' weaker side.
KING: I do not fear it: I have seen you both;
              But since he is better'd, we have therefore odds.
LAERTES: This is too heavy; let me see another.
HAMLET: This likes me well. These foils have all a length?
KING: Ay, my good lord.
(*They prepare to play.*)

a. Invent the actions which will make it clear that Laertes is searching for the poisoned foil, that the first he selects is not the right one, and that he finally gets the right one.

b. If it seems desirable to do so, invent the actions to show that Hamlet might discover the plot.

c. If it seems desirable to do so, invent the actions which would show the King's concern about the choosing of the foils. The King's relief at the outcome of the choosing might also be shown.

d. Perform the scene so that all the significant invented actions are carefully pointed to attract the attention of the audience.

NOTE: The competitive nature of two actions being performed simultaneously will make it necessary for each separate action to be performed separately, not simultaneously with another action.

KING: Set me the stoops of wine upon that table.—
              If Hamlet give the first or second hit,
              Or quit in answer of the third exchange,
              Let all the battlements their ordnance fire:
              The King shall drink to Hamlet's better breath:

And in the cup an union shall he throw,
Richer than that which four successive kings
In Denmark's crown have worn.   Give me the cups;
And let the kettle to the trumpet speak,
The trumpet to the cannoneer without,
The cannons to the heavens, the heavens to earth,
"Now the King drinks to Hamlet!"—Come, begin;—
And you, the judges, bear a wary eye.

HAMLET: Come on, sir.

LAERTES: Come, my lord.   (*They play.*)

HAMLET: One.

LAERTES: No.

HAMLET: Judgement.

OSRIC: A hit, a very palpable hit.

LAERTES: Well:—again.

KING: Stay; give me drink.   Hamlet, this pearl is thine;
        Here's to thy health.—Give him the cup.

(*Trumpets sound: and cannon shot off within.*)

HAMLET: I'll play this bout first; set it by a while.

e. Invent the actions which will make it clear to the audience that the King
    has poisoned Hamlet's cup.

f. If it seems desirable, invent the actions to show Laertes' concern about
    the matter.

g. Invent the actions which will make it clear that the poisoned cup is
    placed where the Queen may pick it up and that this is the cup which she
    eventually does pick up.

h. Perform the sequence so that each separate action is performed separately
    and is pointed.

    NOTE: If the actors rehearsing the scene do not know how to duel, they
    may indicate the actions for rehearsal purposes, but they had better learn
    how to duel before the actual performance.

HAMLET: Come.—Another hit; what say you?   (*They play.*)

LAERTES: A touch, a touch, I do confess.

KING: Our son shall win.

QUEEN: He's fat, and scant of breath.—
        Here Hamlet, take my napkin, rub thy brows:
        The Queen carouses to thy fortune, Hamlet.

HAMLET: Good Madam,—

KING: Gertrude, do not drink.

QUEEN: I will, my lord: I pray you, pardon me.

KING: (*Aside.*)   It is the poison'd cup! it is too late.

i. Invent the actions which will make it clear that the Queen is drinking from the poisoned cup.

NOTE: Apparently Shakespeare saw the possibilities of confusion and so wrote in the melodramatic aside for the King, which sounds like a speech which would be more appropriate in a cheap nineteenth-century melodrama.

j. Invent the actions which show the King's concern prior to his speeches on the subject.

k. If it seems desirable, invent the actions which show Laertes' concern.

l. It might be possible to invent actions which would show that, since Laertes has been hit twice, it is feared that Hamlet will win the duel and that it will be necessary to resort to the poison. These actions could be performed by either Laertes or the King, or by both.

m. Rehearse the scene so that all of the necessary actions are performed separately and clearly.

HAMLET: I dare not drink, Madam; by and by.

QUEEN: Come, let me wipe thy face.

LAERTES: My lord, I'll hit him now.

KING: I do not think't.

LAERTES: (*Aside.*) And yet it is almost against my conscience.

n. If it seems desirable, the Queen might offer the cup again to Hamlet, after she has drunk.

o. Laertes and the King may plot together on these two lines. Care must be taken that any action showing the effects of the poison on the Queen does not detract from other essential actions.

HAMLET: Come, for the third, Laertes. You but dally:
            I pray you, pass with your best violence.
            I am afeard you make a wanton of me.

LAERTES: Say you so? come on. (*They play.*)

OSRIC: Nothing, neither way.

LAERTES: Have at you now.

(*Laertes wounds Hamlet; then, in scuffling they change rapiers, and Hamlet wounds Laertes.*)

p. Work out the action to show that Hamlet is wounded.

q. Work out the action of dropping the swords.

r. Work out the action of Hamlet picking up Laertes' sword.

s. Work out the action of wounding Laertes.

NOTE: Here is where all the actors of the company must take care that each action and its import are clearly presented to the audience. Remember that the Queen took poison only a few lines before these actions and that after two more lines she will fall. The appropriate action for

the Queen must be continued, but it must not blur the wounding of
Hamlet and Laertes.

KING: Part them! they are incensed.
HAMLET: Nay, come again.
(*The Queen falls.*)
OSRIC: Look to the Queen there, ho!
HORATIO: They bleed on both sides.—How is it, my lord?
OSRIC: How is 't, Laertes?

t. All through these sequences, the reactions, and therefore the actions of
the King, have potential dramatic value. If they are to be included in
the scene, they must be pointed for the audience.

u. The three lines, directed first to the Queen, then to Hamlet, and then
to Laertes, demand that each character, in the moment that the attention
of the audience has been directed to him, use this opportunity to perform
an action that will reveal his thoughts and feelings.

LAERTES: Why, as a woodcock to mine own springe, Osric;
I am justly kill'd with mine own treachery.
HAMLET: How does the Queen?
KING: She swoons to see them bleed.
QUEEN: No, no, the drink, the drink,—O my dear Hamlet!—
The drink, the drink: I am poison'd. (*Dies.*)

NOTE: This entire scene is one of the most difficult to play in all Shakespeare
because it is so poorly and scantly written, leaving almost everything to the
invention of the actors.

4. Reexamine the John of Gaunt speech for pointing words of special poetic
force and vigor and apply vocal techniques to give emphasis to these words.

5 Reexamine Juliet's potion scene for the same purpose.

6. Sequence from *High Tor*,[2] Act III.

The Indian speaks:

> Why, when the race is gone, or looks aside
> only a little while, the white stone darkens,
> the wounds close, and the roofs fall, and the walls
> give way to rains. Nothing is made by men
> but makes, in the end, good ruins.

a. Use vocal techniques to give emphasis to "white stone," "wounds,"
"roofs," and "walls."

b. Use vocal techniques to give special emphasis to "darkens," "close,"
"fall," and "give way to rains."

[2] Copyright by Anderson House.

7. Sequence from *Romeo and Juliet*, Act II, Scene 2.

Rehearse the first fifty lines of the balcony scene, taking care to select those words which have color and interest, or which carry the most meaning; use vocal techniques to give a slight emphasis to these words.

NOTE: It is dangerous to select more than two or three words in a single line, for too many stresses destroy the effect of emphasis and create a monotonous pattern.

8. Sequence from *Saturday's Children*,[3] Act I.

Rims has come for a date with Bobby. He's told her of his plans to go to South America. On the table are the shorthand notes that Bobby's sister has told her to follow if she wants to make Rims propose. Bobby has just answered the phone and turned down a date with Fred, but the phone call was actually from Bobby's sister and was a prearranged part of the plot.

RIMS: You're a brick, Bobby. Are you sure you didn't want to go?

BOBBY: If I'd wanted to—I would have. (*There is a pause.*)

RIMS: I've been wanting to talk to you.

BOBBY: What about, Rims?

RIMS: Do you think it's a good thing—me going to South America?

BOBBY: It's an awfully good opening.

RIMS: Well, what I mean is, don't you think it's a good thing for a young fellow to see the world a little when he gets a chance—Just so he can kind of make up his mind what he wants to do?

BOBBY: Surely.

RIMS: That's why I'm going, really. Oh, I'm not sure it's any great shakes of an opening, but I never have been much of anywhere and it's a chance—well, it's a kind of adventure, don't you see?

BOBBY: Surely.

RIMS: That's why I'm going.

BOBBY: Yes (*A pause.*)

RIMS: And, kid—

BOBBY: Yes?

RIMS: (*Placing a hand on her arm*) You certainly have been wonderful to me.

BOBBY: We did have a good Spring together, didn't we?

RIMS: You were certainly marvellous. (*Bobby looks at him, and then turns away.*)

BOBBY: Well, it's Summer now.

RIMS: Yep, But that's no reason you shouldn't give me a kiss, is it?

[3] Copyright by Anderson House.

Bobby: I guess not. (*They kiss.*) Maybe you'd better run along, Rims.

Rims: Why so, sweetie? The night's young.

Bobby: Well—(*She looks down and her eye falls on Florrie's notebook. She looks at it fascinated. There is a pause.*)

Rims: (*Lightly*) What you studying, Bobby?

Bobby: Nothing. Only—oh, I'm so tired of everything, Rims, and I'm afraid I'm not very good company.

Rims: Oh, yes, you are.

Bobby: Rims, dear—

Rims: Yes.

Bobby: (*She looks back at book*) Rims, sometimes you're the only person in the world I can talk to. Sometimes I can't bear to be with anybody else.

Rims: Gee, kid.

Bobby: Rims, don't you ever get tired of poor me, ever?

Rims: Never, I should say not.

Bobby: You're such a darling.

Rims: Well, I wouldn't say that.

Bobby: But you are, (*She turns and glances at the notebook*) and it's going to be awfully hard. (*A pause.*)

Rims: What is, sweetheart?

Bobby: Marrying somebody else.

Rims: You getting married? (*His hand drops from her shoulder.*)

Bobby: Oh, Rims, a girl's got to get married sometime you know, while she's got chances.

Rims: I suppose you get chances all right.

Bobby: Yes.

Rims: Do they come fast?

Bobby: I've had two—every other week, for two weeks.

Rims: Say, look here, you don't mean you're making up your mind to marry somebody in particular?

Bobby: Well, Fred wants me to marry him, and he's awfully in love with me, and I don't want to go on working forever.

Rims: I see. Yeah, I see. I didn't know you felt that way.

Bobby: (*Breaking away*) Well, I don't, really. I was just—I was just joking. You'd better go, dear. I wouldn't marry anybody. I wouldn't marry —anybody. Not even you.

Rims: You wouldn't?

Bobby: No, I wouldn't!

Rims: Oh, yes, you will. I mean—

Bobby: Do you want me to?

Rims: Sweetheart—I don't want anything else. (*They kiss.*)

Bobby: (*Breaking away and crying on his shoulder*) But you're—you're going to South America—

RIMS: (*Still holding her*) South America can go to the devil—! Somebody else can go to South America!

   a. Play the scene as written. The author has indicated action to remind the audience when Bobby is following her sister's plan.

   b. Devise special vocal emphasis for the lines quoted from the previous scene.
     NOTE: The author has asked that the pointing be done by action, and the extra vocal emphasis will make the scene seem overplayed.

9. Sequence from *Cyrano de Bergerac*,[4] Act I.

Cyrano has just confessed to his friend Le Bret that he is in love with Roxane.

LE BRET: And why not? If you love her, tell her so!
        You have covered yourself with glory in her eyes
        This very day.
CYRANO: My old friend—look at me,
        And tell me how much hope remains for me
        With its protuberance! Oh, I have no more
        Illusions! Now and then—bah! I may grow
        Tender, walking alone in the blue cool
        Of evening, through some garden fresh with flowers
        After the benediction of the rain;
        My poor big devil of a nose inhales
        April . . . and so I follow with my eyes
        Where some boy, with a girl upon his arm,
        Passes a patch of silver . . . and I feel
        Somehow, I wish I had a woman too,
        Walking with little steps under the moon,
        And holding my arm so, and smiling. Then
        I dream—and I forget . . .
                     And then I see
        The shadow of my profile on the wall!
LE BRET: My friend!
CYRANO: My friend, I have my bitter days,
        Knowing myself so ugly, so alone.
        Sometimes—
LE BRET: You weep?
CYRANO: (*Quickly*) Oh, not that ever! No,
        That would be too grotesque—tears trickling down
        All the long way along this nose of mine?
        I will not so profane the dignity
        Of sorrow. Never any tears for me!
        Why, there is nothing more sublime than tears,

[4] Copyright Henry Holt and Company, Inc.

Nothing!—Shall I make them ridiculous
In my poor person?
LE BRET: Love's no more than chance!
CYRANO: (*Shakes his head.*)
No. I love Cleopatra; do I appear
Caesar? I adore Beatrice; have I
The look of Dante?

a. Find the places where a shift from a romantic physical attitude to a comic physical attitude will be most effective. Remember that the nose will appear most grotesque and comical when seen in profile.

b. When Cyrano mentions Caesar and Dante in the last speech, the actor might look for comic physical attitudes that use more than the nose.

10. Sequence from *The Rivals*, Act II, Scene 1.
Rehearse the scene between Captain Absolute and Sir Anthony.

a. Examine the scene carefully to discover all those places where Sir Anthony's protestations of calmness may be effectively placed in juxtaposition to his demonstrations of anger.

b. Search out the instances in which the individual joke depends upon a sequence which ends in an unexpected reversal, or a ridiculous exaggeration, and devise techniques which will point the key words of the sequence.

c. Decide the places where the comedy rests upon the reactions of the son to the father or of the father to the son. Decide how those reactions are to be shown and allow time and room for the reactions to be incorporated into the complete performance.

d. Select the vocal and physical techniques which are necessary and appropriate for the development of each progression, taking care that the same techniques are not used too frequently and too continuously. The scene can be sustained and built to a climax only by using a variety of techniques in a variety of combinations.

11. Sequence from *The Rivals*, Act I, Scene 2.
Rehearse Mrs. Malaprop's definition of an education.

a. Select the key words upon which each joke rests.

b. Wherever possible, invent actions which will help to make the audience think of the intended word.

c. Wherever possible, invent actions which will restate Mrs. Malaprop's pride in her learning at those moments when she is about to demonstrate her ignorance.

d. Select the necessary and appropriate techniques to point each of the key words and also point Mrs. Malaprop's false pride.

Chapter 10. THE INVENTION OF ACTIONS

F UNDAMENTALLY THERE are three sources from which the actor may derive the physical actions which give a scene its visible and outward form and which, having been invented, must be motivated by the actor so that they may be performed as though they were involuntary and inevitable: first, the plot; second, the mood and atmosphere of the scene; and third, the character.

Plot Actions

The major plot actions are obvious, and they are clearly indicated in the script: Brutus stabs Caesar; Hamlet kills Polonius; Juliet drinks the potion. Such actions the actor must perform of necessity, but it remains for him to choose a manner of performing them which will be appropriate to the character he is playing. In the plays of Ibsen, and of many other playwrights, however, most of the action of the plot is antecedent action—that is, action which has been performed before the play begins and which is revealed to the audience only through the dialogue. The Greeks avoided all violent action in their plays and contrived to have all the scenes of violence performed off stage, and then revealed to the audience by means of a tableau or a speech delivered by a messenger.

But even in plays in which most of the action either has happened before the play begins or happens off stage, there is a constantly changing relationship between the characters: they fall in love with each other, or they come to hate each other; they learn things about each other, and come to understand each other to a greater or lesser degree; at the highest level of drama they make self-discoveries and learn to know themselves. But through all of this, whatever the plot development, the main purpose of drama is to enable the audience to get to know and understand the characters and their interrelationships.

Plot Action from Antecedent Events

In the scene between Nora and Mrs. Linden in the first act of *A Doll's House*, which was used as an exercise for Chapter 9, Nora reveals to Mrs.

Linden how the money was obtained. This is no news to Nora, since it has been her secret; although it is news to Mrs. Linden, the play is not concerned with the relationship between Mrs. Linden and Nora, and the audience is not expected to be particularly interested in Mrs. Linden's reactions. She serves merely as a person to whom Nora can relate the antecedent action, so that the audience will have an opportunity to deduce from her manner of relating the past events, and from the events themselves, that Nora is something more than a silly, attractive woman whose sole purposes are to amuse and entertain her husband and to be the mother of his children. In this way the author has cleverly foreshadowed the fact that, sooner or later, the husband will also find out about her actions and that his discovery will cause a conflict of opinions, thoughts, and emotions, which will, in turn, lead to the major climax of the play.

If the actress chooses to derive the action for this scene from the plot source, the action would be a shift from physical attitudes which would be appropriate for a silly, frivolous girl to those suitable for a responsible and mature woman. Ibsen, himself, has implied that this is what he had in mind, for at the beginning of the scene he includes such stage directions as "smiling" and "tossing her head," and at the end of the scene he instructs the actress to speak the lines "thoughtfully." The degree of the change and the duration of the change must be left to the taste and discretion of the actress and the director; the scene comes early in the first act, and this is one of the earliest hints that there is more to the character of Nora than meets the eye.

Plot Action from Interaction of Characters

There is a similar sequence, in which one character relates past events to another, in Act I, Scene 2, of *Julius Caesar*, but in this scene the audience should be much more interested in the relationship between the narrator and listener than in the events described. Caesar and his train have just passed in procession, having been stopped by the Soothsayer. Brutus and Cassius have stayed behind, and Cassius has begun to sow the seeds of the thought that Caesar must be deposed for the good of Rome. From time to time the scene is interrupted by the shouting of the people, and it is learned later that the shouting was for Caesar when he refused the crown proffered by Antony. To convince Brutus that Caesar is but an ordinary man, Cassius relates how Caesar, when he was swimming in the Tiber, became tired and had to call for help, and how Caesar was seized with a fever in Spain and called for a drink "as a sick girl."

In an experimental motion picture of *Julius Caesar*, which was made at Northwestern University, the screen showed the actual swimming episode as Cassius related it—the two men leaping into the river, swimming against the current, Caesar getting tired and being forced to call for help, and Cassius coming to his aid and helping him to the shore.   In this instance the motion picture derived its action directly from the related events, but the attention of the audience should not be focused on the events themselves, but rather on the reaction of Brutus to hearing about the events.

Cassius' objective in the scene is to influence Brutus against Caesar, and much of the physical action of the scene should be derived from Cassius' efforts.   He is tempting Brutus, insinuating thoughts into Brutus' mind. He might well come behind Brutus and whisper into his ear, while Brutus watches what is happening off stage; he might come between Brutus and the off-stage events, trying to interpret those events for Brutus; certainly, if Brutus moved away from him, as well he might, Cassius would follow him.   Brutus, however, is a reserved man and an honorable man; his reactions, to be in character, must be slight, but they must be made obvious to an audience.   The script permits Brutus to show more concern about the shouting of the populace than about the words of Cassius.

This scene differs from the scene in *A Doll's House* in that the character change which makes the plot occurs in the person listening to the telling of the off-stage action.   Nora, on the other hand, both narrates the events and reveals to the audience the other side of her character. The two scenes are also different in that Brutus is actually having thoughts that are new to him, while any change in Nora's character has occurred before the play begins.

Plot Action from Character Reaction to an Event

Another scene which involves similar problems is the meeting of Macbeth and Banquo with the three witches.   When the witches hail Macbeth as Thane of Glamis, Thane of Cawdor, and King hereafter, it is clear that the audience's interest in the scene lies in Macbeth's reactions. Shakespeare takes no chances that the actor playing Macbeth will give too subtle a performance to make his reaction obvious, for he has Banquo say:

> Good sir, why do you start, and seem to fear
> Things that do sound so fair?—I' th' name of truth,
> Are ye fantastical, or that indeed
> Which outwardly ye shew?

He goes on to notice that Macbeth "seems rapt withal."

In all three of these scenes it is evident that the dramatic interest is in the revelation of a character change; in Nora's case it is a character change which has previously taken place, but is being revealed to the audience for the first time; in Brutus' case it is a character change which begins to occur as he listens to the retelling of the incidents; in Macbeth's case it is a sudden, and, according to Shakespeare, an obvious change, which happens when he is directly and immediately confronted with the event itself. In all three instances the character change occurs early in the play and later becomes the motivation for the major plot action, and in each case the actor must find pantomimic actions—movements, physical attitudes, gestures, and facial expressions—which will clearly demonstrate to the audience what that character change is and the amount and the degree of the change. If the actor asks himself, "What should interest an audience in this scene?" and invents actions to dramatize his answer to that question, he will not go very far wrong.

Plot Action Derived from the Immediate Episode

In many instances the action which derives from plot is clearly indicated. For instance, at the end of Act I of *Arms and The Man*, Bluntschli is left alone and cautioned that it is dangerous for him to fall asleep; but he is exhausted, and so he falls asleep. Shaw is, as usual, specific in his directions: Bluntschli nods; his eyes close; Raina forces him to stand; but his eyes close again; he yawns; he stumbles to the bed; he sits on the bed; and finally he lies on the bed and is asleep. If the actor chooses to invent any actions which are not suggested by Shaw, they must be actions which are appropriate to a man falling asleep.

The difference between character action and plot action can be easily illustrated by this scene, for if any other character in the play—Sergius, Major Petkoff, or Nicola, for example—also had a scene in which he was to fall asleep, he would have to go through the same pattern of nodding, closing his eyes, and yawning, but each of these characters would do so in a different manner. The variations in the manner of yawning would be part of the characterization, while the yawning itself would be part of the plot.

In the second act of the same play there is a love scene between Sergius and Louka. A little study of the play reveals that this is a scene in which Sergius makes love to Louka, not a scene in which he falls in love with her. Again there are a series of gestures which suggest the relationship between the two characters: he takes her arm as she serves him coffee; he takes her hand and draws her away from the table; he puts his arm around her; they move to a more secluded part of the scene; again he puts his arm around her; and finally he tries to kiss her. All of these actions, like the falling-asleep actions for the Bluntschli scene, are arranged in a natural and logical sequence. Since they are a necessary part of the scene, the actor must incorporate them into the performance, sometimes using an action to give special emphasis to a line, sometimes using a line to give special emphasis to an action.

There are hundreds of love scenes which, regardless of the time, the period, the characters, or the dialogue, must be played with this same pattern of action: first a look, then a simple and innocent bodily contact, then some hand holding, then an embrace, and finally a kiss. The minute an actor finds a love scene in his part he knows that these actions will probably be available to him in playing the scene. If the lady avoids him by moving about the room, then he will follow, and thus larger movements will be built into the scene. If the scene begins with the actors seated at opposite ends of the sofa, then the distance between must somehow be traveled (and to a shy person the length of a sofa may seem a mile); there will then be the arm dropped carelessly on the back of the sofa and the first casual contact, and so the scene will progress as before to the embrace and the kiss.

There are endless variations in love scenes, but always the actors may be sure that the audience, from its own experience and observation of life, is consciously or unconsciously aware of the basic pattern of action and will note any variations. One of the most poignant and beautiful love scenes in drama occurs in the last act of *The Cherry Orchard*, when Varya and Lopakhin meet for the last time. The powerful appeal of the scene rests on the fact that the characters do not take even the first step of the expected pattern of action.

In previous scenes Varya has admitted that she likes Lopakhin and would be glad if he proposed, and he has made it known that he is attracted to her. The estate has been sold and the packing is in progress; in a few moments Varya will leave forever, so that the love scene must occur now or never. Madame Ranevsky leaves Lopakhin alone as she goes to call Varya; feminine giggles and whispering are heard off stage; then Varya enters; the other characters in the play, the two principals, and the audience all know that now is the moment for the love scene.

Varya explains her entrance by saying that she is looking for something; there are three quick lines, and then the author indicates a pause, and in the pause the actors must do something which will indicate that Lopakhin knows it is the moment to speak and that Varya hopes he will speak. But he does not speak of love; he asks a meaningless question about her journey. There are four lines about where each is going; then the author indicates another pause, during which the action—the facial expression, or the gesture, or the slight movement—must suggest that again the moment has come. But after the pause, Lopakhin remarks, "Well, so life in this house is over now," a heartless, cold statement of fact, the bitter truth of which he himself scarcely recognizes; but Varya knows, and the audience knows.

There follow five more lines of meaningless chatter about the packing, about the journey, and about the weather. When Lopakhin remarks that there were "three degrees of frost," Varya replies, "Were there? I didn't look," and again the author asks for a pause; if Lopakhin could bring himself to speak of love or marriage, or if that first accidental physical contact could be established, the play would end differently. Varya gives him one more chance; she says, "Besides, the thermometer's broken," and there is another pause. Then someone calls off stage, and the scene is over, Lopakhin never having said or done what he might have said and done. Varya sits on the floor by her unfinished packing and sobs quietly.

Perhaps it seems farfetched to discuss this scene in terms of the expected pattern of action for a love scene when its dramatic power comes from avoiding that pattern. How far the actors will wish to go in indicating the pattern is a matter of taste. The scene might be contrived so that at the first pause the "lovers" would be about 10 feet apart; then Varya, perhaps coming around to the other side of the trunk, might be within 2 or 3 feet at the second pause; only a hand reached out would bring the happy ending; then Lopakhin might move away to the window so that there would be a whole room and a whole world between them during the last pauses.

The actors might prefer to play the scene so that they begin close together and, as the scene progresses, move farther and farther apart, or they might choose to begin apart and come closer and closer together. Either of these action patterns could be justified. The important point for the actor to understand is that the changing human relationship can easily motivate actions, and these actions must be incorporated into the performance and made meaningful to the audience.

Dean's Theory of "Picturization"

Alexander Dean, in his excellent book *The Fundamentals of Play Directing*, clearly states the concept that much of the action of any scene should be based on the plot. It is his theory that the stage picture should tell the story of what is happening in the scene as clearly as the dialogue. As the plot progresses, the pictures change, and the movements from one picture to the next provide the action of the scene. Quite properly, he considers the planning of movements to be the function of the director, but it is helpful for the actors to understand the significance of the actions assigned to them and for the director to include meaningful actions suggested by the actors.

In one performance of *Boris Godunov*, as the dying Boris, portrayed by Ezio Pinza, sat on his throne, which was in the center of the stage,

Prince Shuisky, portrayed by De Paolis, crept onto the platform beside and a little behind the throne; when Boris toppled forward off the throne, the off-stage chorus sang, and Shuisky placed his hand upon the throne. The story had been dynamically told: it was Shuisky who had driven Boris mad and who would seize the power of the throne.

In another performance of the opera, in which Rossi-Lemeni sang Boris, the throne was higher and at the side of the stage, and many members of the chorus were on stage. When Boris fell from the throne it was a tremendous fall, down five or six steps, and the chorus immediately rushed to surround the prostrate body. De Paolis was again singing Shuisky, but whether or not he again placed his hand upon the throne, the audience will never know, because all eyes were on the figure of Boris in the center of the stage and on the mass movement of the chorus. The director in both instances was using storytelling action, but he was telling a slightly different story.

Action in Contradiction to the Speeches

It has been assumed that whenever the actor or the director invents actions, those actions are intended to convey the identical meaning expressed by the lines and to demonstrate the same emotion and the same degree of emotion as the spoken dialogue. But this is not always so. Frequently the actor interprets his role in such a way that he intends to express a thought or an emotion which is entirely different from the one indicated by the literal meaning of the lines. This might be true, for example, of the actor who plays Caesar. As stated in the first chapter, Caesar's fear or lack of fear, his cowardice or his bravery, will depend upon the actor's interpretation of the role. Almost all of Caesar's speeches have to do with the subject of fear, and he says unequivocally that he is not afraid; yet it is possible to play Caesar as a fearful man.

In the first act of *Candida*, Marchbanks, the young idealistic poet, argues with Morell, the successful preacher, contending that Morell is unworthy of being Candida's husband. Shaw instructs Marchbanks to show physical fear through such directions as, "Shrinking back against the sofa," and, "He cowers down on the sofa," but Marchbanks' words are brave. In a moment he explains his behavior:

> You think because I shrink from being brutally handled—because (*with tears in his voice*) I can do nothing but cry with rage when I am met with violence—because I can't lift a heavy trunk down from the top of a cab like you—because I can't fight you for your wife as a navvy would: all that makes you think that I'm afraid of you. But you're wrong.

Shaw, of course, is differentiating between physical fear and intellectual courage; the actions belie the words, and the words deny the actions.

Action with Indefinite Meaning

There are many instances in which it is clearly the intention of the author, and therefore it should also be the intention of the actors, to have the dialogue spoken in such a way that other characters in the play, and even the audience, are not sure of the meaning of the lines. In many of the plays of Pirandello, for example, there must be several possible interpretations of the characters' actions, so that the audience may be left to make its own decision concerning the truth about the characters. In both *Amphytrion* and *The Guardsman*, the actress portraying the wife must play the role in such a way that the audience is never quite sure whether or not the character who is presumably her husband is really her husband; in *Amphytrion*, he may actually be a god, and in *The Guardsman*, he may be an actor impersonating her husband.

Hundreds of mystery plays demand that the villain give no sign of his villainy while all the innocent people are busy acting in such a way that they will be suspected. At the opening of *The Thirteenth Chair*, the first-nighters gathered in the lobby during the intermissions to discuss the clues of the mystery and advance their own theories as to which of the characters in the play was the culprit. One of the audience, who was wise to the ways of theatrical producers and who was familiar with the habits of certain actors, said that he was certain the character being played by George Graham was the murderer. When questioned about his reasons, he said that Mr. Graham always wore a hair piece when he was playing a good person, but not when he played a villain, and that the hair piece was missing in this performance; then he added, "Besides, no producer would ever pay Graham his salary unless he had a big, emotional confession speech in the last act."

Action That Confirms, Denies, or Is Indefinite

At the end of the first act of *Hamlet*, just after Hamlet has talked with the Ghost, Horatio and Marcellus are sworn to secrecy regarding Hamlet's future behavior. Hamlet makes them pledge that they will make no comment on his actions,

> How strange or odd soe'er I bear myself,—
> As I, perchance, hereafter shall think meet
> To put an antic disposition on. . . .

In the very next scene Ophelia reports that Hamlet is behaving very strangely, that he came to her room,

> with his doublet all unbrac'd;
> No hat upon his head; his stockings foul'd,
> Ungarter'd, and down-gyved to his ancle;
> Pale as his shirt; his knees knocking each other.

She graphically describes his actions:

> He took me by the wrist, and held me hard;
> Then goes he to the length of all his arm,
> And, with his other hand thus o'er his brow,

(One wonders the exact gesture she demonstrates as she describes this.)

> He falls to such perusal of my face,
> As he would draw it. Long stay'd he so:
> At last,—a little shaking of my arm,
> And thrice his head thus waving up and down,—

(Again the specific movement of the head must be demonstrated.)

> He rais'd a sigh so piteous and profound,
> That it did seem to shatter all his bulk,
> And end his being. That done, he lets me go,
> And, with his head over his shoulder turn'd,
> He seem'd to find his way without his eyes;
> For out o' doors he went without their help,
> And to the last, bended their light on me.

There is no scene in the play in which Hamlet actually wears a costume such as she describes; neither is there any scene in the play in which Hamlet necessarily acts in this manner. When John Barrymore played Hamlet, however, he borrowed the actions described by Ophelia and used them in his scene with Ophelia in Act III, Scene 1; after saying, "I say, we will have no more marriages: those that are married already, all but one, shall live; the rest shall keep as they are," he crossed to Ophelia, took her wrist as she related, held her at arm's length and studied her face; at the moment of the sigh, he said, "To a nunnery, go," and then made his exit across the stage, looking behind as he went. Such actions give Ophelia ample motivation to say, "O, what a noble mind is here o'erthrown!"

The problem for any actor playing Hamlet is to decide how mad he should seem, and in which scenes. Ophelia thinks him mad, as do Polonius, Rosencrantz, and Guildenstern. Should those in the audience also think him mad? Or should they think that he is only feigning madness, as Hamlet has suggested he might do? Is the madness real in some scenes and put on in others? Are there times when both the characters in the play and the audience should not be certain?

However the actor decides he wishes to play Hamlet, or any other role, he must be skilled enough to deliver any line or sequence of lines in such a way that the audience will understand that he means what he says, or that he doesn't mean what he says, or that there is doubt about his meaning. If it were not possible to alter the interpretation of lines, much of the creative function of the actor would disappear.

The meaning of a line may be changed through the process of inventing actions to be associated with the line. The actor must remind himself that "actions speak louder than words." If the action performed immediately before, during, or immediately after the actual speaking of the line has the same meaning as the line itself, the line will seem to be the true expression of the character's thoughts and feelings; if the action is in opposition to the spoken words, the audience will usually believe the action instead of the words; and if the line is spoken without action—without gesture or facial expression—the audience will be at liberty to believe or not to believe.

To illustrate that actions have greater force than words, one might use the extreme, but not impossible, example of a man who tells a woman that he hates her and then kisses her. It is evident that the audience—and probably the girl, too—will believe the action rather than the word. In Hamlet's case, if the actor makes Hamlet behave in the manner that Ophelia describes, he will seem mad. If he behaves in this manner all the time, the audience will consider him really mad; but if he plays some scenes, or parts of scenes, with rational actions, the audience will understand that, when he is acting madly, he is doing so with purpose and design, not because he is actually mad.

The following exercise will illustrate the tremendous variety of interpretations which may be accomplished through the invention of action:

A enters. B is already on the stage.
A: Oh! Hello.
B: Hello.
A: I was looking for my pencil.
B: Oh!
A: Have you seen it?
B: No.
A: I thought I left it here.

Each line has at least three possible variations in meaning, according to the plot actions used. On his first line, A will seem surprised to find B there, or not surprised, according to his actions, and B may be surprised or

not surprised to see A enter; as a second possibility either or both characters may remain neutral, giving no indication of either surprise or ex-
pectation; and the third variant is that either or both may be expecting
to find the other.   The same lines may also show that A is pleased, or
displeased, or doesn't care to see B; and B has the same choices of interpretation concerning his feelings for A.

When A says that he is looking for his pencil, he may actually be looking for it or he may not, and the skillful actor may go on to suggest exactly what he is looking for.   B with a simple "Oh" may indicate that
he believes or disbelieves A's statement.   On the next line A may mean
that he thinks B has either seen or not seen the pencil; and B, when he
says, "No," may mean either yes, no, or maybe.   And A's last line can be
either true or false.   The actors rehearsing this scene will discover that
the easiest way to make the selected interpretation effective is to invent
plot action; that is, storytelling pantomime.

If the actors choose to do so, they may ignore the meaning of the lines
and make the scene mean almost anything.   It can be played, for example, as a love scene: If A is a man and plays "Oh, hello!" to mean
pleased surprise at finding B, a woman, sitting on the sofa, B can move
over to make room for A, as she says, "Hello"; then A can come and
sit beside her, putting his arm around her, and finishing the scene with a
kiss.   The new meaning of the scene will be clear, in spite of the dialogue.
Or the sequence can be played as a scene from a mystery melodrama, with
the words used as some secret code of passwords and actions performed
to show that A gives B the secret papers, or the stolen jewels.   The
potential meanings of the scene are limited only by the actors' powers
of invention and their skill in inventing pantomimic action which tells a
story.

Working from Inside or Outside

This invention of action derived from the plot—that is, from the
changing relationship between characters—is very similar to the system
suggested by Stanislavski in which a scene is divided into units and the
actors find objectives within each unit.   The unit corresponds to a
progression or a sequence of progressions dealing with a single thought or
action, and the objective is the inner motivation which causes the character to act as he does.   Stanislavski recommends that the rehearsal period
be devoted largely to the selection of the correct objectives in each unit,
so that the scene will eventually evolve the necessary, meaningful, outward form.

The technical approach to a scene is first to work out the meaningful
form and then proceed to the inner emotional motivations, just as the

actor knows from the beginning the words he must say but must work toward an emotional motivation for the speeches assigned to him.   Some actors will find it easier to work from the inside out, and others from the outside in; all actors will find that there are times when they must use both systems.

Those who work from the emotional motivations will sometimes discover that the actions which feel right to them are not meaningful to the audience and that the outward form of the scene must be changed and then remotivated; those who work from the outside may discover that they cannot devise the outward form of the scene until they have thoroughly explored the inner motivations.   Ideally the two approaches should be used simultaneously; but both paths lead to the same performance from different directions, and in the finished performance the audience should not be able to tell which path has been followed, the actions having been so carefully motivated, or the emotions so skillfully expressed in action, that the final effect seems the inevitable one.

Action Derived from Mood and Atmosphere

The actions suggested by mood and atmosphere are derived from the time, place, and circumstances of the play.   The same lovers would not behave the same way on a park bench with people passing by as they would at home on a sofa.   All of the characters in Street Scene perform certain actions because it is such a hot day; some fan themselves, some use aprons to wipe away the perspiration, some mop their brows with handkerchiefs; in both the New York production and the motion picture, Beulah Bondi used the wonderfully accurate business of surreptitiously pulling her damp underwear away from her body—but not so surreptitiously that the audience didn't see her do it.   If the actors in the first scene of Romeo and Juliet can give the impression of the hot sun which inflames the tempers and stirs the blood, they will have done much to motivate the later action of the play.   On the other hand, the opening scene of The Merchant of Venice, also a street in an Italian city, where presumably it might be as hot, needs no such actions.

The outdoor pastoral scenes in the Chekhov plays should have a special type of action suitable to the place and the time of day.   In the second act of The Cherry Orchard, for example, each of the characters reacts to the nostalgic beauty of evening by the shore of the lake in the manner appropriate to his particular personality; in these scenes, characters lie on the grass, sit on rocks, loll against fences, and get that far-away look, their eyes focused on nothing in particular but on the view in general.

Dinner scenes and breakfast scenes, tea parties and cocktail parties, all provide special opportunities for the invention of action which the actor may use for pointing and emphasis. Many of these scenes demand a kind of bravura acting because there is so much essential activity in the scene that it becomes more of a problem to accomplish the action without having it detract from the scene than to use the action to reinforce the interpretation of the role.

In *Old English,* George Arliss ate an entire chicken dinner—an action which was also required by the plot, for the doctors had said that if the character overate he would kill himself—using the carving of the chicken, the breaking of the joints, the cutting of the meat, the picking of the bones, and all the other necessary actions to help him point the lines and make the emotional state of the character clear. When the play ran a long time, and Mr. Arliss got tired of eating a chicken dinner every night, he reworked the action of the dinner so that he would be able to have a lobster dinner, substituting the breaking of the claws for the breaking of the joints and the sucking on the smaller legs for the nibbling on a chicken bone. A roast beef dinner would not provide actions of a similar kind, and so Mr. Arliss was not able to vary his diet to this extent.

Often the necessary action derived from the mood and atmosphere has a particular quality which, when associated by timing with a particular line, colors the meaning of the line. If a woman is sewing, for example, the biting or the breaking of a thread has a certain vicious quality which might be interpreted by an audience to characterize her feelings toward a person or a thing mentioned in the line spoken when the action is performed. If a gangster stamps out a cigarette as he speaks of his enemy, the audience knows that he intends to kill him. The adroit actor will find that action of this kind is often useful in the interpretation of a role, and careful attention to such actions will give a reality and verisimilitude to the performance.

Action Derived from Character

The third source from which the actor may derive action is the character. Everybody has individual mannerisms—ways of walking, ways of standing and sitting, habitual facial expressions and gestures, and peculiarities of speech—which are the outward forms by which personality is recognized. Sometimes these mannerisms have deep roots in the intellectual and emotional life of the character; sometimes they are merely mannerisms acquired through habit.

There is always a tendency for the actor thoughtlessly to substitute his own personal mannerisms for those of the character he is playing. This is particularly true when the actor, in trying to arrive at an emotional comprehension of the character, imagines himself to be in the same situation as the character, or in a similar situation, and works out the action on the basis of what he himself would do. There is no harm in this if the personalities of the actor and the character are similar, that is, if the actor has been type cast. If the actor himself, when trying to arrive at a decision, wrinkles his brow, closes his eyes, puckers his mouth, drums his fingers on the table, crosses and uncrosses his legs, or wiggles his toes, there is no reason why he should not give this mannerism to the character he is playing, provided that it is also appropriate to the character. It is the repetition of the same mannerisms in several parts which creates the impression that the actor is always playing himself, but the actor, concentrating upon the emotional situation, is often completely unaware that he has substituted his own mannerisms for those of the character. The late Osgood Perkins, referring to his performance in *Uncle Vanya*, said that on opening night the director, Jed Harris, instructed him to "cut out all personal mannerisms." All through the performance, Perkins found himself wondering, every time he moved or made a gesture, whether he was using a mannerism of his own or one belonging to the character.

Mannerisms Derived from Costumes

Many of the personal mannerisms of a character are derived directly from the kind of clothes that he habitually wears. A man who is accustomed to wearing boots or heavy shoes will learn to walk with his feet relatively wide apart, and he is likely to continue to walk that way even when he is no longer wearing the boots. A young lady who is used to being tightly corseted and to wearing a bustle will not stand and walk in the same way as a girl who has been brought up in jeans and sun dresses. The long flowing sleeves of the court costumes worn during the reign of Richard II dictate certain kinds of gestures and movements. A farmer who usually wears suspenders may acquire the habit of standing with his thumbs hooked under the suspenders. Gentlemen of the Restoration period, who wore delicate lace on their sleeves and carried snuff boxes, were forced to acquire an elegance of gesture that would be inappropriate in a Roman toga.

An actress wearing a train is faced with the necessity, and the opportunity, of shoving it aside with a foot; since the action must be done, she has the option of performing it in relation to some line where it will be effective business. Frequently optional costume accessories are also used to create an opportunity for action. There are purses and pocketbooks to be carried, swords to be worn, coats and hats to be taken off or put on, pipes and cigarettes (with or without cigarette holders), chiffon handkerchiefs for certain types of women, umbrellas, canes, and hundreds of other things to be carried or worn, all of which create action.

Each of these articles, once it has been selected, does something to establish the character of the user. Is he the type of man who smokes a pipe? Is she the kind of woman who carries a purse and never can find anything in it? Should Sergius wear a cape, or Juliet carry a handkerchief? The answer to questions of this type, provided the article in question is not obligatory, lies in the use the actor will be able to make of the opportunities for action created by the article. Eddie Dowling made excellent use of a cigarette in the opening monologue of *The Glass Menagerie* to set the character and to point the lines. Mrs. Fiske made expert use of a handkerchief in several comedies, fluttering it nervously to give special emphasis to words which carried the comic idea.

Action derived from the costume can be tremendously useful to the actor, but it can also be dangerous overornamentation which may obliterate the more important facets of the characterization and impress the audience as nothing more than facile trickery. Whenever this type of action is used, whether required as an integral part of the play or included by the actor merely because it is technically useful to him, it must be performed with great skill and must never be allowed to detract from more important aspects of the performance; it must be made to serve the purposes of the characterization and the play.

Actions Derived from Emotions and Thoughts

The actions which derive from the emotions and the thoughts of the character are of much greater interest than the actions derived from what he is wearing. His personal mannerisms, his habits of movement and gesture and facial expression (the personal mannerisms of the actor himself having been eliminated as far as possible), give the role its lifelike quality, and such actions are almost always exclusively the invention of the actor.

Since actions of this type are the outward manifestation of qualities which may later be used as motivation for the plot actions, they are frequently confused with plot actions. In *The Caine Mutiny Court Martial*, Queeg has the habit of rolling little metal balls in his hand when he is worried and psychologically disturbed. At first this mannerism appears merely as an interesting detail of characterization which reveals his inner tensions. Later it becomes a symbol of Queeg's incompetence, which is a crucial issue in the trial, and therefore essential to the plot as well as to the characterization.

When Ina Claire played *Biography* at the Berkshire Playhouse, having previously starred in the Broadway production, it was found that the stage was not as large as the one in the New York theater and that some of the furniture used in the original set would have to be eliminated.

The designer solved the problem as well as he could. When Miss Claire saw the arrangement he had planned, she asked that Marion Freud's work-table be pulled farther into the room; it was explained that to do so would put the table in front of a door and that it would be necessary for Miss Claire—or Marion Freud—to go around the table when she entered and when she crossed from one side of the stage to the other. Miss Claire said that that was exactly what she wanted, that the character was the kind of person who always avoided issues and went around problems, and that it would help to establish the character if there were actual physical objects to be avoided. This character action never was developed into the plot, in the same manner as Queeg's clicking of the metal balls was, but it aided in creating the impression of the character which Miss Claire wanted.

In *End of Summer*, Miss Claire played a wealthy woman with sudden enthusiasms but no permanent convictions. For this role she developed a bouncy walk which started in one direction and then suddenly turned in a new direction; she would start to go toward the window and then suddenly turn to arrange a vase of flowers on the table. Again the fundamental psychological traits of the character had been brilliantly translated into actions.

The beginning exercise in Chapter 2 illustrated that a change in the character's rate of walking tends to indicate a change of thought or emotion. In the discussion of entrances the possibility of establishing character through a physical attitude was illustrated. Obviously it is important that the emotional and mental states of the character be constantly and consistently illustrated through the movement and the various physical attitudes used during the entire play. One of the first things an experienced actor will do is to hunt for all the possible physical attitudes which would be appropriate to his character in the set where the action takes place. Is there a sofa? how long? how low? does it have a sittable arm? how high is the back? can you lean on it? sit on it? Are there steps to the palace? how wide are they and how high are the risers? can you go up them two at a time? or three at a time? can you sit on them comfortably? if you lie back on them, where do your elbows come? would the character sit back deep in the sofa, or perch on the edge? would he get up slowly and majestically? would he rise briskly?

When Edna Best played in *There's Always Juliet* she evolved an action which was tremendously effective. She was playing a very sophisticated woman who, having had one unhappy and unfortunate love affair, had considered herself above love, but who nevertheless had fallen in love again—happily, foolishly, girlishly in love; she had just seen the man to the door; when she came back, she ran to the back of the sofa, lay along the top of it, rolled down onto the sofa, then onto the floor, and crawled on her hands and knees to her bedroom, while the housekeeper looked on in amazed and horrified silence. There was no doubt in anyone's mind how exuberantly happy she was.

In addition to the larger movements which involve walking and to the general bearing and carriage of the body which produce the physical attitudes, the actor must consider the gestures. A gesture is frequently involved in a larger action, but gestures are often performed separately as well, and the actor would do well to study them separately. The compulsion for a gesture is always a thought or an emotion, except in those instances, rarely handled in drama, where an activity is being carried on which has become entirely automatic and can be performed without thought. A woman may knit, for example, while her thoughts are on some other subject. Even in such a case an unusual new thought, or a strong emotion, will change the manner of the knitting, even if it does not stop the knitting.

Since thought or emotion is the motivation for gesture, the actor must take care not to use gestures which reveal neither thought nor emotion. One of the most frequent faults of the inexperienced actor is to make a movement or gesture when he himself feels the need for it, even though, as the character, he has nothing to express, or to use a gesture which seems to him to have been motivated by the thoughts or emotions of the character but which is meaningless to an audience. It is doubtful whether an actor should ever plan in advance of rehearsals the gestures he will use, but it is essential that he examine carefully the gestures which evolve during rehearsals and reconsider those which are not meaningful.

Translating Stage Directions into Action

Authors rarely give specific stage directions concerning the movements and gestures with which the actor is to express an emotion. Usually the playwright merely inserts an adverb indicating the effect he wishes without making any suggestion as to the means by which it is to be achieved; he says "gladly" or "fearfully" or "sadly," leaving it to the actor to evolve the reading of the line and the accompanying action, if any. There are also many directors who ask the actors to achieve effects without making any suggestions as to the methods. Some actors like this system, since it leaves the creation of the character to them; others prefer that either the author or the director assign specific movements and gestures to them, just as the author has supplied their lines, leaving to the actor only the problems of perfomance.

The actor should be cautioned that in many published acting versions of plays the stage directions are the work neither of the playwright nor of the director; they are merely the stage manager's impression of what the director said to a specific actor during rehearsals. To properly under-stand such directions, one should know exactly what the actor was doing just before the instruction was given. While an actor is rehearsing, a director may say, "Play it proudly—arrogantly," and the stage manager will write either "proudly" or "arrogantly" into the script for whatever guidance it may be to the next actor playing the role.

George Bernard Shaw was one playwright who frequently gave specific instructions about movements, physical attitudes, and gestures, indi-cating not only the effect which was to be created but the method by which the actor was to achieve that effect. Some of his stage directions for Marchbanks in *Candida* are as eloquent as the lines he gave him to speak.

To describe one of Marchbanks' entrances, for example, Shaw wrote, "As he catches sight of a stranger on entering, he stops, and edges along the wall on the opposite side of the room." On the next speech, when Marchbanks says, "Glad to meet you," the directions say, "Nervously backing against the bookcase," which is far more helpful to the actor than the one word "nervously" would be. When Burgess offers Marchbanks his hand, Shaw says that Marchbanks takes it "with a nervous jerk." Later he says Marchbanks "sits down on the sofa, his elbows on his knees and his temples between his fists, with an expression of hopeless suffering." If Shaw had said only, "Hopelessly suffering," how many actors would have invented a physical attitude as expressive as the one Shaw suggests?

In the scene with Morell, Marchbanks says, "I am only (*covering his face desperately with his hands*) full of horror. (*Then, dropping his hands, and thrusting his face forward fiercely at Morell, he goes on threateningly.*) You shall see whether this is a time for patience and kindness." Note that in addition to being specific about the gestures, Shaw has also indicated the timing by placing the gesture after "I am only" and before "full of horror."

George Kelly is another playwright who frequently indicates the specific character action. Kelly is usually his own stage director, and it is clear that he knows exactly what the characters are doing at every moment. This is particularly true of *The Show-off*. Aubrey is the show-off in this play—vain, conceited, boastful, amused at his own humor, which is not very brilliant, and insensitive to the feelings of others. His conversation is full of jargon, trite sayings, and catch phrases, his favorite of the moment being, "Sign on the dotted line," which seems to mean, "Aren't I right?" or, "You must agree with me." His actions, as described by Kelly, have the same quality as his lines: he assumes what he con-siders to be smart attitudes; he preens himself before the mirror; he touches his tie and toupee gingerly; he slaps people on the back; and to

match his favorite phrase he has a favorite gesture of smartly tapping the
table twice with his knuckles or of tapping the tip of his cane whenever
he thinks he has said anything particularly brilliant.

Facial Expressions

Facial expressions are, of course, a part of the physical manifestation
of character; but each actor has entirely individual problems in attempting to use them effectively.   Most actors can learn to perform the same
gestures so that they have more or less the same meaning and the same
effect; but all actors cannot make the same expressions.   Most of the
facial muscles, moreover, seem to be involuntary muscles, responding
unconsciously to the thoughts and feelings.

Some actors with mobile faces have learned to hold their faces in definite facial expressions which are appropriate to the characters they are
playing.   Others rely upon make-up to heighten certain natural features—
to provide wrinkles that would have been acquired by the character, to
change the line of the eyebrows, to create highlights and shadows that
will make the eyes seem sunken or popeyed, and even to change the
shape of the chin or the nose by applying putty.

Most actors, however, seem to rely, entirely or in part, upon their
ability to assume the emotions and the thoughts of the character, letting
the involuntary and unconscious muscles of the face take care of the facial
expressions.   Certainly if the actor is overly aware of his facial expressions, he is likely to give a "mugging" performance, for only the exceptional actor can consciously assume facial expressions and have them seem
to be unconscious.   Try smiling when you don't feel like smiling!

Most authors do not have the facility to invent and describe physical
actions, or perhaps most authors feel that these matters are definitely
part of the creative function of the actors and are best left to their invention.   Shaw and Kelly, it has been noted, are the exceptions.

Before the advent of the modern director, stage directions prescribing
specific physical actions are a rarity, and they are almost nonexistent in
the classics.   Shakespeare, himself an actor, and often his own director,
must have been expert in this phase of theater, but unfortunately no
records have come down to us, and the actors are left almost entirely to
their own inventions.   Writing his plays for a company of actors with
whose work he was entirely familiar, as did Chekhov, Molière, and many
other playwrights, and often creating a character with a specific actor
in mind, Shakespeare must have frequently planned to make effective use
of the individual mannerisms and the special capabilities of the actors.

In *The Merchant of Venice*, no hints are given about the physical
appearance of the Prince of Morocco and the Prince of Arragon, save

what may be deduced from the things they say. They are not included in the list of lovers who are described and mimicked by Portia and Nerissa. Nothing is said of their bearing and carriage and manner of walking, their habits of gesturing, or their facial expressions. It is the actor's task to provide this physical expression of the character. Each actor who is assigned to one of these roles must deduce for himself the kind of man who would have had the thoughts, expressed them in the way, and made the choices that Shakespeare describes. Whether these characters should be plausible as lovers or as unattractive as the suitors whom Nerissa lists is a question of taste and discretion. Whatever the decision, the actors must invent the actions which will give outward form to the characterization.

Having invented the plot action, the mood and atmosphere action, and the character action for a role, the actor now sets about using those actions to change or alter, or merely to clarify, the meaning of the lines, to phrase the thoughts of the character so that the audience will understand them readily, to build climaxes where climaxes are desirable or necessary, and to give special emphasis to particular lines or actions by careful timing and pointing. In other words, the actor is now ready to set about the task of projecting his own interpretation of a role so that it will be clear and comprehensible to an audience.

EXERCISES

1. Sequence from *A Doll's House*,[1] Act I.
   Re-rehearse the Nora-Mrs. Linden scene, which was used as an exercise for Chapter 9, paying particular attention to action which will reveal the dual character of Nora.

2. Sequence from *Julius Caesar*, Act I, Scene 2.
   Rehearse the scene between Cassius and Brutus, beginning, "Will you go see the order of the course?"
   a. Work out action which shows that Cassius is putting thoughts into Brutus' mind, that he is pressing his point, that he is trying to get around Brutus, and that he is tempting Brutus.
   b. Work out action which shows the degree to which Brutus has been influenced. Cassius says he is glad of "thus much shew of fire from Brutus." How much show of fire? When does he show fire? How does he show fire? Which of Cassius' arguments have the most effect upon Brutus?
   NOTE: The actor playing Brutus will do well to spend more time studying Cassius' speeches than his own. These are the lines which will give him his cue for action.

[1] Copyright by Charles Scribner's Sons.

3. Sequence from *Macbeth*, Act I, Scene 3.

Rehearse the scene from the point at which Macbeth and Banquo enter.

a. Invent the actions which will show Banquo's reactions to the words of the Witches.

b. Invent the actions which will clearly show Macbeth's reactions to the words of the Witches. Decide whether or not there should be separate reactions to each prophecy.

NOTE: It is essential that Macbeth's reactions include those which Banquo describes.

Shakespeare allows one and a half lines to the establishment of the off-stage mood. The difference between the attitudes of Macbeth and Banquo at the beginning of the scene and at the end of the scene will denote the progress of the scene and the start of the plot.

Compare the actions of Macbeth in this scene with those of Brutus in the previous scene. Both men take the first step in contemplating an assassination. Would the actions of each be suitable for the other?

4. Sequence from *Arms and the Man*,[2] Act I.

Raina has just left Bluntschli alone with final instructions that he is not to fall asleep.

BLUNTSCHLI: (*drowsily*). Sleep, sleep, sleep, sleep, slee— (*The words trail off into a murmur. He wakes again with a shock on the point of falling.*) Where am I? That's what I want to know: where am I? Must keep awake. Nothing keeps me awake except danger—remember that—(*intently*) danger, danger, danger dan— Where's danger? Must find it. (*He starts off vaguely around the room in search of it.*) What am I looking for? Sleep— Danger— don't know. (*He stumbles against the bed.*) Ah, yes: now I know. All right now. I'm to go to bed, but not to sleep—be sure not to sleep—because of danger. Not to lie down, either, only sit down. (*He sits on the bed. A bliss-ful expression comes into his face.*) Ah! (*With a happy sigh he sinks back at full length; lifts his boots into the bed with a final effort; and falls asleep· instantly.*)

a. Rehearse the scene, making the degrees of sleepiness obvious.

b. Rehearse the scene with a different characterization. Let Sergius or Louka or Raina be equally sleepy. The pattern of action will remain constant, a progression from standing to lying down, but the voice and the mannerisms may vary from character to character.

5. Sequence from *Arms and the Man*,[3] Act II. Raina and Sergius have just played a scene in which she states that they have "found the higher love."

---

[2] Copyright by The Public Trustee and The Society of Authors.
[3] Copyright by The Public Trustee and The Society of Authors.

She leaves to get her hat, waving him a kiss as she goes.

SERGIUS: (*He looks after her with emotion for a moment, then turns slowly away, his face radiant with the emotion of the scene which has just passed. The movement shifts his field of vision, into the corner of which there now comes the tail of Louka's double apron. His eye gleams at once. He takes a stealthy look at her, and begins to twirl his moustache nervously, with his left hand akimbo on his hip. Finally, striking the ground with his heels in something of a cavalry swagger, he strolls over to the left of the table, opposite her, and says*) Louka: do you know what the higher love is?

LOUKA: (*astonished*) No, sir.

SERGIUS: Very fatiguing thing to keep up for any length of time, Louka. One feels the need of some relief after it.

LOUKA: (*innocently*) Perhaps you would like some coffee, sir? (*She stretches her hand across the table for the coffee pot.*)

SERGIUS: (*taking her hand*) Thank you, Louka.

LOUKA: (*pretending to pull*) Oh, sir, you know I didn't mean that. I'm surprised at you!

SERGIUS: (*coming clear of the table and drawing her with him.*) I am surprised at myself, Louka. What would Sergius, the hero of Slivnitza, say if he saw me now? What would Sergius, the apostle of the higher love, say if he saw me now? What would the half dozen Sergiuses who keep popping in and out of this handsome figure of mine say if they caught us here? (*Letting go her hand, and slipping his arm dexterously round her waist.*) Do you consider my figure handsome, Louka?

LOUKA: Let me go, sir. I shall be disgraced. (*She struggles: he holds her inexorably.*) Oh, will you let go?

SERGIUS: (*looking straight into her eyes*) No.

LOUKA: Then stand back where we can't be seen. Have you no common sense?

SERGIUS: Ah, that's reasonable. (*He takes her into the stableyard gateway, where they are hidden from the house.*)

LOUKA: (*complaining*) I may have been seen from the windows: Miss Raina is sure to be spying about after you.

SERGIUS: (*stung—letting her go*) Take care, Louka. I may be worthless enough to betray the higher love; but do not you insult it.

LOUKA: (*demurely*) Not for the world, sir, I'm sure. May I go on with my work please, now?

SERGIUS: (*again putting his arm round her*) You are a provoking little witch, Louka. If you were in love with me, would you spy out of windows on me?

LOUKA: Well, you see, sir, since you say you are half a dozen different gentlemen all at once, I should have a great deal to look after.

SERGIUS: (*charmed.*) Witty as well as pretty. (*He tries to kiss her.*)

a. Rehearse the scene following the author's directions. Note that the action consists entirely of the changing relationship between the two characters, drawing together, separating, and then drawing together again. He is the aggressor and initiates most of the actions.

NOTE: The manner in which the actions are performed will denote the characters, but the actions themselves are telling the story and are derived from the plot.

6. Sequence from *The Cherry Orchard*, Act IV. Lopakhin has been left alone on the stage.

A pause. Behind the door, smothered laughter and whispering, and, at last, enter Varya.

VARYA: (*Looking a long while over the things*) It is strange. I can't find it anywhere.

LOPAKHIN: What are you looking for?

VARYA: I packed it myself, and I can't remember. (*A pause*)

LOPAKHIN: Where are you going now, Varvara Mihailova?

VARYA: I? To the Ragulins. I have arranged to go to them to look after the house—as a housekeeper.

LOPAKHIN: That's in Yashnovo? It'll be seventy miles away. (*A pause*) So this is the end of life in this house!

VARYA: (*Looking among the things*) Where is it? Perhaps I put it in the trunk. Yes, life in this house is over—there will be no more of it.

LOPAKHIN: And I'm just off to Harkov—by the next train. I've a lot of business there. I'm leaving Epihodov here, and I've taken him on.

VARYA: Really!

LOPAKHIN: This time last year we had snow already, if you remember; but now it's so fine and sunny. Though it's cold, to be sure—three degrees of frost.

VARYA: I haven't looked. (*A pause*) And besides, our thermometer's broken. (*A pause*)

(*Voice at the door from the yard: "Yermolay Alexeyevitch!"*)

LOPAKHIN: (*As though he had long been expecting this summons*) This minute!

(*Lopakhin goes out quickly. Varya sitting on the floor and laying her head on a bag full of clothes, sobs quietly.*)

Rehearse the scene so that in each pause indicated in the script the unperformed action and the unspoken line are somehow indicated to the audience.

a. Work out the action so that the characters begin apart but that each pause finds them nearer to each other.

b. Work out the action so that the characters begin relatively close to each other and at each pause are farther apart.

c. Work out the action in both of these patterns so that it is Lopakhin who moves first and Varya who follows.

d. Work out the action so that it is Varya who makes the first moves and Lopakhin who follows.

NOTE: The various action patterns suggested derive from the plot but also affect the characterizations. Each character must be a different kind of person to perform the different action patterns.

7. *Romeo and Juliet*, Act III, Scene 5.

Rehearse the sequence which was quoted as an exercise for Chapter 7, working out action patterns, one in which Juliet goes to each of her parents and the Nurse, and one in which each of them comes to her.

8. Sequence from *Hamlet*, Act III, Scene 1.

Rehearse the sequence between Hamlet and Ophelia.

a. Rehearse the scene inventing actions which will make Hamlet seem to be mad.

b. Rehearse the scene inventing actions which will make it seem that Hamlet is feigning madness.

c. Rehearse the scene inventing actions which will make the audience believe that Hamlet is sane.

9. Exercise.

B is on stage when A enters.
A: Oh! Hello.
B: Hello.
A: I was looking for my pencil.
B: Oh!
A: Have you seen it?
B: No.
A: I thought I left it here.

a. Play the scene with as many variations in meaning as possible, without making any effort to change the characterization.

First speech: A expected or did not expect to find B.
                  A is glad or not glad to see B.
Second speech: B expected or did not expect A to enter.
                  B is glad or not glad to see A.
Third speech: A is or is not looking for the pencil.
Fourth speech: B believes A or does not believe A.
Fifth speech :   A thinks or does not think that B has seen it.
Sixth speech: B has or has not seen it.
Seventh speech: A does or does not think it was left here.

b. Play the scene with as many variations in character as possible. Play it as teenagers, as old people, as society club women, as international spies, as a beggar and a garbage collector, as old maid school teachers, as absent-minded professors, as thugs, as racketeers, as a meek husband and a shrewish wife, etc.

c. By superimposing plot actions, play the scene with as many variations in plot as possible. Play it as a love scene, as a parting scene, as a murder scene, as a death scene, etc.

10. Select any of the scenes from Shakespeare which have been used as exercises and play them in modern dress, substituting the manner of walking which is suitable to the clothes of today. Use revolvers instead of swords. Insert pipe smoking or cigarette smoking.

Use the script of Exercise 9 and play it in Elizabethan costumes, in eighteenth-century costumes, in nineteenth-century costumes, in peasant costumes, etc.

NOTE: This exercise should be done imagining the costumes to be worn and also actually wearing the costumes, if this is possible.

11. Read *Candida* or *Arms and the Man* and practice every action given in the stage directions.

12. Sequence from *The Show Off*,[4] Act I.

AUBREY: (*Coming out of the parlor*) Stay right where you are, folks, right where you are. (*He moves to the mirror over the mantelpiece*) Just a little social attention,—going right out again on the next train. (*He surveys himself critically in the mirror, touching his tie and toupee gingerly. Mrs. Fisher gives him a smouldering look, and Joe looks at his Father. Aubrey turns from the mirror, and indicates his reflection with a wide gesture.*) There you are, Mother! Any woman's fancy, what do you say? Even to the little old carnation. (*He gives the table a double tap with his knuckles, then laughs, and moves up towards the kitchen door, and calls out to Amy.*) Come on, Amy, step on the United Gas out there; customer in here waiting for the old aqua pura. (*Moving down to Mr. Fisher's right*) Man's got to have something to drink—how about it, Pop? (*He gives Mr. Fisher a slap on the right shoulder*) You'll stay with me on that, won't you? (*He laughs and moves to the mirror again. Old man Fisher is very much annoyed.*) Yes, sir. (*Coming forward again at the right.*) I want to tell those of you who have ventured out this evening, that this is a very pretty little picture of domestic felicity. (*He laughs a little and looks from one to the other, patronizingly; but nobody pays the slightest attention to him.*) Father reading,—Mother knitting; (*Mrs. Fisher withers him with a quick look*) But then, Mama is *always* knitting. (*She knits rapidly and Aubrey laughs, and moves up and across back of the table*) And little old Tommy Edison over here, working eighteen hours a day to make the

4 Copyright by George Kelly.

rich man richer and the poor man poorer. (*He gives Joe a tap on the back, then moves back again towards Mr. Fisher*) What about it, Popcorn? (*Slaps him on the back*) Shake it up! Right or raving?

MR. FISHER: (*Starting to his feet violently*) God damn it, let me alone! And keep your hands to yourself. (*He crosses below the center-table and up to the hall-door*) I never saw such a damn pest in my life! (*He goes up the stairs bristling with rage, and muttering to himself. Aubrey is vastly amused. He leans on the back of Mr. Fisher's chair and roars with laughter.*)

AUBREY: Sign on the dotted line! And little old Popsy-Wopsy getting sore and going to leave us flat. (*He laughs again considerably; then turns to Mrs. Fisher*) Nevertheless, and notwithstanding, Mrs. Fisher, I'd like to mention that the kid from West Philadelphia is giving the growing boy the said and done. (*He indicates Joe with a waving gesture. Amy comes in from the right with a glass of water. He turns and acknowledges her with even a wider gesture.*) And there she is herself, and not a moving picture. (*Amy extends the glass of water, laughing, and with a touch of self-consciousness.*) Blushing as she gave it, looking down—at her feet so bare, and her tattered gown. (*Amy giggles, and her Mother looks sharply at Amy's shoes. Aubrey takes the glass of water and turns to Mrs. Fisher*) How's that, Mother Fisher? Can't beat that little old Willie Shakespeare, can you? No, sir,—I'd like to tell the brothers that that little old Shakespeare party shook a wicked spear. (*He laughs at his own comedy, and Amy is immeasurably delighted*) Well, here's laughter, ladies! and, (*Turning to Joe*) Mr. Marconi,—my best regards to you. (*He drinks.*)

NOTE: The author has suggested specific character actions to be performed with specific lines.

Chapter 11. TIMING, RHYTHM, TEMPO, AND PACE

THE FOUR WORDS *timing, rhythm, tempo* and *pace*, may be used to designate four separate, but interrelated, time concepts which are of vital concern to those engaged in theatrical work. All the words have been borrowed from music or the other arts, from sports, or from general human activity and have no precise, accepted definitions when applied to the theater arts. Although these terms are commonly used by actors and drama critics, each person seems to use them to describe slightly different concepts, one person talking about "pace" when he seems to mean exactly what another person means when he talks about "tempo." The battle of semantics has often confused the discussion of time in the theater to the point that an understanding of the problem has been obscured rather than clarified.

Timing has been discussed in a previous chapter, where it was arbitrarily defined as the precise time relationship between a spoken line and an action. A separate chapter was devoted to it because it is regarded as a separate technical device, while rhythm, pace, and tempo are not in themselves techniques but are rather the result of techniques.

Stanislavski devotes two chapters of *Building a Character* to what he calls "tempo-rhythm," one chapter dealing with its application to movement and the other with its application to speech; Boleslavsky discusses rhythm as meaning something entirely different and as having more to do with the effect of acting than with a method of acting; critics of theater performances most frequently use one or another of these words to describe the effect of a performance upon the audience, referring to a slow performance, or a slowly paced performance, when they seem to mean an uninteresting performance.

Pace Is Audience's Sense of Time

Since the purpose of drama is to awaken in the audience a predetermined response, it is well to consider first the problem of time as it relates to the audience. This sense of time in the audience will be the determining factor in settling the time problems in actual performance. Let us arbitrarily use the word *pace* to describe the concept of time for the audience.

The analogy of a clock may help to explain the interrelationship of the different time concepts: inside a clock are many different-sized wheels, all moving at different rates of speed, the purpose of which is to establish a rate of speed for the hands of the clock which will tell the observer the passage of time. The audience is not concerned with the rate of speed of the wheels inside the clock, but only with the movement of the hands on the face of the clock.

The Sense of Speed Is Relative

While hours, minutes, and seconds are recognized measures of time with known mathematical dimensions, the duration of a minute seems to vary according to what one is experiencing during that minute. The last minute of a closely matched football game may seem unendurably long to the rooters on one side of the field, but unimaginably short to the rooters on the other side. In *As You Like It*, Rosalind says, "Time travels in divers paces with divers persons. I'll tell you who Time ambles withal, who Time trots withal, who Time gallops withal and who he stands still withal." The actor's concern, then, is not with the actual duration of the performance, but with the duration perceived by the audience; he will hope that Time gallops, or, at the very least, trots with the audience.

Actually, the purpose of theater is to make the audience forget time entirely, to be completely unaware of the passage of time. In this sense, theater is literally a "pastime." To achieve this goal, it is essential that the attention of the audience be focused constantly on the play; its interest can never be allowed to flag, but must be absorbed by the play at all times.

No doubt each individual in the audience considers himself to be separate and apart from all the other individuals in the audience and believes that his own reactions to the play, his interest and his lack of interest, are peculiar to himself; but the actor soon learns to consider the audience as a mass, subject to mass reactions, even though individual reactions may exist to a limited degree. One cough in the audience is a danger signal; the actor knows that it is likely to be followed by a dozen more. And he also learns that as soon as the play becomes more interesting, as soon as something happens on the stage, the coughing will stop.

Just as the members of an audience tend to laugh together, so they tend to get bored together. The old Copley Theatre in Boston had a convenient peephole through which the director could watch the people in the audience watching the play; they smiled together, they chuckled together, they leaned forward together, and when a dull scene came along, they all together became aware of the hardness of the seats and all shifted their weight from one ham to the other.   Laughter is infectious, and so is boredom.

The actor must learn that speed, the actual time it takes to perform a given scene, is not in direct relation to the audience's sense of speed; indeed, it is frequently in an inverse relation.   The longer it takes an actor to play the scene, the shorter the scene may seem to the audience, if the actor uses the time to increase the interest of the audience.

When one is traveling, the sense of speed is in direct relationship to the number of things that one passes; 50 miles an hour is fast driving in some places, but in western Kansas, where the only things to pass are water towers 25 miles apart, it seems a snail's pace.   If one has been driving on an open road and then comes to a bridge, the sudden noise reflected from the structure of the bridge will give a sense of acceleration, even though the actual speed is unchanged.   An airplane trip, in spite of the tremendous speed, is boring because one sees nothing and passes nothing.

When this analogy is applied to the theater, it becomes apparent that to maintain the play's pace—the sense of speed experienced by the audience—the actors may either hurry over the dull passages, thus getting more quickly from one interesting point to another, or find a way to make the dull passages more interesting.   They can go faster, or they can erect a few water towers, or at least telegraph poles, so that the audience will have something to pass and thus something to maintain its interest.

Pace Maintained by Making Points

The actor must assume from the beginning that the author never intended any of his play to be dull and that he thought that every line he wrote had some important contribution to make.   It is up to the actor to discover what that contribution is.

Aristotle lists the elements of a play as plot, character, thought, diction, melody, and spectacle, the last three being the means by which the first three are developed.   It follows, then, that every moment of the play should be concerned with making the audience understand the plot, the characters, or the thought.   It is by discovering the purpose of each section of a play that the actor will discover what the author hoped would hold the attention of the audience.

There are a series of questions that the actor must ask himself concerning every line he speaks and every action he performs.   Does it further the plot?   If so, how and to what extent?   Does it develop the character?   If so, precisely which facet of the character does it reveal?

Does it contribute to the thought of the play—the meaning of the play? Once these questions have been answered, the actor must then ask, Is the purpose of that moment on the stage accomplished through what is said (diction), through what is done (spectacle), or through both?

Melody as a Means of Making Points

In most modern plays, melody is rarely used as a means of conveying plot or character or thought, unless one wishes to consider the cadence of a line as the melody. But motion pictures frequently use melody in the form of a convenient symphony orchestra, which carries on where the actors leave off—creating suspense, stating emotions which the characters themselves are incapable of stating, and sometimes even contributing to the thought of a production. Everyone is familiar with the motion-picture device of two lovers walking off into the dawn, moving farther and farther away from the camera, and getting smaller and smaller, while a symphony orchestra speaks of their love and their rapture, their hope and their confidence, in a way in which neither the author nor the actors could duplicate.

Perhaps the most brilliant example of the use of melody as a means of developing both plot and character is Leonard Bernstein's triumph in the motion picture *On the Waterfront*. The plot concerns a young man, played by Marlon Brando, who is the brother of a racketeering labor leader and who knows that his brother is responsible for a murder. He is urged by the sister of the murdered man to give the evidence and exhorted by the priest to clear his conscience and tell what he knows. The climax of the plot and the most important part of the characterization depend upon his confession. He tells the priest, after much soul searching, that he will confess to the girl.

He meets the girl on a pile of rock, with a fine view of New York harbor in the background, and the wind from the river whipping their clothes about them. As he begins to speak, tugboat whistles begin to blow, and Mr. Bernstein builds their sound into a full symphony, intentionally blotting out the words which are supposed to be spoken. One cannot question the wisdom of the director who elected to play this absolutely essential scene in this manner, for it is quite probable that Mr. Bernstein and his orchestra were far more eloquent than either the author or Mr. Brando could have been.

It is doubtful that Aristotle ever had anything like a Bernstein score in mind when he listed melody as one of the elements of drama, but in any case this device need not concern the actor any more than a competent substitute sitting on the bench concerns the football quarterback. Occasionally an actor, usually in poetic drama, relies upon the mere beauty of the sound of his voice to hold the attention of the audience. Actors in *Romeo and Juliet* frequently depend upon melody of this sort; Maurice Evans has often been praised for the beauty of his voice; and a critic once described Julia Marlowe's performance in *Cymbeline* as a beautiful organ solo. Usually, however, the actor will leave the question of melody to the director and the composer of the accompanying musical score, if any, and confine himself to the diction and the spectacle—the things he says and the things he does—as a means of interesting the audience in the plot, the characters, and the thought of the drama.

Spectacle As a Means of Making Points

In its more modern and less technical sense, spectacle, like melody, can often be used to hold the interest of the audience. The melodrama of the nineteenth century includes many examples of scenes in which fires, earthquakes, or racing chariots were depended upon to sustain audience interest in a play, but perhaps Belasco's production of his one-act play *Madame Butterfly* provides the most interesting example. In this performance the two scenes of the play were connected by a scene during which the little Japanese wife waits for her American husband to return; there was no motion on the stage, but as she waited by the window the sun set, the stars came out, and then, as the dawn came, the stars paled and the festive lanterns flickered out one by one. It is reported that the scene lasted fourteen minutes without resulting in the slightest loss of audience interest.

Such uses of spectacle need not concern the actor beyond the fact that he must be aware when the substitute has taken over, so that he will not attempt to compete with it. The actress wearing the latest in Paris gowns, perhaps designed by Dior, must not be surprised if the audience, or at least the female portion of it, is not ready to pay attention to the play itself until the dress has been fully appraised; she will do well not to attempt to further the plot, or to develop the characterization, except in so far as the dress itself is an expression of the character, until everyone has had a good look at it; and she certainly cannot expect the thought of the play to receive the concentration of the audience until the dress has been seen both front and back.

Actually every visible aspect of the play is part of the spectacle. The actor himself, as the physical manifestation of the character, contributes to the spectacle. All of his pantomimic actions are a translation of the lines into visible symbols. Every time an actor uses a pause in the dialogue and fills the pause with action—or even with inaction—he has altered the rhythm of his acting and changed the tempo of the scene in order to achieve a calculated effect upon the pace of the play.

Diction As a Means of Making Points

Diction, like melody and spectacle, can sometimes command the attention of the audience, but it can never be entirely divorced from the plot, character, and thought. Since it is spoken by a character, it becomes a revelation of his intellectual and emotional personality; except in rare instances, such as a play by Gertrude Stein, it expresses some thought; and frequently it may also further the plot. In its own right, diction holds the interest of the audience largely by means of the mental images which the words evoke. Thus, diction involves the audience in a kind of thought process which takes a certain amount of time, for the words must not only be heard and understood, but must stimulate the mind, consciously or unconsciously, to recall the images and associations necessary for a full comprehension of the words.

When Cyrano gives his definition of a kiss in the third act of *Cyrano de Bergerac*, for example, the audience must be allowed split seconds of time to comprehend and appreciate what has been said:

> And what is a kiss, when all is done?
> A promise given under seal—a vow
> Taken before the shrine of memory—
> A signature acknowledged—a rosy dot
> Over the i of Loving—a secret whispered
> To listening lips apart—a moment made
> Immortal, with a rush of wings unseen—
> A sacrament of blossoms, a new song
> Sung by two hearts to an old simple tune—
> The ring of one horizon around two souls
> Together, all alone!

Naturally the actor will use all his skill in pointing to give emphasis to the key words, but if spoken without due consideration for the time it takes an audience to understand the vigor, the beauty, and the aptness of the images, the passage may be appreciated only for its melody and not for its diction. Played only for the value of the sound and the melody, the speech may easily seem over long. Played more slowly for the value of the images evoked by the diction, it may well seem much more interesting.

It is a paradox of the theater that, frequently, to go slower is to seem to go faster. To make each definition of a kiss clear to an audience is to make nine points—nine telegraph poles for the audience to pass—but if the passage is delivered in this way it will require a fraction more time than would be consumed if it were played as one beautiful-sounding love speech and thus only one point were made. Actually, the actor will probably want to combine the two methods of playing the scene, making some of the definitions clear and separate points of interest and combining some of the less interesting ones to give a general effect. Many of the plays of Christopher Fry pose the same problem, and the actor is forced to decide whether to take the time to make each point or to play only for the general effect.

Points Derived from the Thought

To use diction and spectacle—speech and action—for the purpose of projecting the thought of the play is one of the most difficult tasks for the actor. Here he is concerned, not with the thoughts of the characters as they are related to characterization and plot, but with the author's thought, the meaning of the play.

Many authors leave the meaning of the play unspoken, contenting themselves with telling the story and presenting the characters, leaving the audience to discover for themselves the significance of the drama; but this is not always so. Many of the choruses of Greek drama depend for their interest upon the projection of the thought and the philosophy of the author. The Trojan women speak of the futility and the meaninglessness of war; the elders in *Agamemnon* discuss the dangers and consequences of false pride.

In the last speech of *Winterset*, Esdras, the old Jew, mourns over the bodies of his murdered daughter and her lover. It is a long speech—thirty lines—and it can be played solely for the grief and loneliness of the old man and his ability to find strength and consolation in his philosophy; but certainly these points can be made in fewer than thirty lines, and there is danger that at the end of the play, after the excitement of the murders, after the pathos and tragedy of the death scenes, Esdras' speech, played in this way, will seem like more of the same thing—too much of the same thing. The new element which will sustain the interest of the audience is the thought which brings strength and consolation to Esdras and which, if properly projected, will carry the audience beyond their grief to an understanding of the meaning and significance of the play:

> On this star,
> in this hard star-adventure, knowing not
> what fires mean to right and left, nor whether
> a meaning was intended or presumed,
> man can stand up, and look out blind, and say:
> in all these turning lights I find no clue,
> only a masterless night, and in my blood

no certain answer, yet is my mind my own,
yet is my heart a cry toward something dim
in distance, which is higher than I am
and makes me emperor of the endless dark
even in seeking!

These are not easy words to speak; at first reading, the passage seems turgid and murky, cluttered with dependent phrases; but once the sentence has been parsed and the essence of the meaning distilled, it becomes a strong and powerful affirmation of the dignity of man and the meaningfulness of life. The actor must be careful to use his techniques of phrasing so that the audience will comprehend the passage fully on one hearing and his techniques of pointing so that the key words will stand out with the necessary emphasis. Again, it will take a bit more care and a bit more time to make the passage seem brief to an audience.

Points Derived from Character

Character is one of the most important elements of drama from the point of view of sustaining audience interest, and it is of prime importance to the actor, whose business is the delineation of character. The invention of character actions has been discussed in a previous chapter. The actor is free to include this kind of action whenever he considers it necessary or helpful to the play, but he should always take care that his inventions are in agreement with the author's original creation. In considering such actions in connection with the problem of time, the question is always whether or not the actor's inventions have sufficient relevancy and interest to hold the attention of the audience.

An inexperienced actress who was playing the role of Juliet came to the line, in Act III, Scene 5, "My husband is on earth, my faith in heaven," and in one performance made a long pause after the word "husband." When the director asked her why, she explained that when she mentioned her husband she suddenly thought how handsome he was and how fine, and how much she loved him. She defended her performance on the basis that Juliet would have had these thoughts. It is true that Juliet might have had such thoughts, but it is also true that Shakespeare might have given her lines to express those thoughts had he considered them necessary to the role.

There are, however, many scenes in which the author himself has introduced material which is primarily intended as characterization. The actor must recognize these passages, must know precisely which phase of his character is being elaborated, and must do all that he can to make that material interesting. These passages most frequently occur in the opening scenes of plays, or in scenes in which a character is introduced for the first time.

When the Nurse makes her first appearance in Act I, Scene 3, of *Romeo and Juliet*, the plot, which concerns Lady Capulet's announcement of the plans of a marriage with Paris, must wait while the Nurse prattles of her memories and her youth. In many ways, the advice Polonius gives his son, in Act I, Scene 3, of *Hamlet*, is largely concerned with establishing Polonius' character. In both these scenes, anything the actor can do to enrich the characterization, any actions he can invent to exemplify the qualities revealed in the speeches, will increase the audience interest.

Points Derived from Plot

Scenes in which the dominant element is the plot are much the easiest for the actor to play, because in a well-written play the author has done most of the work; he has made the audience wonder what will happen next, provided the suspense, and then answered the question in a way that automatically raises a new question.

In plot scenes, the actor will, as usual, use his techniques for providing special emphasis upon important key words; but the necessity of pointing individual words or actions will be much less frequent in these scenes. More important will be the techniques of phrasing, which the actor will use to indicate that the play has moved from the discussion of one question to the discussion of the next. Also important are those actions, which have been discussed in a previous chapter, by which the actors clearly state the changing character relationships, which are an important part of the plot.

In attempting to establish the correct pace of a play to sustain the audience's interest, it is helpful to remember that dialogue, as explained in the chapter on phrasing, tends to be written with three phrases or sentences devoted to a single thought, so that the audience will have time to grasp its meaning; anything of importance which is written more briefly than this will usually require that the actor devise actions which will consume a slightly longer time than would otherwise be necessary, in order to let the audience have enough time to comprehend the thought and its implications; anything written at greater length will need to be hurried over, supported by some additional interest, such as character business, or divided into two thoughts and played for two separate points.

Ibsen is a consummate craftsman in writing dialogue which sustains the interest of the audience by dribbling out tiny bits of information which continuously move the plot, though ever so slowly. In the scene between Nora and Krogstad in the first act of *A Doll's House*, the plot is the dominant element; there is little characterization except in so far as the characters are defined by the things they say and do and threaten to do; there are no lines dealing with the thought of the play, except indirectly, and there are no lines which have much interest from the point of view of either diction or melody; spectacle is absent except in its barest essentials, the fact that the actors are on the stage and will be watched.

The actors in this scene should be cautioned that, since the plot moves so slowly, they may feel impelled to resort to movement, walking about the stage, going here and there, unless they have sufficient faith that the tiny bits of plot in each sequence of lines will be enough to sustain the interest. What is accomplished in the scene is that Krogstad threatens Nora that unless she uses her influence with her husband to have Krogstad retained in his job in the bank, he will expose the fact that she forged her father's signature to obtain the money. It takes twelve pages of dialogue to say this much—probably at least ten minutes of actual playing time.

The first sequence devotes itself to establishing that Krogstad has come to see Nora, not her husband; it consists of three speeches by Krogstad, three by Nora, and a seventh line to settle the point.

KROGSTAD: I beg your pardon, Mrs. Helmer—
NORA: (*With a suppressed cry, turns round and half jumps up.*) Ah! What do you want?

There is no reason why Krogstad should not answer this question directly by saying, "To say a few words to you," but this would be too brief a statement to establish the point with the audience. Ibsen delays the answer:

KROGSTAD: Excuse me; the outer door was ajar—somebody must have forgotten to shut it—
NORA: (*standing up*) My husband is not at home, Mr. Krogstad.
KROGSTAD: I know it.
NORA: Then what do you want here?

The plot is still concerned with the same question, but now it can be answered.

KROGSTAD: To say a few words to you.

Now there follow three short lines during which Nora hurries the children out of the room, establishing the point that there is something dangerous about Krogstad's visit. The sequence is somewhat brief, but Ibsen has called for some action which will lengthen it:

NORA: To me? (*To the children, softly*) Go in to Anna. What? No, the strange man won't hurt Mama. When he's gone we'll go on playing.

(She leads the children into the left-hand room, and shuts the door behind them. Uneasy, in suspense.) It is to me you wish to speak?

The next sequence, again three speeches by each character, establishes that Krogstad has not come to demand another payment on the loan:

KROGSTAD: Yes, to you.

NORA: Today? But it's not the first yet—

KROGSTAD: No, today is Christmas Eve. It will depend upon yourself whether you have a merry Christmas.

NORA: What do you want? I'm not ready today—

KROGSTAD: Never mind that just now. I have come about another matter. You have a minute to spare?

NORA: Oh, yes, I suppose so; although—

KROGSTAD: Good.

Now come twelve unusually short speeches, six questions or statements by Krogstad and six answers or reactions by Nora; each pair of speeches adds a minute particle of information for the benefit of the audience. At first glance it might seem that the whole sequence deals with one subject, but it can be divided into the fact that Nora's husband is with Mrs. Linden and that Mrs. Linden is an acquaintance of both Nora's and Krogstad's:

KROGSTAD: I was sitting in the restaurant opposite, and I saw your husband go down the street—

NORA: Well?

KROGSTAD: —with a lady

NORA: What then?

KROGSTAD: May I ask if the lady was a Mrs. Linden?

NORA: Yes.

End of the first part of the sequence.

KROGSTAD: Who has just come to town?

NORA: Yes. Today.

KROGSTAD: I believe she is an intimate friend of yours.

NORA: Certainly. But I don't understand—

KROGSTAD: I used to know her too.

NORA: I know you did.

Because these lines are so short, it is quite possible to play them all in one sequence, possibly increasing both the rate and the volume to arrive at a minor climax which will justify Nora's next complaint that Krogstad is catechizing her. To do this may increase the sense of excitement in the scene, but it may also decrease the import of what is being said and the audience's interest in the plot. It is also possible to play the scene at quite a slow rate, giving the audience time to understand the significance of everything that is being said. But if the actors feel that the information in each pair of lines is too infinitesimal to sustain the interest, they will assume that this method of playing the scene will bore the audience. This is clearly an instance where the actors must decide whether to go faster, in order to get to the next point, or to go slowly, in order to make points out of the material at hand.

The scene goes on, bit by bit. Krogstad gets Nora to admit that she has used her influence to get Mrs. Linden a job at the bank; then Krogstad asks her to use that influence to save his job; Nora now protests that she has no influence; Nora becomes insulted and orders him out of the house; Krogstad explains why it is so important to him that he keep his job. Each little section of dialogue adds a little more to the knowledge and understanding of the audience.

Unless the audience is to become bored, the actors must make each bit of information seem important and significant. They may strive to add interest by having the characters indicate a rather high degree of emotion. As has been suggested, they may add interest by having the characters move around: Krogstad can pace the floor, or Nora can show nervous agitation. Fundamentally, however, the audience interest depends upon the understanding of the plot and of the changing character relationships which are a part of the plot. As regards pacing the scene, the actors must decide when a point is too small to make, and therefore should be played rapidly, and when it can be made, and therefore should be played as slowly as is necessary.

It is interesting to compare this scene with the Capulet scene from *Romeo and Juliet* in which Capulet says little that the audience does not already know, repeats what he does say three times in three different speeches, and finally threatens Juliet with being disowned and disinherited. Obviously the rate of speaking in such a scene can afford to be much faster—indeed, needs to be much faster—than this scene in which each little section contains a bit of information which is new and fresh to the audience.

Tempo Is the Speed of a Performance

If *pace* is the word used to describe the speed of a play as it seems to an audience, the word *tempo* can be used to describe the actual mechanical speed with which the play is performed. Inexperienced actors are often amazed to learn that a play performed by the same cast rarely varies by more than a minute in the actual time that the curtain is up, but the records of stage managers attest to this fact.

Dressing-room conversation during a performance is often concerned with whether or not the play is going "slowly"; to hear the actors, one would think they were talking about the actual number of minutes it takes to play a scene, but actually they are talking about the pace—the rate of response on the part of the audience. One of the greatest errors for the actor is to attempt literally to go faster, when he thinks the play is going "slowly"—that is, to say the words more quickly and to perform the pantomimic actions in less time. As previously stated, speeding the tempo may well result in a decrease in pace.

One thing to consider in attempting to determine the proper tempo for a performance is that "fast" or "slow" have no actual meanings; "fast" means faster than something else and "slow" means not as fast as something else. It is desirable that any scene, or any act, or the play as a whole seem to go faster as it progresses. Again the actor must be careful not to confuse what we are calling pace with what we are calling tempo. The play only needs to *seem* to go faster.

As those in the audience watch and listen to a performance, their rate of perception will increase; as they become familiar with the characters and know what to expect, they will be quicker to note that a character has or has not deviated from the expected action; as they become involved with the plot, they will be quicker to understand the implications of each episode. It is very difficult, for instance, to get the first laugh in the performance of a farce or comedy, but by the third act the audience is in the spirit of the play and ready to laugh more frequently, and often for less cause: in such a play it may well be that the last act will be played louder, with larger gestures and with more movement, and thus at a slower tempo, but the audience will have speeded the pace of reception.

Since tempo is dictated by pace, it is very difficult to study tempo and perform any classroom or laboratory experiments unless there is an actively participating audience. The actor can be forewarned about the danger of going too fast or too slow to sustain interest, but he must eventually learn from the audience. That is one reason why stage training is so valuable to the radio, television, or motion-picture actor, who must learn to set the tempo of his performance on the basis of past experiences with live audiences.

Rhythm Is Rate of Speed of the Individual Actor

Rhythm is the time value of each individual actor; it includes the concepts of both tempo and pace, and it also includes a concept of distance —how far the character has developed or how much he has changed.

Boleslavsky uses the analogy of an elevator to explain rhythm: if an elevator—one which provides a view of the street from every floor—

stops at every floor in a thirty-story building, the view changes gradually and almost imperceptibly, but the view from the top is noticeably different from the way the world looked at street level; if the elevator makes no stops at all, the view from the top is almost unbelievably different from the view at the bottom; if the elevator stops at every fifth floor, the trip will take a shorter time than the first trip, but a longer time than the second trip, and the changes will be more obvious than on the first trip, but less startling and more believable than on the second trip; but all three trips will cover the same distance and finally arrive at the same perspective. In acting, the change and development of the character, or at least the change in the audience's knowledge and understanding of the character, is analogous to the changing view.

In the Krogstad-Nora scene, the elevator is stopping at every floor, as it does through most of the play; it is not until the third act—when Nora's husband has found out what she has done and why she has done it, when the "miracle" has not happened, that is, he has not protected her by offering to take the blame upon himself—that Nora and the audience realize how far she has traveled and how different the world looks.

Rhythm as Illustrated by the Role of Brutus

The first task for the actor in the study of any play, or any scene in a play, is to discover how tall the building is, or how far the character must develop or change. Then he must decide how many steps are involved in the character's progress from his first appearance to his final scene in the play. The role of Brutus provides an excellent example of this problem. Brutus is an honorable man, an honest, law-abiding citizen; murder and suicide are entirely foreign to his nature, and yet he plots and participates in the assassination of Caesar and eventually takes his own life. How does he get from where he started to where he is at the end of the play? How far has he come in each scene of the play? How much progress does he make during each scene?

The first step or steps are taken during his first-act scene with Cassius, while the cheers of the crowd are heard as Caesar is offered the crown. It has been noted that in one motion-picture version of *Julius Caesar*, the action for this scene was handled in flash backs showing the events Cassius is describing, and it has been suggested that the action might better be a pantomimic dramatization of Cassius' insinuating and plotting; a third alternative is to place the emphasis on the degree to which Brutus is moved.

At first it would appear that Brutus is not moved at all, for he states that he is not jealous, that he understands what Cassius has been trying to do, and that he had previously considered the problem; then he dismisses Cassius:

> for this present,
> I would not, so with love I might entreat you,
> Be any further moved.

He promises to hear Cassius further at some indefinite future time. But then he states that his belief in freedom is more important than his loyalty to Rome.   In Boleslavsky's figure of speech, the elevator has gone up.

> Till then, my noble friend, chew upon this:
> Brutus had rather be a villager
> Than to repute himself a son of Rome
> Under these hard conditions as this time
> Is like to lay upon us.

Cassius is quick to note the progress he has made with Brutus:

> I am glad that my weak words
> Have struck but thus much shew of fire from Brutus.

The questions for the actor playing Brutus are: How much show of fire? Is it noted only by Cassius or also by the audience?   How is it revealed?

In the next portion of the scene, Caesar returns, and, speaking to Antony, says he thinks Cassius is a dangerous man.   Then Casca relates the offering of the crown and Caesar's attack of the "falling-sickness."   Apparently Brutus has been further moved, for he now makes a definite appointment to see Cassius tomorrow, offering either to come to his house or to have Cassius come to his.   Cassius again makes note of the progress in a soliloquy, which informs the audience of what they possibly may not have seen, since Brutus has been all but silent in the preceding scene:

> Well, Brutus, thou art noble; yet, I see,
> Thy honourable metal may be wrought
> From that it is disposed.

Although Brutus does not appear in the next scene, it is important to the development of his character, for the scene prepares the audience for things which are to happen.   First Casca and Cicero describe the wild, stormy night and the strange signs and portents which they have seen; then Casca and Cassius discuss the state of Rome, their fear that Caesar will be crowned, and the state of servility which is being imposed upon them—all arguments which bear on Brutus' decision and prepare the audience to be in understanding agreement with that decision.   Even though Brutus does not participate in the scene, the play moves, and so does the role of Brutus, for at the end of the scene Cassius says:

> I will ere day
> See Brutus at his house: three parts of him
> Is ours already, and the man entire
> Upon the next encounter yields him ours.

In the minds of the audience Brutus is much nearer a decision than he was when last seen.

In the first scene of the second act, Brutus is walking in his orchard, having spent a sleepless night. He calls his servant and orders that a light be lighted in his study. Apparently he has been pondering his problem all night long and has arrived at a momentous decision, for his first words are, "It must be by his death." Brutus has traveled a considerable distance. That one phrase, coming as it does from the context of Brutus' thoughts, poses technical problems for the actor since he must somehow impress upon the audience the full implications of its meaning, as to both the character of Brutus and the plot.

Later in the scene Brutus' wife, Portia, describes his behavior:

> An yesternight at supper
> You suddenly arose and walk'd about,
> Musing and sighing, with your arms across;
> And when I ask'd you what the matter was,
> You stared upon me with ungentle looks:
> I urged you further; then you scratched your head,
> And too impatiently stamp'd with your foot.

Portia's speech may provide useful hints as to what Brutus might do after the servant has left him alone and before he says, "It must be by his death." Note that there is no immediate antecedent for the pronoun *his;* the audience must know immediately that it refers to Caesar. To use Boleslavsky's analogy, it is as though the elevator suddenly arrived at the thirtieth floor, having made no other stops—or at least at the twenty-fifth floor—for Brutus does not have much further to go to become an assassin. In the soliloquy that follows, Brutus goes back over the arguments, then the servant brings one of the notes that Cassius has arranged to come to Brutus' attention; and it is established that the Ides of March has come. Brutus is now ready to take a leading role with the conspirators, convinced that the murder they plan is both necessary and justified.

Brutus has come a long way, but he has traveled swiftly. It is interesting to note that he speaks but fifteen speeches, a total of thirty-eight lines, from the time he says that he does not wish "to be moved further" to his fateful "It must be by his death." The technical problem for the actor, once he has analyzed the role, is to devise the means by which each step in the development of the character may be made clear and meaningful.

Rhythm As Rate of Understanding by the Audience

Not many characters have the kind of growth and development that Brutus has; there are relatively few plays that present this problem, and there are seldom more than two or three characters in any one play that develop in this way.   Usually what is mistaken for true character development is really the development of the audience's understanding of the character.   When two people are introduced to each other they form a first impression, and as the acquaintance grows they learn more about each other—their backgrounds, their families, and their reactions to different things; the first impressions may change or may deepen.   In the same way, the audience meets a character in a play for the first time and forms an impression of him, but as the play continues and more and more about the character is revealed, the first impression may change, giving an illusion that the character has changed.   Nora and, to a certain extent, Torvald are such characters; each scene seems to draw away another veil between the audience and the character, until the complete truth of Nora's personality is revealed to the audience, and to Torvald, in so far as he is capable of seeing the truth.

Portia in *The Merchant of Venice* is like Nora in that her character does not change but is gradually revealed in the course of the play. There is a difference, however, because in *A Doll's House* each scene reveals more of the same qualities in Nora, her independence and her personal integrity, while in *The Merchant of Venice* each scene tends to reveal a different facet of Portia's character.   The amusing, vivacious, and somewhat cynical young lady who mimics the faults of her suitors in the first scene with Nerissa gives no hint of being capable of performing the trial scene with such poise and such wisdom.

Many an actress has had difficulty in reconciling the Portia of the trial with the Portia of the rest of the play.   To play the first scene with the maturity and dignity which is essential for the trial scene is likely to destroy its lightness and charm; to play the trial scene with the light, girlish quality which might be appropriate to the first scene is likely to destroy the power and dignity of the trial scene; to play them with distinctly different qualities is likely to destroy the unity of the characterization and of the play as a whole.   Remember that the fifth act returns to the light-comedy quality of the opening of the play.

The answer to the problem is to discover the rhythm of the role, the steps by which the audience can be made aware that there is a depth and maturity underlying Portia's gaiety in the first scene.   Possibly the opening lines of the scene can be used for this purpose; possibly the first mention of Bassanio can strike the new note; possibly some of the lines in the Morocco scenes and the Arragon scene can show her dignity and her control; possibly the opening of the Bassanio casket-choosing scene can include character actions which will foreshadow the trial scene.   The solution of the problem must rest with the individual actress, but the problem must be solved, and the solution will be found in carefully pointing and placing special emphasis upon those lines and actions which will lead the audience to suspect that Portia is capable of the things she says and does in the trial scene.

A third type of role—and by far the most common—is one which neither changes nor seems to change, but one in which the quality or qualities which are illustrated in the opening scenes are strengthened and intensified in the following scenes.   In these plays the author usually arranges the episodes of the plot in a climactic sequence, each episode involving the character in a more important and consequential test, to which the character responds by continuing to act exactly like himself and exactly as the audience expected he would act.   Here the technical problem for the actor is not one of pointing and emphasis so much as it is one of climaxing.   Just as the author has arranged the episodes in a climactic sequence, the actor must arrange his responses in a climactic order.   As the play progresses, he does not become different; he becomes "more so."

The Nurse in *Romeo and Juliet* is such a character.   She displays in the first scene all the qualities which she will show in later scenes; she is garrulous, hearty, and bawdy; she has a boisterous sense of humor, and she is fond of Juliet.   The only deviation from these qualities occurs in the little moment after Capulet has threatened his daughter with disinheritance when the Nurse goes against Juliet and advises her to marry Paris. The problem for the actress playing the Nurse is to avoid overstating the character in the first scene, so that something fresh and new and "more so" will be left for the later scenes.

Even a role of this type, provided that it is of any considerable length, should give the audience a sense of discovery.   The pace of the play will depend in part upon the audience's awareness of the degree or the intensity of the quality which is the basis of the characterization.   In the old farce, *Nothing But The Truth*, the leading character makes a bet that he can tell the truth for 24 hours, and in each episode the consequences of telling the truth become more severe.   If the pace of the play is to be maintained, the actor playing the role must devise means of showing in each episode a greater temptation to lie, greater strength of character in telling the truth, and a greater reaction to the painful consequences.

It has been illustrated, in the discussions of both progressions and climaxing, that the actor always needs to go forward, always needs to be able to carry his characterization to one higher level, always needs to leave the most forceful statement of a thought or an emotion until the very last. The same fact is the basis of rhythm. In roles where the characterization does not change, the only way the actor can maintain the pace is to make the audience aware of each step in the increase of the degree of the emotions, the intensity of the thoughts, and the qualities of the character.

Pace Determines Rhythm and Tempo

Rhythm, tempo, and pace, as defined in this chapter, are all closely related; pace, the frequency with which the audience receives a new impulse of interest, is the dominating factor that decrees both the tempo and the rhythm. All three of these time concepts are not actually techniques, but rather results to be achieved by means of the basic techniques. They are a system of analysis by which the actor decides what he must do; they are not a method of doing it.

In many acting companies it is the director who settles all matters of time, just as in an orchestra it is the conductor who beats the time, sets the tempi, and calls for the individual instruments to take a more prominent or a less prominent part; but it will help the actor if he understands what effects the director is striving for and has some conception of how they may be achieved.

There is always the danger that the actor will think that, if he analyzes a part perfectly and has the skill to perform it with mechanical precision, he will give an excellent performance; but technique is only half of art; it is the form, but not the content. A study of the time concepts merely helps to define and to make specific the inspirations which will be needed. It points a way for the actor to make maximum use of any inspirations he may have. It is a way of achieving competence, without which, excellence is rarely possible.

EXERCISES

1. Passage from *Cyrano De Bergerac*,[1] Act III.

> And what is a kiss, when all is done?
> A promise given under seal—a vow

[1] Copyright by Henry Holt and Company, Inc.

> Taken before the shrine of memory—
> A signature acknowledged—a rosy dot
> Over the i of Loving—a secret whispered
> To listening lips apart—a moment made
> Immortal, with the rush of wings unseen—
> A sacrament of blossoms, a new song
> Sung by two hearts to an old simple tune—
> The ring of one horizon around two souls
> Together, all alone!

a. Play the first three lines as if there were no more to the speech, using as fast a rate of speaking as seems possible if the meaning is to be kept clear.

b. Play the whole speech, using the rate established in a for the first three lines and then building a progression through increase in pitch, volume, and rate.

c. Play the whole speech, using a decrease in rate to the extent that in the last lines individual words are sustained for a slight duration of time, but not to the extent that there are noticeable pauses between the separate definitions: "a new song," or, "a new song sung by two hearts to an old simple tune."

d. Keep the reading evolved in c, but insert a pause before each separate definition, filling the pause with some slight change in physical attitude or with a small gesture.

NOTE: Exercise d will take longer than exercise b, but will seem shorter to the audience because there has been enough time to comprehend the images evoked by the words.

2. Speech from *Winterset*,[2] Act III.

Esdras, the old Jew, stands before the slain bodies of his daughter, Miriamne, and of Mio, whom she loved. He speaks to his son, Garth, and to a few others who have been attracted to the spot by the shooting:

> Well, they were wiser than you and I.   To die
> when you are young and untouched, that's beggary
> to a miser of years, but the devils locked in synod
> shake and are daunted when men set their lives
> at hazard for heart's love, and lose.   And these,
> who were yet children, will weigh more than all
> a city's elders when the experiment
> is reckoned up in the end.   Oh, Miriamne,
> and Mio—Mio, my son—know this where you lie,
> this is the glory of earth-born men and women,
> not to cringe, never to yield, but standing,

2 Copyright by Anderson House.

take defeat implacable and defiant,
die unsubmitting. I wish that I'd died so,
long ago; before you're old you'll wish
that you had died as they have. On this star,
in this hard star-adventure, knowing not
what fires mean to right and left, nor whether
a meaning was intended or presumed,
man can stand up, and look out blind, and say:
in all these turning lights I find no clue,
only a masterless night, and in my blood
no certain answer, yet is my mind my own,
yet is my heart a cry toward something dim
in distance, which is higher than I am
and makes me emperor of the endless dark
even in seeking! What odds and ends of life
men may live otherwise, let them live, and then
go out, as I shall go, and you. Our part
is only to bury them. Come, take her up.
They must not lie here.

a. First parse the sentences so that you are quite sure of the subjects and predicates and which adjectives modify which nouns. It would do no harm to go back to the eighth grade and diagram the sentences.

b. Choose the techniques of pointing and the devices of emphasis which seem necessary to convey the thought to the audience.

c. Invent actions—gestures and changes of physical attitude—which will help convey Esdras' emotional motivations for the different sections and which may be used by the actor to phrase the whole speech in such a way that its meaning and significance will be clear to the audience.

NOTE: Taking time to clarify the meaning and to give it its emotional significance will slow the speech, but it will increase the audience interest. It is assumed that Esdras, being an old man, would have a slow rhythm in speaking, that he would use a slow tempo. If he does so effectively, the result will be an increase in pace for the audience.

3. Sequence from *Romeo and Juliet*, Act I, Scene 3.

Rehearse the Nurse's speech beginning, "Faith, I can tell her age unto an hour . . . ," and also her next three speeches.

a. On the theory that the Nurse is a garrulous person who talks too much, play the scene at as fast a rate as seems possible, making, in a sense, only the one point that she talks too much.

b. Invent character actions which will be of interest to the audience. Take time for the Nurse to dramatize the story as she tells it. Take time for the Nurse to enact her own emotions and reactions as she remembers the

episode. Let Lady Capulet and Juliet assume an air of tolerant understanding at rehearing the stories which Nurse has told many times.

NOTE: The second version will take longer to play, but it may be of
greater interest to the audience.

c. After the scene has been worked out according to *b*, eliminate those
character actions which seem least effective, so that a compromise between
a and *b* is achieved.

4. *Hamlet*, Act I, Scene 3.

Rehearse Polonius' advice to Laertes beginning, "Yet here, Laertes! Aboard,
aboard, for shame!"

a. On the theory that Polonius is a garrulous person who talks too much,
play the scene as fast as possible, supposing that Laertes is impatient to
leave and that he would do so if Polonius would stop talking.

b. Invent character actions which would interest an audience. Let Laertes
and Ophelia assume a tolerant attitude and wait for Polonius to finish.

NOTE: Again, the second version will probably take longer, but it may be
of greater interest.

c. Work out a compromise between *a* and *b*, keeping those character
actions which seem most effective, and otherwise maintaining a fairly
rapid tempo.

5. Sequence from *A Doll's House*,[3] Act I.

Rehearse the scene between Nora and Krogstad which begins, "I beg your
pardon, Mrs. Helmer. . . ." The William Archer translation is recom-
mended.

a. Play the scene avoiding any pauses that are not absolutely essential.

b. Divide the scene into small sections, each section marked by some new
plot revelation or some facet of characterization. Select the techniques
necessary to point the plot and character developments.

c. Experiment with variations in the tempo of each section and in the rhythm
of the individual actors to gain the most desirable pace.

d. Use a variety of techniques for the small progressions in the scene.

NOTE: A variety of techniques and tempi should sustain the audience's
interest, thus seeming to quicken the pace.

6. Sequences from *Julius Caesar*, Act I, Scenes 2 and 3; Act II, Scene 1.

a. Study the role of Brutus, paying particular attention to the steps by which
he arrives at his decision to participate in the assassination of Caesar.
Brutus himself says, "Between the acting of a dreadful thing and the first
motion, all the interim is like a phantasma or a hideous dream."

Mark the speeches which show the progress in his thinking and select
techniques of emphasis and pointing which seem appropriate to them.

[3] Copyright by Charles Scribner's Sons.

Mark the places where reactions by Brutus to what is being said by others could clarify the progress of his thinking. Devise suitable pantomimic action to reveal these reactions. Pay particular attention to Act I, Scene 3, in which Brutus does not participate, to see what arguments are presented to prepare the audience for Brutus' words and actions in Act II, Scene 1. Try to invent plausible physical attitudes and gestures which will express his emotional and intellectual states.

7. The Role of Portia in *The Merchant of Venice*.
Study the role of Portia. Examine carefully the different facets of her character which are revealed in the different scenes. Search out sequences in the various scenes which can be used to prepare the audience to accept her poise, dignity, and intellectual strength in the trial scene as natural and inevitable. Select techniques of pointing and emphasis which will highlight those passages in the earlier scenes that can be used to foreshadow the trial scene.

Chapter 12. STYLE

At first glance it might seem that style is not properly the concern of the actor, except in so far as he must acquire the technical facility to execute a performance in any style demanded by the author and dictated by the director. Many persons, however, insist that the style of a performance is largely, if not exclusively, determined by the methods or the techniques of the artist; and since the actor, in addition to being an artist in his own right, is also the instrument of both the author and the director, the student of acting would do well to give thoughtful consideration to the complex and confusing subject of style.

The *Oxford English Dictionary* lists twenty-eight different meanings of the noun *style*, so that there would seem to be little hope of arriving at one ultimate definition which would be acceptable to everyone, but there are several concepts which recur frequently in the various definitions and which the actor may profitably examine. A study of these concepts should help him achieve a better understanding of his own art, as well as of both the aims and the methods of the other artists with whom he is in constant collaboration—the author, the director, the other actors, the scene designer, and the costume designer. Ever since the revolution, or evolution, which occurred in the theater during the latter part of the nineteenth century and the beginning of the twentieth—bringing with it an increase in the importance of the scene designer, the advent of the director in the modern sense of the word, the ideal of ensemble playing, and the modern emphasis on careful artistic integration of all the elements of a production—actors have been required to achieve a technical facility which permits them to adapt, not only their methods, but also their aims to the methods and the aims of their collaborators.

Style Determined by Techniques of the Author

One of the most persistent concepts involved in the various definitions of *style* is the idea that style is closely linked to the personality of the artist. According to one definition, for example, style is "the manner of expression characteristic of a particular writer, or of a literary group or period." It should be noted that, in defining style as "the manner of expression," all consideration of subject material is eliminated and style is regarded solely as a matter of techniques and methods. If one accepts this definition of style, as well as the idea that, since a play is first of all the work of an author, the actor and all the other collaborating artists should adapt their own techniques to those of the playwright, it becomes an obligation for the actor to make a careful analysis of the techniques or methods which are employed by the author and which distinguish his work from that of any other author.

Actually, as was suggested in the definition, many of the "manners of expression" which are characteristic of the author are also characteristic of other authors of the same period or literary group; Shakespeare, for example, shares many characteristics with other authors of the Elizabethan period. Sometimes a particular manner of expression seems to have been invented primarily by one man and then taken up and used by other men; Marlowe is usually given credit for the "mighty line," but once he had adopted this metrical form, writing in iambic pentameter became the accustomed practice of many other writers, including Shakespeare. The chorus, which all the Greek dramatists used as a means of accomplishing certain purposes, was inherited from the early rituals that were the forerunners of drama. The different degrees to which the individual dramatists used the chorus—the extent to which they were used as a storytelling device, their participation in the plot, their function as observers of and commentators on the plot—are all manners of expression which help to distinguish the work of one dramatist from another, while the use of the chorus at all distinguishes the Greek dramatists as a group from the playwrights of any other period. To the extent that O'Neill in *Mourning Becomes Electra* uses the villagers to serve the purposes and perform the functions of a Greek chorus, he may be said to have written in the Greek style.

The device, perfected by Ibsen, of relating action which has happened before the time of the play by having one character, who has been involved in that action, tell it to another character may be compared to the similar device, used by many other dramatists, of having the maid and the butler explain the antecedent action to the audience by telling each other what they both know and what concerns neither of them. In more recent plays, such as *Death of a Salesman*, the flash back is used for the same purpose, a scene being inserted into the play which dramatizes a part of the action which is supposed to have happened at some previous time. This manner of expression may possibly have been borrowed from the motion pictures or adapted from the stream-of-consciousness technique used by many novelists. Whatever its source, the use of this device immediately marks the author as a twentieth-century playwright.

Only a very few of the most obvious devices which distinguish the style of one period from that of another have been mentioned, but they will serve to illustrate how the actors' knowledge and comprehension of the distinguishing characteristics of the style in which a play is written will affect the style in which it is performed. No actor should consider himself trained until he has familiarized himself with the history and the development of dramatic literature and has developed a keen appreciation of the methods and devices used by the dramatists of each era. It is only through the acquisition of such knowledge that the actor can hope to become an adequate and intelligent interpreter of the author's work.

Techniques Determined by Physical Theater

It will also profit the actor, particularly if he expects to perform in plays of another period, to have some knowledge of the actual theaters for which the plays were written. The actors who played in the Greek dramas, which were intended to be performed in huge outdoor theaters with the characters wearing masks, obviously could not rely on changing facial expressions to help portray the emotions of the characters. On the other hand, Elizabethan drama is full of references to the characters' facial expressions because the actors were in close enough contact with the audience to make changes in facial expression effective.

There is no necessity for the actor who appears in a modern production of a play which was originally performed in a totally different kind of theater to use the same methods and techniques that were apparently used in the original performance. Certainly Judith Anderson in her performance of *Medea* and Laurence Olivier in his performance of *Oedipus* did not forego using facial expressions and rely exclusively on vocal techniques and large gestures, but both did use a sustained vocal tone that frequently approached the quality and effect of singing.

The actor in an eighteenth-century comedy will look in vain for opportunities to invent actions which make use of the setting and the furniture. In this period the scenery consisted mainly of painted backgrounds, in front of which the actors played, making their entrances from either side and hurrying as quickly as possible to the center and front of the stage, where they would be in the most brilliant light. Platforms and elevations were not used, and one looks in vain for scenes of physical action such as abound in dramas written for the Elizabethan stage, which—with its "inner below" and "inner above" and balconies—lent itself to considerable movement and action, permitting Mercutio to leap a wall, Juliet to lower a rope ladder, and Prospero to open magical caves.

In a modern production of *She Stoops to Conquer*, the scene designer provided a handsome 10-foot flight of stairs, which might well have been

authentic eighteenth-century architecture, but which presented diffi-
culties for the actors, who found that the author had provided neither
entrance lines nor exit lines and that the play was forced to wait while an
actor made his entrance or exit.

These few examples should make it clear that any shift in the physical
conditions of performance from the kind of production which was envisaged by the author automatically forces changes in the techniques
and methods of playing the scene and thus alters the author's characteristic
manner of expression.

Techniques Determined by Style of Dialogue

While these major and obvious differences in the plays of various
styles and periods are of tremendous importance to the actor, he must
also be concerned with the smaller and more specific techniques that are
characteristic of a particular author. The ways in which one author
may differ from another are so many and so varied that it is impossible
either to list or to classify them, but a few examples may serve to illustrate that the actor must learn to understand and appreciate the special
quality of each play and adapt his own work to its specific needs.

In *Romeo and Juliet,* most of the characters usually speak in blank verse,
in unrhymed iambic pentameters, but some of the servants, such as Gregory, Samson, Abraham, and Balthasar, speak in prose. Since the quality of
the speeches written for the different characters varies so noticeably, it
must be presumed that the quality of the acting should also vary, both
in the manner of speaking the lines and in the type of actions selected to
accompany the lines. No one in real life, not even if he were living in
Shakespearean England, would speak in blank verse; the characters who
speak in verse have not been merely transported to the stage as they
might exist in real life; their speech has become somewhat formalized and
exalted, or raised above the common speech. To match the method of
speaking the line to the quality of the line itself, the actor may wish to
prolong the vowel sounds slightly and to accent the stressed syllables
slightly, so that the audience will sense the rhythmic pulsation of the
lines. Since the lines are larger and more sustained than the sentences of
ordinary conversation, the actor may wish to use larger and more sustained gestures than would be appropriate to everyday speech; but it is
not necessary to do so.

There have been many productions of Shakespeare's plays in which the
actors strove to speak the lines in such a natural manner that no one
would guess that they were written in blank verse. This seems to have
been done on the theory that to speak them so as to conceal or destroy
the rhythm is to speak them more naturally and that to be more natural

is to be more truthful. It is obvious that Shakespeare was quite capable of writing in prose when he chose to do so, and it must be assumed that when he deliberately chose to write in blank verse he did so because he hoped thereby to achieve some particular effect. It is equally obvious that when an actor chooses to speak verse as though it were not verse he has deliberately and intentionally changed the style of the play. This was apparently the intention of the actors in the New York production of *Macbeth* in which Michael Redgrave appeared, and they were so skillful in carrying out their intention that the play as well as the characters lost some of their heroic stature. The impression created, according to one critic, was that of seeing Mr. and Mrs. Macbeth at home.

Techniques of Playing Rhymed Verse

Another problem which occurs in *Romeo and Juliet* is the selection of appropriate techniques for playing the rhymed couplets which are frequently used at the ends of scenes, in relation to the exits of important characters, and at the end of certain significant passages. Excluding the speech of the Prologue, the first of the rhymed couplets comes at the end of the street brawl, directly before the entrance of the Prince:

MONTAGUE: Thou villain Capulet,—Hold me not, let me go.
LADY MONTAGUE: Thou shalt not stir a foot to seek a foe.

The Prince's speech is followed by Benvolio's recital of how the fight started. Then Lady Montague again speaks in a rhymed couplet:

O, where is Romeo? Saw you him today?
Right glad I am he was not at this fray.

Benvolio tells what he knows of Romeo's whereabouts and actions, and then Montague adds what he knows on the subject, finishing his speech with another couplet:

Black and portentous must this humour prove,
Unless good counsel may the cause remove.

The lack of any knowledge concerning the cause of Romeo's behavior is discussed in the next eleven lines, which are followed by three more couplets:

MONTAGUE: Could we but learn from whence his sorrows grow,
We would as willingly give cure as know.
(*Enter Romeo*)
BENVOLIO: See, where he comes: so please you, step aside;
I'll know his grievance, or be much denied.

MONTAGUE: I would thou wert so happy by thy stay,
To hear true shrift. Come madam, let's away.

In these passages the dialogue has become noticeably more contrived—more artificial. Coming at the end of a passage or a speech, the couplet gives a certain flair and brilliance that seem to bring the preceding scene or subject to a definite conclusion. The actors, according to their taste, may elect to do what they can to hide the rhymes by placing stresses and accents upon the unrhymed words and by moving as they speak the rhymed words, so that the action will distract the attention of the audience from the rhymes; or the actors may adopt a middle course and do nothing either to conceal the rhymes or to attract attention to them, letting them have whatever effect they have merely in being heard; or the actors may decide both to phrase the sentences so that the accents and the stresses fall on the rhymed words, and to invent actions to complement the effect of finish and finality achieved by the couplets, completing the actions exactly as the last rhyming words are spoken.

The last of these alternatives—matching Shakespeare's lines with actions of a comparable quality—would seem to be most suitable. Although it is not necessarily the best way, the actors should at least experiment with this alternative of playing the couplets in the most effective manner possible, instead of deciding immediately, since they fear the artificiality of the rhymes, that the rhymes should be submerged as much as possible.

The dialogue between Romeo and Benvolio in which Romeo tells of his love for Rosaline is sprinkled with rhymes; they do not come exclusively at the end of specific passages, but are woven into the texture of the dialogue. Is Shakespeare now using them to create a different effect? Benvolio makes very few of the rhymes himself; he is restricted to one at the end of the scene and one at a false ending of the scene, but Romeo frequently makes a rhyme with one of Benvolio's speeches. Are the rhymes meant to suggest that Romeo is not truly in love, that he is merely mouthing the phrases of love and assuming the attitudes of a lover? Is it all a little too neat, a little too contrived, to be entirely believable? Later in the play, when Romeo is in love with Juliet, the rhymes have disappeared; and in Mercutio's poetic flights of fancy, such as the Queen Mab speech, there are no rhymes. The fact that Shakespeare's later and more mature plays dispense with rhymes implies that he found this device unsuccessful, whatever the effect he had hoped it would create.

If the actor wishes to match technique with technique, device with device, manner with manner, he should, whenever possible, invent a movement or a gesture which comes to a definite end in a momentarily posed attitude at the precise moment when the rhyme is closed. When Romeo

makes a rhyme with a speech of Benvolio's, it would be essential for
Benvolio to begin an action which he may continue while he speaks his
part of the couplet and which Romeo may either complete or echo as
he finishes the couplet.   It is likely that this kind of acting will produce a
slightly comic or amusing effect, which might serve to heighten the wit,
or the intended wit, of the scene.   Certainly it would "point" the rhymes
and make the audience aware of them.

Techniques of Differentiating Blank Verse and Rhymed Verse

In later scenes in *Romeo and Juliet*, such as the balcony scene, Act II,
Scene 2, the couplets appear with much less frequency and usually come
at the end of the scene or at the end of a distinct and separate passage.
According to the scene division indicated in most editions of the play,
the first line of this scene is the second line of a rhymed couplet which
is begun in the last line of the previous scene.   At the end of Scene 1,
Benvolio says:

> Go, then; for 'tis in vain
> To seek him here that means not to be found.

Then Romeo, at the start of the next scene says:

> He jests at scars that never felt a wound.

It would seem that the scene division which is usually used must be in-
correct, since it is likely that Shakespeare meant the two lines to be
spoken in an immediate relationship.   Then follows the lyric passage,
unrhymed, which Romeo delivers when he sees Juliet on the balcony, a
passage which finishes in a rhyme:

> her eyes in heaven
> Would through the airy region stream so bright
> That birds would sing and think it were not night.

The scene continues in blank verse until Juliet seems to end the scene with
a couplet:

> Good night, good night! as sweet repose and rest
> Come to thy heart as that within my breast!

But Romeo will not let the conversation end; the scene continues until the
Nurse calls.   Again the scene seems to end with a couplet:

> I hear some noise within; dear love, adieu!
> Anon, good nurse! Sweet Montague, be true.

But Juliet herself cannot bear to leave and instructs Romeo to wait a moment. Again, as the scene seems about to end, the couplets reappear:

JULIET: A thousand times good night! (*Exit above*)
ROMEO: A thousand times the worse, to want thy light!
        Love goes toward love, as schoolboys from their books,
        But love from love, toward school with heavy looks.

Juliet returns, and the lovers make their plans to meet again. The scene finally ends with three couplets, one for Juliet, and two for Romeo:

JULIET: Good night, good night! parting is such sweet sorrow
        That I shall say good night till it be morrow. (*Exit above.*)
ROMEO: Sleep dwell upon thine eyes, peace in thy breast!
        Would I were sleep and peace, so sweet to rest!
        Hence will I to my ghostly father's cell,
        His help to crave, and my dear hap to tell. (*Exit*)

The effect of these couplets, appearing always at the end, or at the apparent end of the scene, is one of satisfying completeness or of inevitable fulfillment, like a piece of music which resolves itself in a final chord. The fact that the scene, partly through this device, seems to end several times, only to begin again, adds a charming note of humor, which the scene can well afford to have. Again, to match the author's technique with a satisfactorily appropriate acting technique, the obvious device would be an action or a gesture timed exactly with the couplet, that would also convey a sense of completeness and finality.

Gesture Adapted to Quality of Dialogue

Most plays are not written with the obvious and diverse changes in style that are characteristic of *Romeo and Juliet*, but each play has, or should have, a distinctive quality which makes it different from all other plays. It is the actor's task to understand that distinctive quality and to select those techniques which will be most effective in making the audience understand and appreciate that quality. All phases of the technique of acting will be employed in evolving the style which is appropriate to each play. The actor must learn to phrase a scene as the author has phrased it, to build climaxes where the author has built them, to place the emphasis upon those parts of the play which are most characteristic of the author, and to point the lines and even the specific words which are most expressive of the particular quality of the play.

The size of a performance is a particularly important factor in determining the style of the performance. The actor will find that a change in the duration of a gesture, for example, will have an immediate and noticeable effect upon the style. When a scene is written with short, crisp sentences, it is likely that short, crisp gestures and movements will best emphasize this quality; when the author uses long, sustained sentences, it is most likely that a sustained gesture will be most suitable. But this is not always so. In some instances a long, sustained gesture might be used with short, crisp sentences to provide a startling and effective contrast, which would give greater emphasis to the lines.

There are no absolute rules in art. The actor may learn by practice and experimentation which effects are most likely to be created by which techniques, but only his own taste, natural or acquired, can tell him which effect he should strive to attain.

Style As Unity of Subject and Techniques of Expression

According to some definitions, style is the essential unity in a work of art which embraces both the manner of expression and the subject material which is to be expressed. When any such definition is used, it is easy to quibble about what constitutes subject material and what constitutes form, since this concept of style treats the two as an indivisible entity. One might say, for example, that *The Trojan Women* and *Lysistrata* deal with the same thought or the same subject material— the futility of war. The similarity of the plays goes further in that both deal with the effect of war upon the women who are left behind. Both plays are also similar in their techniques, since both were written to be performed in outdoor amphitheaters and both employ some of the same devices, such as the chorus.

But the similarity soon ends, for the final effect of *The Trojan Women* is to be tragic, and the effect of *Lysistrata* is to be comic. *The Trojan Women*, therefore, introduces episodes in which the women are to be enslaved, the deaths of husbands and sons are reported, and the women mourn the murder of a child. But *Lysistrata* uses no such serious episodes; the husbands are not killed, they are merely temporarily absent; the women are not enslaved, they are temporarily deprived of the pleasures of married life. Are these episodes part of the subject material? Or are they part of the means and the method of presenting the subject material, which is the effect of war upon the women of a nation?

In the discussions of character it was noted that one important quality that helps to establish individuality is thought. If this is true of the characters in a play, it is also true of the man who wrote the play. If one accepts any definition of style which includes recognition of the author's personality, one must acknowledge that the author's thought, as a most important manifestation of his personality, will also be an important aspect of his style.

Surely the most fundamental difference between the works of Aeschylus and those of Aristophanes is that the plays of one are serious and tragic and those of the other are comic and ridiculous. Each author has used his powers of invention to fill his plays with characters and episodes which will best illustrate his fundamental thought, his point of view toward life. As one considers the plays in their details rather than in their broad outlines, as one examines the smaller character observations which contribute to the full characterizations and the kinds of complications which are introduced into the plot episodes, one discovers that each author has selected those details which are appropriate to the total effect he desired.

The actor need not concern himself with deciding which elements of a play are the subject material and which are the means and the methods; but he does need to learn to observe and evaluate the differences between plays and to adapt himself to the essential quality of each play. Just as the author invents the details of the characters and the plot, so the actor invents actions to convey to the audience what the author has indicated, as well as actions which supplement the creation of the author. To play in the style of the author, the actor must see that all the actions he invents are in keeping with the quality of the writing.

An examination of the role of the Herald in *Agamemnon* may serve to illustrate how a study of the script may help the actor decide the manner of playing which will be most appropriate to the style of the play and the kind of actions which he must invent in order to match the quality of the writing. The Herald has come on ahead of the returning victorious army to announce the imminent arrival of Agamemnon. After his first lines, which express his joy and his relief at his safe arrival home after ten years of war in foreign lands, he pays his respects to the gods—Zeus, Apollo, and Hermes, the special patron of heralds—and next addresses himself to the palace. He then announces the return of Agamemnon, briefly reciting Agamemnon's achievements in war with a soldier's pride in the prowess of his commander.

Presumably in the original production the actor wore a mask, thus limiting his facial expressions to one, which was carefully selected and effectively enlarged or exaggerated to be visible to the back rows. The setting apparently included several altars or statues, for in a previous scene, according to the words of the chorus, Clytemnestra and her attendants were seen lighting and tending them; it is logical to suppose, therefore, that the Herald would turn to the specific altars or statues as he addresses them, and then to the palace as he addresses it. The end of the speech concerning Agamemnon is seemingly addressed directly to the chorus, wherever they may be placed. Thus far, the scene could easily be played with a few large, formal, and sustained gestures. Also, the vocal projection could be loud and sustained, with careful observance of the meter.

In the next dialogue, however, the Herald expresses more individualized, less formal, emotions. The leader of the chorus asks if he longed so much for home and fatherland, and the Herald replies, "So much that now my eyes are wet with joy." For an actor who is wearing a mask this statement can be only a figure of speech; in any case the audience in a large amphitheater would be too far away to see the actor's expression; but if a modern actor were playing this scene in a relatively small theater, or in a motion-picture or television production, he would have to do something to convince the audience that his eyes were at least moist.

In a moment the Herald has a long speech in which he recounts the suffering which has been endured by the soldiers. In Edith Hamilton's very speakable translation, the man emerges as an entirely recognizable individual who, in spite of the thousands of years that have intervened since the play was written, speaks like any, or rather, every returning soldier. He is not entirely grammatical, but his language is colorful and dramatic. He seems to be a Greek version of a GI Joe; he is a hero because he has been to war and borne his part in magnificent and legendary events, but he himself is neither legendary nor remote. He seems intent on destroying any romantic concepts of war. Speaking of the hardship of sleeping in the open in a land where there was much rain and continual moisture, he says:

> Beds in the open, near the foeman's walls.
> Forever rain or dew, the meadow dew.
> Our very clothes were rotting from the wet.

Try speaking these lines with the accent of a city boy from Brooklyn or a farm boy from Nebraska. Listen to the scorn that comes into the romantic and poetic concept of "meadow dew" when the phrase is followed by a statement of the devastating effect of meadow dew upon physical comfort. Couple the speech with a facial expression which conveys the same idea and with a gesture of similar quality.

Translations provide an excellent means of studying style because one finds the same ideas expressed in different words, which means in a different manner, or in a different style. E. D. A. Morshead translates the same passage:

> For where we couched, close by the foeman's wall,
> The river-plain was ever dank with dews,
> Dropped from the sky, exuded from the earth,
> A curse that clung unto our sodden garb.

Those of us who cannot consult the original Greek must take each translator's version at face value. If an actor began with the Morshead translation, it is unlikely that he would invent or create the same manner of speaking and gesturing that he would for the Hamilton version; but once this manner has been invented, he will discover that it can be effectively used for both versions. It is just that a more definite and distinct characterization is conveyed in the diction of the Hamilton translation.

The differences between the two translations, or their distinguishing characteristics, or their respective styles, are even more apparent in their varying versions in the next line: Morshead translates it, "And hair as horrent as a wild beast's fell," while the Hamilton version is more simple, more direct, and more colloquial, "Good for the lice—our hair was full of them." The man who would speak of hair as being "horrent" is a different kind of man from the one who would speak of hair as being full of lice. The George Thomson translation, which is less colloquial than the one and more so than the other, renders this line: "A host of vermin in our woollen cloaks."

In the next three lines the Herald attempts to tell how cold it was. Morshead uses the most exalted language:

> Why tell the woes of winter, when the birds
> Lay stark and stiff, so stern was Ida's snow.

Thomson omits the "stark and stiff" description and the concept that the mountain was "stern":

> If I should tell those winters, when the birds
> Dropped dead and Ida heaped on us her snow

The Hamilton translation is again the simplest and most direct and sounds as though the Herald is a man we might know:

> The winters—well, if anyone could try
> to say how cold it was—the birds fell dead.
> And Ida's snow—enough to break your heart.

It is dangerous to decide that the Hamilton translation is necessarily the better of the two merely because it seems to bring the Herald closer to us and makes him speak as a returning soldier might speak today. Since the entire trilogy is a work of heroic structure, of size and magnitude, it may be that such a mundane, average man as the Hamiltonian Herald does not belong; it may also be, however, that Aeschylus wanted such a character so that the generals and queens and gods would gain stature by contrast. Perhaps Aeschylus is using the same device as Shakespeare uses in *Romeo and Juliet*, in which he makes the servants speak in prose and the other characters in verse.

Leaving the scholarly arguments to the scholars and the translators, let us return to the problem of the actor. If the actor invents an action— a facial expression, a gesture, and a quality of voice—which is appropriate to the line, "Good for lice—our hair was full of them," an action which is easily recognizable as having verisimilitude to the behavior one would expect of any returning soldier in real life, an action which is a specific pantomime of a man who has suffered from having lice in his hair, the actor will be playing in the style and the manner of the Hamilton version. But if the actor were to use the same action—the same facial expression and gesture and manner of speaking—in relation to the Morshead line, "And hair as horrent as a wild beast's fell," the effect would be as though the actor had added the word "lice" because the audience would understand "lice" and would think "lice," even though the word was not spoken. The actor would have altered the style to the extent of having added a small detail of subject material which is not included in the script.

Returning to the Herald's first speech, we do not find in the Hamilton version any such vivid and specific details as occur in the second speech; but if the actor imagines specific concepts of army life and uses them as the motivation for the words he speaks, he will have added new subject material. Indeed, if he adds any meaningful facial expressions, he will have added something which could not have been in the performance if the actor wore a mask. If the actor does not play this speech phrased in relatively long sequences, with gestures of considerable duration, and with a somewhat sustained vocal tone, observing the meter of the speech with the appropriate emphasis and accents, but rather plays with many smaller gestures, making more but smaller points, he will have altered the style by changing his techniques or manner of playing. If he invents actions which have more specific meanings or different meanings from those clearly indicated in the script, he has altered the style by the addition of subject material.

As always in matters of technique, one method is not right and another wrong; the two methods are merely different, and the skilled actor should be able to use either, and know exactly what he is doing, why he is doing it, and what the calculated effect upon the audience is likely to be. The taste and judgment of the actor must determine which techniques are appropriate to each play.

Historical Styles Derived from Costume

Different styles of acting are more difficult to identify than are different styles in other art forms. In architecture, a Roman arch immediately identifies a structure as being, at least partially, Romanesque, and a Greek column immediately shows a classic influence on the building. The music, the painting, and the literature of previous centuries have been preserved; but until the invention of the motion picture, samples of the art of acting could not be preserved, and we know the styles of acting practiced in the past only by reports and criticism. The actor cannot decide to add a classic gesture because he does not know what a classic gesture was.

For the actor, the best approach to an historical style of acting is through a study of the costumes that are known to have been worn. The kind of movement and the kind of gesture which are possible and suitable if one is wearing a Roman toga differ from those which are natural to a person dressed in Elizabethan doublet and hose. An actor playing Richard II in the flowing sleeves of the fourteenth century will find that the quality of his movements is prescribed by his costume. A lady wearing a bustle will find it necessary to sit and stand and walk differently than she would if she were wearing panniers. Many actors and critics have held that to move naturally and easily in the costumes being worn is to achieve an historical style of acting.

In the chapter devoted to the invention of actions, it was pointed out that the sources from which the gestures and movements may be derived are the plot, the character, and the mood and atmosphere. If the actor is looking for extra decorations and embellishments with which he hopes to achieve style, they may be developed from the same sources. If he can adapt himself to the modes and manners of the period of the play, reproducing the kind of gesture which would have been used in that age, he will have helped to establish the historical style.

Pelléas and Melisande and *They Knew What They Wanted* tell essentially the same story; but Melisande is a princess who lives in a palace and wanders through gardens and dark caves and loses her wedding ring in a deep pool, while Amy is a waitress from San Francisco who comes to the unpretentious home of Tony, who raises grapes in the Napa valley. If the same actress were to play both parts, she would find that the actions, derived not only from the costumes, but also from the time and place, the mood and atmosphere, would be different in the two plays. If she ever tried to play Amy with the gestures and movements of Melisande, or vice versa, she would find herself at variance with the style of the play. It could be done, but it seems unlikely that it could be done successfully.

Style is Degree of Deviation from Reality

Still another concept of style is that it is the degree and the direction in which a work of art deviates from being real or natural—the term *realism* or *naturalism* being understood to mean the closest possible verisimilitude to things and people as they are in real life. This concept is used more frequently in connection with theatrical performances than with other forms of art; and when it is so used, it is often called *stylization* rather than *style*. *Stylization* is a comparatively recent word, not having come into use until about the beginning of the twentieth century.

In one sense, the entire history of dramatic literature, from the earliest known plays of Greek drama to those written at the beginning of the twentieth century, represents a steady progress toward verisimilitude to real life as it might be experienced and observed by the audiences. The Greek dramatists told and retold the legends and myths, peopled with kings and queens and mighty warriors, and often with the gods themselves. When characters of less noble birth appeared, such as messengers, shepherds, and nurses, the authors usually included details observed in real life which would help to make them recognizable types, no different from the people one might meet in the course of a routine day. The purpose of the Greek dramatists, however, was to create works of art which would have magnitude and universality, which would be larger than life. And so the principal characters are gods and ancient heroes, whom no one would expect to act like ordinary men; their thoughts are profound, their sentiments exalted, their emotions powerful.

Elizabethan drama, as far as its relationship to reality is concerned, echoed many of the qualities of Greek drama. The plays took place on a stage which was rarely made to look like anything except a stage where plays were performed. The leading characters spoke in poetry, with an eloquence which is far removed from the language of real life. It was only the minor characters—the servants and the comic characters —who seemed anything like the people one might meet in the streets.

During the next three hundred years the mainstream of drama gradually approached verisimilitude; the kings and queens gave place to lords and ladies, then to country squires and city industrialists, then to representatives of the middle classes, then to laborers and workers, and then, literally and figuratively, to the lower depths—the destitute and underprivileged. Poetry became a rarity in the theater, and authors strove to reproduce the actual speech of actual people, even making a virtue of capturing the unimaginative and uneloquent banalities of common speech and sometimes mistaking vulgarity and coarseness of language for truth and reality.

At the end of the nineteenth century and the beginning of the twentieth, many playwrights, actors, directors, and designers—especially the
designers—began experiments and proposed theories in their search for
truth which they thought had not been found, and would never be found,
in realism or naturalism.   This kind of experimentation was not confined
to the theater but was carried on in many of the other arts, such as painting and music and literature.   Many names were invented to identify the
works of art which were created according to these various theories.
Most of the names—expressionism, impressionism, futurism, constructiv-
ism, cubism, surrealism, symbolism, and so on—defy precise definition, but
all the theories share in common a desire to state the truth without re-
sorting to complete and exact verisimilitude.

Difficulties of the Actor in Escaping Reality

The actor, in contrast to other artists, works under a handicap when
his purpose is to achieve an effect which is not real, since he himself is
as real as any piece of furniture that David Belasco ever placed upon the
stage.   There has always been an incongruity between a painted back-
drop and a real actor.

It is easier for the scene designer to build the idea of a house, the concept of a house—instead of a real house—for *Death of a Salesman* or
Desire Under the Elms than it is for the actor to project the idea or the
concept of a character rather than the mere external actuality of the
character.   His face is real and his body is real and his voice is real, and
he is forever limited by his inability to go beyond the capabilities of his
face, his body, and his voice.   His subject material, furthermore, is human actions, human thoughts, and human emotions.   Rarely is the
actor called upon to play Caliban, Ariel, or Puck; and for that matter
these characters, since they are obviously intended to be unreal, are
usually more or less unbelievable because the audience is so conscious of
the reality of the actor who is cast in the role.   Mechanical robot characters like those in *R.U.R.* raise the same problems.

The greatest range of which the actor is capable runs from the casual,
disorganized, and unselected habits of speech and movement that most
people use in daily life to the selected and premeditated vocal techniques
of song, in which every syllable is assigned a definite pitch, a definite
duration, and a definite volume; and from the unconscious and involuntary movements of daily life to the controlled movements of the dance,
in which the size of the movement, the amount of the movement, the
duration of the movement, and the quality of the movement have been
carefully selected and rehearsed for the purpose of achieving a predetermined effect upon the observer.

Style as the Degree of Selectivity

Another possible way to achieve style, or stylization, is to arrive at a deviation from verisimilitude through the degree of selectivity. A photograph is more real than a painting because all the details are present in exactly the same relationship to each other that they have when observed in real life. The minute the photograph is "touched up" by removing some of the details, such as wrinkles in a face, it becomes less a facsimile and more a work of art. If the photographer uses a special lens which blurs the outlines or reduces the details of the picture, the photograph moves further in the direction of art. If the photographer carefully arranges his subject material so that his picture includes only certain selected details, he has become even more of an artist, and when he arranges the lighting on his picture so that certain details are highlighted and certain other details are obscured, he is performing one of the essential functions of the artist.

Like the photographer, the actor may select, not only which kind of detail he wishes to include, but also the number or the quantity of the details. The actor who wears a mask is limited to one expression which may be real, or exactly lifelike, or may be enlarged or exaggerated, either in its entirety or in certain details, such as the nose or the eyes. In real life, small variations in the facial expression may occur frequently or constantly. In the same way, the movements or changes in the physical attitudes of a person in real life might vary considerably in a short space of time, but the actor might select only those movements and physical attitudes which are most meaningful and significant, eliminating the others. As soon as some details are removed, those which remain will have greater emphasis, merely because there are no other details competing for the attention of the audience.

Duration and Selectivity

Because of the time element in the theater, if there are fewer details of facial expression, gesture, or movement, it is inevitable that those details which remain must be sustained beyond the point that they would be in real life. If an old lady sits all day in a chair, she may let her hands rest in her lap, or sometimes on the arm of the chair; sometimes she may nod, and at other times look out of the window; sometimes she may rock and at others sit still; she may read or sew. The photographer or the painter who uses this old lady as a subject must select the one position which he considers most typical and characteristic of her and make the one expression and bodily attitude be representative, or symbolic, of her entire personality. The actress who portrays such a character may make the same choice, but because a theatrical performance extends over a period of time, the one expression and bodily attitude which has been selected as meaningful and significant must be sustained.

The continuation of a single gesture or physical attitude for a notice-able time will tend to create an effect that is formal and statuesque, par-ticularly if the gesture is of considerable size. If one must give names to different manners of playing, one might say that when the gestures which are to be sustained for a duration of time are of themselves real-istic in quality, the manner of playing is *stylized realistic;* when the ges-ture or physical attitude is romantic, the manner of playing may be called *stylized romantic;* or when the gesture is derived from the cos-tumes and the manners of an historical period—the eighteenth century, for example—the manner of playing becomes *stylized eighteenth cen-tury.* The continuation of a single gesture or movement for a longer time will have a profound effect upon the phrasing of the role; and the elimination of many small gestures and movements will limit the amount of pointing which can be accomplished.

Removing Transitions

Another device which is frequently used by actors to achieve an effect of stylization is to eliminate the natural transition movements which would normally be performed as one gesture or physical attitude evolves into the next. A change of attitude which is to be made without the transition movement is usually performed quickly and timed to pre-cede or follow a speech, not performed during a speech.

If, for instance, on Hamlet's first speech, "A little more than kin, and less than kind," the actor is sitting with his chin resting in the palm of his right hand, he could enlarge and romanticize this gesture and attitude by sitting to one side of the chair or stool, so that his left leg could be extended straight down from the thigh to the knee, and extended toward the back of the chair from the knee to the toe, his left hand falling by his left knee. In the middle of the line, after saying, "A little more than kin," and before delivering the remainder of the line, the actor could shift away from the scene so that now his head rests on his left hand, which is on his left knee, and his right arm and leg fall into a position similar to that of his left hand and leg in the preceding attitude. These quick angular shifts from one attitude to another create an effect comparable to that achieved by a modern painter who elects not to use perspective. This manner of playing is rarely used except in plays which were written to be so performed, such as certain expressionistic plays.

To discover for himself how changes in the techniques of playing a particular scene may alter the style of the performance, the student-actor should select certain passages from plays which are written in a definite and recognizable style and deliberately perform these passages with techniques which may at first seem inappropriate to the play itself.

The Cherry Orchard is generally regarded as either a realistic or a naturalistic play, depending on one's definition of these terms. In the second act, Madame Ranevsky, the aristocratic owner of the cherry orchard who is about to lose it because she is incapable or unwilling to adjust to changing conditions and to subdivide the property to build villas for summer visitors, confesses her sins, which include spending her money improvidently, making an unfortunate marriage, running off with another man, and allowing him to squander the remainder of her money. Most actresses, reading the scene for the first time, consider it serious and tragic, or at least pitiful, in spite of the fact that Chekhov himself called his play a comedy. If the actress suffuses the scene with sincere emotion and finds facial expressions, gestures, and physical attitudes to express that emotion, the scene will be serious and tragic in its effect.

But some of the thoughts and ideas in this scene are expressed in a frivolous or comic manner. "My husband died of champagne," for example, is essentially a lighthearted and nonserious way of expressing the thought. Madame Ranevsky's own comment on her actions near the end of the speech is, "So stupid, so shameful." She prays for forgiveness, saying, "Lord, Lord, be merciful! Forgive my sins! Do not chastize me more!" but she immediately takes out a telegram from her lover, saying, "I got this today from Paris. He implores forgiveness, entreats me to return," thus suggesting the possibility that she is not entirely contrite or reformed. Her next line refers to some distant music, and one line later she is suggesting that they should give a dance. If the entire speech uses some light, smiling facial expressions and charming graceful gestures and if the comic phrases, the comic thoughts, and sudden contrasts in the ideas are pointed, the scene will be comic rather than tragic.

Almost every line can be read and acted in such a way that it mirrors several different emotions or degrees of emotions. The following sentence is a good example:

> To my misery I loved another man, and immediately—it was my first punishment—the blow fell upon me, here, in the river . . . my boy was drowned and I went abroad—went away forever, never to return, not to see that river again . . . I shut my eyes, and fled, distracted, and he after me . . . pitilessly, brutally.

A skillful actress could find changes in facial expressions and gestures which would reveal the changing emotions which motivate this speech as Madame Ranevsky recalls the events. "To my misery" could have one expression and vocal projection; "I loved another man" could be spoken in a different way; certainly "It was my first punishment," being a parenthetical clause, could have a special treatment which would set it apart from the rest of the sentence; "The blow fell upon me, here, in the river" could be delivered with three separate actions to reveal the increasing vividness of her memories.

If the entire speech is treated in this manner, with every possible change in the emotions reflected in changes in the actions and vocal techniques, and if all of the actions and readings are as similar as possible to those one might find in real life—no larger and no smaller—then the scene is played realistically or naturalistically, and it will be comic or tragic according to the quality of the actions themselves. If the actress uses the same gestures, but makes them larger than would be normal in real life, then the scene, if it is serious, becomes melodramatic; if it is comic, it becomes farcical.

As the actress begins to eliminate some of the small details, phrasing the passage in longer sequences by maintaining a single gesture for a longer time or sustaining a single action while speaking more of the phrases, she is moving in the direction of stylization. This process, if carried to its ultimate limits, might mean that the entire speech would be spoken while maintaining a single attitude; the actress might, for instance, kneel before the little wayside shrine, which is called for in the setting, and deliver the entire speech without changing her position or her facial expression; or, if she wished to give a stylized comic performance, she might open her parasol, tip her head to one side, smile, and speak the entire speech in this attitude.

Later in the same act of *The Cherry Orchard*, the student, Trofimov, gives his version of what is wrong with Russia. This passage, too, seems at first reading to be serious, and yet it includes several comic inventions, such as the remarks about the intellectuals who "are all serious people, they all have severe faces, they all talk of weighty matters and air their theories." Trofimov needs only to use a mocking imitation on this line to turn it into comedy. Again, having delivered himself of a long, serious speech, he says, "I fear and dislike very serious faces. I'm afraid of serious conversation. We should do better to be silent." Since this opinion is a direct contradiction of his own behavior, the line can be played for its comic possibilities if the actor chooses to point or emphasize that contradiction between his thought and his actions. If the actress playing Madame Ranevsky and the actor playing Trofimov both choose to invent actions of the same quality, of a similar size, and in the same amount, and to sustain their actions for a comparable length of time, whether long or short, they may be said to be playing in the same style.

A final word of warning which cannot be repeated too often—whatever the style of a performance, all of the techniques used must be expressive of the emotions and thoughts which the artist wishes to convey to the audience and must always be meaningful and effective. Whether or not the actor must stimulate his own emotions at the time of a performance so that he himself feels the emotions he is trying to express is a question which each actor must answer for himself. The emotional experiences of the actor himself are unimportant and irrelevant, so long as the audience responds to his performance in the manner he intended.

EXERCISES

1. Sequence from *Romeo and Juliet*, Act I, Scene 1.
Rehearse the scene from Montague's line, "Who set this ancient quarrel new abroach?
Speak, nephew, were you by when it began?" to Romeo and Benvolio's exit.

 a. Invent actions which fit the rhymed couplets, each of these actions beginning with the beginning of the couplet and ending as the rhyme is closed. When the couplet is shared by two characters, let each actor perform a comparable part of the action, the first actor sustaining his gesture and physical attitude until the second actor has completed the rhyme and the action.
 b. Invent appropriate actions for the remainder of the scene, with each of the longer speeches of Benvolio, Montague, and Romeo being phrased in one long progression, a single gesture and physical attitude being either sustained or developed through the entire speech.
 c. Phrase each of the longer speeches in smaller sections, with many small actions timed to the smallest possible thought divisions. *Example:* One gesture for "Many a morning hath he there been seen," another for "With tears augmenting the fresh morning dew," a third for "Adding to clouds more clouds," and a fourth for "With his deep sighs."
 d. Speak all of the lines in as colloquial and as natural a manner as possible, with no sustained tones and no marked emphasis to establish the meter of the lines. When the sense will allow it, deliberately place a special emphasis or stress upon words which would not be accented in the meter.
 e. Speak the lines with more volume and with more sustained tones, and, wherever possible, place the accent and emphasis upon those words which would be accented by the meter as well as the sense.
 f. Combine *d* with *b*.
 g. Combine *d* with *c*.
 h. Combine *e* with *b*.
 i. Combine *e* with *c*.

SUGGESTION: Now that almost the entire first scene of *Romeo and Juliet* has been studied in detail, play the whole scene with careful attention to all of the subjects that have been discussed.

2. Sequence from *Romeo and Juliet*, Act II, Scene 2.

Perform this scene in all the variations suggested for the scene in exercise 1.

3. The Herald's speech from *Agamemnon*, as translated by Edith Hamilton.[1]

> Well ended now.   And yet in those long years
> a man might say the evil matched the good.
> But who except a god can look to be
> free from all trouble all his days on earth.
> Trouble!   If I should tell you how we lived—
> No room on deck, and little more below.
> All in the day's work, but we paid for it.
> Ashore still worse, whatever men hate most.
> Beds in the open, near the foeman's walls.
> Forever rain or dew, the meadow dew.
> Our clothes were rotting from the wet.
> Good for the lice—our hair was full of them.
> The winters—well, if anyone could try
> to say how cold it was—the birds fell dead.
> And Ida's snow—enough to break your heart.
> Hot, too, at noonday when upon his couch
> the sea, windless and waveless, lay asleep.
> But why complain?   All trouble over now.
> All over for the dead.   They will not want
> to live again—not they, never again.
> And we who live will let them lie uncounted.
> Why grieve now because fortune frowned on them?
> A long good-by to trouble, so say I.

The Herald's speech as translated by E. D. A. Morshead.

> 'Tis true: Fate smiles at last.   Throughout our toil,
> These many years, some chances issued fair,
> And some, I wot, were chequered with a curse.
> But who, on earth, hath won the bliss of heaven,
> Thro' time's whole tenor an unbroken weal?
> I could a tale unfold of toiling oars,
> Ill rest, scant landings on a shore rock-strewn,
> All pains, all sorrows, for our daily doom.
> And worse and hatefuller our woes on land;

[1] Copyright by W. W. Norton & Company, Inc.

For where we couched, close by the foeman's wall,
The river-plain was ever dank with dews,
Dropped from the sky, exuded from the earth,
A curse that clung unto our sodden garb,
And hair as horrent as a wild beast's fell.
Why tell the woes of winter, when the birds
Lay stark and stiff, so stern was Ida's snow?
Or summer's scorch, what time the stirless wave
Sank to its sleep beneath the noon-day sun?
Why mourn old woes? their pain hath passed away;
And passed away, from those who fell, all care,
For evermore, to rise and live again.
Why sum the count of death, and render thanks
For life by moaning over fate malign?
Farewell, a long farewell to all our woes.

The Herald's speech translated by George Thomson.[2]

Yes, for the end is well.   Our enterprise
At last is well concluded, though in part
The issue be found wanting.   Who but a God
Might live unscathed by sorrow all his days?
If I should tell those labours, the rough lodging,
The land thwart's scant repose, the weary groans
That were our lot through watches of the day;
And then ashore ills more insufferable,
In camp beneath the beetling walls of Troy,
The rains from heaven and the dews that dripped
From sodden soils with cruel insistence, breeding
A host of vermin in our woollen cloaks;
If I should tell those winters, when the birds
Dropped dead and Ida heaped on us her snows,
Those summers, when unstirred by wind or wave
The sea lay pillowed in the sleep of noon—
But why lament that now?   The toil is past—
Yes, for the dead so past that, where they lie,
No care shall trouble them to rise again.
Ah, those are spent: why count our losses then
And vex the quick with grievance of the dead?
So to adversity I bid farewell.

a. Invent actions and vocal techniques for the Hamilton translation which
are as lifelike as possible.   Use gestures of short duration which are timed

[2] Copyright by Cambridge University Press.

to the individual phrases. Use facial expressions. Borrow the gestures, expressions, and vocal techniques from people you have seen in real life.

b. Repeat, enlarging the performance so that it would be effective in a large theater or in an amphitheater.

c. Invent actions and vocal techniques for the Morshead translation. Concentrate on gestures of size and of extended duration.

d. Try to play the Hamilton translation with the techniques invented for the Morshead translation.

e. Try to play the Morshead translation with the techniques used for the Hamilton translation.

f. Work out the Thomson translation using some of the large, heroic, extended actions best suited to the Morshead version and some of the smaller and more natural actions best suited to the Hamilton translation.

4. Madame Ranevsky's speech from *The Cherry Orchard*, Act II.

Oh, my sins! I've always thrown my money away recklessly like a lunatic. I married a man who made nothing but debts. My husband died of champagne—he drank dreadfully. To my misery I loved another man, and immediately—it was my first punishment—the blow fell upon me, here, in the river . . . my boy was drowned and I went abroad—went away for ever, never to return, not to see that river again . . . I shut my eyes, and fled, distracted, and *he* after me . . . pitilessly, brutally. I bought a villa at Mentone, for *he* fell ill there, and for three years I had no rest day or night. His illness wore me out, my soul was dried up. And last year, when my villa was sold to pay my debts, I went to Paris and there he robbed me of everything and abandoned me for another woman; and I tried to poison myself . . . So stupid, so shameful! . . . And suddenly I felt a yearning for Russia, for my country, for my little girl. . . . (*dries her tears*) Lord, Lord, be merciful! Forgive my sins! Do not chastize me more! (*Takes a telegram out of her pocket*) I got this today from Paris. He implores forgiveness, entreats me to return. (*Tears up the telegram*) I fancy there is music somewhere. (*listens*)

a. Invent actions and vocal techniques which will illustrate Madame Ranevsky's charm and lack of responsibility. Point all of the comedy lines. Let her be pleased that her lover was so determined in his pursuit. Let her be amused at her own stupidity. Let her be both proud and pleased that the lover still sends her telegrams.

b. Convey these sentiments and this characterization by phrases of acting of the shortest possible duration. Invent small gestures, slight changes of facial expression, and small movements which can be suited to short phrases and even to single words.

c. Eliminate as many of the gestures and expressions as possible, playing the scene in longer sequences.

d. Invent actions and vocal techniques which will illustrate Madame Ranevsky's seriousness, the deep emotions which are revived by her memories. Let her be ashamed of her actions. Let her be remorseful at what she has done and sincerely repentent.

e. Convey these sentiments and this characterization with as many small actions as possible, using facial expressions of short duration, small gestures of short duration, and small movements.

f. Simplify the performance by using fewer gestures for a more sustained duration.

5. Trofimov's speech from *The Cherry Orchard*, Act II.

Humanity progresses, perfecting its powers. Everything that is beyond its ken now will one day become familiar and comprehensible; only we must work, we must with all our powers aid the seeker after truth. Here among us in Russia the workers are few in number as yet. The vast majority of the intellectual people I know, seek nothing, do nothing, are not fit as yet for work of any kind. They call themselves intellectual, but they treat their servants as inferior, behave to the peasants as though they were animals, learn little, read nothing seriously, do practically nothing, only talk about science and know very little about art. They are all serious people, they all have severe faces, they all talk of weighty matters and air their theories, and yet the vast majority of us—ninety-nine per cent—live like savages, at the least little thing fly to blows and abuse, eat piggishly, sleep in filth and stuffiness, bugs everywhere, stench and damp and moral impurity. And it is clear all our fine talk is only to divert our attention and other people's. Show me where to find the *creches* there's so much talk about, and the reading rooms? They only exist in novels: in real life there are none of them. There is nothing but filth and vulgarity and Asiatic apathy. I fear and dislike very serious faces. I'm afraid of serious conversation. We should do better to be silent.

a. Play the scene for its comedy values. Let Trofimov imitate the people of whom he is scornful. Let him be pompous and sophomoric in his manner.

b. Play the scene as seriously as possible.

c. In both the comic and the serious versions, play with small actions, small phrases, no enlargement of the tone, and no effort at projection.

d. In both the comic and the serious versions, use larger actions, more sustained gestures. Phrase the scene in longer sequences and enlarge the tone above the normal conversational speech, projecting it so that it could be audible in a large theater.

Chapter 13. THE DESIGN OF A ROLE

A FINAL CONCEPT of style is that it is the essential quality of the entire work, embracing both the subject material and the techniques and methods by which the subject material is expressed. When the techniques are entirely suitable to the subject material and to the purpose of the artist and when the entire work has the desired effect upon the beholder or the listener, arousing the desired thoughts and emotions, the work is said to be a work of art.

In this largest concept, style is the sum of all those qualities which differentiate the work from reality. Regardless of how realistic or nonrealistic a work of art may be, it differs from reality in that the artist, taking his material from life, has imparted to it those qualities which are the characteristics of art and not of reality: he has given it form and organization; he has given it balance and arrangement and proportion, so that the parts are integrated and related to the whole; and he has given it a sense of unity and completeness—nothing that is essential has been omitted and nothing has been included that does not make a valuable and necessary contribution to the total effect.

The Need for a Beginning, a Middle, and an End

Literature and music differ from the other arts in that a time element is involved in expressing thoughts and emotions in these forms. The painter does not know how long his work will be observed by one person, but it is possible for the observer to see it all at one time; a painting may not be comprehended and appreciated in one minute, but it can be seen in one minute. Some statues and some models of architecture are intended to be seen from all sides, but there is no assurance that the casual beholder will ever bother to walk around a piece of sculpture or a building to see it on all sides, and the artist must strive to create the effect he desires even if his work is observed from only one side. But a novel cannot be read and a symphony cannot be heard in one minute: instead of arousing a single emotional response, such works are intended to arouse a series of responses which follow one another in a planned order and sequence. Art works of this kind, in order to achieve a sense of unity and completeness, must have a beginning, a middle, and an end. Drama is in this category.

The Organization of a Play

Usually the organizing agent in a play is the plot, although it can also be character, and sometimes thought. The actor must assume that the author, aided and abetted by the director, is an artist and that the work has a unity and a completeness; he must assume that every sentence he speaks and every action he performs has some direct relationship to the work as a whole and makes a necessary contribution to the over-all effect desired. It is his task to discover and to understand the relationship of the parts to the whole.

Eva Le Gallienne, whose Civic Repertory Theatre gave so many memorable productions of Chekhov plays, reported that she found it almost impossible to cut a single line or even a phrase in any of these plays, because when she tried to do so she found that a line cut in one act necessitated the cutting of lines in the other acts, and that these plays, which seem at first glance to be so formless, are actually like a woven fabric in which the cutting of a single thread will start the unraveling of the whole piece.

Madame Ranevsky's speech in the second act of *The Cherry Orchard*, which was used as an exercise in the previous chapter, actually tells the whole story of her life. Many of the sentences are left unfinished; phrases which at first seem either irrelevant or parenthetical are scattered throughout the speech; but when the speech is carefully studied, one finds that every sentence, every phrase, and even every word makes its contribution to the story of Madame Ranevsky's life and to an understanding of her character. The sudden emotional outbursts which have led her into impulsive and unreasonable actions, her tendency to run away from issues rather than to face them, her lack of financial responsibility, all are clearly stated, and all are important to the play; for Madame Ranevsky is one of the principal agents in the main action of the play, and an understanding of her character is essential to an understanding of her behavior in the scenes to come.

As Madame Ranevsky finishes the speech she remarks, with what seems to be a definite inconsistency, that she thinks she hears music, and when her brother explains that it is the local orchestra, she suggests they should give a dance. What could be more consistent with her previous actions, as she has just related them? In the next act, as the cherry orchard is being sold to pay her debts, just as her villa at Mentone was sold, she will actually invite in the orchestra and give a dance. This is not formless writing; it is closely knit construction. In spite of its surface quality of naturalism, Madame Ranevsky's speech in Act II is artfully contrived to reveal the character and foreshadow a major action of the plot.

The Trofimov speech, which was also used as an exercise in the previous chapter, is devoted more to the thought of the play than it is to character, although character points will inevitably be made by the ideas expressed and the manner in which the actor expresses them. In the speech, Trofimov accurately describes the conditions in Russia which are the subject material of the whole play. Possibly the speech is a little overwritten, but since the thought is that the intellectuals talk too much and work too little, a simultaneous illustration has merit.

In the light of this speech, Madame Ranevsky and her brother are seen to be a symbolical representation of the entire aristocratic class that Trofimov is describing, a class whose "Asiatic apathy" has immobilized them from any participation in the future. The student explains that only by unceasing labor can the past be expiated, and in the very next speech Lopakhin explains how he gets up at six in the morning and works all day long. Thus, within a very short time the audience has seen and heard Madame Ranevsky explain what the past, and specifically her past, has been, has heard Trofimov describe the class of which she is typical and its implications for the future of Russia, and finally has heard Lopakhin explain that he is representative of the new group who, by their energy and willingness to work, will be the leaders of the future.

Stripped of naturalism and seeming casualness, the play reveals its form and structure; these three speeches are the core of the play—the heart and soul of the play—and all the actors, not only the three actors who are assigned to these roles, must recognize that everything they say and do has significance and importance as it relates to and illustrates this central theme; the climactic scene at the end of the next act when Madame Ranevsky is giving a dance at the very moment when the cherry orchard is being sold to Lopakhin is almost anticlimactic, so clearly has it been foretold.

Certainly the three principal actors will wish to design their performances so that they serve as proper contrasts to one another; certainly the actor playing Trofimov will want to take great care in pointing the thought, and the whole production must be planned so that this speech, which is almost a verbal diagram of the entire play, will receive strong emphasis.

The First Reading of a Play

Fortunate indeed is the actor who has learned to read a play without thinking about what role he is going to play or hopes to play. The first reading of a script is the actor's only chance to approach the play with the same attitude and point of view as the audience will have. After that he can never again be as excited by the plot because he will always know what happens next and how the play ends. Never again can he be surprised to find out what the characters are really like. It is a good practice for the actor to learn to read a play at one sitting, because the audience will eventually see the play at one sitting.

What the actor needs first is an over-all impression of the play. And he must hang onto that first impression, in spite of the coming weeks of detailed analysis and worry over small details. Many actors find it valuable to read the play and then not to look at it again for a few days but to think about it often, hoping that the first impression will become embedded in the memory. Often the first impression provides the actor with his sense of direction and purpose while he works on a role; it is like a compass as he wanders in the forest of details.

To consider the problems of a particular role when reading a play for the first time is to court disaster; the actor has thus deliberately forfeited his best opportunity to see the play as a whole. One of the greatest mistakes an actor can make is to consider the small problems of a particular role at the first reading, thinking how he might play a particular sequence or what actions might be used in a certain episode. This would be like starting on a long journey without consulting a map.

This discussion of the technical problems of acting has deliberately begun with the smallest units of acting and progressed to larger units; the smallest and simplest problems have been considered first, and the larger and more complex problems last; but the actor must work the other way, considering first the design of the entire play and the entire production. Once this is done, he may begin to work on the details, confident that the details he works out will be a part of the finished whole.

Understanding the Author

It will be helpful for the actor to read the play several times, provided that he can prevent himself from thinking of specific solutions to specific problems. If he has the opportunity, the actor should read other plays by the same author. The author's point of view as a manifestation of his personality is of vital concern to the actor, and there is no better guide to understanding this point of view than the author's own work. Authors have a habit of using and reusing the same thoughts and concepts, as well as the same methods and techniques, and the actor stands a better chance of grasping the author's point of view if the other writings are studied.

Understanding the Physical Production

The next step for the actor is to find out as much as possible about the physical conditions under which the performance is to be given. How large is the auditorium? What will the sets be like? Where are the doors and the windows, the entrances and the exits? How much furniture will be used? Where will it be placed? Where will the other actors be in relation to you? to your right? in back of you? in front of you? Are there to be steps and levels and platforms? In other words, the actor needs what is known as a "blocking rehearsal," in which he learns what his physical relationship will be to both the settings and the other actors. In most productions, the problem of physical relationships will be settled by the director. Most directors use the first blocking rehearsal merely to indicate the general outlines of the performance, leaving the details to be filled in later, or changed later, as seems necessary.

The actor, knowing his own personality and having become familiar with the play and the physical conditions of the performance, is now ready to begin work on the play. Undoubtedly, in the first rehearsals the director will communicate to the entire company his attitude toward the play, the values which he thinks are important and should be stressed, the manner or style in which he wants it played, and other matters concerning the general interpretation. The actor must reconcile and adjust these opinions to those which he himself may have formed.

The Actor in Relation to Plot

Since plot is the usual organizing agent in a play, the actor's next step is to determine the relationship of the character he is playing to the plot. What major actions is he called upon to perform? Brutus, for example, participates in the assassination of Caesar and later commits suicide—all this in spite of the fact that he is regarded by his fellow men as "noble" and "honorable." What kind of man must he be to perform these actions? Romeo, believing himself to be hopelessly in love with Rosaline. goes to a party and falls in love with Juliet. Shylock signs the contract with Bassanio and then demands its fulfillment. Juliet secretly marries Romeo against the wishes of her parents and risks taking the potion in order to escape yielding to their wishes.

The actor will do well to search out the simplest and most direct statement concerning his relation to the plot. In one sense this is the irreducible minimum that is demanded of him in order to perform his function in the action of the play; but in another sense this is the maximum demand put upon him, for unless he can seem to be the kind of person who would perform this action, he has failed. Even the minor characters have this problem. Arragon must seem the kind of man who would choose silver, and Morocco the kind who would choose gold. The servant in *Romeo and Juliet* must be the kind of person who would show the invitation list to a member of the rival house. The qualities which a character must have in order to fulfill his essential function in the plot become the skeleton of the character; it is the actor's task to add the flesh and blood which will make the character recognizable and believable.

Character Traits as Motivation for the Plot

Once the fundamental story line or outline of the character has been decided upon, the actor must now decide what characteristics—physical, mental and emotional—must be present to motivate the necessary plot actions. Certainly Juliet must be, at least to some degree, a headstrong, impulsive, and willful girl to act as she does. If she is not in the beginning of the play, then she must become so during the course of the play. Romeo must have the same characteristics. Shakespeare has, of course, noted these qualities in his characters. Juliet says:

> I have no joy in this contract tonight:
> It is too rash, too unadvised, too sudden.

If Juliet is to act rashly in this important matter, she must seem to be the kind of person who would do so. Thus it becomes essential for the actress to find other instances, of less import, in which this basic characteristic may be demonstrated, lest in the main action Juliet seem to be acting in a manner which is contrary to her nature and, therefore, in a way which is inconsistent and unbelievable. The skillful author will, of course, have provided sufficient minor instances in which the essential quality of the character can be illustrated, as Shakespeare has done in the case of Juliet.

Character Traits of Richard II

Having decided on the essential qualities of the character and on the places in the script where these qualities can be demonstrated, the actor should now decide on the most appropriate techniques to be used to bring the required emphasis to the lines or the actions which convey the correct impression to the audience. In *Richard II*, Richard is arrogant and egotistical. He summarily banishes Bolingbroke and Mowbray without due consideration of the facts; he confiscates Gaunt's estates; he does not accept the advice and counsel of others. This arrogance is rooted in Richard's belief in the divine right of kings; he considers himself to be God's representative on earth.

As the play progresses we see that he considers himself not only the representative but actually the Son of God, for he has identified himself with Christ. Whether or not this is true at the beginning of the play is difficult to say; certainly the audience is not aware of it; but during the play either Richard identifies himself more and more with the Son of God, or the audience becomes more and more aware of this identification. There would be justification for playing the character either way, but the lines suggest that the idea grows in Richard's mind as he is beset by misfortunes, for it is actually the martyrdom of Christ with which he identifies himself.

The first indication of this character trait in Richard appears in the first scene of the first act. Richard says:

> Now, by my sceptre's awe, I make a vow,
> Such neighbour nearness to our sacred blood. . . .

"Sceptre's awe" implies respect and reverence which might or might not be of a religious nature, but the implications of "sacred blood" are unmistakable. When Bolingbroke and Mowbray refuse to reconcile their quarrel, Richard says,

> We were not born to sue, but to command. . . .

This is a clear statement of the divine right of kings. But these two speeches are the only direct reference in the first two acts of the script to an idea or thought which becomes an important facet of Richard's character in the last three acts. Most actors who play the role will want to use effective techniques to highlight these two short passages.

In Act III, Scene 2, when Richard has returned from Ireland to the coast of Wales and is faced with the evidence of open rebellion against him, he finds refuge and comfort in the idea that, as God's appointed representative, he cannot be deposed, that God will intercede for him:

> Not all the water in the rough rude sea
> Can wash the balm off from an anointed king;
> The breath of worldly men cannot depose
> The deputy elected by the Lord:
> For every man that Bolingbroke hath press'd
> To lift shrewd steel against our royal crown
> God for his Richard hath in heavenly pay
> A glorious angel: then, if angels fight,
> Weak men must fall, for heaven still guards the right.

A few moments later, as more news is reported of the growing revolt, he says, "They break their faith to God as well as us." When Richard learns that his followers, Bushy, Bagot, and Green, have made peace

with the enemy, he calls them names—villians, vipers, dogs, snakes, and—
as the climax of the sequence—Judases. The Christ complex is either
growing or becoming more apparent.

> O Villains, vipers, damn'd without redemption!
> Dogs, easily won to fawn on any man!
> Snakes, in my heart-blood warm'd, that sting my heart!
> Three Judases, each one thrice worse than Judas!

In the next scene at Flint castle, when Richard is forced to surrender
to his foes, the same thought is expressed in several places and in a more
extended form. His opponents have failed to kneel before him, and he
asks if he is not still king:

> If we be not, show us the hand of God
> That hath dismiss'd us from our stewardship;
> For well we know, no hand of blood and bone
> Can gripe the sacred handle of our sceptre,
> Unless he do profane, steal, or usurp.
> And though you think that all, as you have done,
> Have torn their souls by turning them from us,
> And we are barren and bereft of friends;
> Yet know, my master, God omnipotent,
> Is mustering in his clouds on our behalf
> Armies of pestilence; and they shall strike
> Your children yet unborn and unbegot,
> That lift your vassal hands against my head,
> And threat the glory of my precious crown.

Richard is apparently relying upon the heavenly hosts to avenge him, if
not to defend or rescue him. But his enemies are adamant, and no
heavenly armies have come to the rescue. He must submit and be deposed.
Again his mind takes a religious turn:

> I'll give my jewels for a set of beads,
> My gorgeous palace for a hermitage,
> My gay apparel for an almsman's gown,
> My figured goblets for a dish of wood,
> My sceptre for a palmer's walking staff,
> My subjects for a pair of carved saints,
> And my large kingdom for a little grave,
> A little, little grave, an obscure grave.

In the actual deposition scene, Act IV, Scene 1, Richard deliberately
compares himself to Christ:

> Yet I well remember
> The favours of these men: were they not mine?
> Did they not sometime cry 'all hail' to me?
> So Judas did to Christ: but he, in twelve,
> Found truth in all but one; I, in twelve thousand, none.

The climax of this thought, and perhaps its strongest and most vigorous statement, comes when Richard, having resigned the crown, is called upon to sign a confession. He turns in anger upon the assembled nobles and says:

> Nay, all of you that stand and look upon,
> Whilst that my wretchedness doth bait myself,
> Though some of you with Pilate wash your hands,
> Showing an outward pity; yet you Pilates
> Have deliver'd me to my sour cross,
> And water cannot wash away your sin.

The religious theme is continued in the last act. In the scene of parting with the queen, Richard says:

> Our holy lives must win a new world's crown,
> Which our profane hours here have stricken down.

Is he speaking of a life after death? Is that the "new world's crown"? This interpretation would be consistent with what has gone before and with what is to follow, for in the last scene, Richard's thoughts are still on religious subjects. Languishing in prison, he plays with his thoughts:

> The better sort,
> As thoughts of things divine, are intermix'd
> With scruples, and do set the word itself
> Against the word:
> As thus, "Come, little ones," and then again,
> "It is as hard to come as for a camel
> To thread the postern of a small needle's eye."

Richard's last words, as he is dying, end the role on the same theme:

> Mount, mount, my soul! thy seat is up on high;
> Whilst my gross flesh sinks downward, here to die.

The last lines of the play, spoken by Bolingbroke, also echo the theme. In several instances, Richard has used the figure of washing away sin, the most important of which was the line, "And water cannot wash away your sin." Now Bolingbroke says:

> I'll make a voyage to the Holy Land,
> To wash this blood off my guilty hand:
> March sadly after; grace my mournings here;
> In weeping after this untimely bier.

Richard's religious convictions and beliefs are an important indication of his character and personality and help to distinguish him from all other men. This theme is introduced early in the play and is continued throughout the play, like a thread woven into a fabric and making an important contribution to the design of the whole piece.

Looking only at those speeches which are directly related to this single character trait, one discovers that Shakespeare has introduced them in a logical, chronological, and dramatic order. In the first act there are only brief, simple statements which indicate that Richard, believing that he is God's representative on earth, considers himself entitled to certain privileges not given to the common man. In the third act, Richard assumes that God will personally intercede for him and that any attack upon the king is a sacrilege which will be punished by God. But intercession does not come, and Richard feels that he, like Christ, has been betrayed and that those who have betrayed him are Judases. In the fourth act, when he is tried and sentenced, his judges are spoken of as Pilates. After this, Richard talks of other worlds and of a life after death. It can be seen that this one theme has a beginning, a middle, and an end, that it arrives at its own climaxes, and that these climaxes are closely associated with the climaxes of the play itself.

The Relative Importance of Specific Character Traits

Presumably the actor who plays the role will wish to find ways and means of making the audience perceive Richard's Christ complex in relation to his other characteristics. In the Flint castle scene, Act III, Scene 3, Richard notes that his antagonists have not knelt to show their obedience to him. Next comes the passage quoted above, in which he warns them that God will punish them. This is followed by his prediction that England will suffer and be torn by bloody civil wars. Then Richard sends a conciliatory message to his enemies and, immediately thereafter, goes into a passage of self-pity. Then comes another religious passage, but it is also one in which he dramatizes himself, for he says he will renounce his sceptre, his crown, his jewels, and his palaces for the religious life. This leads directly into the self-pity theme again as he asks for a "little, little grave" and imagines himself buried where subjects may trample on him. Next he jokes with Aumerle, suggesting that they should have a contest in weeping. Bolingbroke orders him to come down, and down he comes, dramatizing the episode as he does so and commenting on his own actions. Again, as at the beginning of the scene, he complains that Northumberland has not knelt to show his obedience. Richard then submits to Bolingbroke's orders.

While the scene contains two passages which show Richard's conception of himself as God's representative, they are followed by other passages illustrating other facets of his character, and one assumes that Shakespeare did not consider this trait the dominant one. Shakespeare uses much the same sequence in the trial scene, Act IV, Scene 1. A passage showing Richard's concern about the outward signs of obedience is followed by a religious sequence, in which he calls his enemies Judases. Next there is a sequence in which he dramatizes the event, comparing himself and Bolingbroke to buckets in a well. After another passage of self-pity, Richard renounces the crown and submits to being imprisoned in the tower.

The dialogue preceding the plot action in each of these scenes is devoted largely to the illumination of Richard's character, and in both cases his character traits are presented in more or less the same sequence: first, his concern for the observance of the outward forms of obedience; second, his belief that he is God's representative; third, his self-pity; and, finally, his self-dramatization, which is often tinged with a pathetic humor. Such an arrangement, repeated four times, cannot be regarded as accidental, and one must assume that Shakespeare, either intentionally or instinctively, illustrated the character traits in what seemed to him a climactic order, with the most important and interesting facet of the character shown last.

This detailed analysis of the single character trait has been given as a sample of the kind of study the actor should make of a role. All the other character traits would need similar study and analysis.

Designing the Performance in the Correct Style

Once the actor has discovered what the main character traits are, where and when they are illustrated by the author, and how they serve as motivation for the plot actions, he must devise the means by which he is to project these traits to the audience. By this time, having had a number of rehearsals, he should be familiar with the style in which the play is to be presented. Whatever techniques he elects to use must be consistent with and appropriate to that style, which will be derived partly from the author, partly from the physical production planned by the designer, and partly from the director and the methods of playing used by the other actors.

Designing the Performance in the Correct Rhythm

Next, the actor should consider the rhythm of his role—the amount and degree of change in the character, if there is any change, or the amount and degree of increase in the audience's awareness of the character, if he does not change but merely reveals himself more fully as the play progresses. In the case of Richard's conviction that he is God's representative on earth, it seems obvious that there is no change. He begins the play believing in his own divinity and ends the play the same way. The only change is that the audience gradually becomes aware of the intensity of that belief. His first simple statement, "We were not born to sue, but to command," is merely a statement of the divine right of kings, which was an accepted and not an exceptional belief in Elizabethan England; but the audience does not realize that Richard will extend that concept to the point of identifying himself with Christ, as he does when he calls his antagonists Pilates and says that they have delivered him to his sour cross. The steps by which the audience is gradually made to see that Richard carries this thought to this conclusion are an important factor in determining both the rhythm of the role and the pace of the play.

Designing the Performance with the Correct Actions

Now comes the most creative phase of the actor's work: he invents the actions which he will perform as he speaks the words. If he invents actions, gestures, facial expressions, and physical attitudes which exactly coincide with the meaning of the speeches, he will have reinforced that meaning for the audience. If he invents actions which are contradictory to the meaning of the lines, he will have tended to nullify their meaning.

It would be easy, for instance, for the actor playing Richard to use actions which would indicate self-pity rather than a Christ complex as he delivers all, or at least some, of the lines which seem to express his religious convictions. To do this would increase the amount of self-pity in the part and lessen its religious aspects. On the other hand, the actor might use gestures and physical attitudes which would help the audience recognize the fact that Richard has identified himself with Christ.

Some familiarity with religious painting has made most audiences aware of the common conception of Christ's appearance. Some actors who have played the role have changed their make-up from scene to scene, seeming to grow a beard and striving to look more and more like Christ. Some have taken Richard literally and changed their gay apparel for an almsman's gown. If Richard makes the gesture that is familiar in hundreds of pictures of the crucifixion, spreading his arms wide and tipping his head slightly to one side, as he says that his enemies have delivered him to his sour cross, there is little chance that the audience will miss the point. All the other passages which bear on this character trait may be similarly treated, different gestures and attitudes which have become known and familiar through paintings being used in relation to the specific lines.

Since Shakespeare has arranged the passages in both a chronological and a climactic order, the actor would do well to arrange the accompanying gestures in a similar order. Appropriate actions and gestures must be invented for all the character traits which the actor wishes to bring to the attention of the audience. The actor must assume that the emotional motivation for a particular line also dictates the actions to accompany that line, and he must remember that if he belies his words by his actions, the audience will tend to believe the actions rather than the words.

Planning Phrasing within the Total Design

Once the possible gestures, actions, and physical attitudes which are to be associated with specific character traits, emotional states, and mental attitudes have been invented, the actor is ready to consider the problems of phrasing and of building climaxes within particular scenes. He must understand that he does not design the part coldly and intellectually, basing his decisions solely on his own private study of the script, but that he evolves the design in rehearsal and in collaboration with all the other participants in the production. He may easily begin working on the phrasing of early scenes in the play long before he has conceived the design of the entire role. Actually much which he may discover accidentally in early rehearsals may be of great assistance to him in evolving the over-all design. His final plan for the performance must be one which easily includes all the parts; it must, in fact, be the sum of all the parts.

To arrive at his goal of a complete and unified performance, the actor works from both ends, now working on small and specific details and now on the all-encompassing design. He must be ready at all times to readjust his techniques of playing a specific sequence so that it can be made to fit the total plan, or to revise the total plan so that it may include a specific sequence. Rare indeed is an actor who conceives a role in a sudden flash of inspiration, unless he has first completed the study and the work which are likely to make that inspiration occur.

In the professional theater today, and more especially in the nonprofessional theater, it is the director who is expected to do the work and to have the inspiration. He then communicates the results of his study and his work to the actors, who are expected to assimilate his concept of the play and then to execute it.

Technical Details Should Be Automatic

Throughout the rehearsals the actor will work constantly on the techniques involved in projecting the small details of the performance. There will be a constant problem of adjustment and readjustment as the full design of the part is evolved and as the actor becomes familiar with the work of his fellow actors. The trained actor, however, may do all this unconsciously. From the beginning, the student-actor must pursue his study of techniques for the sole purpose of forgetting what he has learned; he must, in other words, practice his techniques until they become automatic. His aim is to acquire sufficient skill so that he can go directly from the thoughts and feelings of the character to an adequate and appropriate projection of those thoughts and feelings to the audience.

Except in rare instances, the actor's rehearsal time should be devoted to matters of the content of the performance, not the methods, the methods being automatic and inevitable once the content has been decided. The accomplished pianist or violinist, even in rehearsal, is not concerned with matters of fingering, except when he comes to a passage which is so complicated that the technical solution is not immediately apparent to him. As he works on the music, he begins to understand its form, the length of its phrases, the need for special accents, the relationship of melody and countermelody and accompaniment; he finds the places where climaxes should be built and the tempi which are most suited to the individual passages. The process of selecting the methods by which all of this can be projected so that the listeners will understand and appreciate the music in the same way that the performer does should be so automatic that it seems unconscious. In the same way, the actor should be concerned, not with the methods of phrasing, or pointing, or timing, or emphasis, but only with the effect his characterization should have on the audience.

It is regrettable that in many companies, both professional and non-professional, there are never any actual rehearsals. The so-called rehearsal time is often entirely consumed in learning the lines and inventing the actions. By the time this has been done and the minor adjustments necessitated by the costumes, properties, and scenery have been made, it is often time to let in the audience.

The Final Effect

In its final form, any performance must seem entirely spontaneous and inevitable, even though it has been carefully thought out and carefully planned and the specific techniques used in any particular part of the play have been carefully selected and rehearsed. Every work of art must be contrived and artificial, but usually the artist will wish his finished work to create the impression that it has been freshly conceived at the moment of performance. This effect can be achieved partly by perfecting one's techniques so that they are automatic; partly by having sufficient rehearsals, and partly by selecting the correct techniques, each thought and feeling which is to be expressed having the perfect form in which to be expressed.

The actor faces a special problem, for—as pointed out in earlier chapters —he differs from most other artists in that he is his own instrument; whatever he has to say to an audience must be said through the medium of his own personality, and his own emotions are inevitably involved. Unless he himself has great emotional sensitivity and emotional power, he will not be able to conceive of the performance in the first place. At some time during the rehearsals of a play he must have been able to identify his personal emotions with those of the character he is playing, for the emotions of the character are the subject material of the actor's performance, to which his techniques will give the form. If he does not have emotional sensitivity and comprehension, he has no business acting at all.

The actor must never mistake his own feelings and thoughts for those of the character. It is not enough to feel emotions; he must be able to feel the right emotions to the right degree and at the right time and to express those feelings with adequate technical facility. Whether or not it is essential for the actor to experience the specific emotions at the instant of performance is a matter for the individual actor to settle for himself, depending upon his own temperament and his own technical skill. Certainly if he finds this necessary, his technical ability will be a great help to him, for with sufficient technical skill, he will not need to be concerned with techniques during a performance but will be free to concentrate solely on the emotions of the character.

A final word of caution—the only emotions which are important or valid in the theater are those which are experienced by the audience.

EXERCISES

1. Choose a major character in each of the following plays:
   Romeo and Juliet
   Julius Caesar
   The Merchant of Venice
   Hamlet
   Richard II
   A Doll's House
   Arms and the Man
   Candida

a. List the major plot actions which he must take.

b. List the character traits which would motivate these actions.

c. Find the places in the script where these character traits are illustrated by the author.

d. Find other passages which might also illustrate these character traits, but which the author has not clearly used for this purpose.

e. Invent gestures, facial expressions, physical attitudes, and movements which also illustrate these character traits.

f. Work out the timing, so that these actions may be combined with the appropriate lines.

g. Plan the vocal techniques necessary to point and emphasize the lines relating to the character traits.

h. Plan the performance so that the illustrations of a single character trait are presented in a climactic order, usually the order established by the author, with the strongest actions related to the strongest statements of the character traits.

i. Fit all of these plans into the physical production being provided.

j. Rehearse until the actions are natural and automatic and until you can concentrate solely on the thoughts and feelings of the character, the actions being performed spontaneously at each rehearsal or performance.

CHARACTER INDEX

SUBJECT INDEX

Characters in plays mentioned are listed separately in the Character Index preceding the Subject Index.